Innovation and Creativity in a Complex World

Essays published in conjunction with the World
Future Society's annual meeting, WorldFuture 2009:
Innovation and Creativity in a Complex World

edited by Cynthia G. Wagner

published by the World Future Society, www.wfs.org

World Future Society Conference Volume Team

Editor: Cynthia G. Wagner, *cwagner@wfs.org*
Editorial Production: Aaron M. Cohen
Staff Editors: Rick Docksai, Lane Jennings, Patrick Tucker
Consulting Editors: Edward Cornish, Susan Echard,
Timothy C. Mack
Business Manager: Jeff Cornish
Administrative Support: Robin Goodman, Sarah Warner
Art Director: Lisa Mathias

Published by:
World Future Society
7910 Woodmont Avenue, Suite 450
Bethesda, Maryland 20814, U.S.A.
www.wfs.org

ISBN 13: 978-0-930242-66-4
ISBN 10: 0-930242-66-1
Printed in the United States of America.

Innovation and Creativity in a Complex World

Contents

Part 3: Building on Innovation and Creativity 133

Part 4: Assessing and Optimizing Our Resources 205

Preface

One of the staff's slogans at World Future Society headquarters is that, when you run low on resources, you need to be more resourceful.

This explains why innovation and creativity—the feedstock of our resourcefulness—are so important at this time. Not only is complexity accelerating, but our resources for solving the problems created by complexity are also increasingly imperiled.

The following 26 essays from futurists working "in the trenches" illustrate one of the first lessons of resourcefulness: that we can't do this alone. We need each other's skills and perspectives to help navigate our way through complexity. As shipmates on this journey, we must learn to value and enhance cooperation by breaking down the barriers between us, whether it is the silos that compartmentalize different disciplines or the boundaries between nation-states. Your ideas enhance mine; my counterarguments and experiences spark debate. All of this becomes a process for achieving better outcomes.

That said, specialists' expertise has never been more critical to resolving the complex issues now bedeviling us. Particularly troublesome are the twin issues of meeting energy demand and reversing the environmental damage to which the consumption of fossil fuels has contributed. Only with global cooperation and resourcefulness on these issues do we have hope for arriving at solutions.

As our lead author, communications-satellite pioneer Joe Pelton, puts it, "systematic division of research and compartmentalization of our thoughts can only multiply the dangers that we will face in coming decades." And our closing author, Arlington Institute president John L. Petersen, concurs that cooperation is our best hope for surviving the converging crises ahead.

This volume may be one of the most normative editions yet produced in conjunction with a World Future Society conference. Several contributors to *Innovation and Creativity in a Complex World* argue persuasively that, as we build the future, we must be prepared to make moral choices—and to do so, we need a better understanding of morality as well as of the specific trends we are dealing with.

Here is a brief outline of the volume's structure:

Part 1: Accelerating Complexity provides an overview of the critical trends shaping our future and offers a glimpse of the tools we will need to solve the problems created by accelerating change and complexity.

Part 2: Applying Strategic Foresight showcases specific instances of the tools of futuring used to understand and forecast trends, as well as the application of knowledge across disciplines to deliver better outcomes.

Part 3: Building on Innovation and Creativity offers fresh ideas on developing that all-important resource—human imagination—and deploying it for the betterment of our communities and even civilization.

Part 4: Assessing and Optimizing Our Resources hones in specifically on the energy crisis and its role in the environmental future. The complexity is daunting, as the choices are many and the consequences of making the wrong choices are potentially devastating.

Part 5: Futuring and the Moral Imperative tackles the issue of developing our resources of wisdom and morality, which are vital to creating a future that works for everyone.

Part 6: Beyond the Horizon dares to imagine how we—and our future—may evolve.

—cgw, Bethesda, May 2009

Executive Summaries

Reinventing 21st-Century Creativity and Innovation: Ten Fundamental Reforms

by Joseph N. Pelton

This article examines a series of basic reforms that are essential to allow creativity and innovation to thrive in the twenty-first century. Among these reforms are: (1) more systems analysis and interdisciplinary studies; (2) assessing the impact of "thinking machines" and the coming "Singularity" on society; (3) embracing the need for active "futuring"; (4) actively embracing "green" technologies, regulations, and economic pricing systems; (5) Western lifestyle changes; (6) regionalism; and (7) active reduction of global population to the levels of the 1950s.

The Millennium Project as a Method for Dealing with Global Complexity

by Jerome C. Glenn, Theodore J. Gordon, and Elizabeth Florescu

This paper provides an overview of the mission of the Millennium Project, a global participatory futures research think tank organized as an independent, interdisciplinary, transinstitutional, and multicultural information system. The paper outlines the Millennium Project's methodology for tracking global challenges and opportunities through a "strategic global intelligence" comprising 32 Nodes (groups of institutions and individuals) and participants from around the world. The Millennium Project is designed—both in its organizational structure and research content—to address increasing global complexity.

GrrRANK! The World's Largest System Shifts Gears: The Inertial Realities That Are Transforming the American Economy

by David Pearce Snyder

Although a techno-economic wave of creative destruction produced an accelerating loss of middle-income jobs in America since 2000, U.S. consumer spending rose sharply between 2000 and 2007, because of easy access to credit and unsustainably low tax rates. But now that the 2008 financial crash has eliminated more than $50 trillion from the world's capital supply, both commercial and consumer credit will cost more and be harder to get for the foreseeable future. Simultaneously, shrunken capital markets will curtail public-sector borrowing, forcing all levels of government to raise taxes and fees in order to restore our decaying infrastructure and renew the integrity of our regulatory mechanisms.

As a consequence of tighter credit and higher taxes, even after we recover from the current economic downturn (2011) consumer spending will remain 5% to 10% below pre-recession levels. From now on, America will spend less on housing, cars, and vacation cruises, while spending more on infrastructure, health care, and home entertainment. Spreading suburban sprawl will come to a halt, and most new residences will be in high-density, mixed-use infill developments—"urban villages"—typically clustered around rail transit stations throughout an increasingly car-free urbanized America.

Meanwhile, even as society adapts to our austere new circumstances, economic history suggests that, within five years, the U.S. will enter the "creative" phase of the wave of creative destruction, during which the economy should begin to generate a growing number of new high-value products, services, and jobs. The paper concludes with an exploration of five possible scenarios for the future evolution of the postindustrial economy.

Through the Crisis of Maturity: Forecasts of an Economic Boom in 2015

by William E. Halal

Drawing on forecasts from the TechCast Project, this article sketches out how the green revolution, global e-commerce, and other emerging business sectors are likely to pull the world out of recession about 2012. Charting the 35-year Kuznets business cycles also suggests that the next economic boom based on this sustainable growth will start about 2015. These innovations should begin to resolve the global "crisis of maturity"—energy shortages, climate change, environmental decline, weapons of mass destruction, etc.—that must be overcome to move civilization to an advanced stage of development.

PART 2: APPLYING STRATEGIC FORESIGHT

Disruptive Innovation: The Future of Primary Health Care

by Jay Herson

Health-care reform is likely to provide incentives in primary care for electronic medical records, e-prescribing, and use of evidence-based disease management protocols. These innovations require large information technology infrastructures and levels of medical supervision and computer expertise. There are currently about 2,000 walk-in clinics, with services provided by nurse practitioners and physician assistants, located at chain retail pharmacy sites.

This paper makes the case that health-care reform and market forces will cause these walk-in clinics to evolve, via a disruptive innovation, into retail pharmacy-based primary care group practices with physicians added to the provider team. This transition will create a more patient-centric system and attract a new generation of physicians interested in practicing medicine without the need to be involved in business issues. A retail pharmacy clinic patient can have his/her medical record accessible from any location of that RP chain, including at the workplace, as retail pharmacy clinics expand to run employee health offices for large companies. Retail pharmacy clinics are likely to find their way into areas that are currently medically underserved. The transition will result in a standardization of primary care processes and changing the doctor–patient relationship. Retail pharmacy based clinics offer the scale necessary to bring about many innovations in health-care reform and to offer reasonable, although perhaps not optimal, care for most primary-care indications.

Future Patterns of Work and Retirement: The Evolving Third Age

by Anna M. Rappaport

Citizens in all developed countries are living longer, and life-spans are continuing to increase. Many countries will have relatively more older persons than at any time in the past, and communities, workplaces, and families will be very different. This trend will continue, and over the next 25 years the change will be dramatic. This paper looks at how people retire, how that may change, and how retirement plans are likely to fit in. It discusses efforts to move to new models and includes recommendations for the future. It is primarily based on U.S. data and the U.S. environment, but many of the issues also apply in other countries.

The Maryland Law-Enforcement and Mental-Health Systems

by Barbara Parker

This essay examines the respective roles of the partnership between Maryland's law-enforcement system and its mental-health system in assisting victims of family violence. It also addresses why advocates for victims of family violence say coordinated action is necessary. It offers a synopsis of legal options for victims of family violence and discusses the points at which mental-health experts become involved in the law-enforcement process. These legal options include civil and/or criminal remedies, as well as counseling provided by mental-health professionals. Effective intervention has proven to be successful in decreasing the number of family violence cases, because it calls for a strategic response from this team of experts. Their primary goal is to stop the cycle of family violence.

A Foresight Method for Enhancing Competitiveness of Brazilian Industrial Sectors

by Cláudio Chauke Nehme, Adriano Galvão, Antonio Vaz, Gilda Coelho, and Lélio Fellows

Governments all over the world hope to make their industrial sectors more competitive in the global economy. This paper introduces a sectorial foresight methodology created to define long-term strategy plans for six industrial sectors in Brazil, each of which is aligned with an industrial policy that aims to reorganize strategic sectors, enhance their competitiveness in the global market, and increase foreign sales of value-added products.

The method was created while Centro de Gestão e Estudos Estratégicos (CGEE) developed prospective studies for the six sectors. It is based on the development of strategic and technological road maps, adapted to accommodate unique requirements for each sector. It consists of four phases: Foresight Planning, Understanding the Present, Futuring Perspectives, and Prospecting Future Opportunities.

Foresight Planning includes (1) defining a work plan and foresight approach, and (2) negotiating with stakeholders. Understanding the Present includes (1) data-hunting and gathering, and (2) segmentation and prioritization. Futuring Perspectives includes (1) scanning and detecting trends, and (2) developing vision and action goals. Prospecting Future Opportunities includes (1) defining strategies and road maps, and (2) making recommendations.

This paper focuses on formalizing this process so that it can be more broadly disseminated and more easily used. It starts by introducing the meaning of foresight concepts relevant in the industrial context of Brazil, and subsequently introduces an adaptation of the road-map technique to the broader scope of the industrial sectors. This paper emphasizes the challenges and results obtained while working with the aeronautical, shoe, plastic, furniture, medical equipment, and textile sectors of Brazil. The final recommendations for prospective studies are not shared, due to the sensitive nature of the information.

PART 3: BUILDING ON INNOVATION AND CREATIVITY

Globalization 3.0: A New Urgency for Building Creative and Innovative Communities

by John M. Eger

A major consequence of the "flat world" that Thomas Friedman writes about is the worldwide competition between cities and regions around the world positioning themselves to capitalize on the new global information economy. The winning cities and regions will be those that not only have the broadband technology of the new age, but also have in place aggressive plans to use technology to transform their regional economy and society. The best ones are those looking to play a leadership role and recognize that creativity and innovation will be the hallmarks of the new global economy, in order to attract, retain, and nurture the most entrepreneurial, creative, and innovative workforce. Those communities placing a premium on cultural and ethnic diversity, and reinventing their educational systems for the creative age, will likely burst with innovation and entrepreneurial fervor. These are the ingredients so essential to developing and attracting the type of bright and creative people that generate new patents and inventions, innovative world-class products and services, and the finance and marketing plans to support them.

The Telecommunications Explosion: Toward a Global Brain

by José Luis Cordeiro

This article gives a global summary of the evolution of telecommunications around the world. It is a quick review of this vital industry from its past to its future.

The invention of the telephone allowed the immediate and simultaneous interconnection of many people around the world for the first time in human history. This produced many major benefits, such as the unprecedented rates of economic growth experienced in the last century. Therefore, the twentieth century could be called the "Age of the Telephone."

Finally, some implications of an increasingly interconnected world are considered, such as even faster development and knowledge creation. New mobile forms of communication in the twenty-first century are substituting the old fixed landline telephones of the twentieth century, bringing cheaper, faster, better, and more-efficient ways to communicate in our rapidly connecting planetary civilization.

Anime: Art Form of the 21st Century

by Lane Jennings

As poetry in Elizabethan England, the novel in nineteenth century Europe, or silent film at the start of the twentieth century, so animation—the presentation of stories without live actors, using drawn and/or computer-generated artwork with two- or three-dimensional modeling, and voice-over dialogue—is today emerging as the art form of our times.

Signs and Wonders: Information Technology, Cybernetics, and the Dawn of the Postliterate Age

by Patrick Tucker

This paper questions if the written word and traditional literacy can survive the coming era of instantaneous communication and the advent of human-level artificial intelligence. It explores current trends in information technology and IT's influence on literacy. The paper further examines potential future trends in cybernetics and artificial intelligence in terms of their possible effects on education.

PART 4: ASSESSING AND OPTIMIZING OUR RESOURCES

Sustainable Development: Tomorrow's Salvation or Today's Hype?

by Richard MacLean

This essay examines the growing controversy over what government, industry, and the public are doing to protect the fate of Earth's ecosystems. Climate change is just one aspect, and possibly not even the most significant dimension. Some experts argue that, if we are not vigilant, humans will overshoot ecological limits and enter a period of collapse. Others believe that this doomsday scenario is preposterous. They argue that technological advances, new resource discoveries, and shifts in consumptive patterns will ensure that future generations' needs will be met.

The analysis briefly examines the positive and negative forces in play, such as technology, population, and affluence. In addition, it offers a critical examination of society's attitudes toward protecting the environment and its capacity to achieve the elements necessary to realize a sustainable future. The analysis ultimately presents a forbidding scenario of what the future may hold unless society rises to a challenge the likes of which humankind has not faced before.

Sailing and Surfing through Complexity: Emerging Contexts of Energy, Environmental, and Society Transitions

by David J. LePoire

About every 100 years since the scientific revolution, both the technological basis and the global center of political leadership have shifted. If this pattern continues, a transition might occur soon, but two recent interpretations and extrapolations of technological trends have led to widely differing predictions.

To gain a broader perspective of these possible interpretations, historical trends are explored to identify emerging properties of an underlying large complex adaptive system. For example, the leadership transitions often show competition between two new ways to organize societies with increased technology and energy use. The leaders might alternately explore the boundaries of the two options in a manner analogous to the tacking strategy of sailing against the wind.

Also, historical wave-like trends have been identified in a range of important topics, including energy, environment, and technology. For example, the energy source sequence (wood, coal, oil, natural gas, efficiency, and renewables/nuclear), which seems to coincide with major transitions in international leadership, has been interpreted as periodic waves. These transition waves help set the context of social dynamics (demographic, democratic, and developmental transitions) analogous to surfing ocean waves.

This work was supported by the U.S. Department of Energy under Contract No. DE-AC02-06CH11357.

The Future of Nuclear Energy

by Vladimir Knapp and Gioietta Kuo

After more than two decades of rejection, often unjustified, nuclear power is now advocated by even some of the most ardent green scientists, aware that other forms of energy (non-CO_2-emitting sources) cannot be developed in time, apart from the unresolved backup problem. Scientists and engineers in the nuclear field who are aware of the unique advantages of nuclear energy are certainly happy with the change, yet must be careful should support overlook issues associated with the large-scale development of nuclear power.

Questions about nuclear power can be divided into those of the near or intermediate term and those associated with the long-term development. Questions of the first group are on nuclear electricity cost, investment costs, safety, and waste disposal. They are discussed in the first part of the paper. Answers are either positive already, or expected to be in the intermediate term on the basis of current development. Longer-term issues include the contribution of nuclear energy in transport and industry, sufficiency of nuclear fuel, and nuclear proliferation. It is shown that with more efficient use of uranium and thorium resources there is no limit to the large-scale use of nuclear power. Proliferation safety, on the other hand, is primarily a political issue that cannot be resolved by technical fixes; however, it is an essential precondition for the large-scale use of nuclear power. Believing that solutions should be sought on the lines similar to those of the old, but farsighted American (Baruch) UN proposal in 1946, which envisaged internationalization of nuclear fuel cycle, some possible steps in this direction are discussed.

Energy: The Grand Strategic Joint of the 21st Century
by Tsvi Bisk

Reducing dependence on oil would impact positively on the economy, the environment, and the security of the entire world, as well as reinforce the moral robustness of the West by liberating it from dependence on countries ruled by thugs. This would also be a key factor in achieving a Middle East peace and normalizing the West's relationship with the Muslim world.

We now have the means to make liberation from oil a reasonable policy aim. This essay demonstrates how a rational/doable energy strategy might achieve this. What can we do and when can we do it are the standards—not visions of a perfect world. Policy criteria must be concerned with time (when something can be done) and doability (what can be done). Time refers to short term, intermediate term, long term, and deep long term. In other words, how do we get from here to there and what would be the intermediate (or bridging) steps. Doability relates to practicality—a policy that reflects how real people actually live. This paper tries to show how this might be implemented in the real world.

The Post-Scarcity World of 2050-2075

by Stephen Aguilar-Millan, Ann Feeney, Amy Oberg, and Elizabeth Rudd

We are all quite familiar with the concept of peak oil—the notion that oil is a finite resource and that we are soon coming to the peak in its historical production. It also is the case that the production of a number of other key resources will peak in the same time frame. This convergence of peaking production is likely to lead to an age of scarcity. And yet that age of scarcity is unlikely to herald the end of the world. So what lies beyond scarcity?

The purpose of this paper is to examine what the post-scarcity age may look like. We examine the issue from the perspective of the post-scarcity company, post-scarcity society, post-scarcity geopolitics, and the post-scarcity financial system. While the work is highly speculative, there are sufficient common threads between the present and the future that we can usefully start to consider the main outlines of what a distant future might look like. It is only through a conversation about the deep future that we can improve life for future generations.

PART 5: FUTURING AND THE MORAL IMPERATIVE

The Next Generation of Forecasters: The Future Futurists

by Irving H. Buchen

As often happens, an initial pioneering group gradually is replaced by those they have set standards for and even helped to succeed them. But what will be different about this next generation of forecasters? Many things, but at least three. These future futurists will be more adept at repositioning so that all that they study will be inevitably and greedily holistic; the micro will always be given its macro extent. Then, too, they will constantly situate their work at intersections—crossroads of many different academic disciplines and national cultures—and simulate 360. Finally, they will become intense advocates for creating a system of systems as comprehensive and decisive as the Human Genome Project. Hopefully, their legacy to those who come after them will be one of greater clarity and hope.

The Future of Holocaust Memorialization: Altruism in Extremes

by Arthur B. Shostak

Innovation and creativity—the overarching focus of this volume—are vital components in meeting a most unusual and quite consequential challenge. In the very near future, the last of the direct survivors (and perpetrators) of the 1933-1946 Holocaust will pass away. In the aftermath, we will inherit responsibility for shaping a fresh telling of the greatest crime of the twentieth century, a persuasive retelling that should lend a special meaning to twenty-first-century life. This essay shares a unique candidate approach, one that emphasizes not the horror as true of almost all such memorialization work, but instead calls attention as well to the help that victims shared with one another. A case is made for its employ as an aid to creating a more optimistic future for our complex world.

Applying and Prioritizing Moral Values in the Creative Process: Some Important Threshold Issues

by Michael Blinick

Creativity is supposedly a good thing, but can have extremely negative results when whatever is created is put into action and effect in the "real world" without having been screened for compliance with ethical and moral values. To protect intellectual and artistic freedom, which indeed are in themselves fundamental values, the point at which possible implementation of a proposed innovation starts being considered is where inquiry as to relevant values can properly and prudently occur. The relevant issues are set forth and discussed as preliminaries to development of protocols for accomplishing such reviews and evaluations.

Why Replace the UN with a Directly Elected Parliament?

by Brian Coughlan

More than 60 years after the creation of the United Nations, the world is more at risk than ever. Why? What on earth are we doing wrong? The halting progress afforded by the League of Nations, the UN, and the EU were bought at a terrible and increasing cost, 20 million lives in World War I and 55 million in World War II. We may not be able to afford the next step forward, so let's take it without the butcher's bill. We need to face the reality that a world permanently Balkanized into nuclear-armed (or worse!) camps simply cannot survive in the long term. It has no future. This is not hyperbole, but simply an expression of statistical reality. We need to take a long, hard look at our options, start thinking seriously about a future in which war is criminalized, and finally take the obvious step of embracing our collective interdependence through a genuine global democracy.

Power, Responsibility, and Wisdom: Exploring the Issues at the Core of Ethical Decision Making and Leadership

by Bruce Lloyd

Decisions taken today are driven by our visions of tomorrow and based on what we learned yesterday. This basic rule applies to all decisions, irrespective of size. Every time we take any decision we are involved in some element of leadership, but the bigger the decision the more critical are our leadership credentials.

The Wisdom of Future Consciousness

by Tom Lombardo

Wisdom is the highest expression of future consciousness; it is the normative ideal toward which we should aspire in the development of future consciousness. Heightened future consciousness and wisdom go hand-in-hand.

I support this central thesis by describing the many parallels between these capacities. First I examine the holistic nature of wisdom and future consciousness. Then I describe how both capacities involve an expansive level of consciousness. Next I look at the knowledge base and similar cognitive abilities associated with each capacity, as well as parallels in their motivational and emotional structures. Then I examine the ecological context of wisdom and heightened future consciousness, again pointing out similarities.

After ecology, I introduce a key feature of both wisdom and heightened future consciousness: both capacities are grounded in a set of key character virtues. Then I move to self-identity, pointing out how each capacity impacts a person's overall sense of self. I summarize by presenting comprehensive descriptions of wisdom and heightened future consciousness, noting the overall degree of resonance between the two capacities. I conclude with some thoughts on the further evolution of wisdom and future consciousness, connecting these capacities and their future development with the theory of the new enlightenment.

PART 6: BEYOND THE HORIZON

The Fifth Engine of Creation

by David Harper

Over the past 13.7 billion years, the universe has gone from an exploding, hot mass of quarks to being populated with all the objects and systems we know of today. Galaxies, planets, molecules, plants, animals, brains, cars, computers, etc., exist because the universe's evolution has started four basic methods of producing things. These four engines of creation—physics, chemistry, biology, and technology—all have unique materials and engineering techniques that produce an ever evolving and expanding array of structures.

The recent invention of computers has now started a fifth basic, unique path of evolution—a fifth engine of creation. The computer's new materials (information) and methods (software) are following their own evolutionary path and have a great potential to take the pinnacle of the universe's evolution to new heights. Physics produced chemistry, chemistry produced biology, which in turn started technology, and recently technology has created the information realm. At each new stage, the resulting structures were dramatically more sophisticated than those of prior stages. The potential for evolving future virtual structures is similarly to be much more sophisticated than technology's, or biology's, structures.

This article offers a new paradigm for understanding universal evolution, which provides a context for understanding the impact that the introduction of computers will have in the future. It discusses the material and methods of the virtual realm and some possibilities for what its evolution will produce.

One Giant Leap for Mankind: Terrestrial and Extraterrestrial *Hominina* Evolution

by Julian F. Derry

The human capacity for buffering ourselves from environmental effects only goes part of the way to divorcing ourselves from the natural world, Darwinian evolution, and the pressures of natural selection. This paper first examines how human society has weakened our susceptibility to evolutionary pressures, then looks forward to the most significant modern development and the most likely cause of those pressures being remade stronger. Finally, predictions are made on the future of human evolution, on Earth and in space, including one scenario under which humanity is so externally controlled that selection occurs quite unnaturally.

A New End, A New Beginning

by John L. Petersen

Numerous indicators suggest that big change is on the horizon. These huge, extraordinary trends—such as the collapsing financial system, global climate change, and peak oil production—any of which would be enough to derail our present way of life, are converging to precipitate a historically big transition event. The challenges are complex, structural, and global, well beyond the means of a single government to resolve. But global cooperation appears unlikely, and protectionism may prevail as countries eye only their own short-term interests. The time is now to plan for the new realities, by not only thinking how we will provide for ourselves, but also by engaging in more cooperative ventures, for we cannot succeed alone.

Part 1

Accelerating Complexity

Reinventing 21st-Century Creativity and Innovation

Ten Fundamental Reforms

Joseph N. Pelton

Confronting the Tower of Babel Issue and Embracing the Concept of "Futuring"

We—i.e., the scientists and engineers, the research institutions, the politicians, and the industrialists—have step-by-step created a twenty-first-century "Tower of Babel" problem. Increasingly, specialized and ultra-technical science and engineering courses of study and projects have served to splinter our understanding of a coherent, mutually reinforcing, and self-healing world.

In contrast to the strictly disciplinary schools of studies we find, in most research labs, a different school of thought about how to understand the complex world in which we live. These thinkers have come to think in terms of multidisciplinary research and integrated concepts. These more "philosophical researchers" express themselves in terms of the "Gaia" concept of the earth. They advocate interdisciplinary studies and the study of nonlinear math, chaos theory, and complexity. These thinkers give rise to new schools of thought that are born of multidisciplinary study centers, such as the Santa Fe Institute where Nobel laureates from many disciplines have assembled

---

Joseph N. Pelton is the former dean of the International Space University. E-mail joepelton@verizon.net.

to probe the unknown using a multiplicity of skills.

During the twentieth century, traditional researchers within various departments of learning—such as physics, electrical engineering, chemistry, biology, and mathematics—have built, block by block, a modern Tower of Babel, where specialized technologies and scientific cubbyholes not only have sundered our ability to think creatively and synoptically, but also have stifled truly innovative and integrated solutions to our complex global problems.

What do economics, restructured markets and commodity pricing, trade agreements, "green" energy and transportation systems, demographics, architecture, communications systems, computer science, artificial intelligence, education, ecology, material sciences, birth control, medical research, health sciences, arts and literature, linguistics, biology, genetics, the physical sciences and chemistry, psychology, sociology, philosophy and religion, astronomy, and space travel have in common? What they have in common is that the integration of these diverse fields of study into unified systems and interrelated social and political problems is more and more essential to understanding our complex world.

We must teach educators to break the mold of the past and embrace new modes of learning, and to appreciate the value of interdisciplinary research and education. Those who insist on relying solely on "vertical research" based on traditional academic disciplines miss key connections that bind our world and different disciplines together. Those who believe we can rely on research based on single-minded and compartmental disciplines separated in "stovepipe mode" stand in danger of conducting research that ultimately can represent an exercise in futility. X-rays discovered and applied in medical fields are now critical to astronomy. Nonlinear math discovered by mathematicians is now being applied by stock-market analysts, biologists, cartographers, and physicists. God, physical and biological evolution, or the entity responsible for "intelligent design" all seem to have studied in interdisciplinary systems.

Future research and questing for knowledge and new solutions must become much more like the process found within an integrated biological system. Certainly this makes more sense than the segregated research efforts one typically finds being conducted within the largely separated and even hermetically sealed-off departments in a conventional university. Approaching the future by examining the unknown via a single disciplinary pathway may often produce more harmful results than helpful answers.

This article seeks to explain via a series of arguments, plus a platform of 10 specific actions, how we can better approach the future. This Ten-Point Program not only seeks to outline a better pathway to future innovation and creativity but even boldly dares to present a way forward to achieve the longer-term health and survival of the human race.

The central thesis is that we require an integrated and interdisciplinary systems approach to the future. We need a combination of perspectives—plus a unity of scientific, artistic, and philosophical thought—in order to solve our mounting twenty-first-century problems. In short, this is a call to pursue in a systemic way what Edward Cornish, the founder of the World Future Society, has elegantly called "futuring."

If this article has one message, it is as follows: Integrated, multidisciplinary research and technology is in! Stovepipe division of different disciplines into disconnected independent studies is out! Such systematic division of research and compartmentalization of our thoughts can only multiply the dangers that we will face in coming decades. And the problem is not of just science and technology. It spreads across all modes of arts, sciences, philosophy, and especially business as defined by free-market capitalism. It then goes on to boldly suggest we reduce the human population of the planet, restructure the nature of cooperation among nation-states, reform free-market capitalism, restructure how goods and services are priced, and prepare ourselves for the impacts of the coming "Singularity." Kenneth

Boulding suggested that the twentieth century was a time of fundamental transition. He was right in suggesting that such a fundamental transition was necessary. His timing was off, however, in that we
will belatedly have to get around to reshaping the world in a really,
really, really important way in the twenty-first century since we
screwed up by not doing it about a half century ago.

"STRUCTURED MARKET" CAPITALISM FOR THE 21ST CENTURY

One of our keenest current problems is that our technical, industrial complex is tied to a laissez-faire, shopworn, and increasingly
outmoded form of free-market capitalism that often dogmatically
drives our current scientific research and engineering development.

The current crop of capitalists, who gave us the present-day
world recession and invented some $63 trillion in derivatives when
thinking up ways of creating really serious financial mischief within
the global economy, seem to have some serious values problems.

These Wall Street capitalists have a limited and single-minded
view of what a free market's function is in today's world. First of all,
they think the world is their oyster and its purpose is to allow them
to live a rather extravagant lifestyle filled with huge bonuses and a
very large carbon footprint that goes well beyond extravagant shopa-
holic consumption.

They also believe that the single function of the global economy
is to increase economic throughput. This translates into the need for
always increasing the size of global markets, enlarging industrial output, consuming more calories, and incidentally increasing the carbon
footprint of the entirety of human society, and, as a byproduct, the
exponential ramping up of industrial pollution.

It is now time to recalibrate the purpose of innovation and creativity and tinker with the current form of free-market capitalism as
defined for us by Wall Street bankers and hedge-fund managers. We
need some fresh thinking about markets and market efficiencies. In

short, it seems that *New York Times* essayist Paul Krugman and Nobel laureate Joseph E. Stiglitz may have some ideas that are more relevant to twenty-first-century innovation and market economies than, say, Adam Smith, Thomas Hobbes, and John Locke, who, as smart as they were, have been dead now for a few centuries.

The intellectual heritage of a free-market economy and laissez-faire defined concepts of democracy and capitalism that were first set forth by Hobbes, Locke, and Smith. We tend to idolize Locke as one of the great advocates of democracy, but for Locke there really was no higher value than private property. As political philosopher Victor Ferkiss once said: "John Locke would have supported putting billboards on the sides of the Grand Canyon."

Ever since the time of the high Renaissance and the rapid rise of scientific research and industrial development, we have seen a close linkage between and among a free-market economy, industrial development, and scientific research. These elements have worked well in tandem to spur growth and raise the standard of human living—especially for the capitalists, the research establishments, and the investment bankers.

The alliance of researchers and innovators, capitalists, and political advocates of free-market economies within democratic societies has worked reasonably well for the last two to three hundred years. In short, this process worked extremely well during the period of human society when industrialization and human enterprise was a modest part of the world's ecosystem. We now seem to have come to a major branching point in human societal development where adjustment to some new realities seem necessary. Some really big changes have been happening, and very quickly, over the past half century. The next half century represents a real humdinger of a time of accelerated change.

COPING WITH MEGA-CHANGES—THE NEW REALITIES

Today, however, humans and their consumption of livestock, plants, trees, drinking water, and more are increasingly out of scale with the biosystems on which we depend. Operational research and systems analysis conducted first by the Club of Rome (i.e., by Dennis Meadows and Jay Forrester of MIT) more than three decades ago initially sounded some alarm bells. But those obsessed with industrial throughput and the accumulation of private wealth chose to shoot the "canaries in the coal mine" rather than accept the warnings that these studies of future trends first seriously raised. These initial studies and those that followed projected that human lifestyles and industrialization were causing increasing damage to the very systems on which we depend to survive.

In the twentieth century, several things changed—and rapidly so. These changes, as outlined below, have not only endangered the human race and large mammals but also increasingly imperil the flora and fauna of the entire world. What is alarming is that these changes are following exponential growth patterns that suggest our responses to the dangers they pose may well be too slow to be effective.

What are these changes?

1. **Demographics.** For many thousands of years, human population was stable at around 100 million people. The first "green revolution" allowed one seed to generate many seeds for the next crop, enabling human population to expand by millions. Then the second "green revolution," based on modern agricultural research, allowed our global population to reach a billion at the start of the twentieth century, about 3 billion by the middle of the twentieth century, and around 6.5 billion today. Population projections suggest that human population may reach some 12 billion before it stabilizes before the end of the twenty-first century. Some believe that such staggering numbers may spell a death sentence for humanity in terms of greenhouse gases discharged into the atmosphere by humans, cattle, and various machines; the thinning of the ozone layer; or the various demands for energy, potable water, or other vital resources, from food for people and livestock to trees for paper and fuel. In short, if we could magically return the earth's

human population to levels of the 1950s, it would have enormous benefits in almost every way, from climate change to access to renewable energy to drinkable water. Human survival may depend not so much on stabilizing human population before the end of the twenty-first century, but actually seeking to reduce it to the level achieved in the 1950s.

2. **Rapid proliferation of nation-states and independent territories.** The United Nations now has some 200 entities that participate in its deliberations and seek worldwide consensus on many issues, such as orbital debris, airline safety, food safety, nuclear proliferation, or control of global disease and pandemics. The spread of nation-states, the reality of "rogue states" that do not respect global norms of behavior, and, in effect, a world that is seemingly more and more lawless does not help address key problems of air and water pollution, the spread of weapons of mass destruction, etc. Countertrends such as the formation of the European Union and the expansion of the political strength of regional systems to control fiscal policy, trade regulations, immigration, and pollution may be critical to addressing global warming, population control, and other key issues of the twenty-first century.

3. **Energy and calorie consumption.** Westerners of the Organization for Economic Co-operation and Development tend to consume on the order of 2,000 calories a day and about 10 liters of gasoline a day and produce on the order of 1 ton of carbon-based gases a year. Each year as the standard of living and intensity of energy and food consumption rises in the industrializing countries of the world, and as overall global population relentlessly expands 1% to 2%, the result is the negative impacts of climate change ineluctably pushing forward. The indisputable impact is an exponential increase in calories and energy around the world. Each week some 10,000 vehicles are added to the streets of Beijing alone. In countries like China, India, Brazil, Thailand, and Indonesia, the increase of population, energy, and calories is creating a global-

warming juggernaut that cannot be offset by conservation measures among the most-developed countries. Green and renewable energy and transportation systems are moving ahead, particularly in the OECD, but the pace today is discouragingly slow. The consumption of high-carbon-impact foods, like beef and other meats, remains steady in the West and is escalating in the industrializing countries.

4. **Industrialization.** The increase in population and the consumption of calories by humans is one thing, but industrialization that results in people driving gasoline-powered vehicles, living in larger houses and modern offices with heating and air-conditioning, and using a complex of equipment that tends to run on fuels that produce carbon-based greenhouse gases only accentuates the negative impacts that come with more and more people.

5. **Style of life.** The nearly doubling of the global population from about 6.5 billion to about 12 billion around 2075 does not mean a doubling of the carbon footprint of humanity. It would be optimistic to suggest that greenhouse-gas emissions under such a scenario might only increase by a factor of four. This is to suggest that human survival may hinge not only on population reduction, but also on a redefinition of "success" and a "desirable" lifestyle in the twenty-first century.

6. **Environmental change and meteorological disturbances.** The level of greenhouse gases continues to rise. The average temperature of the earth's atmosphere has increased 1 degree centigrade over the past century as the amount of carbon-based gases have steadily increased from 300 parts per million to more than 500 parts per million. As a result, the ice caps are melting. The Northwest Passage now allows direct shipping from Japan to Europe, without the use of the Panama Canal. The power of El Niño and La Niña increases along with the number of hurricanes, monsoons, tropical thunderstorms, and tornadoes. Forest fires will continue to threaten increasing areas of drought as rain water supplies dry

up. As the ice caps, glaciers, and icebergs melt, the sea level rises and seacoast cities are endangered. Once the ice caps are melted into seawater, refreezing becomes much more difficult because of the salt component. Further oil spills eventually drift to the ice caps and serve to change the reflectivity of the ice, thus accelerating the melting process. As we know from the experience of Venus, trapped gases continue to accelerate the heating of the atmosphere for thousands of years and risk a runaway process that could literally spell humanity's doom along with the doom of all life-forms on earth.

So what do all of these supertrends mean for humanity? Are we doomed? Can creativity and innovation save us? Can some form of planning and "futuring" help us ensure the survival of the species?

The good news is that there are indeed positive steps to take that can save us. The bad news is that a free-market-driven capitalist type of economy, focused on maximizing industrial throughput and fostering traditional forms of wealth accumulation, will not get us to where we need to go. Yes, creativity, innovation, and new technology can preserve life longer. But without some basic reforms of lifestyle, redefining concepts of wealth, restructuring how we arrive at economic pricing, and restructuring of government regulation, we will be in big trouble. A good deal of new technology could actually make the problems of longer-term survival even more difficult. The longer that technology puts off the need for political and economic reform, the more difficult the problem will be. Approaching the issue of population reduction should be front and center as a top priority now. The larger our population grows, the more difficult it will be to reduce it without harsh regulatory and economic measures.

The keys to the future transcend creativity and technology. Systems analysis and interdisciplinary planning, futuring, integrated technology systems, new economic incentives, and new acceptance of regulatory reforms are all necessary elements to creating a sustainable society that outlives the twenty-first century.

Top 10 Changes We Need to Face the Future

Clearly, creativity and innovation will be of critical importance for improving the quality of life and addressing environmental, health, and well-being issues of the twenty-first century. The point is that new technologies alone will not be enough. Interdisciplinary processes that combine technology, economics, pricing incentives, and governmental and international regulatory reform need to be a part of an integrated solution. Some of the most-profound new technical breakthroughs (i.e., the so-called Singularity) will give rise to huge problems of employment (e.g., unemployment, underemployment, and job retraining). Other technical needs may require massive, governmentally backed undertakings equivalent to the Manhattan Project that developed the atomic bomb. Here are some of the key changes we need to allow twenty-first-century creativity and innovation to possibly achieve higher-level goals of world peace and energy independence, and to avert climate catastrophe.

1. Interdisciplinary Studies

Twenty-first-century universities and research labs can no longer pretend that technological research and new industrial developments exist independently of one another and that one new development does not impact on energy consumption, global warming, educational needs, architectural concepts, the design of new utility systems, transportation planning, or dozens of other parts of our physical or intellectual infrastructure. Just try to imagine how much Google or the Internet have impacted such things as telework, libraries, education, health care, or governmental services.

The Santa Fe Institute, which has brought together Nobel laureate scientists from fields as diverse as economics, physics, chemistry, biology, and computer science, has led the way in trying to understand how complexity, chaos theory, and nonlinear math hold the key to understanding how things work at the level of "fundamental truth" within the cosmos. The International Space University, founded in the 1980s, has pioneered breaking down the barriers of traditional university disciplines and "stovepipe" education. Futurist and computer-science guru Ray Kurzweil, together with NASA Ames Research Center head Pete Worden and X Prize CEO Peter Diamandis, has just announced the formation of the Singularity University as a way to bring rising new governmental leaders, economists, and scientists together to cope with the implications of the likely invention of self-aware machines that possess the thinking ability of humans. These new intelligent robots of the 2020s may redefine labor, service jobs, and technological research within the next decade and a half.

This is not just another innovative or creative breakthrough, but a window into the future that impacts everything from government, health care, and education to economics or even the nature of the world order. The pretense that fields of advanced study, innovation, and creativity are unrelated and have no spillover effects can no longer be realistically maintained. Cultivating new ways of undertaking interdisciplinary and multidisciplinary studies is one of the more important needs of our times.

2. Strategies for Coping with the Coming Singularity

There are now forecasts that, within 15 years, we will see computer processors that can operate at many petaflops/second (a petaflop represents 10^{15} operations a second) and heuristic algorithms that equate to the reasoning and thinking skills of human intelligence. This translates into the capacity to create cybernetic organisms that can discharge the tasks that most industrial workers or service workers now perform across the world.

It is hard to conceive of what it would mean for employment, economic growth, R&D, education, and health care if we could create self-aware machines that could perform the jobs of more than half the people in the world. It could lead to a multitude of possibilities—massive unemployment or underemployment, significant new research capabilities, new types of man–machine interfaces and cooperation, cost-efficiency gains, new patterns of consumption, and a range of options yet to be conceived or understood. If the current worldwide fiscal meltdown were considered a three on a scale of 10, then the achieving of the Singularity could turn out to be a 10 unless full attention is given to what this major innovation means to the world economy and to see how the impacts could be mitigated.

3. Lifestyle Changes to Leverage Maslow's Hierarchy of Survival Needs

The following graphic represents a visual presentation of Maslow's investigation of human motivation, starting with physical needs and rising to self-actualization. The current professional and service worker in Western society (i.e., within the OECD) almost assumes the first three levels of needs will rather automatically be met. The business leaders in a market-driven, capitalist-motivated economy more often than not tend to seek self-actualization in terms of material wealth. The business elite frequently seek to express their sense of success through fancy homes, swimming pools, vacation homes, country club membership, or perhaps endowing a university, a museum, or some other institution—perhaps with their name attached. The problem is that, in the early part of the twenty-first century, this self-actualization is being expressed in a way that contributes to global warming and environmental pollution, and the aspirations of others seeking to emulate them in similar anti-environment actions that support a non-sustainable approach to environmental survival.

In an article in the *Washington Post* entitled "You Can Cap the Pay, But the Greed Will Go On" (February 8, 2009), Harvard Business School professors suggest that American businessmen are still locked into a mind-set that says "success" is defined in terms of how much money you make. The challenge of our times is to change the mind-set and redefine what is a "cool" lifestyle. Living in a "smart

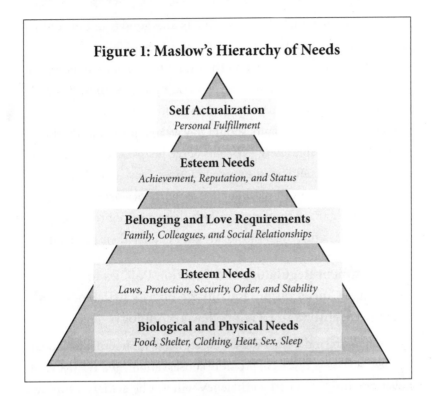

Figure 1: Maslow's Hierarchy of Needs

Self Actualization
Personal Fulfillment

Esteem Needs
Achievement, Reputation, and Status

Belonging and Love Requirements
Family, Colleagues, and Social Relationships

Esteem Needs
Laws, Protection, Security, Order, and Stability

Biological and Physical Needs
Food, Shelter, Clothing, Heat, Sex, Sleep

and green" house that is not large but rich in energy-efficiency and media features needs to become the status symbol of the future. Likewise, electric sports cars like the Tesla and staying at "green spas" can replace the wasteful status symbols of the past. Self-actualization can become "green."

4. Economic Pricing to Stimulate Efficient and Green Energy, Transport, Offices, and Housing

The straight market pricing of goods and services today is inconsistent with long-term human needs. An easily replenishable liter of wine can cost 10 times as much as a nonreplenishable liter of gasoline. There is no market-based premium placed on energy-inefficient houses and offices or polluting or gas-guzzling cars. This needs to be addressed either through taxation systems or environmentally linked pricing systems. Europe has been a leader in trying to "price in" sustainability for products and goods, and in finding ways to provide cost incentives for living a green lifestyle.

This does not mean that in the future people cannot use paper, live in large houses, and drive gas-guzzling limousines. It merely means that they should pay a premium to do so. Likewise, coal-fired electricity-generating plants should pay a large premium until they convert to renewable energy systems. Urge people and companies to do the right thing and pursue green practices, recycle, and drive electric vehicles, and they think about it. Charge them a penalty for maintaining large carbon footprints or give them a price break for going green, and it is amazing how quickly they change their behavior.

5. Government Regulatory and Taxation Policies to Encourage Conservation, Encourage Energy Efficiency, and Provide Incentives to Develop New Technology

Changing individual and corporate behavior in order to encourage desirable new research; promote conservation, creativity, and innovation; and find energy efficiency will not be achieved through "jawboning" but through price incentives, tax penalties, or regulatory processes that either discourage unwanted behavior or stimulate wanted behavior. Pricing, taxation, and regulation/laws are powerful tools that can be deployed to modify simply wide-open market processes to apply where maximizing profits or industrial throughput is the lone motivator of behavior.

For centuries since Adam Smith wrote *The Wealth of Nations*, the popular credo of business has been to let the almighty market decide. But in truth, even Adam Smith conceded that the market can be deficient and that governmental regulation may be necessary. Such intervention may be to provide some form of health protection or inspection against food contamination or police protection against swindlers or legal scams. The truth is that those who argue against governmental taxation, regulation, or market interventions are often those who see profit maximization as the ultimate purpose of economic activity. Such bottom-line, economic-throughput hard-liners are willing to ignore the other social values—even the protection of human life or ecological preservation as a part of a balanced economic equation.

In the twenty-first century, there is a need to retool economic systems and market mechanisms to recognize more complex values. Consumption, faster economic throughput, and unrestrained markets worked to create complex industrial systems in the nineteenth and twentieth centuries, but these mechanisms need to be reworked to respond to twenty-first-century needs to preserve the environment, narrow the information and welfare gaps between the wealthiest and poorest inhabitants of the world, meet energy needs, and extend our knowledge of our world and the cosmos. In short, the operation of a free and open market without concern for social values, scientific pursuits, and ecological needs is too crude an instrument to respond to the complex needs of a twenty-first-century world. It was observed at the end of the 2008 presidential election that the Republican Party looks to prevent and stave off the problems of the past and the Democratic Party looks to the future and its potential. This is the dynamic tension found in many nations around the world today.

6. Embracing of "Futuring"

The admonition of Gaston Berger, the futurist and head of the Prospective Movement in France, is that one should not only embrace the future but aggressively grab hold of it and seek to shape it, almost like an adversary in a war. There are a variety of techniques available to actively confront the future. These include the DEGEST approach, which suggests that active planning must first inventory current conditions and assess key trends related to (D)emographics, (E)conomics, (G)overnmental policies and systems, (E)nvironment, (S)ocial-cultural and religious values, and (T)echnology. This article actually represents an operational example of the process.

7. Develop New Analytic Tools, Including Integrated Systems Analysis, Operational Engineering, and Simulation and Modeling to Help Understand Complexity in Global Systems

We have developed amazingly useful computer-based tools, such as MatLab, to help us with simulations and modeling. We have created increasingly sophisticated tools for analyzing growth patterns and the interactions among population, industrialization, resource use, environment, and national trade since the original Club of Rome studies as carried out by Jay Forrester and Dennis Meadows in the 1960s. The best researchers from organizations—such as the Santa Fe Institute and the International Institute for Applied Systems Analysis in Laxenburg, Austria—and interdisciplinary projects—such as the International Space University and the Singularity University—need to redouble their efforts to learn how to better project future development trends, as well as to help identify new innovations and creative enterprises that are needed for us to not only survive the twenty-first century but to aspire to even greater achievements in the twenty-second.

8. Address the Issue of Rising Number of the World's Nation-States and the Need for Key New Global Treaties

The rise of more rather than fewer nation-states, some with populations under 10,000, and the result of fractured countries alienated by warring ethnic and religious sects, creates a pattern of tensions, adversarial rifts, and even fanatical terrorist attacks. Such warring factions make it difficult to maintain peace and undermine the opportunity for concerned international agreement on ways to combat environmental pollution, regularize global trade, limit the spread of weapons of mass destruction, or even limit the impact of gaps in education, information, or regional wealth.

The only hope comes from regional coalitions and even integration, such as is occurring with great effectiveness in the European region—first in western Europe and now even in eastern Europe. Regional trade agreements, most-favored-nation provisions, and symbiotic relationships born of mutual interest can help not only to preserve peace but also to allow pacts that can address issues such as pollution, energy consumption, transportation, and even urban planning and cooperation on employment related to an entire region. The people of Planet Earth travel on a single spaceship through the cosmos and depend on a common ecosystem. The fostering of tensions and warring interests based on conflicting religions, ethnic backgrounds, languages, and cultures—and even patriotic appeals—can often intercede against a populace's longer-term interests and well-being.

9. Undertake Research for True Breakthrough Technologies

It is possible that, over time, nations can coalesce around regional interests and even agree to global treaties that allow the best interests of all peoples to be pursued in terms of preserving a livable environment and sustaining a viable biosphere with an ozone layer to protect us against genetic mutation, and reducing greenhouse gases so as to avoid climate catastrophe. There is currently a good deal of scientific evidence that suggests modest efforts to move toward using clean and renewable energy, converting to electric vehicles, and reducing our carbon footprint could well be too little and too late.

Major new and heroic technological developments may be necessary. This could be new, massive ways to generate oxygen biosources in the oceans. It might be space-based heat-transfer systems that extend thousands of kilometers into outer space to provide us clean and cheap access to orbit as well as to transmit atmosphere heat out into the cosmos. It might be to create space colonies in a Moon–Earth Lagrangian point that provides us solar energy 24 hours a day and to create a "space ark" to protect humans from catastrophic destruction from the strike of an asteroid or weapons of mass destruction.

The creation of a new level of international cooperation to take on megaprojects that far outstrip the scope of an International Space Station or a supercollider is one of the challenges of the twenty-first century that we have yet to seriously consider. A world with self-aware machines that will, within a period as short as the next 20 years, perhaps exceed the intelligence of human beings might be able to do many things. This might be to colonize the Moon or Mars, find world peace, or even aspire to colonizing our galaxy in a hundred thousand or a million years. The potential is great if we can find a way to channel our creativity and patterns of innovation into constructive projects and truly productive tasks.

10. Reduce the World's Population Back to 1950s Level

One can conceive of hundreds and even thousands of ways to advance human potential, expand our education and health-care systems, control weapons of mass destruction, or create new and clean energy and transportation systems that help us preserve the livability of our planet. It is ironic that the one project that could be undertaken for perhaps the least cost and with the minimum of new technology has eluded our political leaders and our scientific community. This single initiative could almost guarantee the survival of humanity and make the challenge of climate catastrophe perhaps an order of magnitude less difficult. This would simply be to create a pact among all nations to seek to lower global populations back to the level that existed some 60 years ago. This would be to offer aid packages and educational programs to seek a steady but progressive reduction of global population back to about 3 billion people. With the advent of smart and self-aware machines, the need for human labor can be greatly reduced, and new occupations related to research, innovation, creativity, and the arts could flourish.

Conclusion

This then is a modest list of 10 steps we need to take to ensure a better future for our progeny a century or so from now. Indeed, these are the steps we need to undertake to hope that humanity can survive for the next billion years. Our pathway to the future passes through a narrow neck within the hour glass of cosmic time. Of all these steps, specific action to limit global population, build new regional cooperatives among proliferating nations, and seek new international agreements to accomplish all of the above 10 steps to the future are the most important. In short, the plea is for humans to embrace the concept that futuring is possible and that it is time we use our intelligence to preserve a future worthy of thinking beings. Creativity and innovation are not enough. We must embrace the future and ensure that it fulfills our destiny.

BIBLIOGRAPHY

Boulding, Kenneth. *The Meaning of the Twentieth Century: The Great Transition.* New York: Harper and Row, 1964.

Cornish, Edward. *Futuring: Exploration of the Future.* Bethesda, MD: World Future Society, 2004.

Ehrlich, Paul. *The Population Bomb.* New York: Ballantine Books, 1968.

Gleick, James. *Chaos: The Making of A New Science,* New York: Viking Press, 1987.

Khurana, Rakash, and Andy Zelleke. "You Can Cap Pay, But the Greed Will Go On." *Washington Post,* February 8, 2009, p. E1.

Kurzweil, Ray. *The Age of Spiritual Machines: When Computers Exceed Human Intelligence.* New York: Viking, 1999.

Pelton, Joseph N. *E-Sphere: The Rise of the World Wide Mind.* Westport, CT: Quorum Press, 1999.

The Millennium Project As a Method for Dealing with Global Complexity

Jerome C. Glenn, Theodore J. Gordon,
and Elizabeth Florescu

The Millennium Project is a global participatory futures research think tank organized as an independent, interdisciplinary, trans-institutional, and multicultural information system, providing an international capacity for early warning and analysis of global long-range issues, opportunities, and strategies. The purposes of the Millennium Project are to assist in organizing futures research, to improve thinking about the future, and to make that thinking available through a variety of media for consideration in policy making, advanced training, public education, and feedback—ideally to accumulate wisdom about potential futures. It is a "strategic global intelligence" that interconnects global and local perspectives through its network of 32 Nodes (groups of institutions and individuals) and participants from around the world.

In 1992, when the pre-feasibility study for a Millennium Project was launched (followed by a three-year feasibility study), the idea of looking at the future of the world through many different institutions, cultures, and disciplines seemed too idealistic and unmanage-

Jerome C. Glenn is director of the Millennium Project of the World Federation of UN Associations. E-mail jglenn@igc.org.

Theodore J. Gordon is a senior fellow of the Millennium Project.

Elizabeth Florescu is director of research for the Millennium Project.

able. Many assumed it would produce an incoherent mess. Some people still criticize the Project for being too biased in one way or another, or not profound enough, or giving some subjects too much attention and others too little. However, there is no longer any question that global participatory and cumulative futures research is possible and should be done—the only issue now is how to do it better.

The Millennium Project is designed—both in its organizational structure and research content—to address increasing global complexity.

A New Organizational Approach for Global Futures Research

The accelerating complexity of global change makes it difficult to sense the "big picture" and design beneficial strategies. Climate change cannot be turned around without a global strategy. International organized crime cannot be stopped without a global strategy. Individuals bent on creating designer diseases and causing massive deaths cannot be stopped without a global strategy. It is time for global strategic systems to be upgraded to help make important transitions, notes the *2008 State of the Future*.[1]

The challenges confronting humanity are increasingly complex, and they cannot be fully addressed by any government or institution acting alone. They require collaborative action among governments, international organizations, corporations, universities, NGOs, and individuals. Therefore, global futures research should draw on all these sources without being too attached to any one of them.

The Project got early support from organizations like EPA, UNESCO, UNDP, UNU, and some enthusiastic futurists from Australia, China, Iran, Italy, Japan, Russia, the United States, and Latin America in creating the first transnational, transdisciplinary, and transinstitutional futures research think tank to address the issues and their possible future impact for humanity as a whole.

A planning committee of 30 futurists—acting like a board of

directors—was established after the three-year feasibility study to counsel and oversee the Project's direction. "Nodes" were created to connect global and local perspectives. The concept of working with Nodes as intersections of two or more networks in a country or region has proved to be a successful organizing principle for a geographically dispersed think tank. Millennium Project Nodes are groups of individuals and institutions that identify key futurists, politicians, scientists, business planners, and scholars in their regions to participate in Millennium Project research. They conduct interviews, translate and distribute questionnaires, and conduct research and conferences. It is through their contributions that the world picture of the Millennium Project emerges. Today there are 32 Nodes: Argentina (Buenos Aires); Australasia (Melbourne, Australia); Azerbaijan (Baku); Bolivia (La Paz/Santa Cruz); Brazil (São Paulo); Brussels-Area (Brussels); Central Europe (Prague, Czech Republic, and Bratislava, Slovak Republic); Canada (Kingston); Chile (Santiago); China (Beijing); Dominican Republic (Santo Domingo); Egypt (Cairo); Finland (Helsinki); France (Paris); Germany (Cologne/Berlin); Gulf Region (Kuwait); India (New Delhi/Madurai); Iran (Tehran); Israel (Tel Aviv); Italy (Rome); Japan (Tokyo); Korea (Seoul); Mexico City (Mexico); Peru (Lima); Russian Federation (Moscow); Silicon Valley (United States); Slovenia (Ljubljana); South Africa (Pretoria/Johannesburg); Turkey (Istanbul); UAE (Dubai); UK (London); Venezuela (Caracas). There is also an experimental Cyber Node and the coordinating office in Washington, D.C. With the participation of the Nodes, more than 2,500 experts from around the world, from different domains and backgrounds, have contributed to the Project's work.

The Project can be seen as a "coalition of the willing" of like-minded individuals concerned with global issues. The main principle that unites the "Millennium Project family" is an interest in identifying strategies for building the best possible future for humanity as a whole. Most of the work is volunteered.

There are one or two meetings per year, at which the planning

Figure 1: Millennium Project Nodes

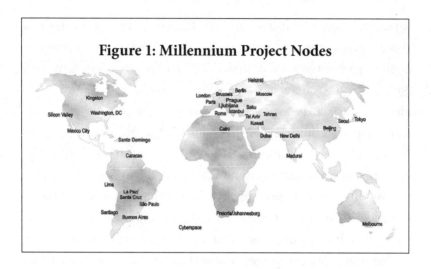

committee members and the Nodes get together face-to-face to discuss the past year's achievements (and shortfalls) and plan the work and priorities for the next year. These are two to three days of intensive brainstorming sessions where, in addition to discussing the Millennium Project work, the Nodes present highlights of their own futures-related activities for encouraging cooperation and seeking ideas from the others. Feedback from the participants indicates that the meetings are getting better and more intense each year. Additionally, due to the broad involvement of the Project and its members in different future-oriented activities around the world, many members meet on other occasions to discuss cooperation and Millennium Project issues and to influence work priorities. Outside meetings are also an opportunity for disseminating Millennium Project findings and to involve other experts from different domains in the Project's activities.

The Project maintains two Web sites: *www.millennium-project .org,* for general information on the Millennium Project and featuring all of its studies, and *www.mpcollab.org,* for more internal collaboration and use of experimental Internet tools for improving work flow. Communication among the Project's Nodes, participants, and the headquarters is facilitated by several Listservs used for internal announcements as well as for discussions and input for research. Some Listservs are dedicated only to the Nodes and the planning committee, some have larger public access, and others are devoted to specific subjects.

The Millennium Project has demonstrated that it is possible to conduct participatory global futures research across nations, institutions, and disciplines. Furthermore, the Nodes themselves have begun to cluster around different regional issues or subjects. For example, some European Nodes collaborate on joint projects for the European Union and organize conferences on the future of Europe. Sometimes Nodes participate in specialized studies, such as Millennia 2015, which addresses the status of women. Latin American Nodes are cooperating in organizing futures research and conducting various studies in their region, while same-language Nodes collaborate on translation of the *State of the Future* reports. All these activities help to further collaborative global futures thinking and address world and regional complexity.

Addressing Global Change through Systematic Cumulative Work

A systematic and cumulative approach to futures research is essential for designing strategies and managing global issues. Futures research studies should not begin from scratch each time, but should build on the results of all that has gone on before. Therefore, the Millennium Project's work is cumulative—building on previous work, updating, developing, and expanding it. Studies tracking change are continuously updated, and new studies are added and published in annual *State of the Future* reports. The first edition of *State of the Future* was published in 1997, followed by a new updated version each summer. Each edition contains an executive summary in print, accompanied by a CD-ROM designed to serve as a reference document—containing the Millennium Project's cumulative research and methods (note, the CD-ROM of the *2008 State of the Future* has more than

6,000 pages).

The *State of the Future* is a "very useful integration of a vast amount of information from many sources. Continues as the best introduction—by far—to major global issues and long-term remedies," says Michael Marien, editor of *Future Survey*. The reports are an overview of global change and prospects for civilization that the public, researchers, and policy makers may use to improve their own global understanding and strategic decision making.

Editions of the *State of the Future* have been published in Arabic, Chinese, Farsi, French, Korean, and Spanish, while the executive summaries are available online in many more languages. The publication in other countries has had numerous impacts. For example, Chinese editions published since 1999 have stimulated some sectoral, regional, and national State of the Future scenario studies in China (such as for water, energy, and population) by the Chinese Academy of Natural Sciences, and provided important input to the National 11th Five-Year Plan.

The Millennium Project methods can be highly quantitative (such as the State of the Future Index), a combination of quantitative and qualitative (such as the RealTime Delphi), or primarily qualitative (such as the scanning used for the Global Challenges and the emerging environmental security issues).

Presented below are thumbnail sketches of some Project studies that illustrate its work and seem relevant as means for identifying and dealing with global adaptive complex systems.[2]

The 15 Global Challenges

The 15 Global Challenges identified and updated by the Millennium Project provide a framework to better understand the present and to assess the global and local prospects for humanity. They emerged through the broadest and longest-lasting ongoing set of feedback processes in the history of futures research. These Challenges have provided input to nearly all heads of state and governments prior

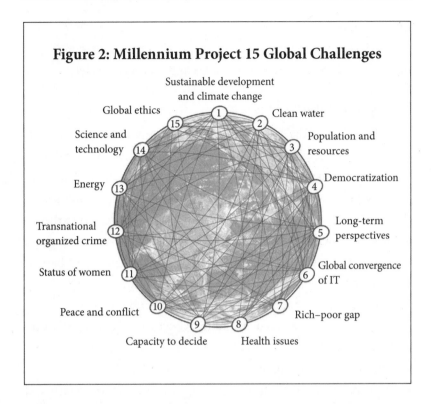

Figure 2: Millennium Project 15 Global Challenges

to the UN Millennium Summit and to the subsequent selection of the eight Millennium Development Goals, and they may have stimulated the creation of similar lists put together by other groups. They have been used extensively in education—from primary to graduate levels—in many institutions and countries.

The Global Challenges address the world situation regarding sustainable development and climate change, water, population and resources, democratization, long-term policy making, globalization of information technology, rich-poor gap, health, decision-making capacities, conflict resolution, improving the status of women, transnational organized crime, energy, science and technology, and global ethics.

The 15 Global Challenges build a comprehensive system of equally important issues and opportunities. They are interdependent: Improvement in one makes it easier to address others; deterioration in one makes it harder to address others. No institution, state, or organization can successfully address any of the challenges alone. They have to be addressed across all spectra and sectors of society.

State of the Future Index

The State of the Future Index is a measure of the 10-year outlook for the future based on the previous 20 years of historical data. It is constructed with key variables and forecasts that, in the aggregate, could show the directions and intensity of change and identify the factors responsible. It provides a mechanism for studying the relationships among the elements of a complex system—how making a single change ripples throughout a system, creating some positive and intended consequences as well as unintended results.

The unique combination of features of SOFI includes:

- The subject: SOFI is a quantitative forecast of the general future outlook.
- The elements/variables: determined by groups of experts.
- Probabilistic nature: The forecasts of the constituent variables and the SOFI are displayed.
- Set of "standards": allowing nation-to-nation comparisons.

The index has been constructed for the global level as well as for individual countries.

SOFI was first presented in 2000 and has since been continuously updated and improved. A set of 29 variables was identified by an international panel of experts selected by the Millennium Project Nodes around the world during a study conducted in 2006–2007. Participants were asked to rate the variables, give worst- and best-scenario estimates, suggest new variables to be included in the SOFI, and suggest sources that could provide at least 20 years of historical data. The following graph shows the SOFI 2007 using trend-impact analysis.

Combining many variables into a single index number can lead to loss of detail. Creating an index requires judgments both in selecting the variables to include and in weighting them. An index of global

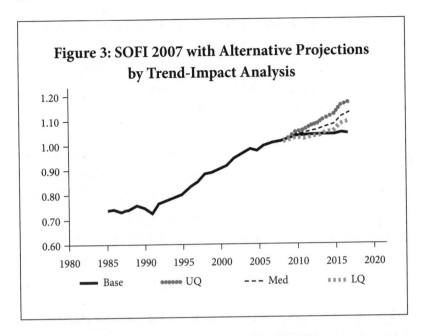

Figure 3: SOFI 2007 with Alternative Projections by Trend-Impact Analysis

conditions can mask variations among regions, nations, or groups. The apparent precision of an index can easily be mistaken for accuracy. For these reasons, great attention has to be given to the variables that make up the index, and to seeking accurate data sources and tracking changes when they occur.

Yet, assessing the world's key indicators over the past 20 years and projecting them for the next 10 gives the basis for a report card on humanity's future, showing where we are winning or losing, and hence, helps to set policy priorities.

RealTime Delphi

The RealTime Delphi is a relatively new and efficient method for collecting and synthesizing expert opinions. It is designed to speed up the Delphi process while still maintaining the principle of anonymous group feedback to bring forth the best thinking of the group. The respondents participate by filling out an online questionnaire—both numerical and qualitative—that is updated as new responses are recorded. The respondents can—and are encouraged to—revisit the questionnaire as many times as they want within a specific time period.

If a leader wanted to know the best thinking on an issue or to understand the range of thinking on an issue, top experts could be invited to sign on to the RealTime Delphi Web site and answer a series of questions about the issue. They would add their judgments to the group's and edit them on a continuous basis in response to other comments within a deadline. The distribution of the group's responses and the reasons they have provided for their answers can be available to the leader immediately. The process can be synchronous or asynchronous and can involve a worldwide panel. A tutorial on how to use a RealTime Delphi questionnaire was developed and is available at *www.mpcollab.org/learning/course/view.php?id=3.*

NEW ORGANIZATIONAL FORMS TO IMPROVE GLOBAL STRATEGIC THINKING

Over the years, the Millennium Project made several suggestions for organizational structures that could advance global futures thinking and strategic forecasting. Following are outlined the most recent ones, which could improve the process of addressing global complexity.

Government Future Strategy Units and Potential Coordination

In order to make good national decisions, heads of state and government have to consider complex and rapidly changing global factors that are beyond their control. As a result, an increasing number of governments and government components are creating future strategy or foresight units to contribute to their national policy process. Typically, the future strategy unit is placed within the office of the prime minister or president of the country to integrate the futures research from other government sections and external institutions. These units often manage a network of other executive councils and future strategy units within ministries to provide inputs to national strategy.

The Millennium Project has prepared brief overviews of 28 such future strategic units. Based on some general observations, it suggests that the efficiency of these units might be improved if they were to use the RealTime Delphi to quickly collect and synthesize best judgments, create national SOFIs, develop collective intelligence for continuity between administrations, and better link these units with each other and their counterparts in UN organizations to improve international strategic coordination.

Some advocate that climate change should be the first topic for such systematic strategic development and coordination. Some steps could include:

- Connect government and UN agency future strategy units via Web/intranet with the offices of the secretary-general and president of the General Assembly.
- Create an interoperable global futures scanning system for the secretary-general's office and the major UN organizations.
- Design a global situation room for the secretary-general that might initially focus on global climate change.
- Develop a UN-integrated or collective-intelligence system for climate change to provide for "just-in-time knowledge" to support decision making and management.
- Use the RealTime Delphi to rapidly collect best judgments worldwide to support decision making that is integrated into the collective intelligence and global futures scanning system.
- Integrate the UN secretary-general's situation room with the UN government strategic intranet and the climate change collective intelligence system.

Global Energy Collective Intelligence

The options to create and update national, global, and corporate energy strategies are so complex and rapidly changing that it is almost impossible for decision makers to gather and understand all of the information required to make and implement coherent policy. At the same time, the environmental and social consequences of incoherent policies are extremely serious. Therefore, a new global system for the identification, analysis, assessment of possible consequences, and synthesis of energy options for decision making is urgently needed.

The Millennium Project has outlined a Global Energy Network and Information System (GENIS) as a collective intelligence to help understand the whole energy picture and get "just-in-time" knowledge about specifics, thus leading to better questions and decisions. The proposed system would be composed of two integrated elements:

- The Global Energy Network, providing communications and collaboration capabilities for a worldwide community of experts and others working on or concerned with energy issues.
- The Global Energy Information System, a repository (knowledge base) and associated interactive access facility for as much of the world's total knowledge about energy (actual content, pointers to external systems, and ability to mashup from other databases into one integrated set of outputs) as can be accumulated.

The two components would work together to support a variety of needs, such as those for politicians during energy hearings; for policy makers creating national, bilateral, or multilateral energy strategies; for businesses and universities supporting R&D; for media fact-checking; and for the general public.

SOME CONCLUDING THOUGHTS

After 12 years of the Millennium Project's global futures research, it is increasingly clear that the world has the resources to address our common challenges, but coherence and direction are lacking. However, ours is the first generation with the means for many to know the world as a whole, identify global improvement systems, and seek to improve such systems.

The "transinstitution" is a new type of organization to address an issue that could be more effective than current institutional approaches. An organization would be registered as a "transinstitution" if can demonstrate that it: (1) receives its funds from at least four of the following categories but not a majority from any one: governments, for-profit corporations, nonprofit organizations (NGOs), UN or other international organizations, foundations, universities, and/or individuals; (2) has a board of directors whose members come from all these institutional categories but without a majority from any one institutional category; (3) pays associated employees and consultants who come from all these institutional categories but does not have a majority from any one institutional category; and (4) has products, services, and/or other outputs that are purchased or used by all these categories but without a majority being used by any single institutional category. This definition could be used as an amendment to a country's corporate laws.

Groups of Nodes working together could create a "space of action" or "field" that does not fit in the usual concepts for organizational structures. For example, three European Nodes created a project with the European Union for futures methodological applications. Such "fields" could conceivably connect with other fields to make synergies that would have been impossible in previous institutional forms. This could itself become a more complex adaptive system with an emerging collective intelligence, which is self-improving and increasingly interconnected with media and decision making.

Clustering information in Global Challenges, their continuous update and interdependency assessment, as well as computing a State of the Future Index, could help clarify the complexity and changes of the global system and set priorities.

Creating collaborative collective intelligence systems improves information flow, accessibility, and accountability, and expands brain horizons, enhancing decision-making capacity.

Cumulative research with executive summaries for policy makers and detailed background material for researchers will help to bring the research to larger and more sophisticated audiences and increase interest in futures studies in general.

Holding awards ceremonies for students on the 15 Global Challenges is a unique and efficient way to teach long-term global thinking to the next generation in schools. (See Global Millennium Prize, *www.globalmillenniumprize.org.)*

"Time-to-impact" is a key to decision making. Therefore, future research should provide complete information on forecasts highlighting the best solutions that can provide the fastest positive impact and the actors that should be involved.

Decision science is primitive, and decision making needs to be improved. More information is becoming available about the role of information and the psychology and mental processes involved in decision processes. Since the future of the world rests largely in the hands of decision makers at all levels, it is important to follow paths that will result in better decisions that anticipate issues, achieve goals, and avoid unpleasant surprises.

The current mission and structure of the Millennium Project focuses more on generating content and futures methods than on connecting content and methods to decision makers, policy advisers, and educators. However, increasingly the Project is becoming more helpful to those who are the means by which its research finds consideration and application.

Through its research, publications, conferences, and Nodes, the Millennium Project helps to nurture an international collaborative spirit of free inquiry and feedback for increasing collective intelligence to improve social, technical, and environmental viability for human development. Feedback on its work (both methods and content) is most welcome at *http://millennium-project@igc.org.*

NOTES

1. Most of the material in this article is from the *2008 State of the Future* by Jerome C. Glenn, Theodore J. Gordon, and Elizabeth Florescu (Washington, D.C.: Millennium Project, WFUNA, 2008).

2. Since most of this article is drawn from the *State of the Future,* more details on each study are available in the report.

GrrRANK! The World's Largest System Shifts Gears

The Inertial Realities That Are Transforming the American Economy

David Pearce Snyder

As we travel through life—out of the past, through the present, and into the future—the pace of tangible change is typically so incremental that there seems to be little evidence to distinguish the future from the recent past. And, while the slow arrival of apparent change frustrates many futurists, attitude surveys suggest that the general public is much more comfortable with evolutionary change than with revolutionary change.

Of course, as history makes clear, there have been a number of noteworthy eras in the past when combinations of trends and developments have coalesced in such a way that they have provoked accelerated, system-wide adaptation and innovation. During such times, the rate of change often becomes so rapid that it cannot be accommodated within the existing paradigms of daily life and work—or of organization and operation. According to the Austro-American economist Joseph Schumpeter, such periods are characterized by "waves of creative destruction," as old ways of doing things are modified or abandoned and new ways of doing things are created or adopted, tan-

David Pearce Snyder is a consulting futurist and principal of The Snyder Family Enterprise. E-mail david_snyder@verizon.net.

gibly changing life for most people in a single generation or less.

There is growing evidence to suggest that the United States—and with it, the entire human enterprise—has entered a historic period of accelerated innovation and change, and that we will soon find ourselves living in a near-term future that will be strikingly different from the recent past.

The following scenario begins in our recent past, passes through the present, and on into the middle of the next decade. The dynamics driving this scenario are not speculative; they are built into the existing demographic, econometric, and technological realities of the system in which we all live. These dynamic forces are therefore inertial to the ongoing existence of the American enterprise, and the following scenario can be expected to play out regardless of any unpredictable random events that will occur. Such events—political

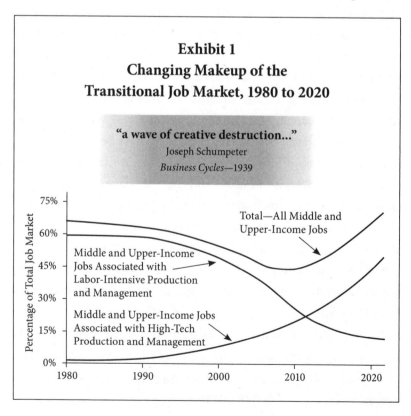

Exhibit 1
Changing Makeup of the
Transitional Job Market, 1980 to 2020

"a wave of creative destruction..."
Joseph Schumpeter
Business Cycles—1939

Exhibit 2
Signs of Techno-Economic Change

Average Annual U.S. Productivity Improvement Rates

1974-1994	1995-1999	2000-2007
1.4%	2.5%	3.1%

Average Annual Inflation Rates

	1990-1994	1995-1999	2000-2007
U.S.	3.6%	2.4%	2.3%
World	30.4%	8.4%	4.1%

developments, natural disasters, technological breakthroughs, etc.—may serve to either accelerate or slow the following sequence of events. They are unlikely, however, to prevent the following scenario from occurring.

OUR INERTIAL PATH INTO THE FUTURE

1980–2016: As a consequence of the internationalization of the U.S. economy and the technologically driven restructuring of work itself, real median income in America has been stagnant or falling for most of the past 30 years (see Exhibit 1). While household income did rise significantly during the second half of the 1990s, it has since fallen in seven of the past eight years. Meanwhile, because of steadily rising U.S. productivity and the offshoring of high-tech job growth, current U.S. Bureau of Labor Statistics projections reflect a slowing U.S. job-creation rate and little or no structural increase in median personal income between now and 2016 (see exhibits 2 through 4).

2000–2007: In spite of constrained household income growth, U.S. consumer spending rose robustly until 2008. Personal consumption rose from 67% of GDP in 2000 to a record-high 72% in 2007, after having averaged 63% from 1960 through the mid-1990s.

Exhibit 3

"We're doing more work with less labor!"
Comparative 10-Year Projections for
U.S. Population and Job Growth

	Projected Population Growth		Projected Job Growth		Job Creation Rate
	Numbers	%	Numbers	%	
2000 to 2010	28.1 million	10%	22.2 million	15.2%	100:79
2002 to 2012	28.8 million	10%	21.3 million	14.8%	100:74
2004 to 2014	29.4 million	10%	18.9 million	13.0%	100:64
2006 to 2016	30.9 million	10%	15.6 million	10.4%	100:52

Source: U.S. Bureau of Labor Statistics (BLS)

2000–2007: Since 2000, easy access to low-cost credit, plus the lowest tax rates among all industrial nations, have permitted U.S. households to consume more goods and services than their European and Japanese counterparts. (For years, economists have observed that Americans were living beyond their means.) At the same time, low interest rates on bank deposits reduced U.S. propensity to save from 3.7% of all personal income in 2000 to less than 1% in 2007.

2008–2013: The sudden "evaporation" of $50 trillion from the world's capital supply in 2008 is widely expected to reduce the availability—and increase the cost—of both consumer and commercial credit for at least three to five years.

2009–2010: Tighter government regulation of all financial markets will substantially curtail high-risk investing, reducing the financial services sector's ability to create new sources of credit.

2009–2013: The long postponement of infrastructure maintenance and the chronic underfunding of regulatory mandates resulting from the nation's suppressed tax rates and curtailed government revenues have begun to produce growing examples of infrastructure and regulatory failures that demand immediate remediation. Because of the global recession and the collapse of the world's credit markets, the government will be unable to raise sufficient capital needed for essential infrastructure improvements. As a result, the next four years will see rates of taxation, user fees, road tolls, etc., rise at all levels of government jurisdiction. Increased federal taxes on surplus corporate profits and capital gains—along with higher gasoline taxes, plus carbon taxes on all forms of energy consumption—will underwrite substantial public investments in new transportation, energy, and environmental infrastructure. The taxes to pay for these investments will, in turn, increase the average cost of living in America, reducing the discretionary income in the hands of U.S. consumers.

2006–2016: Meanwhile, workforce demographers project that, from now on, there will be a growing shortage of new recruits to fill all types of skilled positions—from pediatricians to plumbers (see Exhibit 5). Labor economists routinely warn that the scarcity of skilled workers will inevitably constrain U.S. economic growth. Moreover,

---

Exhibit 4

But, most service jobs earn less than median pay and don't require college!
BLS forecasts indicate that, of the 15.6 million service jobs created between 2006 and 2016 ...

Number	%	will require:
5.8 million	37.7%	A two- or four-year college degree
1.1 million	6.9%	Trade school or internships
8.7 million	55.4%	No postsecondary education

Source: U.S. Bureau of Labor Statistics, 2008

Exhibit 5

BUMMER!
BLS expects job growth to outpace labor supply in U.S. between 2006 and 2016!

	Employment (in 1,000s)		Projected Change	
	2006	**2016**	**(1,000s)**	**%**
Total—All Jobs	150,620	166,220	15,600	+10.4%
Total—All Workers*	51,428	164,232	2,804	+8.5%
Labor Surplus/Shortfall	+808	-1,988		

*Includes undocumented foreign-born workers

Source: U.S. Bureau of Labor Statistics, 2008

while the intensifying competition for skilled recruits will predictably boost the wages of people with readily employable skills, it will also fuel wage inflation and increase the costs of a wide range of professional, commercial, and consumer services (see Exhibit 6).

2012: Not only will higher taxes and the rising price of credit demand a greater share of consumer income in the years ahead, but also the underlying levels of inflation are widely expected to rise following the global recession, over the long term, as growing worldwide consumption of middle-class goods and services generates ever greater marketplace demands for basic commodities—food, fabrication materials, fuel, and water—that will increasingly outstrip readily available supplies, putting upward pressure on commodity prices.

Together, the preceding set of eight inertial realities implies a three- to five-year economic outlook in which household income is projected to stagnate, while taxes will rise, credit will become more costly, and the underlying global rate of inflation will move slowly but steadily upward. Several major economists have written that, after years of profligate consumption, altered circumstances will now force Americans to live within their means. The current downturn in the business cycle reflects the initial downshifting of the consumer engine that has driven the U.S. economy for the past decade. Even after we recover from the current recession (2010–2011), levels of consumer spending can be expected to remain 5% to 10% below pre-recession levels for at least five years.

2009–2014: To offset the effects of the recession, Congress is expected to authorize the expenditure of hundreds of billions of dollars on social-support services and on infrastructure improvements—including urban water systems, highways and mass transit, renewable-energy research and production, pollution abatement, and greenhouse gas reduction. In addition, Congress can ultimately be expected to enact a single-payer national-health-insurance system with universal standards for electronic medical record-keeping—reducing the costs of health care in America while improving its quality.

2009: From now on, Americans will be spending less on hous-

Exhibit 6
The rising cost of everything!

• Growing global demand for consumer goods will drive up costs of commodities—food, materials, and energy, DRIVING UP THE UNDERLYING COST OF LIVING!

• Shrinkage of global capital supply will raise long-term costs of consumer and commercial credit, DRIVING UP THE UNDERLYING COST OF LIVING!

• Growing shortage of skilled workers—especially in health, education, and construction—will increase labor costs, DRIVING UP THE UNDERLYING COST OF LIVING!

• Need to replace/expand infrastructure will require higher taxes, user fees, tolls, etc.

ALL DRIVING UP THE UNDERLYING COST OF LIVING!

---

ing, cars, and designer clothing, and spending more on infrastructure, health care, and home entertainment. Spreading suburban sprawl will grind to a halt; most new residences will be built in high-density, mixed-use, in-fill developments clustered around rail-transit stations throughout an increasingly urbanized nation. The coming building boom in energy-efficient urban villages will mark America's adoption of new middle-class lifestyles that will be both ecologically and economically sustainable. For the foreseeable future, economic necessity will lead growing numbers of Americans to purchase smaller, more energy-efficient homes and vehicles and to substitute communications for transportation via telecommuting, virtual vacations, distance learning, and e-playing.

A RENDEZVOUS WITH AUSTERITY

In many respects, this moment is remarkably similar to the opening years of the Great Depression. Franklin Delano Roosevelt famously said, "We have always known that the heedless pursuit of self-interest was bad morals; we now know that it is also bad economics." He also said, "This generation of Americans has a rendezvous with destiny." Nearly three-quarters of a century later, it would appear that today's generation of Americans "has a rendezvous with austerity."

Our rendezvous with austerity is presaged by system-wide inertial forces that cannot be altered. These forces may, however, be either ameliorated or exacerbated by unpredictable random developments, including political actions, technological breakthroughs, and marketplace adaptations—about which we can only speculate.

Some economic historians, for example, argue that political actions by the Hoover and Roosevelt administrations during the early 1930s deepened and prolonged the 1929 stock market crash into a depression by shutting down foreign trade, preventing bank consolidations, delaying technological innovation, and barring improvements in labor productivity. While historians have concluded that the New Deal workplace programs—NRA, WPA, CCC, and Social Security—

were instrumental to cutting unemployment in half (from 25% to 12%), the economy as a whole was not lifted out of the Depression until the massive public expenditures associated with another random event, the Second World War.

Ben Bernanke, the current chair of the Federal Reserve Board, is widely recognized as one of the most knowledgeable experts on the 1930s Depression. Bernanke finds much to applaud in the New Deal initiatives, but he concludes that the Depression was unnecessarily prolonged by Roosevelt's failure to maintain the liquidity of the nation's banking system. Clearly determined to avoid that mistake, the Federal Reserve and the Treasury Department pumped more than $1 trillion into financial institutions during the past 12 months. Chairman Bernanke and Treasury secretaries Geithner and Paulson have urged that massive infusions of capital should continue until credit is again flowing freely.

Problematically, it is widely acknowledged in the business press that 2009 is likely to witness additional meltdowns in the credit markets—arising this time from defaults on student loans, municipal bonds, commercial real estate mortgages, corporate debt, and underfunded pensions. If this happens, even more trillions of dollars in taxpayer money might not be sufficient to restore liquidity to America's commercial and consumer credit markets, especially in light of the fact that the United States would, itself, have to borrow most of those trillions from the shrinking global capital supply. In short, the immediate future of the global financial markets—and of governments' responses thereto—is fraught with uncertainty and incalculable risks. Because the bulk of the world's troubled assets are in exotic, unregulated areas of the financial marketplace, the degree of risk and the extent of the system's exposure to loss is not yet knowable. This uncertainty raises the legitimate concern that, in bailing out failing banks and manufacturers, the government (and the taxpayers) may be pouring good money after bad.

By comparison, the Obama administration's February 2009 economic stimulus package is considerably more comfortable territory, involving such familiar components as unemployment benefits, tax cuts, public works, infrastructure improvements, and basic scientific research. While there was widespread bipartisan support for governmental economic stimulus, fiscal and political conservatives sought to scale back the legislation. An even broader array of economists and politicians, meanwhile, continue to argue that the $787 billion stimulus will scarcely be sufficient to offset the economic impact of a $12.7 trillion loss in U.S. housing and stock values, plus the added losses that many experts believe await us in 2009.

At the Bottom of a Deep Hole

As we contemplate the near-term future, we can be reasonably certain that the next 24 to 36 months will be characterized by high unemployment, weak economic growth, and a wide array of unpredictable political, financial, and international developments that may either improve or degrade our circumstances. But even when we emerge from the current recession, we will still find ourselves in the trough of Joseph Schumpeter's "wave of creative destruction" (see Exhibit 1). The rising tide of prosperity that has historically accompanied the closing years of previous techno-economic revolutions can be traced to the fact that, as a new technology matures, it begins to generate more new high-value jobs while eliminating fewer old high-value jobs. Given the maturity of computer technology, history suggests that a rising tide of technology-driven prosperity is not far off—24 to 36 months—which suggests that the long-prophesied high-tech boom may turn out to be a significant factor in ending the current recession, in much the same way that World War II was instrumental in lifting the nation out of the Great Depression.

In fact, various politicians and interest groups—and futurists—are publicly promoting three different visions of a prosperous twenty-first-century high-tech American economy:

1. A high-tech manufacturing economy. In this vision, while the United States will continue to mass-produce vehicles, appliances, farm equipment, etc., new growth in the industrial sector will largely be driven by the production of new hard goods, including biomedical technologies, robots, and nanomaterials.

Meanwhile, many "Rust Belt" states have been peddling:

2. A green industrial economy. This vision is popular with many political leaders and involves U.S. industrial growth being largely driven by the production of environmentally beneficial goods and materials—e.g., wind turbines, fuel cells, solar panels, electric cars, cellulose-based plastics, etc., plus energy-efficient appliances and structures.

3. A professional, managerial, scientific, and technical services economy. In the 1970s and 1980s, this was essentially the only vision of a postindustrial economy, but only futurists, academics, and the IT industry believed in it. The long-term assumption behind this vision was that—just as with agriculture—mechanization and automation would ultimately minimize the labor required to produce all of the goods we need. Employment would shift to the service sector, where knowledge-based work would generate the professional, managerial, scientific, and technical jobs that would become the basis of an ever more prosperous Information Age middle class. This perception of the future, in turn, gave rise to the widespread acceptance of the notion (never proven) that in the future a postsecondary education would be required in order to earn a middle-class income.

Major elements of both the $787 billion economic stimulus package (the American Recovery and Reinvestment Act) and of President Obama's five-year federal budget are clearly intended to foster the development of high-tech manufacturing and green industries. The recent elimination of the federal ban on stem-cell research will also be instrumental in increasing U.S. high-tech manufacturing. In fact, without these kinds of substantial government commitments, neither high-tech manufacturing nor green industries are likely to become large-scale economic activities anytime soon. The most recent Bureau of Labor Statistics long-term jobs forecasts indicate that pharmaceutical manufacturing is the only class of high-tech industrial enterprise that is expected to experience any employment growth at all between now and 2016.

On the other hand, current BLS employment projections show that professional, managerial, scientific, and technical (PMST) occupations, including health care and education, are expected to grow rapidly through 2016. At first glance, this would appear to validate the classic futurist vision that the postindustrial economy will literally be *past*-industrial. Today, only 9% of all U.S. workers are in manufacturing, down from nearly 40% in 1950, and the BLS projects that manufacturing will shrink to 7.6% of all work by 2016. Meanwhile, service work already makes up more than 80% of the current workforce, and 97% of all new jobs between now and 2016 will be in the service sector—roughly one-third of which are expected to be in professional, managerial, scientific, and technical positions.

Unfortunately, large numbers of PMST jobs—including elementary school teachers, social workers, and paramedics—pay less than skilled blue-collar jobs, such as autoworkers, miners, and machinists. Moreover, the actual numbers of many PMST occupations—forensic scientists, substance-abuse therapists, pharmaceutical technicians, database administrators, computer game designers, etc.—are so small that even with their rapid growth rates these occupations will not add nearly enough new, well-paid jobs to replace the millions of skilled blue-collar jobs that have vanished over the past decade. In short, the Labor Department's job forecasts offer no indication that we are about to experience a significant increase in high-wage employment in either blue-collar or white-collar work.

Of course, because BLS employment projections are largely extrapolated from past trends, it would not be terribly surprising if these forecasts failed to anticipate the rise of new types of jobs in new industries—all made possible by new technologies. Over the next three to four years, federal and state tax incentives, along with sustained government investments in initiatives like alternative energy, mass transit, and a national electronic medical record system, should help to accelerate growth in high-tech employment.

Meanwhile, an innovative form of work organization has, in recent years, gained sufficient system-wide momentum to merit attention: the growth of microbusiness.

THE GROWTH OF VIRTUAL ENTERPRISES

The IRS and the Small Business Administration define microbusinesses as non-incorporated firms—sole proprietorships, partnerships, consortia, etc.—reporting "taxable earned income, but having no employees." The number of these firms rose 30%, from 15.4 million in 1997 (the first year the Census Bureau began to publish data on microbusinesses) to 20.0 million in 2006. During that same period, the number of U.S. businesses with one or more paid employees grew just 4%, from 6.9 million to 7.2 million. While the annual revenue of firms with employees ($27 trillion) vastly exceeds the annual revenue of firms without employees ($1 trillion), average revenue growth of firms with no employees exceeds that of firms with employees (5.1% growth per year, compared to 4.4% per year).

Microbusinesses are truly virtual enterprises. To minimize overhead costs, most organize themselves along the model of today's independent Hollywood film producers, who typically assemble temporary teams of writers, designers, actors, and technicians for each motion-picture they turn out. Microbusiness owners (often salaried employees themselves) use the Internet to identify potential projects and mobilize collaborators. They employ groupware to develop proposals and execute their work commitments, frequently in conjunction with contributors they have never met, living in countries where they have ever been. These transitory enterprises are ideally suited to a wide range of multidisciplinary consulting projects. Microbusinesses also commonly engage in developing and marketing software and applets for Web-enabled devices, in designing online games and even producing short-run manufactured goods using contract industrial job-shops in both the United States and abroad. The primary characteristic of microbusinesses is that they come together, do the work, and then disperse.

Many observers believe that recent initiatives to offer software and computing capacity as on-demand services over the Internet point to a future in which most firms will routinely purchase their computing services from giant information utilities (IBM, Oracle, and H-P) or from system conglomerators (Amazon and Google). These new business services permit individual firms to eliminate their own in-house IT staff and costly computing facilities. The looming shortage of skilled IT personnel will certainly encourage these developments, even though most corporate IT executives argue that a company's own proprietary computer system is too intrinsically important as a strategic asset to be outsourced.

Whether or not the on-demand availability of cheap-but-powerful information services will eliminate corporate IT departments, the truly revolutionary implications of these new Web-based information services—and of the plunging telecommunications costs made possible by the ongoing integration of the Internet and telephony (WiFi, 3-G Mobile, VoIP, Skype, Google Voice, etc.)—must be thought of in terms of their relationship to Coase's law, an economic concept first advanced by British economist Ronald Coase in 1934, which holds that "the cost of gathering information determines the size of organizations." Specifically, under the fundamental principles of Coase's law, when the cost of gathering information falls to zero, then the optimal size of enterprise, theoretically, falls to one person.

If Coase's law accurately characterizes commercial marketplace behavior, then, as access to growing amounts of information becomes easier, faster, and cheaper, the numbers of self-employed and micro-businesses will continue to grow faster than will the numbers of large firms. For the same reasons, large organizations are expected to become smaller. Major employers are creating electronic, online "hiring halls"—virtual spaces where free agents can match corporate requests for input with their expertise. InnoCentive, for example, was originally created by drug maker Eli Lilly to augment its in-house research capacity. This online network now serves a number of major firms and is routinely used by more than 100,000 independent consultants looking for problems they can solve or questions they can answer—often for fees of $10,000 or more. "In the emerging marketplace of free agents and spontaneous collaboration," says Reid Hoffman, CEO/founder of LinkedIn, a social-networking Web site for the workplace, "every individual will be a small business or a brand."

Many futurists—including this author—have long forecast that free agency would ultimately replace wage slavery in the information economy. But this development was not possible without a supporting infrastructure. That infrastructure (or *infostructure*)—in the form of ubiquitous, low-cost broadband Web access, open information systems and services, and groupware—is now largely in place. Spontaneous workplace collaboration is on the rise. The strategic question is, Is the current boom in free agentry and open sourcing simply a transitional stage in our passage from a mature industrial economy to a mature information economy—which will ultimately be dominated by large, formally structured enterprises? Or are we currently creating a new and different twenty-first-century world of work, in which each individual will be a continuously evolving small business throughout his or her life? And, if microbusinesses truly are about to become a primary feature of the twenty-first-century workplace, can we really expect such an unstructured job market to ultimately restore the general middle-class prosperity and economic security of the Industrial Era?

CODA

Today, the answer to all these questions can only be a matter of speculation. Five years or so from now, the next stage of our future will be much closer, and we will be able to see it more clearly. Five years from now, we will know whether our current efforts to jump-start high-tech manufacturing and green industries in America have been successful. But right now, we are in the middle of a techno-economic revolution, and things are likely to get a good deal more squirrelly before we begin to converge on a specific direction for the American enterprise. Most complexity theorists would argue that, in light of the number of major dynamic variables currently in play throughout the American economy, chaotic developments should not be unexpected. After all, revolutions have historically been untidy affairs.

Through the Crisis of Maturity

Forecasts of an Economic Boom in 2015

William E. Halal

The constant drumbeat of cascading business failures is certainly daunting, but technology forecasts suggest that a green revolution, advanced auto designs, surging e-commerce, and other new business sectors are poised to lead the global economy out of today's recession, producing a new economic boom at about 2015.

We have poured trillions of dollars into reviving economic life, and President Obama shows the temperament to lead. But in the rush to be practical, we have slighted the need for a guiding vision of a viable economic system beyond the one that is failing. We lack a clear understanding of what is taking place and what it means.

The financial meltdown is part of a larger "global crisis of maturity," whose symptoms include energy shortages, climate change, weapons of mass destruction, terrorism, and other yet unforeseen threats that are straining old systems to the breaking point. These are interrelated elements of a failing global order that increasingly looks like a train wreck in slow motion. If not subprime mortgages, then some other flaw in today's economic system would likely have caused roughly the same failures. Just as the collapse of communism resulted

William E. Halal is professor emeritus at George Washington University and president of TechCast LLC. E-mail halal@gwu.edu.

from an over-controlled planned economy, today's "collapse of capitalism" is the result of an under-controlled market economy.

I lead a research team that forecasts the evolution of technology and its massive impacts that are changing the world. We've developed an intelligent Web site *(www.TechCast.org)* that pools the knowledge of 100 experts worldwide to forecast breakthroughs in all fields. Technology forecasts are especially useful because our collective "tools" form the economic foundations of the social order. Technological progress is insulated from economic cycles because R&D projects often have long-term support from governments, foundations, and universities. Entrepreneurs may delay product launches during recessions, but they also discount temporary downturns in favor of long-term prospects.

The relentless power of technology can be seen in the fact that the dot-com bust of 2000 didn't faze the Internet, which has now entered a more sophisticated "participative" stage of Web 2.0 sites, like Facebook and YouTube, influencing even the election of Barack Obama. Today's recession is but a two- to three-year year dip as globalization continues to be driven on by the exploding forces of information technology. As Andy Grove, chairman of Intel, put it so well: "Technology always wins in the end."

Our forecasts show that today's surging interest in green business should take off in four to five years, and governments are likely to take serious steps to curb global warming about the same time. Entrepreneurs are working on alternative energy sources—wind turbines, biofuels, nuclear plants, and solar cells. This entire "green revolution" is growing by 30%–50% per year, roughly the same rate of the famous Moore's law that predicts information technology to double every two years. Al Gore was right that the transition to sustainability could be made substantially in 10 years or so.

Because these complex issues are so intertwined, Obama should use his political capital to invite major corporations and other governments to work together on innovative solutions. Green technology is roughly a $500 billion market and expected to reach $10 trillion in 2020—larger than autos, health care, and defense. In short, the present energy and environment mess actually offers a great opportunity in disguise. It may be that the resulting economic growth in a noble cause to protect the earth could even defuse the race toward weapons of mass destruction and conflict, as diverse cultures are more closely integrated into the global community.

Almost all sectors of the economy are likely to be rejuvenated with high-tech advances in roughly the same time frame. A new wave of green autos powered by hybrid, electric, and fuel-cell engines should enter the mainstream about 2013–2018, and we are likely to see "intelligent cars" that may even drive themselves. So there are growth opportunities for automakers if Detroit can get its act together and make needed changes in corporate governance—just as financial institutions must do.

The information technologies driving globalization are gaining momentum as publishing, entertainment, virtual education, and other forms of e-commerce reach the critical 30% adoption level where new businesses usually take off. The huge populations of China, India, Brazil, and other developing countries are moving in droves to PCs, the Internet, smart phones, and global media, for better or for worse. Our forecasts show that 3 to 4 billion people will soon inhabit a digital world that is smarter, faster, and interactive, creating online markets of several trillion dollars and forming a fine web of global consciousness.

The year 2015 seems to mark the serious beginning of all this innovation because it is the next inflection point in the 35-year cycles that roughly govern U.S. markets. The Roaring Twenties were the peak of a 35-year cycle that ended with the stock market crash and Great Depression. The boom that started about 1945 and lasted through the Sixties was followed by the Reagan boom that began with his election in 1980. Today's collapse marks the end of the Reagan 35-year cycle, and it is likely be followed by the "global boom" outlined above starting about 2015. The economy may recover its recent losses, but five or six years may be needed to begin a major new growth cycle.

These are enormous challenges, of course, so it's hard to imagine how they can be achieved in a world that celebrates power politics, money, consumerism, and self-interest. The 2008 financial crisis, however, is widely understood to mark an end to that era, and the outpouring of goodwill around the world for the Obama presidency signals the possibility of global support. Polls show that 70%–80% of Americans are also united behind him.

Beneath the surface, deep rivers of fresh thought are bubbling up. Pollster John Zogby analyzed his data over the past 20 years to conclude: "We are in the midst of a fundamental reorientation of the American character ... away from wanton consumption and toward a new global citizenry in an age of limited resources." Zogby finds that the 18- to 29-year-old cohort, "millennials," constitute the "First Globals." This "digital generation" accepts all races, genders, and cultures equally, and they are intent on living sustainably in a unified world.

This global megacrisis may not be catastrophic if acted on in time, but a major turning point seems inevitable as these multiple threats reach critical levels over the next decade. Global GDP is expected to double by 2020, increasing all these threats to the breaking point. We can no longer muddle through, because the world is poised at the cusp of a great discontinuity—much like a teenager when thrust into the passage to adulthood. Whether a teenager shedding the baggage of youth to become a responsible adult or a civilization facing the imperative to form a mature, functioning society, the imperative is much the same—grow up or perish.

Things look bleak because that's the normal situation facing any system struggling through maturity, whether a youth or an entire civilization. The transition seems to possess a life all its own that is unfolding rapidly, and it is precisely because so many people are so deeply concerned that serious change is under way. The world has accepted women in power, transformed planned economies into free markets, begun to protect the environment—and Americans have elected a black president. Now the tough challenge of forming a sustainable, collaborative, and intelligent global order lies ahead. Hardly a perfect world, of course, but a mature world that works.

Part 2

Applying Strategic Foresight

Disruptive Innovation

The Future of Primary Health Care

Jay Herson

The U.S. problems with health care in general relate to access, affordability, quality, and continuity. Current health-care reform efforts seek to correct deficiencies in these areas (Daschle 2008). The thesis of this paper is that a partial solution to this problem will be a market-driven migration of primary care from physician-centric to patient-centric. The emerging venue for primary care will be the retail pharmacy (RP), with the physician being just one member of the health-care team at the pharmacy. This change will come about by group practices moving from professional office buildings to selected retail pharmacies. This trend will be driven by the need for cost-effective care through protocol-driven, evidence-based disease management (DM) and an information technology infrastructure (IT) needed for electronic medical records and e-prescribing. These important components of primary care are best achieved through regional and national administration of a large enterprise. Clinics based at RPs fit this profile.

Jay Herson is a senior associate at the Johns Hopkins Bloomberg School of Public Health and at the Institute for Alternative Futures. E-mail jay.herson@ earthlink.net.

DRIVERS OF CHANGE

Conventional wisdom on health-care reform indicates that a re-designed system will need the following. We may consider these items as drivers of change.

1. The need for technologies such as electronic medical records to optimize continuity of care regardless of who the provider of care happens to be and e-prescribing to minimize prescription errors and provide warnings on drug interactions.

2. The need for formal, protocol-driven, evidence-based disease-management systems to standardize care to cost-effective procedures for diagnosis and treatment.

3. The interest in third-party payers reimbursing physicians on performance metrics of accepted treatment protocols derived from evidence-based medicine.

4. Motivations for grassroots programs of preventive medicine to keep the people well.

5. The need for modern clinic facilities in medically underserved areas, such as inner cities and rural areas.

6. The need for physicians to concentrate on medicine, free from partnership, business, and paperwork issues. Many recent medical school graduates are hoping to practice medicine with this freedom.

EARLY SIGNALS

There are several early signals of an emerging trend of primary care being delivered at RPs. These early signals are dominated by the parallel growth of the retail pharmacy clinic industry and the disease-management industry.

Walk-in clinics in RPs are becoming popular. These clinics are sometimes referred to as "Doc in a Box" even though there is most often no physician present. Instead, the clinics are often staffed by nurse practitioners and physician assistants. These clinics treat minor emergencies and acute conditions, screen for diabetes and cholesterol, provide childhood, flu, and travel vaccines, etc.

There are now about 2,000 RP in-store clinics of this limited service type operating in the United States. They are operated by national chains such as Wal-Mart, Walgreens, CVS, and Target. This number is expected to increase to 6,000 by 2011 (Mehrotra et al. 2008). At that time, Wal-Mart projects having RP clinics in 55% of its stores (Scott 2007). The current distribution of clinics by host store is: drug stores (65%), supermarkets (15%), and mass merchandise stores (20%) (Scott 2007). In the period 2000-2007, the clinics served 3.5 million patients (Convenient Care Association 2008). In the case of CVS, the clinics are operated by a wholly owned subsidiary known as Minute Clinic. Similarly, the Walgreens clinic subsidiary is Take Care. The walk-in clinic industry has developed enough to be represented by a trade association, the Convenient Care Association.

The expansion of health-care services from walk-in clinic to primary care described in this article is an example of a "disruptive innovation." The latter occurs when a service or technology enters a market at a niche low end, then moves upstream to capture the whole market (Boehmer 2007; Christensen et al. 2000). An example of a disruptive innovation in the automotive industry would be Toyota, which had developed methods to manufacture small, inexpensive automobiles but grew to be a manufacturer of trucks and mid-size and luxury cars. In the software industry, Microsoft developed an operating system for the IBM personal computer and then branched into all types of software.

A recent survey by the Deloitte Center for Health Solutions (Deloitte Center 2008) found that 34% of patients who have never used an RP clinic would consider using one for routine acute care or for vaccination, and a Rand Corporation report found that more than 80% of patients using RP clinics have insurance that is accepted by the clinics (Mehrotra et al. 2008). The clinics accept cash payments from the uninsured. Insured patients will often pay for services such as flu shots or suture removal with cash at RP clinics because the costs are reasonable and they can avoid the paperwork hassle of insurance. Patients with high-deductible health insurance policies are now becoming frequent users of RP clinics (Scott 2008). Few patients come to the RP clinic when they should have gone to an emergency room (Mehrotra et al. 2008; Boehmer 2007). This indicates that the clinics are at present being used as intended.

Loyalty of patients to a particular physician or practice is decreasing among middle-class patients, as physician changes are often mandated by change of employment, residence, or insurance.

Physicians are beginning to appear at RP clinics. Initially, "moonlighting" physicians were employed at these clinics for limited hours. However, currently in New York City, the MDs working at the Duane Reade RP chain are regular primary-care practitioners with admitting privileges at St. Luke's-Roosevelt Hospital Center and Beth Israel Medical Center (Kershaw 2007). In Houston, RP clinics are operated as an outreach program by Memorial Hermann Hospital. A similar program is operated in northern California by the Sutter Hospital System. These programs have physicians located at the RP clinic, and there is a referral pattern to the hospital for specialized care (Scott 2007).

Disease management (DM) is a term for evidence-based, protocol-driven medical practice that seeks to avoid costly hospitalization and complications. DM protocols exist for diseases such as asthma, diabetes, congestive heart failure, chronic obstructive pulmonary disease, coronary artery disease, etc. New diseases are constantly being added to the DM inventory. A depression protocol was recently added. A list of available DM protocols can be found at *www.guidelines.gov.* The protocols provide a basis for diagnosis, proper sequence of behavioral modification, nutritional changes, and drug treatment and methods for monitoring medication adherence. There is a developing DM-protocol-provider industry dominated by companies such as Healthways and LifeMasters, and is expected to be a $30 billion industry by 2013, with a global rollout likely. Customers of the DM providers are health maintenance organizations (HMOs), employer groups, and insurance companies (Deloitte Center 2008).

THE ROLE OF RETAIL PHARMACY CLINICS IN PRIMARY CARE

RPs are an ideal place for group practices of primary-care practitioners to provide care using DM, electronic records, and e-prescribing. Not all RP locations will have clinics, but in the select locations they will be staffed by a combination of physicians, nurses, and physician assistants. Most RP clinics will be open seven days per week; some will be 24/7, and some will be located in medically underserved areas.

There are several characteristics of RP chains that give them a competitive advantage in the process of reform of primary-care delivery. Their IT infrastructure affords them considerable experience in efficient processing of medical and insurance documents. This IT infrastructure, together with their regional and national administration, can provide quality control, DM protocols, and cost containment. The IT prowess can create "members only" Web sites providing individualized DM instructions to the patient, incorporated with the patient's own medical record and lab results. The huge national database of medical records will allow RP clinics to advance primary-care knowledge through outcomes research studies to add to knowledge of cost-effective treatments for different populations of patients. Some of this research may be done in collaboration with academic institutions and third-party payers, but, rather than static research published in journals, knowledge technology can allow for continuous clinical decision support on the best treatment for each individual patient. Analysis by ZIP code can allow the RP chain to study where in their primary-care-clinic market is obesity or diabetes most prevalent, or in which neighborhoods patients are more or less likely to comply with asthma medication, etc. Pooled data from several RP chains can provide even more powerful analysis. There should be no reason for a patient's health data to reside with a single provider as long as data can be anonymized for data analysis (Rowley 2008).

RP clinics should have lower costs of care due to economies of scale, competition with other RP chains, attracting physicians with more modest income expectations (including foreign-trained physicians), and efficient use of nurse practitioners and physician assistants. RPs can enter into national agreements with insurers. These agreements may mandate cost-effectiveness using DM protocols, which RP clinics can deliver.

RPs are used to doing market research and holding focus-group meetings with customers to learn how to improve customer service and merchandise. These skills can be applied in their clinics to both clinical staff and patients. Private practices do not have this introspection, and a single group practice offers neither the environment nor the scale to collect this information.

ADVANTAGE OF RP CLINICS TO CONSUMERS (PATIENTS)

There are many advantages to consumers of primary-care clinics in RPs. Lower cost of care is expected, and no appointment is necessary for many services. During flu season it is common for RP clinics to run "flu shot sales" with reduced fees or bundled services. This brings customers into the retail store. Patients can take a number or a vibrating pager and shop in the store until they are called. Many will consider shopping a better use of time than sitting in a dreary waiting room reading an outdated issue of *People* magazine.

The RP chains are likely to attract younger, more recently trained medical staff that is better schooled in nutrition, exercise, and other means of prevention and more eager to follow DM protocols than physicians who have been in private practice for several decades.

Suppose a patient of an RP clinic in Nashville is moving to Minneapolis. When this person and family arrive at their new home, they can walk into the closest clinic operated by that chain and the complete medical record will already be on the computer at that location. No need to sit in a waiting room with a clipboard and complete a perfunctory new-patient form. As people travel around the United States for business or vacation, if the need for medical care arises while in transit, they can go to the nearest RP of their chain and be treated, with the medical record in place on the computer screen. Similarly, RP clinics will allow domestics and construction workers to get medical attention while working in neighborhoods far from their own. Further expansion of RP clinics is likely to see these clinics take over employee health operations, under a contract agreement, at large companies and student health facilities at universities. This would be similar to American Express employees forming the travel department of a large company or UPS employees forming the shipping department. If employees know that Walgreens, for example, is taking over employee health at their company, they may want to receive primary care at a Walgreens pharmacy so that the clinical staff at their workplace will have access to their medical record should an emergency arise. These RP-run health services will resemble mini-RPs, with pharmacist, physician, and nurses and shelves with over-the-counter products and health and beauty aids for sale.

The RP chain will be of the scale to offer telemedicine; i.e., enrolled patients can call an 800 number and receive advice from a nurse practitioner on symptoms that they may be experiencing. Some health insurance companies offer this service today, but the RP clinic nurses would have the patient's electronic health record in front of them during the call. Insurance company telemedicine staffs do not have access to this important element of a counseling session. Similarly, the RP chains will be able to support the "health home" concept (Miller 2009).

The choices offered by the presence of RP clinics means that the patient is now in charge of his or her care. Some may prefer to not have an allegiance to any particular RP chain but choose a different one for each service. Of course, they will go to specialists in private practice when needed or, for certain primary-care indications, they may also prefer to go to a primary-care physician in a traditional private-practice setting. This freedom of choice is analogous to consumers taking their car to a local service station for an oil change but to a dealer-based service facility for an emission-system problem. When patients go to private-practice physicians, they will be able to request that the RP clinic and private-practice medical records be continuously merged, with the RP clinic being granted trustee rights. This would give the RP clinic the responsibility for maintaining merged records and making them available to all clinicians authorized by the patient.

RP stores also offer several health-care advantages for senior citizens and minority patients. The chain RP store is a social "leveler." People of all age groups, races, and social classes know where the neighborhood RP is located and, due to standardization, feel comfortable in any location of the chain. For this reason the RP clinics should fit in well with Medicare and Medicaid as we now know them.

If patients are attracted to a particular RP clinic in an inner-city neighborhood not currently served by a satisfactory community health center, perhaps social-service agencies, mental-health clinics, health-food stores, etc., will open up next door. The RP chain could benefit by being landlord or primary leaseholder for the space occupied by these organizations. This will not only be of enormous health-promotion value but also contribute to inner-city development.

Underserved rural areas would, presumably, be able to attract primary-care staffs by the RP chain providing a fully furnished modern clinic and IT support.

ADVANTAGE OF RP CLINICS TO PROVIDERS (CLINICIANS)

Many physicians and nurses will be attracted to practice at RP clinics because it will enable them to be involved in the treatment of patients on a reasonable work schedule and free of making business decisions. If the providers want to relocate in another city, they should be able to attach themselves to a clinic operated by the same RP chain in their new city. RP chains have the scale to offer clinicians state-of-the art software and DM protocols with 24/7 IT support. Specialists will still remain in private practice, but if RP clinics take the primary-care load, these specialists will be able to spend more time with their patients on the diseases of their specialty. Emergency rooms are already experiencing a reduction in nonemergency walk-ins due to the growth of RP clinics (Boehmer 2007; Scott 2007).

ADVANTAGES TO BUSINESS

For the RPs, the addition of primary care would certainly be expected to increase traffic in the store in all departments, but the ease of filling a prescription in the same store as the prescription was written should certainly boost pharmacy sales.

Shopping malls that are losing retail tenants might benefit from the traffic that an RP with a primary-care practice could generate. Once the RP clinic is in place, there is the opportunity for the developer to rent space, continuing the vertical integration with optometrists (next door to opticians of course), podiatrists, chiropractors, dentists, day surgery centers, home health agencies, yoga studios, fitness centers, health-food stores, etc. If the shopping mall is losing a department store anchor tenant, there is the possibility to expand the RP clinic into an RP-centric health care and wellness center.

ORGANIZATIONAL ISSUES

It must be understood that the RP clinic is being seen as the endpoint of a trend beginning with walk-in convenience clinics. This trend is expected to result in RP primary-care clinics staffed by physicians, nurses, and physician assistants. Private-practice primary care will still exist, and the RP clinic would not include specialists. In many states, physicians are not permitted to become employees of corporations such as a retail pharmacy chain. Hence, in most states, the RP clinic physicians will be provided by a group practice. In some cases the group practice, although separate, will be formed by the RP chain. When the RP clinic is part of an outreach program of an existing hospital chain, no further organization would be necessary. Similarly, in some cases the group practice may already exist, and the RP location will be just one location where the group practice provides services. The other locations will likely be traditional professional office buildings. Indeed, the entire clinical staff of the RP clinic should be employees of the group practice. Physicians at the RP clinics will be family practice and internal medicine certified, but given this organization, it is likely that pediatricians and obstetrician/gynecologists who practice elsewhere might be present at RP clinics during certain hours. This would round out the primary-care team. Given this model, it is presumed that the RP chain would not be at risk for malpractice claims, although they must always be prepared to defend themselves when plaintiffs' lawyers file suits. Market forces will determine compensation for clinic staff. Salaries should settle somewhere between private-practice earnings and the salaries that RP chains would pay if the physicians were to be employees of the RP chain.

More space will be needed if an RP is to include a primary-care clinic. Some RPs will have no clinic at all. Some may have only the walk-in type of clinic that exists today. The primary-care clinic, which is the focus of this article, will exist at strategically located sites. Such a facility would probably retain the walk-in clinic on the first floor, but a second floor would house the primary-care clinic. The second-floor space would include a meeting room, where the public would be invited for presentations on health-promotion topics like exercise and nutrition, living with chronic disease, prenatal care, etc. The RP chain network of RP walk-in clinics and primary-care clinics would mean that a patient who has an appointment for his or her annual physical at the primary-care location could drop into any walk-in clinic location for the blood draw and urine sample a week before the appointment. When the patient reports to the primary-care location for the annual physical, his or her latest blood and urine chemistry information will already be part of the electronic medical record for the clinician to view and discuss with the patient.

A patient who lives in Richmond might be in Los Angeles a week before the annual physical to be done in Richmond. He could get the blood/urine sample work done at a walk-in clinic in Los Angeles. This patient should not be surprised if the nurse at the Los Angeles walk-in clinic, upon viewing his electronic health record, reminds him that the prescription for his statin drug is due for refill or asks if he still bicycles 20 miles per week.

Of course, there will be many internal RP chain corporate conflicts. Current management is retail-oriented rather than clinically oriented. These two groups will see the world differently, and this will frustrate the newly arrived clinical executives. As more space is demanded by clinical staff, these conflicts will escalate for a while, but market forces and competition should eventually determine the optimal space allocation.

This national RP chain clinic model should not be confused with health maintenance organizations (HMOs). The latter is a prepaid health-care-delivery model where, for a fixed annual fee, patients receive the care they need at centralized clinics. The RP model will be fee for service. HMOs are expected to exist well into the future. A complete analysis of why they have not been more successful is beyond the scope of this paper. However, it is sufficient to mention that, like many third-party payers, HMO plans have underestimated costs. Preventive medicine was a good selling point for HMOs, but the savings from preventive medicine cannot be seen for decades; the patients who partake in preventive medicine programs at HMOs are long out of the plan by the time some of these costs savings might be seen. There are many diseases we don't yet know how to prevent, and, for those about which we have some knowledge, prevention must begin at an early age. Prevention programs beginning at age 45 for a patient who has just entered an HMO might not prevent a heart attack at age 50. Although they operate on a fee-for-service basis, RP clinics might be able to enroll patients when they are young and retain them for long periods of time even as patients move from city to city and, thus, see some payoff for prevention.

SCENARIOS: 2010-2025

The next 15 years suggest the following as possible scenarios for primary care.

1. Alpha—Extrapolative, Business as Usual

Due to political and interest-group pressure, health-care reform creates legal and cost barriers for full development of RP clinics. The clinics remain as they are today, with limited services provided by nurse practitioners and physician assistants. In some states, a single physician may be present for limited hours and can give advice to staff through a video over Internet connection at other times.

Signposts for this scenario would be failure of health-care reform to pass and, thus, not enough patients with insurance to interest the RP chains for expansion into primary care. Other signposts would include lack of federal support for clinical IT and telemedicine and failure of the physician community to embrace DM.

2. Beta—Challenging Times

As a result a combination of political and interest-group pressure, cost of services, judicial decisions regarding malpractice, and conflict of interest, RP clinics exist in a few states but only to provide flu shots and treat minor emergencies.

Signposts to watch for under this scenario would be state laws discouraging RP clinics, and organizations like the American Medical Association and the American Academy of Family Practice failing to endorse RPs for primary care and discouraging MDs in their residence years from working in RP clinics. Another manpower blow to RP clinics would be visa obstacles for foreign-trained physicians to come to the United States. If we see clinical IT finding its way into private practices in traditional settings, RP clinics would lose one of their selling points.

3. Delta—Paradigm Shift

To remain competitive and to take advantage of the national health-care-reform legislation, the RP clinics grow too fast. There are too many clinics, and at least half of the clinics include more than primary care. The typical clinic is a six-story building with a retail pharmacy and optometry/opticians on the first floor, with independent group practices representing primary care, surgery, ophthalmology, psychiatry, etc., on the remaining floors. Due to the power wielded by the practices, the RP chain has little say in how they practice medicine. Indeed, group practices have the option to contract with a rival RP chain when their current contract runs out, and a bidding war ensues like the expensive competition between the New York Yankees and the Boston Red Sox to sign up a star player. The RP chain becomes merely a landlord and IT provider, thus losing its ability to improve health-care delivery.

Signposts to watch for under the delta scenario are the passage of health-care reform that includes universal health insurance, federal and consumer demand for clinical IT, and telemedicine. Another sign would be that third-party payers create standards of care that include evidence-based DM and telemedicine. Another supportive factor would be an increasing percentage of women graduating from medical schools and more foreign-trained physicians entering the U.S. labor market. This is the labor pool that is expected to prefer the type of practice that RP clinics offer. If private practices find they can invade and dominate RP clinic management by entering into agreements with the RP chains to run the primary-clinic program, there will be less objections to RP expansion into primary care from the

American Medical Association and the American Academy of Family Practice.

4. Most-Likely (Normative) Scenario

Given cost and efficiency considerations, health-care reform creates mergers among RP chains so that they will be large enough to provide efficient primary care on a national basis. Third-party payers and federal health-care authorities will now have to deal with no more than a dozen companies nationwide for financing and monitoring 40% of primary-care services. These dozen companies will be more than the RP chains we see today. They will represent mergers between clinical laboratories, supermarkets, department stores, shopping malls, etc. The remaining primary care will be delivered as it is today from independent practices, with IT support provided by the hospitals, third-party payers, or the RP chains under contract agreements.

EFFECTS OF MOST-LIKELY SCENARIO

Social

Health care becomes patient-centric, with the consumer deciding among alternate primary-care models. The patient–doctor relationship changes to a patient–RP chain relationship, with physicians being mere representatives of RP health-care policy. It is the RP chain that monitors cost and quality according to federal and third-party standards. The individuality of the patient is marginalized as mergers between RP chains are created, because the RP chains will find that it is easier to "buy patients" on Wall Street than to compete for them in the open market.

Government-sponsored community health centers may ultimately be replaced by RP clinics in their neighborhoods. The RP clinics will be self-sustaining and may be able to retain clinical staff longer than the community health centers.

Technology

Health care becomes computer and Internet driven. It is now feasible for most citizens to have cradle-to-grave electronic health records. This would not require allegiance to a single RP chain, because records can be easily interchanged between providers. DM continues to grow as an industry, creating standardization but marginalizing physician judgment and reducing the value of physician experience. The economies of scale allow some of the RP chains to have specialists in select cities to do remote diagnosis and even computer-driven day surgery at RP clinics.

Economic

The RP clinics create a new business model, and this model creates jobs and careers in finance, health-care administration, software development, outcomes research, etc. Retail development will create jobs in architecture, construction, law, and finance. Not all jobs will be created in the United States, as foreign companies continue to compete in software development, customer service, etc. Many shopping centers that provide homes for the RP clinics will be owned by global financial empires based in foreign countries.

Retail development will be generated by the growing RPs, including in inner cities, with related development described above.

Competition between RP chains controls cost and quality, but health care becomes a commodity like automobile maintenance. As a result, many physicians and nurses at RP clinics are now foreign-trained, while U.S.-born physicians go into specialties or other fields completely, such as law and business consulting, where they can have the autonomy that medicine once offered.

Environmental

Suburban areas will see uglier big-box stores, as RPs will need more space. RPs are typically located on major thoroughfares. Thus, mass transit is likely to be the way most patients commute to and from the clinics, leading to less use of individual means of transportation regardless of the type of energy they use. Economies of scale are likely to produce more efficient handling of medical waste.

Political

The RP clinics will be one aspect of health-care reform, and there will be many legislative and legal challenges at federal, state, and local levels. Isolated problems in patient care, privacy and confidentiality, and conflict of interest will be exploited by those who try to eliminate or at least control the growth of RP clinics. The RP chains themselves will need political support to prevent hospital chains, nursing-home chains, and third parties from forming national primary-care clinics. There is no reason that these types of organizations could not use available technology, hire pharmacists, and create something very similar to the RP clinic model.

CONCLUSIONS

The RP clinic development discussed here is seen as a market-driven consequence of proposed health-care reform and the digitalization of medicine. RP clinics will develop into a cost-effective and reasonable primary-care model. As this trend progresses, the personal doctor-patient relationship will be present only for those who wish to pay a higher fee for more personalized care at private practices. For most people, the care given at the RP clinic will be adequate. Many people look back fondly on the days of small neighborhood stores that sold groceries, clothing, hardware, etc., where a personal relationship existed between merchant and customer. These same customers probably made doctor visits to a physician who practiced in an office attached to his or her home. Most consumers realize that we cannot go back to the old days and that market forces dictate that retail purchases today are made on an impersonal basis, either online or in big-box stores understaffed by minimally trained low-wage employees.

The same market forces that created these retail changes are operating within governmental health-care reform efforts, and consumers will have to adjust to a more impersonal protocol-directed clinical approach.

These changes, although not optimal, will be accepted as a convenient means of implementing cost-effective and continuous care. Although the care will be continuous, it will not necessarily be with the same physician in the same office. This, too, will require consumer adjustment, but acceptance should come quickly as the public realizes that the new system, although different from the past, offers many worthwhile advantages.

REFERENCES

Boehmer, R. 2007. "The Rise of In-store Clinics—Threat or Opportunity?" In *New England Journal of Medicine,* 356: 765-768.

Christensen, C. M., et al. 2000. "Will Disruptive Innovations Cure Health Care?" In *Harvard Business Review,* 78:102-112.

Convenient Care Association. 2008. http://www.ccaclinics.org/index. php?option=com_content&view=article&id=4&Itemid=11.

Daschle, T. 2008. *Critical: What We Can Do About the Health-Care Crisis.* New York: Thomas Dunne Press.

Deloitte Center for Health Solutions. 2008. "Disease Management and Retail Pharmacies: A Convergence Opportunity," http://www.deloitte .com/dtt/cda/doc/content/us_chs_RetailPharmacyandDMConvergence .pdf.

Kershaw, S. 2007. "Drug Store Clinics Spread and Scrutiny Grows." In *The New York Times.* August 23.

Mehrotra, A., et al. 2008. "Retail Clinics, Primary Care Physicians and Emergency Departments: A Comparison of Patients' Visits." In *Health Affairs,* 27: 1272-1282.

Miller, C. C. 2009. "Doctors Will Make Web Calls in Hawaii." In *The New York Times.* January 6.

Rowley, W. 2008. "Health Care Knowledge Technologies Transform

Health Care in 2020." http://www.altfutures.com/pubs/Health_Care_
Knowledge_Technologies_in_2020.pdf.

Scott, M. K. 2007. "Health Care in the Express Lane: Retail Clinics Go
Mainstream." http://www.marykatescott.com/pdf/HealthCareInThe
ExpressLaneRetailClinics2007.pdf.

Future Patterns of Work and Retirement

The Evolving Third Age

Citizens in all developed countries are living longer, and life spans are continuing to increase. Many countries will have relatively more older persons than at any time in the past, and communities, workplaces, and families will be very different. This trend will continue, and over the next 25 years the change will be dramatic. The United States had 37.3 million persons over age 65 in 2006, and that is projected to grow to 86.7 million in 2050, or from 12.4% of the population to 20.6%. The percentage of the population over age 85 is projected to more than double, from 1.8% in 2006 to 5.0% in 2050.[1] The benefit structure, data, and legal issues in this paper are drawn from U.S. experience. There are parallel issues in developed countries, including population aging; multi-tiered retirement financing systems that use a combination of social security and private benefits, with a range of benefit structures; and extensive policy influence on retirement security. The issues combine in different ways, but there is substantial overlap in the issues.

Key questions as we think about the new demographics and emerging society include:

Anna Rappaport is an actuary, consultant, author, futurist, speaker, and founder of Anna Rappaport Consulting. E-mail anna@annarappaport.com.

- What will retirement mean, and how will it be defined?
- Under what circumstances will public programs offer support to all or virtually all elderly persons in a country? How will "elderly" be defined?
- What will be the expectations about work at higher ages? What obstacles will there be to working to later ages, and how capable will people be of working longer?
- What kind of benefits will employers offer for retirement, and how well will they work? Are programs that provide for earning benefits over 30–40 years of work and collecting them over the next 30 years reasonable?
- How do we encourage individuals to save for their own retirement? What can be expected on a voluntary basis?
- How will families be involved in supporting their senior members? What alternatives will there be for people without family members to offer help?
- What must we do to deal with future instability? How much stability can we count on?
- How similar are the issues between countries?
- What can developed and developing countries learn from U.S. experience?

TRADITIONAL RETIREMENT SYSTEMS

In developing countries and preindustrial society, there were no formal retirement systems. Many people had large families, and the retirement system was that people worked as long as they could; when they could not work any longer, other family members or people in the local community cared for them. The unit over which risk was pooled was the family (including the extended family and local community). People lived near their families.

In developed industrial countries, formal systems for retirement developed based on governmental social security systems (Tier 1), added private benefits (Tier 2), and personal savings (Tier 3). Retired persons had a means of support based on pensions and would live independently away from their families. Tier 2 benefits are based on two types of plans: defined benefit (DB) and defined contribution (DC). DB plans usually pay a benefit of an income guaranteed for the life of the retiree and spouse, with the income most often based on a formula linked to pay and length of service. DC plans are more like a savings account and provide a benefit based on the amount saved plus investment earnings. Often DC benefits are payable as a lump sum, leaving the individual totally responsible for managing them in retirement.

The level of benefits varies by country, as does the role of the public and private sector. In many countries, there has been a shift away from DB plans to more DC plans. As a result of retirement programs in industrial countries, during the past century, most citizens expected to retire at ages 60 to 65. The expected life-cycle pattern was that work would be followed by leisure and retirement. In the last decade, it has been recognized that, without change in these norms, periods of retirement for some would be as long as periods of work, financial security systems were becoming extraordinarily expensive, and meaningful activity was important throughout life. Increasingly, people are moving from full-time work to full-time retirement in steps, with a transition period that can include work on a reduced schedule, and interspersed periods of work and leisure. This period is often called the third age.

The economic conditions of 2008 make the landscape far more challenging. As of December 2, 2008, U.S. retirement accounts had lost 32% of their value.[2] Many countries are confronted with aging populations and difficult economic conditions. As people age, fertility rates have dropped in many countries, and in some are as low as 1.2 or 1.3.[3] The balance between workers and retirees is shifting, making many systems unaffordable and leaving countries with severe potential labor shortages.

PERSPECTIVE ON RETIREMENT BENEFITS

Many experts believe that a new generation of retirement systems is coming. Retirement systems at the start of 2009 can be viewed as representing a mix of success and failure. We will look first at successes and then at failures.

Key successes include the following:

1. For the last two decades, many people in various countries (far more than 50 or 100 years ago) could afford to retire and live a good life in retirement. In the United States, 35.2% of the 65-and-over population was in poverty in 1959; 15.7% in 1980; and 9.4% in 2006.[4] For the 85-and-over population, the percentage in poverty dropped from 21.2% in 1982 to 11.4% in 2006. However, with the present economic crisis, it is unclear how much the number who can retire reasonably will be reduced and how those already retired will be affected.

2. People are living longer in many countries, and it is not uncommon for people to be retired for 25 years or more. Life expectancies at age 65 for men in the United States increased from 11.5 years in 1900 to 12.7 years in 1950 and to 17.1 years in 2004. For women the corresponding years are 12.2, 15.0, and 20.0.[5]

3. People most likely to have good retirement resources are those living in countries with good social benefits and those working for larger companies and governmental bodies over their career.

4. Support of retirement savings by employers and sponsorship of pensions and retirement savings plans has greatly increased the number of people with retirement savings and the amount they have available.

5. Health care today in the United States is better than ever before, but health-care costs are a challenge in many countries. In the United States, the number of uninsured is growing. This reflects a mixed success.

The United Nations Department of Economic and Social Affairs says about the global situation:

- Population aging is unprecedented, without parallel in human history—and the twenty-first century will witness even more rapid ageing than did the century just past.

- Population aging is pervasive, a global phenomenon affecting every man, woman and child—but countries are at very different stages of the process, and the pace of change differs greatly. Countries that started the process later will have less time to adjust.

- Population aging is enduring: we will not return to the young populations that our ancestors knew.

- Population aging has profound implications for many facets of human life.

Key failures include the following:

1. Poverty rates are still too high in many countries. Widows and divorced women are far more likely to be living in poverty than married couples in many countries.
2. Portions of populations are left out of retirement plans. This may be the result of work history and/or personal decisions.
3. Existing programs are growing rapidly in cost as a result of population aging and difficult economic times and are unsustainable in many cases.
4. Many traditional DB pension plans have been frozen or terminated.[6] Generally, employees get benefits earned prior to the termination or freeze date, but this is not always the case. Some, but not all, of the terminated and frozen plans are replaced with new benefits, often at a lower level.
5. Current retirement ages need to increase in many countries, but politically this is a very difficult task. This is under way in some

countries, but more increases are probably needed. Opponents of increase point to the needs of people in hazardous and strenuous jobs.

6. Many people in the world do not have access to good health care, and affordability of the system is an issue in many places.[7]

CHOICE AND INDIVIDUAL RESPONSIBILITY

There has been a vast increase in individual responsibility for retirement, with a major shift in pension structure from DB plans to DC plans. Some social security systems have made similar changes. It is difficult to describe this as either a success or failure, but lessons have been learned. DC plans generally offer far more choice than DB plans. Choices include whether to enroll, how much to save, and how to invest funds. Both types of plans can offer choice at retirement or plan exit. While it was once expected that choice would be a big plus for DC plans, experience with choice has demonstrated that many people choose default options—they do what happens without having to take positive action. And further, the average citizen is not knowledgeable about investment choices and can be nudged quite easily. The result of this is that DC plans are now structured to work better without individual action, and common defaults include automatic enrollment, increases in savings, and balanced investment options. Under this system, employees must opt-out, otherwise they will be in. Offering a wide range of choice has not worked well.

THE ENVIRONMENTAL AND SOCIETAL CONTEXT

Across countries, common factors define the landscape for work and retirement in the third age, and help us think about the future and the potential for discontinuity and major changes. The tables below describe these factors and the type of change they are subject to and provide examples of change.

GOALS FOR THE FUTURE

The author is focused on the following goals as retirement-plan structures are considered. Societal systems should provide:

- Financial systems, public and private, to support retirement that works without too much individual decision making. Systems that support better work options, later retirement, and retirement security for as many citizens as possible. Systems designed to recognize that many individuals will not do good long-term planning.

Table 1: Political Structure

Factor and Its Importance	Description	Type of Changes	Examples
A change in structure could mean radical change in and even the end of Tier 1 benefits if a country ceases to exist, and big change in how Tier 2 and 3 benefits are governed.	Government defines and provides social security benefits and has a big influence over health benefits. Government regulates employer retirement plans and tax preferences for individual retirement savings. But, the structure of a country or its government may change, or the country may cease to exist in its current form.	Change in philosophy of those in power. Change can also occur when countries band together. The EU will be a source of policy for that region in the future. Discontinuity occurs when structure of countries change or they break up. As a result of change in political structure, people may spend part of their working lifetime in one country and part in another, or they spend their working lifetime in one country and their retired life in another.	Shift from liberal to conservative government or vice-versa. Looking ahead, changes are hard to predict and many are possible. Examples of last 50 years: Breakup of the Soviet Union and of Yugoslavia. Formation of the EU. Possible future split of Canada if Québec withdraws. There have been several referenda on this.

Table 2: Economics

Factor and Its Importance	Description	Type of Changes	Examples
Both DB and DC pensions as well as personal savings depend on having a currency and investment markets with reasonable stability and predictability over time.	The economic structure includes rate of growth, inflation, investment returns, etc. Business cycle sets normal change.	Much greater change has occurred in some cases. Some cycles seem to be very long.	In early 2009, it is very difficult to predict whether future will be similar to recent decades. Equity market downturn, mortgage foreclosures, and real-estate downturn in 2008. Many countries have experienced major inflation—e.g., Germany in 1920s.

- Better work options for third-age Americans as they move toward full exit from the labor force.
- Later retirement and full exit from the labor force that gradually adjusts to changing life spans and helps make the idea of retirement more affordable for more people.
- More individuals thinking about the long term and doing better personal planning for retirement, with more analysis as part of that planning.

ONGOING EFFORTS: THE FUTURE OF RETIREMENT SYSTEMS AND RETIREMENT

Different groups are focused on the next generation of retirement systems and are involved in efforts to create a better future for retirement. The Society of Actuaries is sponsoring a major effort to look at retirement systems (Retirement 20/20) in order to define and search out a better system in the future. The ERISA Industry Committee (ERIC), a group of major employers in the United States, has

Table 3: Demographics

Factor and Its Importance	Description	Type of Changes	Examples
Demographics drive who is working and who is eligible for benefits. Demographics and related matters include the age structure of the population, life spans, fertility rates, immigration rates, etc. As a result of immigration, people may not spend their entire working life in one jurisdiction, and they may not spend their retired life in the same jurisdiction where they worked.	Traditional systems use retirement ages defined as "fixed numbers" even though life spans are rising. Traditional systems do not make formal provision for gradual retirement. Government policy has a major role in defining retirement ages and it has been extremely difficult to make changes to increase these ages.	Demographic change occurs gradually and is generally predictable several years before it happens. Exceptions would be a major epidemic or war wiping out many people, or big sudden change in the immigration policy.	Retirement ages need to increase in the future—far more than accepted to date. Retirement ages need to be redefined as number changing with life spans. Populations in Japan, Hong Kong, Europe, and North America are all aging, and life spans are increasing. Fertility rates are very low in Japan, Germany, Italy, and Spain.

put forth a New Benefits Platform. Various other groups have put forth proposals to offer savings programs to Americans not covered by employer plans. These proposals vary, but several call for mandating employers to at least offer an IRA, or call for automatic enrollment in an IRA with an opt-out. Only the Society of Actuaries initiative and the ERIC proposals are discussed further in this paper.

This paper describes four scenarios for the future of retirement. These scenarios will interact with the next generation of retirement programs, so that both patterns of retirement and the benefits provided interact.

The Society of Actuaries Retirement 20/20 initiative focuses on some important concepts for the future of retirement systems. There

Table 4: Family Role

Factor and Its Importance	Description	Type of Changes	Examples
Family includes the role of the family in caring for older family members and in providing support for them. This can range from virtually no responsibility to nearly total responsibility.	Family role is intertwined with rising life spans, a mobile population, and divorce. People have multiple families over their lives and often do not live near family members. The family unit during the time benefits are earned may be different from the family unit when they are paid. Traditionally, in Asia, the family has played a major role in the care and support of older family members, although this is gradually changing in many countries.	Change is generally gradual and reflects changes in custom and values as well as demographics. Divorce is also a factor in driving such change. Declining fertility rates mean that fewer children are available to care for aging parents. Multiple marriages over time are common in some countries. In some countries, significant parts of the elderly population are alone and elderly women are mostly likely to be alone. Of U.S. women over age 85, only 15.4% were married in 2007 and 48.8% of women over age 75 were living alone.[8]	Shrinking institutional systems point to the need for more family involvement, but for many it may not be a reality. New forms of support will be key: In the U.S., many of the very old are divorced women and widows, often with no family members to provide care. For Asians who would formerly have relied on the family, but where this will not be a future reality.

are four major stakeholders whose needs and interests interact: society as a whole, individuals, markets, and employers. The Retirement 20/20 initiative brought together a diverse group of experts to think about the future. In 2006, after they discussed the needs of the stakeholders, they focused on six key themes of importance:

1. Systems should align stakeholders' roles with their skills;

2. Systems should be designed to self-adjust;

3. Systems should consider new norms for work and retirement and the role of the normative retirement age;

4. Systems should be better aligned with markets;

5. Systems should clarify the role of the employer; and

6. Retirement systems will not succeed without improvements in the health and long-term care systems.[9]

In 2007, this effort focused on the roles of society, markets, and employers. Society's role includes helping individuals make the right decisions, setting guidelines about what should happen, and protecting consumers. The experts felt that society should encourage lifetime income, help individuals build wealth for retirement, and provide oversight and regulation. The experts focused on markets supporting the retirement system by working with groups who could negotiate with the markets, providing incentives for agents that aligned with the interests of those they were serving, offering products with standardization, and innovating. There were various views about the role of the employer, and consensus about several roles. These roles included being a facilitator of individual savings, serving as an unbiased educator and trusted advisor, and participating in a range of elective roles included guarantor of benefits, purchasing agent, and distributor of income. It is expected that this effort will provide information about a range of options for future models and systems.

ERIC has proposed a model where employers could retain their traditional role, but could also choose to delegate management of benefits to regional purchasing cooperatives. Under their proposals, individuals would be mandated to save beyond Social Security, and that would enhance retirement security. A benefit design is included in this model as well. This model offers individuals without benefits access to benefits comparable to what individuals with employer-provided benefits get. The proposal combines a market-based structure with individual choice and enhanced group risk sharing, ensuring the voluntary continuation and expansion of the employers' role. It leaves employers to do what they do best and administration to those that do it best. The following is a brief description of the New Benefits Platform as it was described in testimony to Congress:[10]

1. Benefits Administrators would manage benefit plans, competing for business and customers on the basis of product quality, service, and cost.

2. Retirement, short-terms savings plans and medical plans would be included. Other benefits such as life insurance and disability could be added at a later date. We believe that integrating retirement, savings, and health coverage is critical.

3. A uniform national regulatory structure would be established to ensure that there is effective and fair competition among administrators and that there is total transparency for consumers. The structure could be developed by the Federal government or a federally enabled non-governmental entity.

4. Employers would have the option of continuing in the current system, purchasing benefits for their employees from a regional Benefit Administrator, or providing "benefit funding" to their employees who could purchase benefits from the Administrator of their choice.

5. Individuals would be guaranteed the opportunity to purchase benefits directly from Benefit Administrators on the same basis as those accessing benefits through employers.

6. Benefits would be portable among Benefit Administrators.

7. Employers and individuals would share in funding; the tax treatment of qualified lifetime security benefits would be uniform for all Americans.

8. Benefit Administrators would provide financial planning services through salaried financial planners to optimize the potential for retirement security.

9. All individuals would be required to establish a retirement savings account apart from Social Security. We would support a subsidy for low-income savers.

The efforts described above are two of the ongoing efforts to build a new generation of retirement plans. One is from the actuarial profession, and the other from a group of large business organizations. Both recognize the importance of risk pooling and the need for an organized retirement system. Some observers of the current situation indicate that we could go back to where we were prior to industrialization. The author believes that this is impossible for two reasons—first, we are living much longer than at that time, and, second, the family and community structures that supported those who needed help no longer exist. Many people live away from their families and may not have much family at all. However, as we live longer, adjustments are needed in how and when we retire and how we organize for retirement.

Scenarios for the Future of Retirement

As we think about the shifting environment, we can define several scenarios for the future of retirement within the United States. This section explores four scenarios:

- Scenario 1: Continuation of present trends—retirement is generally accepted part of the life cycle.
- Scenario 2: Increase in retirement ages.
- Scenario 3: End of retirement.

- Scenario 4: Move to new patterns of retirement—much later total retirement, but introduction of a third age, where people work at a reduced level with more choices before total retirement.

These scenarios reflect the author's opinions operating in the context of increasing life spans and are built on a combination of intuition and interpretation of research findings. While these scenarios have been built to fit the situation in the United States, issues surrounding retirement ages and the third age are applicable in many settings. The same types of scenarios can be considered in other industrialized countries linking to their demographics, laws, retirement systems, and family structures.

Scenario 1: Continuation of Present Trends. Retirement Is Generally an Accepted Part of the Life Cycle

Under this scenario, many people will have access to regular retirement income, and the expectation is that between ages 60 and 67 most people will leave the full-time paid labor force, and often they will leave all employment.

There is a substantial difference in individual circumstances with regard to access to pension benefits. People with long-term employment in major firms and/or government employment are likely to have good resources for retirement, including their Social Security, and to do well in retirement. The situation is much more mixed with regard to people who had many different jobs or who worked primarily for smaller firms. People without substantial attachment to the paid labor force are unlikely to have retirement benefits, although they could have family assets.

People seeking work during retirement have different experiences with regard to their ability to find work. Professionals are most likely to find work based on contacts from former employment and professional associations, and are quite likely to be able to find contract work. Retailers often use part-time and/or older workers, and firms such as Home Depot are known for their hiring of older workers. Many older persons seeking employment have difficulty finding work.

Scenario 2: Increase in Retirement Ages

Under this scenario, there would be a significant increase in retirement ages. Retirement may be defined as it is now, or it might be defined to include much more phased retirement and different patterns of work and activity. As in Scenario 1, there are substantial differences in individual circumstances with regard to retirement resources and employability. This scenario will create problems for people in very strenuous jobs who wear out early and are unable to do jobs later.

Scenario 3: End of Retirement

Under this scenario, many people will need to continue working, and there will be no (or very inadequate) formal systems for retirement income. When people become disabled, they will usually stop working. Hopefully, disability benefit plans will be extended to higher ages. For some people, families will be available to help them out. While this scenario seems politically impossible, some commentators talk about people working much longer, and baby boomers not retiring.

People with adequate personal assets will have the choice to stop working, but those without will not, or they may find a bleak existence. People with larger families are more likely to be able to live with family members and to have help from them. Widows are particularly likely to have problems in old age.

This scenario could well lead to an increase in fertility rates in the long run, as adult members of society would recognize the importance of children in helping to care for them as they get older. This scenario will likely lead to conflict between generations, as members of society fight over allocation of governmental resources, and will

(continued on page 98)

Table 5: Comparison of Scenarios—The Work and Retirement Experience

	1 - Continue present trends	2 - Increase retirement ages	3 - End of retirement	4 - Move to new retirement patterns
Labor force participation at ages over 70	Minimal	Somewhat greater than at present	Very substantial	Somewhat greater than at present
How people leave the labor force	Retirement, death, or disability	Retirement, death, or disability	Death or disability	Retirement, death, or disability
Need for development of alternative work options	Moderate	Much greater than at present	Much greater than at present—people will prefer reduced work after some point	Much greater than at present, depends on how scenario is developed
Relationship to disability programs	As at present	Would probably need to extend benefits to higher age	Disability programs would be much more important	Would need to adjust disability benefits
Likely work alternatives	Part-time, part-year, project work, telecommuting, some special project work	Similar to present situation	Part time, part year, project work, telecommuting, some special project work; likely to see great demand for flexible job options as people try to work at much older ages	Similar to present situation

Table 6: Comparison of Scenarios—Demographics and Personal Choice

	1 - Continue present trends	2 - Increase retirement ages	3 - End of retirement	4 - Move to new retirement patterns
Impact of personal choices on old age economic success	Moderate and increasing	Moderate and increasing	Total, since there are only individual efforts	Greater than at present
Impact on retirement ages	Small increases	Major increases	Retirement no longer common pattern	Retirement is more multi-step, with complete retirement at later ages
Role of family in retirement	Families are an economic unit, pool risk and help each other Unmarried people are more likely to need to buy help in the marketplace	Similar to present situation	Greatly increased, families will need to step in when people are no longer able to work as retirement income systems will not exist This scenario could encourage increases in fertility as families recognize the importance of children to help care for parents	Similar to present situation
Special issues for different groups	Unmarried and childless people need more money as family help is much less likely to be available	Similar to present situation	Groups in physically demanding jobs and those without families are very vulnerable in this scenario	Similar to present situation

(continued on page 98)

Table 6, continued

	1 - Continue present trends	2 - Increase retirement ages	3 - End of retirement	4 - Move to new retirement patterns
Link of scenario to longer life spans	Current system does not adjust to life span increases	Can track changes in retirement ages to increases in life spans	Individuals are totally responsible for themselves, regardless of how long they live	Can index retirement ages and link to increases in life spans, would need to link to new definition of retirement

probably lead to more demands on government and a focus on increased programs for the poor.

Scenario 4: New Patterns of Retirement

This scenario provides for a move to much later total retirement, with general acceptance of a third age. The third age is a period of transition from full-time work to total retirement and includes a reduced level of work and lifestyle choices. This scenario builds on Scenario 2 and takes it much further. As in Scenarios 1 and 2, there are substantial differences in individual circumstances with regard to retirement resources and employability. This scenario redefines patterns of work in a later period of work stage and introduces more work options and phased retirement. It introduces the concept of the third age and anticipates that new careers and different activity patterns will be used widely. This scenario will work much better for some jobs than for others.

The author's preference is for Scenario 4, "Move to new patterns of retirement," as her choice for the future. This would encompass eligibility for full benefits under public systems (such as Social Security) indexed to increases in longevity starting from age 67. Employ-

Table 7: Comparison of Scenarios—Economics: Earnings and Retirement Income

	1 - Continue present trends	2 - Increase retirement ages	3 - End of retirement	4 - Move to new retirement patterns
Responsibility for old age and retirement security	Shared with government and employer playing important roles	Shared but with diminished costs due to less retirement	Totally with the individual	Shared but with diminished costs due to less retirement
Economic role of retirement systems	Enable people to leave paid labor force, often when they choose to, and often when they could continue to work	Same idea but at a later age	Would not apply	Depends on system
Role of benefit systems in work and retirement choices	For people with good benefits, major role Health care availability is key; employer health care for retirees enables retirement and the lack of it is a barrier to retirement	Similar to present situation	Not applicable	Similar to present situation
Fit of defined benefit plans to scenario	Good fit, but adjustment to more flexible retirement would be needed	Retirement ages would need to increase and support of flexible retirement would be very helpful	Not applicable	Plan could continue to work well, but would need to be designed to fit new structure
Impact of defined contribution plans	Provides assets for retirement, but people likely to retire at higher ages with only DC plans	Similar to present situation	Not applicable	Similar to present situation

ers are fully allowed to pay benefits under DB employer systems while people continue to work after age 62, with that age indexed in parallel with the full benefit retirement age under public systems. For DC, there is no set retirement age, but ages are set below which there are tax penalties if funds are withdrawn and above which there are tax penalties if no funds are withdrawn. Currently the ages of interest in the United States are 59.5 and 70.5. These ages could be adjusted upward, and there could be more limits on the time when retirement funds could be used.

Scenario 3, "The End of Retirement," is viewed as very unfortunate, and it is the author's opinion that this would lead to many more poor women in old age and an undesirable greater dispersion in wealth. There would be major transition problems if society moved to Scenario 3, but these problems are beyond the scope of this paper.

RECOMMENDATIONS FOR THE FUTURE

It is the author's view that an organized retirement system is very important to society. The best systems are based on a partnership of public and private benefits, or mandated and voluntary private benefits. Diversification in the "total retirement and wealth portfolio" is necessary to diversify risk. In diversifying risk, it is important to go beyond traditional investment risk. A floor of protection should be offered to everyone, through either a public benefit or a mandated private benefit. Encouraging savings is important, but it is also important to be realistic about the limits on what will be saved. Combined DB and DC approaches balance the needs of older and younger workers, and can be very efficient. It is very possible that new designs different from traditional DB or DC will emerge. Choice has a role to play, but it makes sense to limit the amount of choice that is offered.

For a good retirement future, it is important that a country:
- Accept and include in public policy the importance of an organized retirement system and its value to society. Without such a system, there would be many more poor people in old age and a

great deal more stress on society. Disabled individuals would be severely disadvantaged unless there was good coverage for them.

- Build integrated retirement policy, including cash, medical, and long-term-care elements. The benefits are interrelated and should be dealt with in a unified way.

- Understand that innovation is important—support it, but don't get rid of the basics. It is important to accommodate new ideas and support emerging designs, but at the same time to remember system goals and support what has worked well previously.

- Remember the widows and divorced women. Women alone are most likely to be poor and need protection. One person needs about 75% of what a couple needs! Families can be important in caring for family members, but those who spend their lives caregiving also need retirement benefits. It also needs to be remembered that not everyone has a family when he or she retires.

- Support DB plans or other plans that offer substantial risk pooling. DB plans remain the most efficient way to provide regular income to longer-service employees. They are important to retirees today, and in spite of the rhetoric to the contrary, turnover patterns have not changed that much over time.

- Maintain Social Security as a system that pays out regular retirement income. For many people, this is the only retirement income guaranteed for life, and this will be true for a greater percentage of the population in the future.

- Facilitate work options and work later in life. Under the emerging patterns of retirement and all of the scenarios, this is very important.

- Facilitate phased retirement. Part of later retirement and part of the idea of working in retirement is to have systems that support phased retirement, allowing people to use retirement resources for part of their support as they continue to work on a partial basis.

- Encourage full retirement at later ages. This is called for under some of the scenarios, and is important as we adjust to longer life spans. At the same time, this requires a balanced approach and a focus on how to handle disability and demanding jobs. Adjust to increasing life spans on a gradual basis.

- Facilitate auto-pilot DC plans. Auto-pilot DC plans are those that work well without employee decisions. They would include auto-enrollment, good methods of handling investment mix, and, ideally, good distribution options.

- Support and encourage regular income with survivor benefits as a distribution option in DC plans. As DC plans have become important, regular income remains very important.

- Make life simpler for plan sponsors. Many of the problems of the last few years are rooted in complexity and uncertainty.

- Try to improve financial literacy, and remember the diversity of the people who need the messages. Offer education to increase personal savings, but recognize the realities. There is ample evidence that many Americans are not positioned to make good retirement decisions. No amount of education can completely solve this, but let's do our best.

- Provide health care access for all. If private individual insurance markets are central to this, use a method of risk adjustment so that individual insurance markets can function. If there are no such private markets, make sure public programs are available to cover people who do not have employer coverage.

NOTES

1. Older Americans, 2008, Tables 1a and 1b, Federal Interagency Forum on Age Related Statistics.

2. Mauricio Soto, *How Is the Financial Crisis Affecting Retirement Savings?*, Urban Institute, 2008.

3. Countries with particularly low fertility rates include Japan, Hong Kong, Italy, Germany and Spain. U.S. fertility rates have remained much higher than Europe.

4. Older Americans, 2008, Tables 7a, Federal Interagency Forum on Age Related Statistics.

5. Older Americans, 2008, Tables 14a, Federal Interagency Forum on Age Related Statistics.

6. In the United States, benefits under DB plans are insured up to a certain level. On termination of a pension plan, these benefits are provided through paying a lump sum equal to their value, through purchase of an annuity, or through a Federal Agency, the PBGC. Benefits earned and above the insured amount are provided if assets are adequate to do so.

7. United Nations Department of Economic and Social Affairs, Population Division, World Population Ageing, 1950-2050, 2002.

8. Older Americans, 2008, Tables 3 and 5b, Federal Interagency Forum on Age Related Statistics.

9. Report from Retirement 20/20: Resolving Stakeholder Tensions: Aligning Roles with Skills, Society of Actuaries, 2008

10. From November 8, 2007, testimony by Michael Stapley, Chairperson, ERIC Task Force on the New Benefit Platform for Life Security to the Subcommittee on Health, Education, Labor and Pensions of the United States House of Representatives.

The Maryland Law-Enforcement and Mental-Health Systems

Barbara Parker

This essay examines the respective roles of the partnership between Maryland's law-enforcement system and its mental-health system in assisting victims of family violence. It also addresses why advocates for victims of family violence say coordinated action is necessary. It offers a synopsis of legal options for victims of family violence and discusses the points at which mental-health experts become involved in the law-enforcement process. These legal options include civil and/or criminal remedies, as well as counseling provided by mental-health professionals. Effective intervention has proven to be successful in decreasing the number of family violence cases because it calls for a strategic response from this team of experts. Their primary goal is to stop the cycle of family violence.

The partnership between law enforcement and mental-health professionals in the state has been crucial because mental-health experts have a very important role to play in stopping family violence. The mental-health system is essential to help implement the directives of the law enforcement system that declares that family violence must stop. It can do this by informing victims (patients) about their

Barbara Parker is a graduate student at the University of Maryland, College Park, and a Professional Member of the World Future Society. E-mail ddg21@ comcast.net.

legal options and offering treatment to the abusers who are referred through the court system. In turn, the law enforcement system has the police power and authority to impose the criminal law stating that an adult cannot commit an act of violence toward another family member.

Without the help of the mental-health experts, law enforcement cannot monitor and rehabilitate the criminal defendants (abusers). Cross-training for mental-health professionals and civil and criminal justice personnel is important for victims and batterers because family violence creates about 100,000 days of hospitalization, 30,000 emergency room visits, and 40,000 trips to the doctor's office each year in the state of Maryland. Coordination and cooperation are only effective when these two systems have the same goals and objectives. Meanwhile, advocates argue that this abuse is a form of gender inequality because most of these victims are women and children.

BACKGROUND

Family violence, sometimes known as intimate violence, is a serious and widespread social problem in America. It refers to violence between individuals in a significant relationship. The violence can be directed toward former or current spouses, children, elders, partners, or dates. The victims and batterers are found in all social-economic groups. Victims may be psychologically, verbally, physically, and/or sexually abused. Family violence is very destructive, especially for children. It may cause physical, mental, or emotional illness and even death. It is a serious crime. A collaborative and coordinated response to family violence from the law-enforcement system and mental-health professionals can provide protection and safety for victims, and can hold abusers accountable.

Before the 1970s, family violence was basically ignored by the law-enforcement system. Law-enforcement professionals refused to intervene in family violence, because it was considered a private matter that should be handled within the family. For instance, a victim of marital abuse could obtain a divorce on the grounds of cruelty, or petition the court for a legal document that warned the abuser to stop the violence. The mental-health community responded similarly by treating the violence as a relationship problem within the family unit, rather than a crime committed by the abuser. As in the past, victims of family violence today are disproportionately women and children, although some men experience family violence. Statistics show that men are usually the batterers, whose actions represent a form of gender inequality. Biological studies show that activity levels and aggression are higher in boys consistently. It is a biological inequality.

In some communities, law enforcement still remains hesitant to intercede in family violence. In most states, however, there are legal tools that victims can use to change their situation. Through the local court system, the victim may obtain a civil protection order (restraining order) to force the abuser to stop the violence. If the abuser violates the order, he or she can be jailed. A protection order can also require the abuser to receive counseling from a mental-health professional or pay a fine or civil support to the victim; the batterer can also be ejected from the residence. In 1976, Pennsylvania was the first state to legislate orders of protection against family violence. A victim of family violence may also file criminal assault charges against the batterer, which may lead to jail, fines, or an order into counseling programs. In 1977, Oregon became the first state in America to pass a law ordering that an arrest be made in family violence cases. These same laws exist in the state of Maryland. Some places use what is called a "peace bond."

LEGAL SYSTEM

Maryland has its own laws and court system. There are two types of laws: civil and criminal. They are usually enforced in different courts. A number of states allow victims of family violence to choose to initiate both civil and criminal charges in accordance with the abuse that was suffered. Civil court remedies are normally faster and less formal, but they may not be as effective as the criminal penalties in preventing family violence. The state of Maryland is trying a new approach that will expand access to legal services for civil orders of protection, peace orders, and family law cases that include separation, divorce, custody, and financial and child support. This process will decrease the rate and number of victims of family violence. In Wicomico County, Maryland, the state's attorney has hired more assistant attorneys to handle family violence felony cases in district and circuit courts. This was funded with money from the Violence Against Women Act.

The purpose and proof for civil proceedings is different from criminal proceedings in Maryland. The civil court's purpose is to settle disputes between individuals and to compensate for injuries, and the violation of the law must be proven by a preponderance of the evidence; in other words, the legal standard of proof in civil court is "more likely than not." Some victims of family violence have sued the police for improper response. Their accusation is that the police officers respond differently to family-violence calls than to other calls for help, or that the police officers have breached a duty of care toward victims *(Watson v. Kansas City* 1988, and *Thurman v. The City of Tarrington* 1984). Similar to Maryland's civil court proceedings, victims of family violence requested money damages for injuries that they received because the police failed to act. In several cases the victims have reached a settlement out of court, opting for the police departments to provide a better response to family violence *(Bruno v. Codd* 1979). Unlike the civil court, the criminal court's purpose is to punish abusers for acts that are considered disruptive to social order; to convict, the violation must be proven beyond a reasonable doubt. The criteria here are much higher than in a civil case.

In recent years, law enforcement's response to family violence has been more appropriate because it is no longer considered a private matter between the victim and the batterer. Working with the Police Foundation, a research organization in Washington, D.C., criminologist Lawrence Sherman and sociologist Richard Berk designed an applied research study to test which actions by the police actually reduced the chances that a spouse abuser would be involved in future family violence incidents. When police officers responded to the call of family violence in Minneapolis, Minnesota, they had three alternatives: (1) to arrest the accused individual; (2) to separate the couple by asking the alleged abuser to leave the household; or (3) to try to serve as a mediator between the couple to resolve the dispute. Sherman and Berk's basic findings supported the policy of arresting the accused. Batterers who were arrested were significantly less likely to be involved in repeated occurrences of family violence. Research studies like this have caused a shift in policy and can be seen in the International Association of Chiefs of Police (IACP) Training Manual that now maintains a policy of arrest in cases of family violence. Maryland has adopted these policies.

MENTAL-HEALTH SYSTEM

As the above discussion of the legal enforcement system indicates, there are many circumstances in which the legal and mental-health systems work together to address instances of family violence in Maryland. Mental-health experts play a vital role in both civil and criminal cases. Before, during, and after a family violence case goes to court, the mental-health system is involved in different ways with the law enforcement system. A basic concern for mental-health professionals who work with the legal system is their attitude toward abuse. Experts in this field who treat family violence as a crime can assist in stopping the cycle of violence. But those who try to solve a dispute without addressing the acts of violence only aid in continuing the cycle of violence. In the majority of cases, a relationship that continues results in continuing violence. To intercede and treat victims and abusers of family violence, mental-health professionals need continuous special training in psychological and social-emotional battering, and the legal resources available within the state. The special training allows them to make the right choices when making referrals for their patients to other programs.

Experienced mental-health providers who work with law enforcement systems use effective tools and tactics to prevent and treat mental illness. They normally ask questions about family violence, whether they observe signs of abuse or not, especially since they understand that victims and batterers go to extreme measures to make light of and reject family violence that they have experienced or perpetrated. Through education they improve and build on school mental-health programs. They constantly screen for co-occurring mental and substance disorders. These health providers also connect with integrated treatment strategies, while strongly recommending that screening for mental illness should take place in primary health care across a lifetime that connect treatment and support services. Early prevention and intervention by the mental-health system can stop and prevent family violence from occurring and reoccurring.

PARTNERSHIP AND COORDINATION

Family violence impacts all institutions in American society. Systems working together, like the Maryland law enforcement and mental-health systems, can prevent and reduce the cycle of violence within the family unit. No single department is capable of addressing the needs of the victims. When the police are called to the scene, the officers should be trained to collect proper evidence and conduct interviews effectively. A mental-health professional should have an ideal model for screening victims and batterers involved in family violence.

Maryland has formed a network against family violence. When a victim calls for help, she or he should expect a comprehensive systemic response. If implemented correctly, communities can:

1. Significantly decrease the number of family-violence homicides.
2. Encourage teamwork among departments and agencies.

3. Promote responsibility for coordinated and effective intervention.

4. Encourage innovative future ideas from law-enforcement agencies and mental-health professionals.

5. Support increased arrests, penalties, education, and supervision of offenders.

6. Construct formal and informal networks for communication and partnership between systems.

7. Assist the implementation of solutions that can affect the policies as they are developed in the state.

Systems working together, through cross-training, screening, treatment, and referrals, promote mental-health and law enforcement programs that serve the needs of victims of family violence. The state of Maryland supports this type of partnership and coordination and has established Lethality Assessment Programs and Domestic Violence Fatality Review Teams in many communities.

CONCLUSION

In this essay, the analysis reveals that there should be collaboration between agencies (law enforcement and mental-health systems) in the state of Maryland to support the victims of family violence. In Maryland, and in other states, victims of family violence may use any of the legal options that are described above or they may decide to use more than one. For instance, a protection order is often used when a victim files criminal charges against her partner. The victim's decision about what legal actions to take depends on her goals. Most victims want the violence to stop. They may want to press charges against the batterer, get the batterer professional help, end the relationship, or all of these options.

The mental-health system has a very important role to play in the law-enforcement system. Mental-health programs are designed to promote the prevention and treatment of mental illness with tools, analysis, and treatment. At the same time, they are faced with the victim's challenges, such as combating stigmas and discrimination. By working with a mental-health professional, the victim will better understand her legal alternatives in stopping the cycle of violence. During counseling, a batterer can learn what behaviors are criminal, the penalties for those behaviors, and the moral lesson that family violence is a serious crime.

The law enforcement system and the mental-health system can work together to stop family violence. However, coordination and cooperation are only effective when these two systems have the same goals. The best response from the mental-health system is when it supports the law enforcement system in communicating that family violence is wrong, that it is a serious crime, and that those who commit this crime will suffer severe penalties.

REFERENCES

American College of Obstetricians and Gynecologists (ACOG). 1989. *The Battered Woman.* Technical Bulletin Number 124. Washington, DC.

Brannen, S. J., and E. R. Hamlin. 2000. "Understanding Spouse Abuse in Military Families." In *The Military Family: A Practical Guide for Human Service Providers,* eds. J. A. Martin, L. N. Rosen, and L.R. Sparacino. Westport, CT: Praeger Publishers.

Brewster, A. L. 1997. "Research That You Can Use." Briefing presented at the USAF Family Advocacy Prevention Conference, San Antonio, TX.

Brewster, A. L. 2000. "Responding to Child Maltreatment Involving Military Families." In *The Military Family: A Practical Guide for Human Service Providers,* eds. J. A. Martin, L. N. Rosen, and L. R. Sparacino. Westport, CT: Praeger Publishers.

Brooks, T. 2008. *The Global Justice Reader.* Malden, MA: Blackwell Publishing.

Collins, R., and M. Makowsky. 1998. *The Discovery of Society.* Boston: McGraw-Hill.

Flowers, R. Barri. 2000. *Domestic Crimes, Family Violence and Child Abuse.* Jefferson, NC: McFarland & Company Inc.

Gimbel, C., and A. Booth. 1994. "Why Does Military Combat Experience Adversely Affect Marital Relations?" In *Journal of Marriage and the Family,* Vol. 56, No. 3, 691-703.

Kilpatrick, D. 1992. *Rape in America: A Report to the Nation.* Washington DC: The National Victim Center and the Crime Victims Research and Treatment Center at the Medical University of South Carolina.

Kymlicka, W. 2002. *Contemporary Political Philosophy.* New York: Oxford University Press.

Martin, J. A., L. N. Rosen, and L. R. Sparacino. 2000. *The Military Family: A Practical Guide for Human Service Providers.* Westport, CT: Praeger Publishers.

Moore, A., D. Gibbons, and J. Higgins. 1986-1987. *Watchmen.* New York: DC Comics.

Salas, M., and L. Besetsny. 2000. "Transition into Parenthood for High-Risk Families: The New Parent Support Program." In *The Military Family: A Practical Guide for Human Service Providers,* eds. J. A. Martin, L. N. Rosen, and L. R. Sparacino. Westport, CT: Praeger Publishers.

Stark, E., A. Flitcraft, and W. Frazier. 1979. "Medicine and Patriarchal Violence: The Social Construction of a 'Private' Event." In *International Journal of Health Services,* 9, 461-493.

Strauss, M. A., and R. J. Gelles (eds.). 1990. *Physical Violence in American Families: Risk Factors and Adaptations to Violence in 8,145 Families.* New Brunswick, NJ: Transaction; William Morrow.

U.S. Bureau of Justice Statistics. 2005. *Family Violence Statistics: Including Statistics on Strangers and Acquaintances.* Washington, DC: U.S. Department of Justice.

U.S. General Accounting Office. 2000. *Military Dependents: Services Provide Limited Confidentiality in Family Abuse Cases.* Washington, DC: General Accounting Office.

Walzer, M. 1973. "The Problem of Dirty Hands." In *Philosophy and Public Affairs,* Vol. 2, No. 2 (Winter), 160-180.

A Foresight Method for Enhancing Competitiveness of Brazilian Industrial Sectors

Cláudio Chauke Nehme, Adriano Galvão, Antonio Vaz,
Gilda Coelho, and Lélio Fellows

In the era of globalization, the four BRIC countries—Brazil, Russia, India, and China—are expected to have a growing global presence and influence on major international trade negotiations and agreements. In this context, Brazil already dominates as a major supplier of raw materials and agricultural goods (Goldman Sachs 2003), and in the near future it has the potential to reap new opportunities in manufacturing and services while improving its industries' competitive position. The Brazilian government has an urgent and strong desire to make several industrial sectors more competitive in the global economy by leveraging their strengths and overcoming their weaknesses.

This paper introduces a foresight methodology developed by the Center for Strategic Studies and Management of Science, Technology and Innovation (*Centro de Gestão e Estudos Estratégicos*, CGEE) to envision opportunities for, and avoid threats to, six industrial sectors in the next 15 years. The methodology was created during six future-studies projects requested by the Brazilian Agency for Industrial De-

The authors are all futurists at the Centro de Gestão e Estudos Estratégicos (CGEE) in Brasilia, Brazil. E-mails Cláudio Chauke Nehme, chauke@cgee.org.br; Adriano Galvão, abraun@cgee.org.br; Antonio Vaz, avaz@cgee.org.br; Gilda Coelho, gmassari@cgee.org.br; Lélio Fellows, lelio@cgee.org.br.

velopment (*Agéncia Brasileira de Desenvolvimento Industrial*, ABDI), a nonprofit organization with a mission to promote Brazilian technological and industrial development. The main results of these studies provided guidelines to implement industrial development policies.

The basis of the sectorial foresight method is the road-map technique (Galvin 2004; Price et al. 2004; Laat 2004), which was adapted to accommodate the unique requirements of each industrial sector. The aeronautical sector, for example, places a strong emphasis on technology, engineering, and innovation; therefore, their foresight study involved an analysis of the significant developments that have been made in aeronautical science and technology. In contrast, the shoe sector's study focused on new technologies and processes that were emerging to acquire the best quality leather shoes, while being aware of environmental sustainability.

This paper starts with a brief description of concepts present in the industrial context of Brazil. Subsequently, the customization of the road-map technique and its application for the industrial sectors are introduced. Finally, the paper presents the results and examines the new challenges of introducing an implementation plan, based on the future study, which can increase the industrial sectors' competitiveness. The content of this paper focuses exclusively on the foresight methodology and the environment for its application. The final outcomes of these studies are not shared, due to the sensitive nature of the information.

Concepts Used in the Sectorial Foresight Method

This section sets the stage for introducing the sectorial foresight method by briefly introducing the meaning of important concepts used in the foresight technique.

Innovation and Sustainable Development

The term "innovation" is ubiquitous nowadays. While the concept has undergone some transformations during the last few decades, the essence of its meaning remains unchanged: It is society's acceptance of a new product, service, or process. Many companies and organizations in Brazil already understand and seek innovation as the promise for prosperity. In the future studies presented in this paper, innovation is also related to the concept of sustainability, where it is not just about developing new things and enhancing competitiveness, but also preserving the life-support systems of the planet while improving living standards for all. For instance, a new product targeted at a specific market segment may be rejected by consumers if it causes a serious negative impact on the environment.

Organizational versus Sectorial Learning

Organizational learning is a characteristic of an adaptive organization—i.e., an organization that is able to detect changes in signals from its environment and adjust accordingly. This concept, borrowed from the area of organizational theory, was expanded in future studies to include a broader perspective of each industrial sector. Sectorial learning patterns emerged when advisory committees were formed to oversee each study. These advisory committees, composed of major representatives from each sector, had the major task of making strategic decisions for their sectors based on strategic intelligence from observed trends and market drivers. The scope of sectorial learning is therefore defined appropriately, considering the focus of each sector, their management requirements and shortcomings, and the capacity to implement strategic planning at a broader level.

Strategic Intelligence for Industrial Sectors

Strategic intelligence is often needed to form policy plans at the national and international levels. In this paper, strategic intelligence is considered from the perspective of knowledge management, covering five activities of organizational intelligence: reasoning, cognition, learning, memory, and communication (Kirn 1995; Akgün et al. 2007). Reasoning deals with the main goal of expressing the major issues of sectorial strategy and their relations to, and impacts on, businesses. Cognition provides the sector with the means of conducting the core business with the necessary knowledge to reach the best results with quality. Learning prepares the sector to sustain and improve its capacity to deal with world changes. Memory is based on the need to document and recover important facts that have the potential to support complex decision-making processes. Finally, communication is essential to disseminate knowledge for strategic actions. In order to provide the best guidance to sectorial stakeholders, different kinds of capacities and resources are used to (1) scan and interpret relevant signals from the global market, (2) analyze business strategies among companies and within market segments, and (3) help decision making, for instance, with computer simulation.

Strategic Foresight Approaches and Tools

One of the biggest challenges in assisting decision makers seeking to navigate the complexity of today's world and to stay competitive is to anticipate needs and uncover relevant trends. In strategic foresight, several approaches and tools, such as Delphi surveys, scenario workshops, surveys, etc., can be used to elicit the opinions of experts and generate potential future options that decision makers can choose from (Schlossstein and Park 2006). The key to success in the case of ABDI's studies was to avoid a set of standard and rigid methods; instead, it chose to select and customize the methods and tools for each sector.

PROGRAM TO ENHANCE THE COMPETITIVENESS OF INDUSTRIAL SECTORS

In contrast to the most dynamic emergent countries, Brazil hasn't followed the evolution of modern industrial sectors. Its average annual growth rate has been well below those of China and India, and, in some industrial sectors, industry is consolidating and being acquired by multinational corporations. Cumbersome regulations, a high-tax environment, administrative hassles, infrastructure bottlenecks, and skill gaps collectively add unnecessary costs to doing business and have driven investments out of the country. In response to this condition, the Brazilian government announced a new industrial policy—*Política de Desenvolvimento Produtivo* or PDP—which aims to recover accelerated economic growth and reduce overall financing and tax burdens currently withering several industrial sectors. The overall goal of PDP is to reorganize strategic sectors, enhance their competitiveness in the global market, and increase foreign sales of value-added products.

The PDP was launched early 2008 by ABDI and was partially based on the foresight studies that CGEE developed for six industrial sectors: aeronautical, shoe, plastics, furniture, medical equipment, and textile. Some guidelines were considered in choosing each industrial sector. First, the sector had to have elements that would justify efforts to enhance its competitive position over the next 15 years. For example, it would have to have a developed production system, a supply chain with some competitive advantage, and updated research and development initiatives that could support incremental and/or radical innovations. Leader associations and industrial communities also had to manifest their desire to embrace the study and to commit themselves in supporting the recommendations. Finally, each industrial sector selected had to be capable of creating positive synergy among government, science and technology institutions, universities, and industry. The main goal was to agree on implementing and maintaining the suggested strategic plans.

For each study, an advisory committee was formed to oversee the development of the strategy and make sure it could be implemented. ADBI carefully chose key stakeholders from each industrial sector to be part of the project. Representatives from the Ministry of Development, Industry and Foreign Trade *(Ministério do Desenvolvimento, Indústria e Comércio Exterior,* MDIC), the National Council of Industrial Development (*Conselho Nacional de Desenvolvimento Industrial*, CNDI), and the Brazilian Ministry of Science and Technology (*Ministério da Ciência e Tecnologia*, MCT) were also involved in each study.

CGEE's APPROACH TO PROSPECTIVE SECTORIAL STUDIES

Over the course of one and a half years, during which CGEE developed these studies, the strategic-foresight approach was adjusted and improved to incorporate the varied needs of each industrial sector. An overview of CGEE's four-phase sectorial foresight method is shown in Figure 1. The tools and outputs of each phase are shown directly under their respective activities.

Foresight Planning

In the Foresight Planning Phase, the work plan and the appropriate foresight tools are defined. One of the characteristics of CGEE's sectorial foresight method is the involvement and commitment of key decision makers in the foresight development and evaluation. The Brazilian Agency for Industrial Development (ABDI) had a major role in negotiating with the sector in this initial phase. As a political entity that navigates through all levels of the government, ABDI's major goal was to persuade, and gain commitments from, the advisory committee representatives who could help organize the sector while improving its global competitiveness. The advisory committee was in charge of advising and validating the outcomes of each phase of the study and had representatives from major industrial associations, leading companies, government institutions, universities, and non-profit organizations.

Understanding the Present

The first phase of CGEE's foresight methodology is about describing current characteristics and market dynamics of the indus-

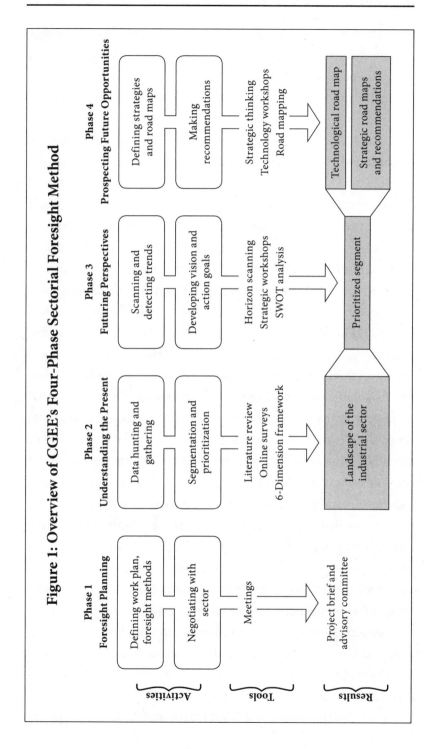

Figure 1: Overview of CGEE's Four-Phase Sectorial Foresight Method

trial sector in as much detail as possible. Understanding the present is a key element to creating a common vision of the future, one that portrays a place where the industrial sector wants to be in years ahead, particularly in issues of technology and productivity development.

Data hunting and gathering are the two major activities in this phase, to describe the landscape of each industrial sector by looking at issues around technological advancements and socioeconomic developments. The focus of the study at this phase must be already well defined or the information collected could be overwhelming and lead to inconsistent, faulty recommendations. A structured gathering plan is therefore the basis of this stage. The frame of reference shown in Figure 2 illustrates the plan of action used in the future studies.

Two important views are described above: (1) the industry sector's view, which includes the sources that describe the industrial sector, and (2) the general view, which positions the sector in the global economy through the lenses of specific dimensions. The data hunting and gathering starts with the identification of complete, relevant, and reliable data sources. Even though this appears to be an easy part of the prospective study, there are several challenges in choosing data sources in Brazil, including outdated statistics and a lack of reliable secondary sources. If data gathering is not well structured, and if it does not cover a broad range of sources, it can compromise the foresight results and give decision makers faulty information.

As the first stage of the foresight exercise, information hunting and gathering has to be complete in its scope and detail. It should provide a 360-degree view of data sources that can establish a good foundation for the decision-making process. For example, when considering global competition, it is important to examine new players, main competitors around the world, leading companies, Brazilian companies, and Brazil's environment for business, such as Brazil's productive chain structure. A good amount of detail will guarantee an adequate confidence level for the foresight exercise.

The interpretation of the information collected is organized

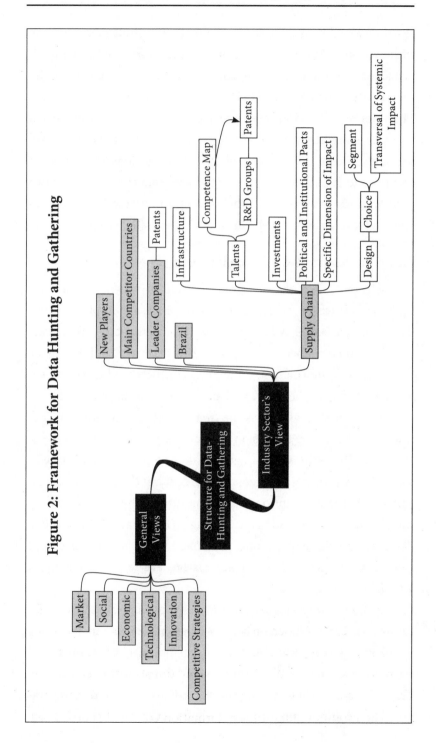

Figure 2: Framework for Data Hunting and Gathering

based on key dimensions, which should have a strategic connection with the foresight exercises. For industrial sectors, the following dimensions were used: Market, Technological, Investment, Human Resources, Infrastructure, and Political and Institutional Environment. The amount of data allocated to each dimension is sufficient when it provides enough evidence about the industry's sector and its market segments. The last step in this phase is the prioritization of market segments to gain focus for the next phase. Focusing on one or two product lines or technologies helps to optimize research resources and align the sector's stakeholders toward one single goal.

Futuring Perspectives: Doing a Puzzle

The purpose of the Futuring Perspectives phase is to gain foresight intelligence for the decision-making process. This phase is similar to doing a puzzle, where pieces of information are carefully selected and then put back together to see how they fit. By choosing the right pieces of information, untangling conflicts, and exploring solutions, a vision of the future and an action plan can be created.

A vision of the future is the first element that needs to be defined by each sector. The vision statement is used to determine how to achieve the sector's chosen goal. It describes a desirable place in which manufacturing is better positioned and, at the same time, challenges existing assumptions about the future, thereby motivating stakeholders to plan and act accordingly (Hines and Bishop 2007). Elaborating a vision of the future statement with a large group of representatives from an industrial sector is, however, extremely complex and risky.

As the first strategic decision, the visions created in CGEE's future studies were based on certain types of information, including key findings from the landscape description; latest trends; and strengths, weaknesses, opportunities, and threats within each sector. The vision statement was made of key words arranged into a few paragraphs; its composition involved a lot of discussion.

For the purpose of illustrating the end result of this exercise, here is a vision of the future for the cosmetic sector: "To be a world class industry enhancing the quality of life and prosperity of the community through sustainable development, and contributing to the economic growth of Brazil."

The risk involved in creating a long-term vision is that it may point the industrial sector in a direction that may be completely different from how events really unfold. As the world is unpredictable, the future will almost certainly not occur exactly as it is described in a vision statement. Single-point forecasting is doomed. With visions, however, executives from each sector will be better served in preparing for the places where they want to be. If the major goal is to be more competitive in 15 years, then they will need to take it seriously in the coming years and continue monitoring the environment for leading changes that will likely suggest adjustments to their vision and goals.

In the next section, the set of action goals required to make a vision of the future come true are described.

Futuring Perspectives: Defining Action Goals

As described earlier, the competitiveness of industrial sectors is driven by innovation and sustainable development. Consequently, the foresight puzzle could be assembled in many ways. The approach used in ABDI's prospective studies was to consult experts about market and technology drivers. Experts from industry, academia, and government were grouped in panel sessions to assess market conditions and to formulate action goals targeted toward realizing the industrial sector's vision of the future.

The action goals created were short sentences made up of major tasks that have the potential to organize the industrial sector's environment and produce positive synergies. The sentences originated from SWOT (Strengths, Weaknesses, Opportunities, and Threats) analyses and were organized based on the market dimension so that

Table 1: Examples of Action Goals

Action Goals	Sector
Incorporate strategic technologies (e.g., nanotechnology and biotechnology) into the production chain.	Shoe
Expand market share of commercial aircrafts and parts in the national and world markets.	Aeronautical
Gain market share in the high-tier segment in the United States and European countries.	Furniture

Source: Ministério do Desenvolvimento, Indústria e Comércio Exterior (MDIC).

the discussion could focus on how to increase the competitiveness of the sector. The analysis provided indicators for the overall strategy, which were the main pieces of the development of the strategic road maps for each sector. Table 1 shows examples of broad action goal from some of the sectors.

Among all studies, there were recurring goals addressing current challenges. These include, for example, the need to significantly improve the performance of Brazilian education systems and to directly invest in logistical infrastructure.

The final product of this step is a set of action goals capable of improving the industrial sector's position. The exercise of formulating action goals reveals that the market dimension can be used to link together goals from other dimensions and to promote synergies among them. The last step is to create a communication piece in the form of a road map, in order to align high-level strategies, development efforts, market needs, and technology development plans.

Prospecting Future Opportunities

The last phase of CGEE's sectorial foresight method is the development of strategic and technological road maps based on the opportunities identified in earlier phases (Camarinha-Matos 2004; Rezgui and Zarli 2002). Road maps are generally used in the context of enterprises, within well-defined boundaries of the enterprise's environment of influence. In the case of creating a road map for several industrial sectors, the concept has to be adapted to include fewer control variables. In other words, in order to take advantage of the synergetic connections among macro objectives toward a vision of some industrial sectors, it has been necessary to review and be in control of few variables. This adaptation introduces the risk of losing influences among macro objectives that structure the synergy of the strategy. In order to mitigate this risk, the next phase is an elaboration of a detailed plan to be executed, introducing as many variables as necessary so as to produce a business plan for specific industrial sectors.

The basic elements of the strategic road map were the action goals from the market dimension defined in the previous phase. These action goals had to be interpreted in terms of their impact on the competitive system of each sector, and redefined as directives or macro strategies toward the vision of the future. The starting point for this exercise was to define a set of criteria for selecting and evaluating opportunity areas that would guide the development of strategic road maps. Extracting objective criteria from subjective judgments included filtering questions, such as:

- Are there fundamental and critical aspects that could either introduce or maintain the industrial sector in the competitive environment?
- Does the strategy stimulate a competitive environment to organize the industrial sector for global competition?
- Could specific technologies renew opportunities for the industrial sector, in order to maintain or improve its competitiveness?

The directives provide the structure for several possible routes into the future. Each route is formed in the following manner:

- Define the main strategy for increasing global competitiveness.

- Organize the strategy into directives that have individual and systemic impact on the industrial sector's competitiveness.
- Structure each proposition into a route, organized by macro actions from strategic objectives considering all dimensions of the foresight exercise. This organization must be complete, clear, and objective for the purpose of creating synergies and fostering a strong ability for the industrial sector to attain the vision of the future.

THE CHALLENGES OF CONDUCTING THE ADAPTED FORESIGHT APPROACH

The foresight exercises provide insights and opportunity areas to enhance the competitiveness of the industrial sectors considered. The road-map development for each industrial sector was a major challenge. The nature and maturity of each sector required a flexible approach toward the foresight methodology and differed on two major levels:

1. **At the organizational level.** Some industrial sectors have fragmented production chains, while other sectors are organized with major stakeholders and well-defined roles that follow the processing of commodities from the extraction of raw materials through the production of finished goods. In the first case, the strategy focused more on action goals to solve short-term problems and less on future opportunities. With a fragile production chain, the strategic road maps mainly suggested ways to organize the industrial sector as a first step toward increasing competitiveness. In the case of the organized sectors with mature production chains, the strategic road maps were designed to include and leverage global competition, focusing more on action goals for middle-term and long-term gains.

2. **At the technological level.** The focus of the vision will impact the recommendations for new technologies and how they may be used to improve the competitiveness of each industrial sector. For a set

of industrial sectors, the vision of the future was broad enough to include strategies in technology and innovation that ranged from investments in specific research areas to the promotion of certification and testing. For other sectors, where the visions included a specific market segment or a product line, the strategies were more focused and supported by a technology road map in addition to the strategic road map.

Another challenge to conducting ABDI's future studies was managing the various key stakeholders of the project. In some cases, stakeholders took action before the results of the strategic plan were officially released. As the stakeholders helped to elaborate action goals, they were also planning strategies related to their own interests. This behavior can damage the strategy to enhance the industrial sector's competitiveness as programs are implemented without leveraging the synergies. Future studies should consider this fact to avoid disruptions of strategies and actions.

FINAL RESULTS AND CONCLUSIONS

These foresight studies for multiple sectors of Brazilian industry provided several results regarding processes and products. The first result relates to the ability to change perceptions and motivate stakeholders to proactively implement recommendations. Most of the industrial sectors chosen for the foresight exercises initially lack competitiveness, but their leaders are open to the need to enhance their position with respect to global competition. For this reason, industrial stakeholders initially showed disbelief in any government support and were unable to evaluate the potential of the study. This behavior changed during the elaboration of the road maps, and, as they got involved, they started to promote the political environment to implement the foresight recommendations. This was considered to be an excellent result of the foresight exercise, because the main stakeholders have periodically declared the relevance and importance of each foresight study.

In terms of final deliverables, the strategic road maps and recommendations were applied as the basis for the new industrial policy. This result surpassed the initial expectations, and hopefully it will support stakeholders with the best decision-making process under a clear, objective, and complete executive plan to enhance the competitiveness of several industrial sectors.

As for methodology adaptation, successful implementation of the foresight approach depends on the reasoning used to structure it and the ability to represent global aspects. In ABDI's future-studies experience, the best results were driven primarily by the constraints of the present, and less by the recommendations of the specific methods applied. It seems paradoxical, because the long-term goals are competitiveness and innovation; why, then, would the current constraints drive the methodology? One simple reason is that the desired future is created based on the present conditions and necessities and depends on current plans and actions. The desire to be more competitive is not sufficient to guarantee a successful future. In most industrial sectors of Brazil, there are many basic necessities that need to be fulfilled before the sector can implement programs and actions to achieve a desired future. Planning, in cases like this, is a dynamic process, and has to be done by finding a balance between the present necessities and future desires, and by generating intermediate demands.

Acknowledgements

The authors wish to acknowledge many individuals whose help and commitment aided in the completion of each industrial sector study and development of the methodology presented in this paper. Special thanks to the technical team, including Elyas Medeiros, Flavio Albuquerque, Kleber Alcanfor, Lilia M. Souza, Liliane Rank, Marcio M. Santos, Marco Lobo, Elenita Nascimento, Milton da Paz, Regina Silvério, and Rosana Pauluci. The authors also thank Brianna Sylver for thoughtful insights in the writing revision process.

REFERENCES

Akgün, A. E., J. Byrne, and H. Keskin. 2007. "Organizational Intelligence: A Structuration View." In *Journal of Organizational Change Management*, vol. 20 No. 3.

Camarinha-Matos, L. M., H. Afsarmanesh, H. Löh, F. Sturm, and M. Ollus. 2004. "A Strategic Roadmap for Advanced Virtual Organizations." In *Collaborative Networked Organizations*. Springer US.

Galvin, R. 2004. "Roadmapping: A Practitioner's Update." In *Technological Forecasting & Social Change*, no. 71, pp. 101-103.

Goldman Sachs. 2003. "Dreaming with BRICs: The Path to 2050." In Global Economics Paper no. 99 (October). http://www.gs.com/insight/research/reports/99.pdf (accessed January 2009).

Hines, A., and P. Bishop. 2007. *Thinking about the Future: Guidelines for Strategic Foresight*. Washington, D.C.: Social Technologies.

Kirn, S. 1995. "Organizational Intelligence and Distributed AI." Research report of the Institute of Business Informatics, University of Münster.

Laat, B. 2004. "Conditions for Effectiveness of Roadmapping: A Cross-sectional Analysis of 80 Different Roadmapping Exercises." EU-US Seminar: New Technology Foresight, Forecasting & Assessment Methods. Seville (May 13-14).

Ministério do Desenvolvimento, Indústria e Comércio Exterior (MDIC). "Política de desenvolvimento produtivo 2008-2010." http://www .desenvolvimento.gov.br/pdp/index.php/sitio/inicial (accessed January 15, 2009).

Price, S., P. Conway, P. Palmer, and R. Summers. 2004. "Technology Roadmapping—A New Perspective." EU-US Seminar: New Technology Foresight, Forecasting & Assessment Methods. Seville (May 13-14).

Rezgui, Y., and A. Zarli. 2002. "Roadcon—A European Strategic Roadmap Towards Knowledge-Driven Sustainable Construction." In proceedings of ICE, *Civil Engineering*, 150 (November).

Schlossstein, D., and B. Park. 2006. "Comparing Recent Technology Foresight Studies in Korea and China: Towards Foresight-Minded Governments?" In *Foresight*, vol. 8 no. 6.

Part 3

Building on Innovation and Creativity

Globalization 3.0

A New Urgency for Building Creative and Innovative Communities

John M. Eger

INTRODUCTION: IT IS A FLAT WORLD

Thomas Friedman, *New York Times* foreign-affairs columnist and author of *The World Is Flat: The Globalized World in the 21st Century*, says "Globalization 3.0 is shrinking the world from a size small to a size tiny and flattening the playing field at the same time." It is "a force that gives it its unique character—is a newfound power for individuals to collaborate and compete globally. And the phenomenon that is enabling, empowering and enjoining individuals and small groups to go global so easily and so seamlessly is what I call the flat world platform...." Friedman points out that this platform is the by-product of the convergence of personal computers and a new information infrastructure, the Internet, which suddenly allowed individuals worldwide to collaborate regardless of distances between them.[1]

No one anticipated this convergence. It just happened—right around the year 2000. And when it did, people started waking up all over the world and realized that they had more power than ever to go

---

John M. Eger is the Lionel Van Deerlin Endowed Chair of Communications and Public Policy and Director of the Creative Economy Program at San Diego State University. E-mail jeger@mail.sdsu.edu.

global as individuals, they needed more than ever to think of themselves as individuals competing against other individuals all over the planet, and they had more opportunities to work with those other individuals, not just compete with them.

Friedman cites a number of applications, such as accounting, radiology, and banking, that are done out of Bangalore for a price that is considerably lower than if they were done in the United States. For example, during the evening in the United States, a radiologist in Bangalore who makes less than $15,000 a year can read an MRI and have it back to the attending physician in the United States to read the next morning. Perhaps most important, he can do it for a fraction of what it would cost in the United States. This outsourcing of jobs, and what has been called offshoring—shifting more work including the relocation of business processes usually because of labor cost advantage—is on the rise among global corporations around the world.

This worldwide competition for jobs is multiplied by a number of cities and regions around the world positioning themselves to capitalize on the new global information economy. Singapore's Intelligent Island project, Dubai's Internet City, or Canada's Smart Communities—no matter what they're called—these new enterprise zones not only have the broadband technology of the new age, they also have in place aggressive plans to use technology to transform their regional economy and society. The best ones are those looking to play a leadership role in this new age. Recognizing that it is creativity and innovation that will be the hallmarks of the new global economy, they also have strategies to attract, retain, and nurture the most entrepreneurial, creative, and innovative workforce.

Cities across the world have been struggling to reinvent themselves for the new, postindustrial economy and society foreshadowed in the 1960s by economists Fritz Malcop and Marc Porat[2] and by sociologist Daniel Bell.[3] In their efforts to prepare themselves for the twenty-first century, many communities focused on updating their data infrastructure to accommodate the needs of an age in which information is the most valuable commodity. Now the stakes have gotten higher.

Those communities placing a premium on cultural and ethnic diversity, and reinventing their educational systems for the creative age, will likely burst with innovation and entrepreneurial fervor.

BACKGROUND

In his biography *Cicero: The Life and Times of Rome's Greatest Politician*, author Anthony Everitt writes, "even the largest empire the world had seen was created slowly because communications were slow and unreliable." He points out that, although a network of "well engineered roads were constructed, travel was limited," and since Rome had no public postal service, "letters—which were scratched tablets or written on pieces of papyrus—were sent at considerable cost by messenger. The trick by a private correspondent was to persuade a traveler going in the right direction to take his or her post with him and deliver it."

It wasn't until the Rothschilds, the wealthy French financiers, deployed racing pigeons around 1813 that the value of timely communications accelerated the concept of multinational business and finance. The family established a European-wide network of carrier pigeons to capitalize, among other historical events, on Napoleon's loss at Waterloo, which they knew about first.

Within a decade, the telegraph reduced the reliance on pigeons, but it wasn't until undersea cables, originally laid for the telegraph and subsequently used for telephony, that multinational trade and commerce began to accelerate. In 1927, with cooperation between American Telephone & Telegraph ("the Bell system") and the British Post Office, a program of transatlantic communications between New York and London was begun, and a new undersea cable communications infrastructure was created that still exists today.

The next great leap forward occurred in 1957 with the Soviet launch of the Sputnik I satellite. "About the size of a basketball, but weighing 184 pounds, Sputnik whipped around the globe," according to space writer Leonard David. "Every 98 minutes and with every orbit, Sputnik I thumbed its nose at America's technological prowess, political esteem in the community of nations, as well as military strength."

Sputnik I started the so-called "space race." President John F. Kennedy declared the United States would put a man on the Moon within a decade. The National Aeronautics and Space Administration (NASA) invested heavily in technology, creating today's communications satellite-based system. In 1962, the Kennedy administration formed the Communications Satellite Corporation (Comsat) with the passage of the Communications Satellite Act. This legislation enabled the government, as fifty-percent owner, to create a vehicle for the start-up of a new domestic carrier in competition with the existing AT&T monopoly, and a global organization called INTELSAT (the International Consortium of Satellites). INTELSAT was the predicate for the first worldwide communications system available to every country in the world based upon their individual use and investment.

Within 10 years, more than 80 countries had joined the INTELSAT system, further shrinking the globe and enabling broadcasting as well as telephony to expand exponentially. This innovative effort created yet another communications wave, encouraging the growth of multinational and transnational enterprises of all kinds. The global presence of these new multinational corporations accelerated the deregulation and demonopolization of so-called PTTs (postal, telephone, and telegraph) or government-owned and run telephone monopolies.

COMPUTERS AND THE DIGITAL AGE

While there is no doubt that the development of satellites contributed greatly to the expansion of commercial broadcasting throughout Europe in the 1980s and had a similar effect worldwide, it also created the avenue for the global expansion of trade and commerce.

The real threat to national hegemony and the spur to "globalization 3.0," as Friedman and others have called it, was the development of the computer. The computer enabled creation of the Internet, and with the Internet came media convergence and a vehicle for the distribution of voice, video, and data over a single system.

Currently there are close to 2 billion Internet users in the world. Depending on the growth of the mobile Internet, with the cell-phone industry quickly embracing Internet-based protocols, it is not unlikely that the whole world will be connected within the next 10 years.

THE PERIOD OF INTERNET BOOM AND BUST

It was the creation of the World Wide Web, the graphical user interface superimposed on the Internet, in 1990 that presaged the tremendous growth of the modern-day Internet. The Web, as it came to be called, allowed graphics, documents, audio, and video files to be loaded onto servers and exchanged among users worldwide, revolutionizing business and industry, which today cannot exist without a Web presence. The Web has also transformed education, health care, government, and the leisure and entertainment industries.

Creation of the Web, along with passage of the Communications Act of 1996, the first major rewrite of the law governing ownership and use of the telecommunications infrastructure since 1934, led to the widespread perception that almost any business plan that proposed using the Internet was going to be an instant success. The 1996 Communications Act, while allowing cross-investments between existing players, clearly invited new players to the field of telecommunications. It has often been said that, once the regulatory gates were opened in Washington, the capital markets in New York were quick to follow with financing.

Millions and millions of investment dollars poured into Internet start-ups as business, government, organizations, and institutions scrambled to increase their presence on the "national information highway." Paradoxically, however, although the world's information infrastructure was built in record time, as the *Wall Street Journal* reported, only about 3% of the new infrastructure was actually being used, due to federal regulatory barriers.

This period of Internet investment in the United States and elsewhere in the world is referred to as the "dot-com boom." Sadly, the "dot-com bust" followed soon after. Many of the business plans were built on the hopes and dreams of those proposing a new way of doing business. They lacked, however, real-world applications, or were based on applications whose time had not yet arrived. The net result of these investments—by one estimate, hundreds of billions of dollars or close to the cost of building the entire U.S. national highway system—was that they had to be written off. Many of the fledgling companies had to file for bankruptcy or simply go out of business altogether. The good news is that the dot-com bust set the stage for yet another telecommunications revolution as many of these facilities and systems, expensive to build, were resold for "pennies on the dollar." Now, literally thousands of new communications links have been established at a fraction of the original cost.

THE NEW ECONOMY

In the wake of the rapid spread of computers and telecommunications, and the development of global corporations, yet another demand on nation-states, and especially cities and regions across the world, was created. That demand was, and is today, to create the twenty-first-century information infrastructure so vital to the wealth and well-being of all cities and communities in a new global knowledge economy and society. As the economies of the world become more integrated, one of the realities is that political power devolves to cities and regions worldwide. Information or knowledge becomes the new wealth, replacing gold as the monetary standard. As former Citibank Chairman Walter Wriston put it, "information technology [becomes] the tools of wealth creation."

Even before the dot-com boom and bust era of the late 1990s, President William Jefferson Clinton and Vice President Albert Gore were sounding the alarm. Gore particularly was promoting not only increased commercialization of the Internet, but also the development of the broadband, high-speed Internet. He called it simply Internet II and was seeking federal funding from the Congress to develop such a high-speed broadband system.

Both Clinton and Gore were keenly aware that we were entering a new uncertain era in which information or knowledge would become the most important indicator of national wealth. They knew it was important for America to awaken to this basic shift in the structure of the global economy and that as a country we begin to change institutions, both public and private, to respond to the challenges presented by the new global information economy.

Although the Clinton–Gore initiative, called the National Information Infrastructure (NII), clearly involved reforming the law to allow existing players to invest in the future and allowing new players to participate in that information age as well, the administration was aware that real growth had to take place within communities across America and that all sectors of the economy and society needed to be involved. Toward that end, billions of federal research and development dollars were targeted toward public projects across the country in health care, education, business, and "e-government." The Clinton administration tried to put the spotlight on community development.

The tiny country of Singapore in many ways created the model for what is occurring, indeed what must occur, worldwide to succeed and survive in the new global economy. As the technology of telecommunications and computers converges with the forces of the new global economy, political, social, and economic power is devolving rapidly to smaller and smaller entities. Probably the best geopolitical entity for a rebirth or reinvention of a governing system that encourages knowledge-based production and activity is the city. Not surprisingly, the city in many ways has always been the center of commerce and the crucible of civilization. Today, in the new economy where ideas themselves are the basis for the new wealth, the city becomes the most likely incubator of creative and innovative products and services.

Over 25 years ago, Singapore created a National Computer Board whose goal was to create "an intelligent island." By that, government leaders and policy makers meant not only the infrastructure of the new age but a mind-set that used technology as a tool of social, political, and economic transformation. As Prime Minister Goh Chok Tong stated in announcing the formation of a community-wide, government-created Intranet—an internal network—called Singapore One, the network "will empower Singaporeans to work efficiently in a smart environment to facilitate the use and access of information to enhance their business, personal, and family lives." The government saw use and deployment of technology as crucial to the "next great leap forward." While only a small nation of fewer than 3 million people, Singapore aggressively began wiring the country and targeting key industry sectors for transformation. Eventually every sector of the Singapore economy and society was automated.

Today, Singapore has launched what is called Infocomm 21, a broad strategic plan to take the country to the next level of the digital future. To use Singapore's stated goal, it is "to develop Singapore into a vibrant and dynamic global infocomm capital with a thriving and prosperous e-economy and a pervasive and infocomm savvy e-society."

Next door to Singapore, Malaysia, a far bigger country primarily dependent on agriculture, launched the Multi-Media SuperCorridor Project. An area of approximately 10 by 20 miles and including the Kuala Lumpur International Airport, it is, in effect, a free-trade zone for IT and telecommunications research, development, and manufacturing. As with Singapore's government, Malaysian officials are appealing to global corporations to make the Multi-Media SuperCorridor their Pacific-region headquarters and have offered a package of incentives to companies in the IT and telecom fields. For example, the SuperCorridor guarantees IT and software developers duty-free importation of all related equipment and a 100% investment tax allowance. These kinds of incentives are obviously attractive to IT companies such as IBM, Microsoft, and Google.

Like Singapore, Malaysia also promises world-class physical and IT infrastructures within the Corridor; no censorship of the Internet, and no taxes for the first five years of operation for those earning so-called "Pioneer status." Malaysia garnered major attention in the United States by inviting companies to its Corridor and reportedly had several billion dollars in investments promised when it first launched the initiative. By providing globally competitive tariffs, freedom of ownership, exemption from state and local ownership requirements and other permits, and by ensuring intellectual property protection and a series of legal innovations such as digital signatures and so-called new cyber laws ensuring and enhancing online security, Malaysia sought to position the Corridor as an attractive location to invest and operate.

In the Middle East, the Gulf state of Dubai was taking out full-page ads in the *New York Times*, the *Wall Street Journal,* and other major publications proclaiming itself as a "city of the future." In October 2000, Dubai opened its "Internet City" in a technology and media "free zone." Like Malaysia's Multi-Media SuperCorridor, Internet City provides tax-free locations for further development of knowledge-based industries and duty-free import and export of media and information products and services.

Through an arrangement with U.S.-based company Cisco Systems, which provided technological vision and expertise, Dubai built what has been labeled the world's largest Internet facility, allowing the highest technically practical transmission speeds throughout the Internet City. These amenities and others have attracted Microsoft, IBM, Dell, Siemens, Sony, Ericsson, and other global corporations.

Dubai's strategy is comprehensive. In addition to its telecommunications facilities, it also boasts a first-rate transport and shipping infrastructure, free health care for all its citizens, and virtually no crime, along with countless modern shopping malls. Despite its roots in Islam, Dubai has very few cultural and religious restrictions and serves a diverse population of 150 different nationalities, factors that make Dubai a truly cosmopolitan world city.

There are other cities all over the world attempting to replicate the successes of Dubai, Singapore, and Malaysia in one respect or another. Canada has launched a "Smart Communities" program, and Europe has an aggressive "digital cities" project. In the United States, despite the Clinton–Gore NII, which funded billions of dollars of innovative digital cities projects, significant progress has not been made. Sadly, in the second half of 2006, the United States had fallen to 25th in the world in household penetration of broadband technology.

However, the effort of Silicon Valley to create a private–public regional consortium is noteworthy. As author Kenosha Ohmae put it in his book *The End of the Nation State*: "There are no national economies, only the global economy and constellations of regional economies with strong cities at the core." This national ability to encourage regional infrastructure development, and indeed an economy based upon the use and production of media and information products and services, is the key to success for those regions and nations most likely to succeed in this new global economy. Silicon Valley succeeded without the kind of federal support offered in other countries. Perhaps the lesson here is that the concept of devolution really works if communities can organize themselves to take advantage of the power they actually have.

As Friedman has said, "The world is flat." All communities are suddenly competing with every other community around the world for basic manufacturing requirements and provision of high-tech and biotech services. With this flattening taking place everywhere, we must accelerate the change taking place within our communities and reinvent our centers of learning at every level and at an unparalleled pace.

This is not about technology for its own sake. San Diego, for instance, even commissioned a "City of the Future" committee[4] in 1993 to make plans to build the first fiber-optic-wired city in the country in the belief that, as cities of the past were built along waterways, railroads, and interstate highways, cities of the future would be built along "information highways," wired and wireless information pathways connecting every home, office, school, and hospital and, through the World Wide Web, millions of other individuals and institutions around the world.

For the new technologically sophisticated city, the information infrastructure it is not so much about technology as it is about jobs, dollars, and quality of life. In short, it is about organizing the community for the new knowledge economy and society; preparing its citizens to take ownership of their community, and educating the next generation of leaders and workers to meet these global challenges.

THE DEMAND FOR CREATIVITY AND INNOVATION

Today, the demand for creativity and innovation has outpaced America's ability to produce enough workers simply to meet the needs of Silicon Valley or the Hollywood entertainment community. For example, the Alliance of Motion Picture and Television Producers asked the governor of California to declare a state of emergency to help Hollywood find digital artists. There were enough people who were computer literate, they claimed, but they could not draw. In the new economy, they argued, such talents are vital to all industries dependent on the marriage of entertainment to computers and telecommunications.[5]

Worrying about the lack of qualified workers in this day and age may sound unusual. With the globalization of media and markets in full bloom, America is beginning to see the outlines of yet another out-migration of American jobs, unleashing new concerns about rising unemployment. Many economists are alarmed that the latest round of losses, unlike the earlier shift of manufacturing jobs to Taiwan and less developed East Asian countries, will have a dramatic impact on the West's economic wealth and well-being.

Twenty years ago it was fashionable to blame foreign competition and cheap labor markets abroad for the loss of U.S. manufacturing jobs, but the pain of the loss was softened by the emergence of a new services industry. Now that the service sector also is beginning to automate, banking, insurance, and telecommunications firms are eliminating layers of management and infrastructure as the traditional corporate pyramid disappears and is replaced by highly skilled professional work teams. State-of-the art software and telecommunications technologies now enable any kind of enterprise to maximize efficiency and productivity by employing foreign workers wherever they are located, making the retention of service-sector jobs in the United States even more precarious.[6]

IBM, the world's largest computer maker, acknowledged that "a significant number" (the unions claim several thousand) of software, chip development, and engineering jobs were being moved to India and China. In 2004, industry stalwarts like Microsoft, Hewlett-Packard, and Dell Computer announced that they, too, were either outsourcing their software development or beefing up their foreign subsidiaries in China, India, the Eastern bloc, and Russia to do the same.

Marketing research firm Forrester Research Inc. estimated some 3.3 million service jobs will move out of the United States over the next 10–15 years. Others, such as the Hass Business School at the University of California, Berkeley, have put that number at 15 million, warning that the results would be devastating for America's economy.[7]

While CEOs, economists, and politicians are telling us that these are short-term adjustments, it is clear that the pervasive spread of the Internet, digitization, and the availability of white-collar skills abroad mean potentially huge cost savings for global corporations.

Consequently, this shift of high-tech service jobs will be a permanent feature of economic life in the twenty-first century, but this does not necessarily mean the news is all bad. On the positive side, some economists believe that globalization and digitization will improve the profits and efficiency of American corporations and set the stage for the next big growth-generating breakthrough. But what will that be?

A number of think tanks, including Japan's Nomura Research Institute,[8] argue that elements are in place for the advance of the "Creative Age," a period in which America and the West should once again thrive and prosper because of their relative tolerance for dissent, respect for individual enterprise, freedom of expression, and recognition that innovation, not mass production of low-value goods and services, is the driving force for the economy.

Developing the human mind to its fullest potential and educating people so they are capable of success in the information age requires that we rethink the role of community broadly defined; retool our knowledge factories—starting with our universities—concentrating all our energies on educating the public for the coming knowledge age; and restructure education to incorporate what we now know about enhancing creativity. Unless we do so, we will not develop the skill base we so desperately need in the workforce for the new millennium. Richard Florida, author of *The Rise of the Creative Class*, more optimistically argues that the United States is already churning out large numbers of creative workers.[9]

We can meet the challenges of globalization and the needs of a creative and innovative workforce best by helping our communities renew and reinvent themselves for this new global age in which the Internet, knowledge creation, and innovation are key and where collaboration and connectivity are the hallmarks of the most successful communities.

CREATIVE AND INNOVATIVE COMMUNITIES

In less than a decade, the great global network of computer networks called the Internet has blossomed from an arcane tool used by academics and government researchers into a worldwide mass communications medium, now poised to become the leading carrier of all communications and financial transactions affecting life and work in the twenty-first century. Cities the world over are struggling to gain prominence in the wake of a global knowledge economy. Philadelphia, for instance, put in place one part of its global telecommunication strategy: a plan to offer inexpensive wireless Internet as a municipal service to the whole city—a bold move that is the most ambitious yet by a major U.S. city.

Not surprisingly, the Philadelphia plan collided with commercial interests, including the local phone company. The Telco and cable interests have now joined hands to make sure no other city in Pennsylvania gets as "creative." As dozens of cities and towns have either begun or announced similar ambitions, these competing interests have intensified a national campaign to quash municipal wireless initiatives like Philadelphia's.[10]

New York City, too, is looking at ways to provide broadband access to all their citizens. In a briefing paper released before they began public hearings, the city through its experts made it unequivocally clear that "broadband is a necessity for every resident," and that having it "improves the quality of life of everyone who has access."[11]

Other cites in the United States, Europe, indeed everywhere in the world are developing plans to be so-called "connected communities," or as California called them almost a decade ago, "smart communities."[12] In the wake of globalization and with yet another out-migration of American jobs, there is a new urgency. The demand is for a creative and innovative workforce.

Those communities that develop aggressive broadband strategies for this new age by reinventing their educational systems, recognizing the role of art and cultural assets in the community, and creating highly livable and walkable communities will attract and nurture the type of bright and creative people who generate new patents and inventions, innovative world-class products and services, and the finance and marketing plans to support them.

THE CREATIVE ECONOMY

John Howkins, author of *The Creative Economy* (2001), acknowledges that anyone with a good idea can make money. He tends, however, to limit the creative industries to things like advertising, architecture, graphic design, filmmaking, authors, painters, and the like.[13]

Richard Florida claims to count 38 million creative people. In what is clearly a more expansive definition of the term "creative," Florida includes creative professionals in "business and finance, law, healthcare and related fields." These people "engage in complex problem solving that involves a great deal of independent judgment and requires high levels of education or human capital ... all are members of the creative class," he says.

Given the outsourcing of jobs and offshoring of whole businesses, people are understandably worried about these kinds of things, confused as to whether Howkins or Florida is right. Perhaps some index clearly defining the creative class and the creative industries they make up is needed. In fact, several economists are working on such indexes as we speak.

In truth, however, it does not matter in the short term. In truth, both authors are right. Both are attempting to define not only an industry category and people who populate those industries, but rather a new age requiring creativity and innovation as never before. That is a trend shaping our world, and our workforce, as never before.

Now, nearly four decades after Daniel Bell described the coming postindustrial society, we are struggling to define yet another shift in the basic structure of the world's economy. We know it's global, and, as Friedman has told us, "flat."

This age is "digital," for computers have transformed every sector of our economy and society or are about to, and we know, too, that the new age is more than the age of information, which for many years has been what followed the postindustrial era. It is also the Age of Knowledge, for those who are able to sift through the tons of information one can get by "Googling" almost any subject, and who can add value and thus invention or innovation to a product or service, will, too, find new wealth.

But it is creativity—simply defined as "the quality or ability to create or invent something, originality"—that best defines the quality most of us need to succeed in the new economy. But again it is not as important what we call this new age. Call it The Creative Age, as *Business Week* once did, or The Age of Innovation, which *Business Week* later did, thinking that might appeal more to the business reader, or call it The Age of Creativity and Innovation and make everyone happy.

What is important is that we recognize that a whole new economy and society based upon creativity and innovation is emerging and that, as a consequence, we recognize the vital importance of re-inventing our communities, our schools, our businesses, and our government to meet the challenges that such major shifts are compelling.

CONCLUSION AND OBSERVATIONS

The agenda to renew our cities is huge. Working either in partnership with the existing cable or Telco providers or through some alternative strategy, cities must aggressively look for ways to provide the wireless "hot spots" often found in downtowns, coffee shops, and other public gathering places. In the belief that having broadband is as necessary as water, electricity, and a telephone, and, indeed, that such broadband Internet service may be the missing link to reinventing and renewing themselves, cities are developing plans for comprehensive, wired, 24/7, broadband infrastructure.[10]

But having such broadband infrastructures in place is only a first step. As discussed earlier, the effort to create a twenty-first-century city is about economic development and quality of life, not technology per se. In short, it is about organizing one's community to reinvent it for the new knowledge economy and society. Cities must prepare their citizens to take ownership of their communities and educate the next generation of leaders and workers to meet the new global challenges of what has now been termed the Creative Economy.[14]

The message is becoming clear: Rather than economic stimulus tools such as subsidies for footloose corporations and taxpayer-underwritten industrial parks, the successful cities and metro areas of the twenty-first century will be stimulated by their attractiveness to young, talented people. The traditional economic development push to lure big corporations and build large factories was characteristic of the twentieth-century economy. The prize of the future will be the ability to attract, nurture, and retain bright and creative people.

For the past 10 years, the California Institute for Smart Communities has looked at hundreds of smart communities in the making worldwide. Each community's approach is different, as each community itself has its own unique characteristics and demographics. But there are three overarching conclusions or observations that the Institute believes make the critical difference for success in the creative age.

First, the effort to remake our cities as we shift from an agrarian and industrial economy to a knowledge economy should not be seen simply as an effort to deploy technology. Rather, it is an attempt to understand how people use technology, and then, importantly, how to deploy technology as a catalyst to transform every sector of the community's economy and society.

Second, an outgrowth of this new understanding is the recognition of the importance of collaboration. While competition surely existed between industry and government, and clearly in the telecommunications field between different industries—cable versus telephone, wired versus wireless communications firms, and so forth—in this new environment, cooperation is essential among governments and between governments and industry. Indeed, it is clear that the City of the Future cannot be built without the active participation and cooperation of all of its stakeholders. Many people believe that, as the world has become more competitive, a competitive strategy that is not based on a spirit of cooperation will not be competitive very long.

Last, but most importantly, is the lesson about empowerment, or shared governance. Under this principle, all the stakeholders, including individual citizens, have a voice in the dialogue and discussion about their city and region, and indeed even in establishing a governance structure that allows them to participate in the decisions that are made. The most successful cities and regions will find a way to empower their citizenry.

NOTES

1. Thomas L. Friedman, *The World Is Flat: A Brief History of the Twenty-first Century* (New York: Farrar, Straus and Giroux, 2005).

2. Marc Porat, "The Information Economy: Definition and Measurement." Special Publication 77-12 (1), U.S. Department of Commerce, 1977.

3. Daniel Bell, *The Coming Post-Industrial Society* (New York: Basic Books, 1977).

4. John Eger, "San Diego: The City of the Future—The Role of Telecommunications." Report of the Mayor's Advisory Committee on the City of the Future, March 11, 1994, http://www.smartcommunities.org/research_future.htm.

5. John Eger, "Forget Manufacturing Slump, America Is Entering Creative Age," Insight, *San Diego Union-Tribune*, September 7, 2003.

6. Stephanie Armour and Michelle Kessler, "USA's New Money-Saving Export: White-Collar Jobs," *USA Today*, August 5, 2003.

7. Juan Carlos Perez, "IBM Aims for Desktop Outsourcing," *Computerworld*, November 4, 2005.

8. "Japanese Tasks in the 1990s," *NIRA Research Output,* Vol. 1, Number 1, 1988.

9. Richard Florida, *The Rise of the Creative Class: And How It's Transforming Work, Leisure, Community and Everyday Life* (New York: Basic Books, 2004).

10. Reuters, "Philly Wi-Fi Clash Pits City against Telcos, " *ZDNET,* November 3, 2004. Available: http://news.zdnet.com/2100-1035_22-5471853.html.

11. John M. Eger, "New York City Holds Hearings on Affordable Broadband," *Government Technology Magazine,* July 18, 2005.

12. John M. Eger, editor, *The Smart Communities Guidebook. Report to the California Department of Transportation,* SDSU International Center for Communications, 1997.

13. John Howkins, *The Creative Economy: How People Make Money from Ideas* (New York: Penguin, 2001).

14. John M. Eger, *The Creative Community* (San Diego: California Institute for Smart Communities, SDSU International Center for Communications, 2003). Available: http://www.thecreativecommunity.org/.

The Telecommunications Explosion

Toward a Global Brain

José Luis Cordeiro

THE INFORMATION REVOLUTION GROWS

Study the past, if you would divine the future. (Confucius, Chinese philosopher, circa 500 BCE)

In recorded history there have been perhaps three pulses of change powerful enough to alter man in basic ways: the introduction of agriculture ... the Industrial Revolution ... and the revolution in information processing.... (Herbert A. Simon, Nobel Prize in Economics, 1978)

While the agricultural revolution took millennia to spread around the world, the Industrial Revolution needed less than a century to spread in many other countries, thanks also to the advances in knowledge and technology, particularly telecommunications. Now, with the new Information Revolution, the time needed is not millennia, nor even centuries, but decades and sometimes just years.

José Luis Cordeiro is founder of the World Future Society's Venezuela Chapter, co-founder of the Venezuelan Transhumanist Association, chair of the Venezuela Node of the Millennium Project, and former director of the World Transhumanist Association and the Extropy Institute. E-mail jose_cordeiro@yahoo.com.

Since the second half of the twentieth century, several authors have been writing about a new revolution. Not just a second or third industrial revolution, but something completely different. For lack of a widely recognized and better term, the "information" revolution is an appropriate name for the current era.

While the agricultural revolution started in the Fertile Crescent in the Middle East, and the Industrial Revolution began in England, this new information revolution originated in the United States during the twentieth century. And it is spreading faster and farther than the previous two revolutions.

Figure 1 clearly shows the evolution of the main economic sectors in the United States from the time since such statistics are officially kept. The decrease of the agricultural sector can easily be noticed, while the industrial and service sectors have grown. It is interesting to notice that more than half of the U.S. population was employed in the agricultural sector at the beginning of the nineteenth century. Today, U.S. agricultural employment is less than 1%, and that is enough not just to feed the U.S. population but also to export many food products (since the United States is currently a net food exporter). Figure 1 also indicates the constant increase of the service sector, which is the main component of the economy during the Information Revolution.

This new information revolution is dependent on technology, particularly telecommunications, since the speed and spread of knowledge are fundamental to the creation of wealth today. In fact, the telecommunications sector basically did not exist two centuries ago, but today it represents about 3% of the global economy. And the telecommunications sector is growing consistently, even as the price of telecommunication services are falling dramatically.

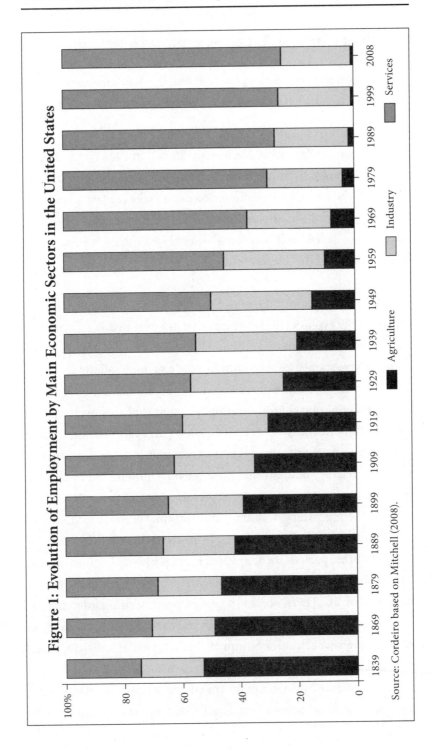

Figure 1: Evolution of Employment by Main Economic Sectors in the United States

Source: Cordeiro based on Mitchell (2008).

THE BEGINNING OF TELECOMMUNICATIONS

> Well-informed people know it is impossible to transmit the voice
> over wires. Even if it were, it would be of no practical value. (*The
> Boston Post*, 1865)

The word *télécommunication* was coined in 1904 by the French engineer Édouard Estaunié. It comes from the Greek prefix τηλέ (télé), "far," plus the Latin suffix *communicare*, "to make contact." The original French word was soon adopted in English and most other languages. The word itself was spread quickly by the increasing speed and reliability of the telecommunication systems of the early twentieth century.

Biologically speaking, one of the first forms of telecommunications was the evolution of languages that allowed advanced symbolic communications from one individual to another. Even though some animals have sophisticated communication systems, all the way from ants and bees to chimpanzees and dolphins, human language is an advanced symbolic communication tool that probably evolved with our first human ancestors at least 100,000 years ago. Certainly many animals also have different systems of communications, from audiovisual to olfactory mechanisms; however, only humans have perfected telecommunication systems based on technology.

In the prehistory of human civilization, there are examples of cave paintings with designs dating from about 30,000 BC in the Upper Paleolithic period. By definition, human history begins with the invention of writing systems, which can be traced back to the fourth millennium BC. (Even earlier, however, proto-writing, ideographic and mnemonic symbols, emerged in the early Neolithic period, as early as the seventh millennium BC, if not earlier.) Writing itself emerged in a variety of different cultures in the Bronze Age, around 3000 BC, mainly Mesopotamian cuneiform scripts, Egyptian hieroglyphs, and Chinese characters. Finally, during the Iron Age, around

1000 BC, the first alphabets appeared: first the Phoenician alphabet (only consonants, not really an alphabet but an abjad), then the Greek alphabet (also with vowels), and later the Latin alphabet and many others. Documents were first written in stones, wood, and shells, followed by papyrus in Egypt and then paper in China. The first postal system was developed in Egypt, where pharaohs used couriers for the diffusion of their decrees in their territory since 2400 BC. Persia, India, China, and Rome also created their own postal systems since the first half of the first millennium BC.

In terms of audio signals, there is some evidence of drums and horns in parts of Africa before 3000 BC. Similarly, for visual signals, there are remains of light beacons (fires) and possible smoke signals since 3000 BC and earlier in several parts of the world. The Greeks, and later the Romans, also perfected the heliographs for telecommunications since 490 BC, and heliographs could reach until 50 kilometers in good weather conditions.

The Chinese probably invented paper in the second century BC, but it was only standardized by Cai Lun in about AD 100. The first movable-type printing press was developed by Pi Sheng in China around AD 1041, and the first alphabetic movable-type printing press was invented by Johannes Gutenberg in Germany around AD 1439. Postal systems continued to evolve, including sometimes the use of homing pigeons (evidenced in Baghdad in AD 1150) and many land and sea transports.

In the late eighteenth century, the first telegraphs came in the form of optical telegraphs, including the use of smoke signals and beacons, which had existed since ancient times. A complete semaphore network was invented by Claude Chappe and operated in France from 1792 through 1846. It apparently helped Napoleon enough that it was widely imitated in Europe and the United States. The last commercial semaphore link ceased operation in Sweden in 1880.

The first electrical telegraphs were developed in the 1830s in England and the United States. Sir William Fothergill Cooke patented it in May 1837 as an alarm system, and it was first successfully demonstrated on July 25, 1837, between Euston and Camden Town in London. Independently in the United States, Samuel Morse developed an electrical telegraph in 1837, an alternative design that was capable of transmitting over long distances using poor-quality wire. The Morse code alphabet commonly used on the device is also named after Morse, who developed it with his assistant, Alfred Vail. On January 6, 1838, Morse first successfully tested the device in Morristown, New Jersey. In 1843, the U.S. Congress funded an experimental telegraph line from Washington, D.C., and Baltimore. The Morse telegraph was quickly deployed in the following two decades, and the first transcontinental telegraph system was established in 1861, followed by the first successful transatlantic telegraph cable in 1866.

In only three decades, the telegraph network crossed the oceans to every continent, making instant global telecommunications possible for the first time in history. Its development allowed newspapers to cover significant world events in near real-time and revolutionized business, economics, science, and technology. By now, however, most countries have totally discontinued telegraph services, like the Netherlands in 2004 and the United States in 2006. The invention of wireless telegraphy, as radio was originally called, also decreased the importance of electrical telegraphy in the twentieth century. After more than a century and a half, with incredibly high success, the electrical telephone has given way to more efficient and newer means of telecommunications, including the Internet.

Figure 2 shows the theoretical evolution of telecommunications in the last few centuries, from smoke signals to Internet, passing by optical telegraphs, electrical telegraphs, fixed telephone landlines and mobile telephones. It is worthwhile to note that each new system is on average faster, cheaper, more accurate and reliable, and also has a wider bandwidth than its predecessors. The changes in telecommunications are now very rapid, and the efficiency of the systems is generally increasing.

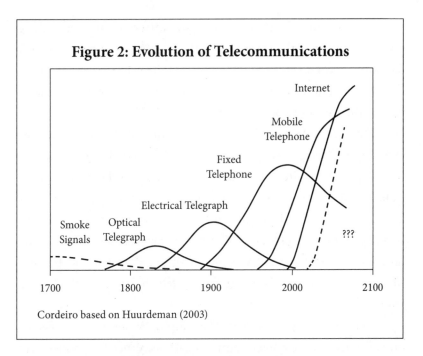

Figure 2: Evolution of Telecommunications

Internet

Mobile
Telephone

Fixed
Telephone

Electrical Telegraph

Smoke   Optical
Signals   Telegraph

???

1700   1800   1900   2000   2100

Cordeiro based on Huurdeman (2003)

THE INVENTION AND GROWTH OF AN INDUSTRY

> Mr. Watson, come here, I want to see you. (Alexander Graham
> Bell "telephoning" his assistant Thomas Watson, March 10,
> 1876)

The first telephones, from the Greek words tele (τηλέ) "far" and
phone (φωνή) "voice," arrived in the second half of the nineteenth
century in the middle of claims and counterclaims of the individuals
working on similar or related inventions. As with other great inventions, such as radio, telegraph, television, light bulb, and computer,
there were several inventors who did pioneer experimental work on
voice transmission over wires and improved on each other's ideas.
Chronologically, Innocenzo Manzetti, Antonio Meucci, Johann
Philipp Reis, Elisha Gray, Alexander Graham Bell, and Thomas Alva
Edison, among others, have all been credited with pioneer work on
the telephone.

The continued belligerence of the different and conflicting groups involved in the invention of the telephone delayed the quick development of a standard system during its very first years. However, the Bell and Edison patents were finally victorious and later proved themselves to be commercially profitable.

During the 1876 Philadelphia Exhibition, Bell received the unexpected and decisive support of Emperor Pedro II of Brazil, who was traveling in the United States at the time. Emperor Pedro II was curious about the telephone and recited into it Shakespeare's famous line from Hamlet—"To be or not to be"—and then exclaimed with surprise: "This thing speaks!" The emperor was so impressed that he ordered the installation of a telephone in Brazil, which thus became the second country in the world to have telephones, after the United States.

In the high days of electrical telegraphy, Western Union was the unquestionable leader of telecommunications. When telephones were first invented in 1876, Western Union circulated an internal memo saying:

> This "telephone" has too many shortcomings to be seriously considered as a means of communication. The device is inherently of no value to us.

When Alexander Graham Bell approached Western Union in order to sell his telephone patent for $100,000, the committee charged with investigating the potential purchase wrote in a report to the president of Western Union:

> Why would any person want to use this ungainly and impractical device when he can send a messenger to a local telegraph office and have a clear written message sent to any large city in the United States?

Against all odds, Bell continued with his patent and eventually founded, with the help of financiers, the American Telephone & Tele-

Table 1: Telephones Growth in the 19th Century

Year	United States	Europe	Rest of the World	Total
1880	47,900	1,900	-	49,800
1885	147,700	58,000	11,800	217,500
1890	227,000	177,000	31,500	435,500
1900	1,355,000	800,000	100,000	2,255,000

Source: Cordeiro based on Huurdeman (2003).

graph Company in 1885. He also bought a controlling interest in the Western Electric Company from his rival, Western Union, which only a few years earlier had turned down Bell's offer to sell it all rights to the telephone for $100,000.

After the acquisition of Western Electric, AT&T expanded quickly and founded similar companies in many countries, such as Canada, France, India, and Japan. Thus, the former competitor Western Union remained the leader of the eventually shrinking telegraph industry, while AT&T became the leader of the growing telephone industry.

AT&T, together with its subsidiary Western Electric, oversaw an explosive growth of telephones during the late nineteenth century, first in the United States, later in Europe, and finally in the rest of the world. In just about two decades, the number of telephones passed the 2 million mark, more than half of them in the United States, but with increasing numbers in Europe and other regions. Table 1 shows the telephone growth during the end of the nineteenth century.

In the 1880s, AT&T began creating a national long-distance network from New York City, which was eventually connected to Chicago in 1892. The AT&T national long-distance service finally reached San Francisco in 1915, thus connecting the east and west coasts. Transatlantic services started in 1927 using two-way radio, but the first trans-Atlantic telephone cable did not arrive until 1956, with the TAT-1 undersea cable between Canada and Scotland.

In the 1960s and 1970s, AT&T grew and grew, thus becoming a quasi-national monopoly in the United States and some other countries where it operated. In 1982, "Ma Bell" was broken up in the United States and was split, following a famous antitrust suit against AT&T, into seven independent regional Bell operating companies known as "Baby Bells." Less than two decades later, with all the new technologies and more global competition, the natural monopoly status disappeared. SBC (one of the original Baby Bells, known by successive names as Southwestern Bell Corporation, later SBC Communications) reabsorbed some of the other Baby Bells, plus the older but then much smaller AT&T Corp., and renamed itself as AT&T Inc. The new AT&T Inc., however, was not totally vertically integrated as the previous Ma Bell.

Figure 3 shows the evolution of telecommunications in the United States, with telegraphs dominated mostly by Western Union, fixed telephone landlines by the near monopoly of AT&T, and mobile telephones and Internet supplied by a larger variety of newer companies, both national and international.

Similar technological "waves" can be seen in other industries, such as in the energy sector. Figure 4 shows the evolution and forecasts of the energy sector in the United States from 1820 to 2040. Several waves or cycles can be clearly identified: first, energy based on wood; second, coal; third, oil; fourth, natural gas; and finally, new energy sources. It is worthwhile to note that each subsequent cycle is faster, and the waves become shorter with time. A similar conclusion could be reached about the telecommunications industry, with the new technologies having shorter and faster cycles.

Just as the twentieth century has been called the century of oil, the twentieth century will also be remembered as the century of the fixed telephone landlines. It is true that fixed telephone landlines have gone through major changes, but the general concept remained the

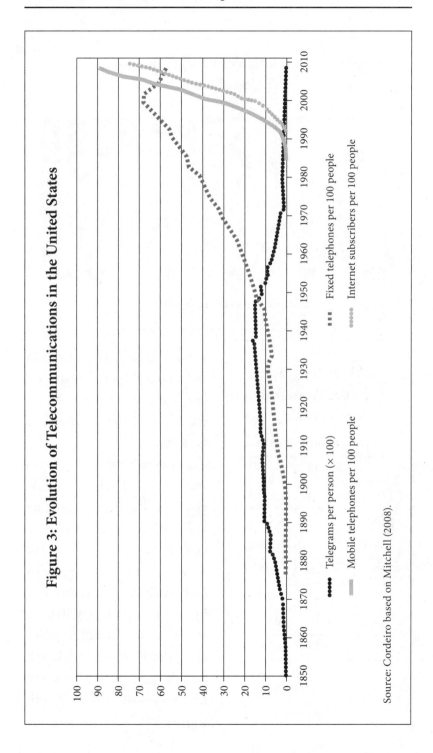

Figure 3: Evolution of Telecommunications in the United States

Telegrams per person (× 100)

Mobile telephones per 100 people

Fixed telephones per 100 people

Internet subscribers per 100 people

Source: Cordeiro based on Mitchell (2008).

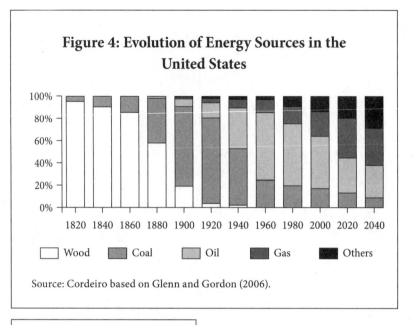

Figure 4: Evolution of Energy Sources in the United States

Source: Cordeiro based on Glenn and Gordon (2006).

Table 2: Telegraph Rates per Word from New York City

Year	London	Tokyo
1866	$10.00	-
1868	1.58	-
1880	0.50	$7.50
1890	0.25	1.82
1901	0.25	1.00
1924	0.20	0.50
1950	0.19	0.27
1970	0.23	0.31

Source: Cordeiro based on Odlyzko (2000).

same. The telegraphs before and the mobile telephones later are very different, but fixed telephones continue with the same basic model.

Historic analogies seem to indicate that telecommunications will continue changing at faster rates. Additionally, the costs have been rapidly going down, particularly when an older technology is substituted by a newer technology. Table 2 shows the drastic fall in prices after the electrical telegraph service between New York and London was started in 1866 with the first successful transatlantic

Table 3: Telephone Rates for a Three-Minute Call from New York City

Year	Philadelphia	Chicago	San Francisco
1917	$0.75	$5.00	$18.50
1926	0.60	3.40	11.30
1936	0.50	2.50	7.50
1946	0.45	1.55	2.50
1959	0.50	1.45	2.25
1970	0.50	1.05	1.35

Source: Cordeiro based on Odlyzko (2000).

telegraph cable (all the prices are in nominal current dollars of the year considered). A similar drop in price can be seen after telegraph service started between New York City and Tokyo. Additionally, there is an important downward and long-term convergence in prices before the telegraph services were discontinued later on.

Just like for telegraph messages, telephone calls have also become much cheaper over time. Table 3 shows the costs of a three-minute daytime telephone call between New York City and Philadelphia, Chicago, and San Francisco. Since the AT&T transcontinental telephone connection was finalized in 1915, the telephone rates between New York City and San Francisco have gone down considerably. Additionally, prices have converged downwards, and today most telephone companies in the United States have flat rates and unlimited calling programs that make the marginal cost of calling to almost any city equal to almost zero.

Figure 5 shows similar results for the telephone rates for a three-minute call between New York City and London since 1927, when the first public transatlantic phone call (via radio) was started. Most in-

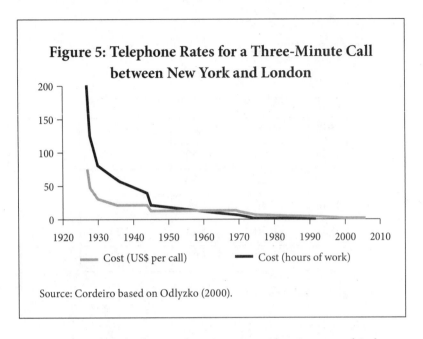

Figure 5: Telephone Rates for a Three-Minute Call between New York and London

Cost (US$ per call) ▬▬ Cost (hours of work) ▬▬

Source: Cordeiro based on Odlyzko (2000).

teresting is to see the bigger drop in prices when measured in hours of work, from almost 200 hours in 1927 to almost nothing today. Indeed, using the new VoIP (Voice over Internet Protocol) services like Skype, it might actually cost basically zero to make such transatlantic calls now.

Not only might transatlantic calls cost today practically zero, but also transpacific calls and international calls to just about anywhere with a phone, fixed or mobile, or even just a computer with an Internet connection. Niklas Zennström, the Swedish entrepreneur who co-founded KaZaA peer-to-peer file sharing system and then co-founded in Estonia the Skype peer-to-peer Internet telephony network, is famous for saying:

> The telephone is a 100-year-old technology. It's time for a change.
> Charging for phone calls is something you did last century.

Telephone rates have in fact dropped to almost zero in just over a century, but this trend can again be observed in several other sectors. Lighting is an important sector that was studied by Nordhaus

(1997), starting briefly with the biological origin of the eyes and their long evolution to allow organisms to use light (since many lower life-forms do not have eyes or other light receptors). Nordhaus estimated the price of light as measured in hours of work per 1,000 lumen hours (lumen is a measure of the flux of light), including estimates for the fires in the caves of the Peking man using wood, the lamps of the Neolithic men using animal or vegetable fat, and the lamps of the Babylonians using sesame oil. After reviewing the labor-time costs of candles, oil lamps, kerosene lamps, town gas, and electric lamps, he concludes that there has been an exponential decrease of lighting costs, particularly during the last 100 years. These outstanding cost reductions are shown in Figure 6: close to a 10,000-fold decline in the real price of illumination.

Another example of the exponential increase of capabilities and the corresponding reduction of costs is commonly called Moore's law for the semiconductor industry. Caltech professor and VLSI pioneer Carver Mead named this law in 1970 after Gordon Moore, co-founder of Intel. According to Moore's original observations in 1965, the num-

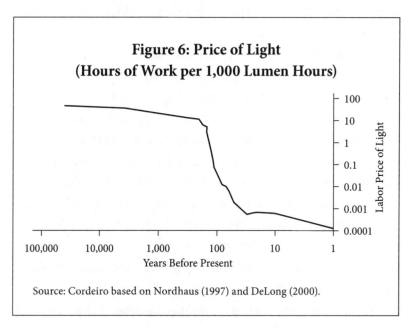

**Figure 6: Price of Light
(Hours of Work per 1,000 Lumen Hours)**

Source: Cordeiro based on Nordhaus (1997) and DeLong (2000).

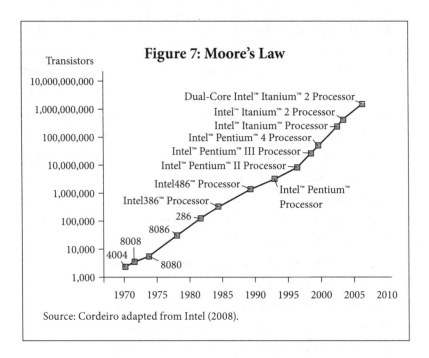

Figure 7: Moore's Law

Source: Cordeiro adapted from Intel (2008).

ber of transistors per computer chip is doubling every two years, even though recently this trend has accelerated to just about 18 months. Figure 7 shows the Moore's law with an exponential scale in the vertical axis.

Moore's law and similar conjectures have been observed for the number of transistors per integrated circuit, cost per transistor, density at minimum cost per transistor, computing performance per unit cost, power consumption, hard disk storage cost per unit of information, RAM storage capacity, network capacity, and pixels per dollar. In the case of computer flash memories, the South Korean company Samsung follows Hwang's law, named after a vice president of Samsung.

According to Moore himself, his "law" should still be valid for the next 20 years or so, until we reach levels of transistors at the nanoscale. For the telecommunications sector, this is very important, since we are currently witnessing the convergence of the information and communications technologies, usually referred together as ICT.

Such trends of increasing capabilities, decreasing costs, and convergence are happening not just with ICT, but also with other major industries. For example, there are currently fast price reductions in some innovative energy technologies (with rapid efficiency increases and cost decreases for solar energy and other renewable sources), nanotechnology, and biotechnology. The case of biotechnology is also an example of the fast rate of change both in time and costs in order to sequence the human genome. The publicly funded Human Genome Project, begun as a 15-year project, was estimated to cost about $3 billion, and it took 13 years, from 1990 to 2003. There was an additional privately funded project led by biologist Craig Venter that took a little less time and significantly less money. In early 2008, the genome of Nobel laureate James Watson was published: It took about two months and cost more than $1 million. By late 2008, it was possible to sequence a complete human genome in only four weeks at a cost of $100,000. Now there are some companies already offering to sequence a general genome for $1,000, and it is estimated that by 2012 it will take just two days and cost $100 or less. Table 4 shows the diminishing trend in time and costs to sequence the human genome.

Table 4: Time and Cost to Sequence Human Genome

Year	Cost	Time
2003	$437,000,000	13 years
2007	10,000,000	4 years
2008 (early)	1,000,000	2 months
2008 (late)	100,000	4 weeks
2012	100	2 days

Source: Cordeiro based on Kurzweil (2008).

Across many technological fields, trends of convergence, increasing efficiencies, and decreasing costs can be observed. They will obviously have a major impact on the continuous economic growth of different countries around the world, from wealthy OECD countries to poor African countries, from Asia to Latin America. Just as the nineteenth century, which experienced a rate of economic growth unprecedented in human history, was followed by a twentieth century with even more growth, the twenty-first century might have the highest rate of growth yet to be recorded. The recent *Growth Report* commissioned by the World Bank and chaired by Nobel economist Michael Spence (2008) has actually qualified signs of hope for the future. In fact, the rise of China and India, plus other developing countries, is a reality. This is good news not just for those countries, but also for the entire world; as a Chinese saying explains: "a rising tide lifts all the boats." Telecommunications have played a very important role in faster, cheaper, and better connections for all the regions of the world. Now the accumulated knowledge of all mankind is becoming accessible, almost for free, from Tokyo to Timbuktu.

IMPLICATIONS FOR THE FUTURE

> It is my heart-warm and world-embracing Christmas hope and aspiration that all of us, the high, the low, the rich, the poor, the admired, the despised, the loved, the hated, the civilized, the savage (every man and brother of us all throughout the whole earth), may eventually be gathered together in a heaven of everlasting rest and peace and bliss, except the inventor of the telephone. (Mark Twain, *Boston Daily Globe*, Christmas Greetings: December 25, 1890)

The history of telecommunications suggests strongly that there is a very high correlation between the number of telephone lines and economic growth during the twentieth century. Over the long term, the fixed telephone landlines network has remained a relatively stable communication system, and it has also become a landmark in the telecommunications history of human civilization. In fact, the twentieth century could be called the century of the telephone for the telecommunications industry, just like it was the century of oil for the energy industry.

There are also some significant simple causality relations between telephones and GDP growth, as evidenced by the previous statistical analysis. However, the relationships are not always the same and not necessarily unidirectional. For the 41 countries considered here, and for the 100-year period analyzed, the causality sometimes goes from telephones to GDP, but more often it goes from GDP to telephones. Nonetheless, some sort of relationship is certainly present, and it might probably increase with time, together with the increase in interconnectivity among individuals, institutions, and nations.

The continuous growth of ICT is worth notice. From its very humble human beginnings as smoke signals and drum beats, telecommunications has grown into a modern industry representing 3% of the world economy. Telecommunications is also one of the fastest-growing sectors, particularly among the poorest countries, who are just jumping from no telephones to mobile telephones and soon wireless Internet connections. In fact, some of the highest growth rates of cellular networks are in poor African countries that are completely bypassing expensive landlines, and they are leapfrogging into newer, better, and cheaper telecommunication systems. The mobile telephones are having a positive impact on growth, which is very significant for developing countries, as well as the smaller rate for developed countries. This is also a sign of rapid convergence in mobile telecommunications. Mobile telecommunications are indeed powering a peaceful economic revolution in poorer countries, where people might not even know how to read and write. For example, illiterate farmers and merchants in Africa and India are using their new mobile telephones to make better decisions about the prices of their outputs and the costs of their inputs. The same for fishermen who, using their mobile telephones, find out about weather conditions and higher demand for certain products, for example, thus changing their daily decisions based on more informed and immediate sources of knowledge.

Telecommunications are once again reducing transaction costs and increasing the amount of available information to all people, even illiterate people. The additional convergence of information and communications technologies and development economics has created a new interdisciplinary research field known as ICT4D (information and communications technologies for development), which investigates how to transform the so-called "digital divide" into a "digital dividend." The United Nations has taken a special interest in this field, just like financial organizations (for example, the World Bank), academic institutions (like the University of California, Berkeley), private foundations (like the Bill and Melinda Gates Foundation), and many government and nongovernmental organizations in several countries. Some initiatives, like the OLPC (one laptop per child) by Nicholas Negroponte at the MIT Media Lab, are widely known, but they are just the tip of the iceberg of the many possibilities offered by the new technologies. In fact, the newer generations of telephones will probably be better than many current laptops, and also faster and cheaper. Additionally, the technological convergence will continue adding new features to the telephones of the future.

The world is increasingly becoming an interconnected place. British author Frances Cairncross (1997) has considered *The Death of Distance: How the Communications Revolution will Change our Lives.* American author Thomas Friedman (2005) has written *The World Is Flat: A Brief History of the Twenty-First Century.* Technology experts Tapscott and Williams (2006) have explained the new economy in *Wikinomics: How Mass Collaboration Changes Everything.* The fact is that the world is indeed becoming more interconnected, and perhaps a new economy is also emerging based on more open-source projects and sharing of knowledge. The farfetched success not just of mobile telephones, but also of the Internet, and newer applications like Google and Wikipedia, is a clear indication of the faster changes to come, both in telecommunications and in the more general and converging ICT fields.

The theory of network effects should be considered in order to understand the full potential of the interconnected world. Theodore Vail, president of AT&T from 1885 to 1889 and again from 1907 to 1919, was an early proponent of the importance of network externalities. More recently, Robert Metcalfe (co-inventor of Ethernet and co-founder of 3Com) has popularized the concept as Metcalfe's law, stating that the value of a telecommunications network is proportional to the square of the number of users of the system (n^2). Metcalfe's law follows a considerable improvement over Sarnoff's law, which states that the value of a broadcast network is proportional to the number of viewers (n). David Sarnoff, a longtime executive of RCA and founder of NBC, conceived his law based on his practical network experiences.

Metcalfe's law explains many of the effects of communication technologies and networks such as the Internet and social networking. This law has often been illustrated using the example of fax machines: A single fax machine is useless, but the value of every fax machine increases with the total number of fax machines in the network.

Metcalfe's law has been criticized for overestimating the total number of contacts and confusing it with the *potential* number of contacts. For example, Odlyzko and Tilly (2005) emphasize that the social utility of a network depends upon the number of nodes really *in contact*. Nodes that do not interact, which are many, do not contribute to the total number of contacts. Thus, they argue, the (n^2) term is actually closer to ($n\log(n)$):

> This growth rate is faster than the linear growth, of order n, that, according to Sarnoff's Law, governs the value of a broadcast network. On the other hand, it is much slower than the quadratic growth of Metcalfe's Law.

There is yet no general academic consensus, but even if the previous argument turns out to be true, the total number of possible contacts in a multidirectional network is certainly larger than (n), maybe

($n$log(n)) in many cases, and perhaps as large as (n^2) in some cases. This is obviously more significant for larger numbers. David Reed, a computer scientist at MIT, formulated his own law for groups-forming networks (GFN):

> [E]ven Metcalfe's Law understates the value created by a group-forming network [GFN] as it grows. Let's say you have a GFN with n members. If you add up all the potential two-person groups, three-person groups, and so on that those members could form, the number of possible groups equals 2^n. So the value of a GFN increases exponentially, in proportion to 2^n. I call that Reed's Law. And its implications are profound.

Sarnoff's law, Metcalfe's law, and Reed's law, even with criticisms such as those by Odlyzko and Tilly, do indeed have profound implications for networks and all their possible and potential combinations—as nodes, connections, and groups—and particularly for group-forming networks in multidirectional environments where many types of communications are simultaneously possible. The value of nodes, connections, and groups increases with the size of the network, and there are increasing returns and path dependence considerations in such multidirectional new world of fast and cheap telecommunications. Figure 8 illustrates the value creation theories according to Sarnoff's law, Metcalfe's law, and Reed's law.

TOWARD THE BIRTH OF A GLOBAL BRAIN

> The empires of the future are the empires of the mind.
> (Winston Churchill, British Primer Minister, 1944)

In the December 1900 issue of *The Ladies' Home Journal* there were several predictions for the year 2000. John Elfreth Watkins, an American civil engineer and railroad expert, wrote then an article called "What May Happen in the Next Hundred Years":

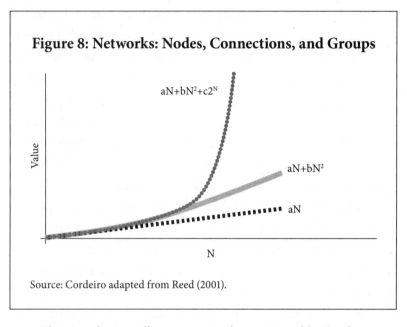

Figure 8: Networks: Nodes, Connections, and Groups

$aN+bN^2+c2^N$

$aN+bN^2$

aN

Value

N

Source: Cordeiro adapted from Reed (2001).

These prophecies will seem strange, almost impossible. Yet, they have come from the most learned and conservative minds in America. To the wisest and most careful men in our greatest institutions of science and learning I have gone, asking each in his turn to forecast for me what, in his opinion, will have been wrought in his own field of investigation before the dawn of 2001—a century from now. These opinions I have carefully transcribed.

Prediction #18, concerning telephones in the year 2000, transcribed the following idea by scientists at that time:

Telephones Around the World: Wireless telephone and telegraph circuits will span the world. A husband in the middle of the Atlantic will be able to converse with his wife sitting in her boudoir in Chicago. We will be able to telephone to China quite as readily as we now talk from New York to Brooklyn. By an automatic signal they will connect with any circuit in their locality without the intervention of a "hello girl."

It is interesting to see what has actually happened in the last 100 years. In fact, this specific prediction was not so much off the mark, even if happened actually earlier than expected by the writer. Now, however, with the continuous growth and the increase of telecommunications, many things will be possible much faster than before.

H. G. Wells, British science-fiction writer, proposed the idea of a world encyclopedia, or world brain, and this dream seems to have become a reality today with Wikipedia. Tim Berners-Lee, British computer scientist and co-inventor of the Web, was inspired by the free associative possibilities of the brain for his invention. The brain can link different kinds of information without any apparent link otherwise; Berners-Lee thought that computers could become much more powerful if they could imitate this functioning—i.e., make links between any arbitrary piece of information. Now, with telecommunications becoming faster, cheaper, and better, plus the convergence of telecommunications with other technologies, it might be possible to create a global brain. Alan Turing, often considered to be the father of modern computer science, was interested in artificial intelligence and the possibility for creating computer brains:

> No, I'm not interested in developing a powerful brain. All I'm after is just a mediocre brain, something like the President of the American Telephone and Telegraph Company.

Nobel laureate Robert Fogel, who partially inspired me to write this analysis, expanded his idea of "technophysio evolution" in his book *The Escape from Hunger and Premature Death, 1700–2100: Europe, America, and the Third World.* He refers to technophysio evolution as the relationship between technology (techno) and the human body (physio). He finished his 2004 book with the following prescient words:

> The outlook for new and more effective technologies to deal with chronic disabilities through the marriage of biology and

microchip technology is very promising. Indeed, some devices that combine living cells and electronics to replace failed organs are already at the stage of human trials. Somewhat further off, but even more promising, are advances in genetic engineering that will produce cures for what are now untreatable diseases.

Thanks to the rapid advances of the current telecommunications explosion, the world is changing faster than many expect, and a new global brain of network telecommunications is emerging. As a reputed ancient Chinese proverb and curse says:

May you live in interesting times.

May you come to the attention of those in authority.

May you find what you are looking for.

REFERENCES

AT&T. Several years. *Telephone and Telegraph Statistics of the World*. New York, NY: AT&T, Office of Statistician.

Bairoch, P. 1982. "International Industrialization Levels from 1750 to 1980." *Journal of European Economic History* 11 (Fall 1982), pp. 269-333.

Bell, D. 1976 (1973). *The Coming of Post-Industrial Society*. New York, NY: Harper Colophon Books.

Benkler, Y. 2006. *The Wealth of Networks: How Social Production Transforms Markets and Freedom*. New Haven, CT: Yale University Press.

Brooks, J. 1976. *Telephone: The First Hundred Years*. New York, NY: Harper & Row, Publishers.

Cairncross, F. 1997. *The Death of Distance: How the Communications Revolution will Change our Lives*. Cambridge, MA: Harvard Business School Press.

Cordeiro, J. L. 2008. *Telephones and Economic Growth: A Worldwide Long-Term Comparison—With Emphasis on Latin America and Asia*. Tokyo, Japan: VRF Series No. 441. Institute of Developing Economies, IDE–JETRO.

Cordeiro, J. L. 2007. *El Desafío Latinoamericano ... y sus Cinco Grandes*

Retos. Segunda Edición. Bogota, Colombia: McGraw-Hill Interamericana.

DeLong, J. B. 2000. "Cornucopia: The Pace of Economic Growth in the Twentieth Century." NBER Working Paper 7602. Cambridge, MA: NBER.

Diamond, J. M. 1997. *Guns, Germs, and Steel: The Fates of Human Societies.* New York, NY: W.W. Norton & Co.

Fogel, R. W. 2004. *The Escape from Hunger and Premature Death, 1700–2100: Europe, America, and the Third World.* New York, NY: Cambridge University Press.

Friedman, T. L. 2005. *The World Is Flat: A Brief History of the Twenty-First Century.* New York, NY: Farrar, Straus and Giroux.

Glenn, J., and T. Gordon. 2006. *The State of the Future 2006.* Washington, DC: The Millennium Project.

Halal, W. 2008. *Technology's Promise.* New York, NY: Palgrave Macmillan.

Huurdeman, A. A. 2003. *The Worldwide History of Telecommunications.* New York, NY: Wiley Interscience.

International Telecommunication Union. Yearly. *World Telecommunication Indicators.* Geneva, Switzerland: ITU.

International Telecommunication Union. Yearly. *Yearbook of Statistics—Telecommunication Services.* Geneva, Switzerland: ITU.

Kennedy, P. 1987. *The Rise and Fall of the Great Powers: Economic Change and Military Conflict from 1500 to 2000.* New York, NY: Vintage.

Kurzweil, R. 2005. *The Singularity Is Near.* New York, NY: Viking Adult.

Landes, D. 1998. *The Wealth and Poverty of Nations.* New York, NY: Norton.

Maddison, A. 2007. *Contours of the World Economy 1-2030 AD: Essays in Macro-Economic History.* New York, NY: Oxford University Press.

Maddison, A. 2004. *Historical Statistics for the World Economy: 1–2030 AD.* Paris, France: OECD. Statistics available online at http://www.ggdc.net/maddison.

Mitchell, B. R. 2008. *International Historical Statistics 1750–2005.* London, UK: Palgrave MacMillan.

Nordhaus, W. 1997. "Do Real Output and Real Wage Measures Capture Reality? The History of Lighting Suggests Not" in T. Bresnahan and

D.R.J. Gordon (eds.). *The Economics of New Goods*. Chicago, IL: University of Chicago, pp. 29-66.

Odlyzko, A., and B. Tilly. 2005. *A Refutation of Metcalfe's Law and a Better Estimate for the Value of Networks and Network Interconnections*. Preliminary electronic version. Available online at http://www.dtc.umn.edu/~odlyzko/doc/metcalfe.pdf.

Odlyzko, A. 2000. *The History of Communications and Its Implications for the Internet*. AT&T Labs. Preliminary electronic version. Available online at http://www.dtc.umn.edu/~odlyzko/doc/history.communications0.pdf.

Rostow, W. W. 1990. *Theories of Economic Growth from David Hume to the Present*. New York, NY: Oxford University Press.

Tapscott, D., and A. D. Williams. 2008 (2006). *Wikinomics: How Mass Collaboration Changes Everything*. New York, NY: Portfolio Hardcover.

Toffler, A. 1990. *Powershift: Knowledge, Wealth, and Power at the Edge of the 21st Century*. New York, NY: Bantam Books.

United Nations. Yearly. *Statistical Yearbook*. New York, NY: United Nations.

United Nations Development Program. 2001. *Human Development Report: Making New Technologies Work for Human Development*. New York, NY: Oxford University Press.

World Bank. Yearly. *World Development Indicators*. Washington, DC: The World Bank. Available online at http://www.worldbank.org/data/wdi/index.htm

World Bank. 1999. *World Development Report 1994: Knowledge for Development*. New York, NY: Oxford University Press.

World Bank. 1997. *The Information Revolution and the Future of Telecommunications*. Washington, DC: World Bank.

Anime: Art Form of The 21st Century

Lane Jennings

Almost since writing began, storytellers have tried to record exactly, and in permanent form, the narrative events and characters that filled their own imaginations. Homer used music and rhythmic repetition of sound to make memorable his tales of the Trojan War. Dramatists like Aeschylus and Euripides added multiple speakers in costume to bring these and other stories still more vividly to life. And for more than two thousand years, on stage, screen, and television, the tradition of live actors depicting real or imagined events has effectively made audiences suspend their disbelief and accept the evidence of their own eyes.

Occasionally, words alone have done the same job just as well or better. A perfect line of poetry can sometimes capture a mood or a scene so vividly that a reader/listener not only sees but feels what is being described. And in the hands of a novelist like Tolstoy or Trollop or Tolkien, entire worlds teeming with events and characters have become convincingly real to readers, with a degree of elaborate detail that no visual presentation can ever match.

But to make such deep impressions, even the finest writing demands a reader willing and able to shut out all distractions—and in our present age of multitasking, texting, and Twittering, such readers are proving increasingly hard to find. Actors, on the other hand, how-

Lane Jennings is managing editor of *World Future Review,* published by the World Future Society. E-mail lanejen@aol.com.

ever skilled, have one annoying trait in common: They are seldom content to play one role exclusively. Once audiences see the same actors repeatedly in different costumes and settings, they begin to see the people behind the characters. The storyteller's magic spell is broken.

The late-eighteenth-century German writer and dramatist Heinrich von Kleist suggested one intriguing way out of this dilemma: a theater whose performers were not human beings at all but lifelike puppets.[1] In his age, of course, the technology did not exist to create such a mechanical marvel—what we today would likely call a robot— nor does it yet, although experiments in theatrical robotics have already taken place.[2]

What is possible today, however, is the matching of expressive human voices with nonhuman figures, created especially for the purpose of telling one particular story. Enhance the action with music, visual settings of every imaginable kind, and dialogue or narrative as minutely accurate or suggestively lyrical as a writer can produce, and you have an art form equally capable of showcasing the combined input of scores of talented individual artists simultaneously, or reflecting the multiple facets of one individual's dream vision in perfect clarity, undiluted by considerations of cost, time, or artistic differences. This medium, once known as "the cartoon film," is now more appropriately called graphic animation or *anime*.

Based on examples from past and present masters in this field, I believe that anime stands poised to become *the* characteristic art form of the twenty-first century, just as live-action film and television can reasonably be considered to have been the artistic media that best reflected the values, technological achievements, and spiritual limitations of human society worldwide in the twentieth century.

A Thumbnail History of Animation

Early experiments with the technology for moving-picture presentations were based on simplified drawings, and cartoon comedies were a staple of early cinema shows. Walt Disney and his many talented collaborators expanded the entertainment potential of cartoons by adding music, color, and a host of technical innovations that gave scenes depth and a lifelike quality unmatched by any other practitioners.

After World War II, partly in reaction against Disney's "perfectionist" drawing style and relentlessly upbeat storylines, new schools of animation arose in Eastern Europe and elsewhere that focused more on bizarre appearance and content. A major source of humor in these short films was whimsy or outright absurdity—often with cynical or bleakly pessimistic overtones.

Yet no one matched Disney for the complex full-length features that his organization produced starting in 1937 with *Snow White* and extending (after a gap in the early 1940s, when most of even Disney's studio resources were co-opted to produce propaganda pieces and public information shorts) into the 1960s and beyond. By this point, television was a major competitor with movies in the mass entertainment field, and most cartoons produced in the United States between about 1970 and the 1990s were created specifically for viewing on the small screen by an audience consisting mostly of young children.

Japanese Animation

The father of animation in Japan was Osamu Tezuka, probably best known in America as creator of the *Astro Boy* series of popular children's cartoons and comics. Beginning in the late 1930s, Tezuka drew comic book stories and short animated cartoons featuring characters with simplified body shapes and disproportionately large eyes. Tezuka based his style on American cartoon figures like Betty Boop, Mickey Mouse, and the many humanized animals featured in various Disney productions. As with their American precursors, the simplified shapes of Tezuka's characters made them easier to draw quickly, while exaggerated facial features allowed them to convincingly convey a wide range of emotions.

Tezuka's work increasingly gained popularity in the years following World War II, as Japan's cash-strapped movie industry perceived the advantages of using artwork to replace expensive sets, and cartoon figures in place of live actors (whose obvious Asian appearance often made them seem unconvincing in any story set outside the borders of Japan). The advent of television (widely available in Japan about a decade after its introduction in the United States), with its insatiable demand for new programming, added still more to anime's popularity.

While in the West, cartoons and comic books were most often aimed at children and teenagers, in Japan, *manga* (books of narrative told in illustrations and/or collections of humorous/bizarre sketches by wood-block artists) and animated features have consciously tried to appeal to a far wider range of tastes—including sports fans of every age, married women seeking escape into a world of mystery and romance, and adult males hungry for adventure tales, crime thrillers, and pornography. Because examples of this latter segment of the market, often combining violent and frankly erotic content, were among the first to be imported to the West, the anime genre quickly acquired a reputation in the United States and England in particular for being morally depraved, or at least irresponsible—a reputation that, by and large, it does not deserve.

Two Modern Masters

One can find many examples of outstanding Japanese work in the anime genre (see Appendix for a few tips on where to begin looking). But here, I'll single out just two individuals whose films I believe clearly demonstrate anime's unique potential to become *the* art form of the twenty-first century: Hayao Miyazaki and Mikoto Shinkai.

As director, writer, and head of his own studio, Hayao Miyazaki (b. 1941) has long been active in the field of animation. He and his colleagues at Studio Ghibli, which he founded in 1984, are responsible for some of the most original, artistically impressive, and, at the same time, commercially successful anime features produced anywhere in the world. These include works like *Castle in the Sky, Porco*

Rosso, Princess Mononoke, and the Academy Award–winning *Spirited Away.* Miyazaki is also a writer and manga artist, whose multivolume graphic novel *Nausicaa of the Valley of the Wind* (which he also directed as an anime film) tells a powerful story of a future world struggling to recover from the ecological devastation wrought by mechanized war.

Starting from his original designs and storyboards, Miyazaki painstakingly guides and orchestrates a large team of illustrators and assistants to produce an anime. His characters and story lines are complex, and he makes excellent use of music and sound effects to enhance and complement the dramatic visual content of his films. He also teams with inspired colleagues, whose work, though different in emphasis and style, is every bit as effective as his own. Overall, productions from his Studio Ghibli are consistently adult, yet thoroughly entertaining for viewers of all ages. His sources include not only traditional Japanese tales and myths, but also modern stories written by European and American writers. In 2008, Miyazaki's studio produced an anime movie based on Ursula K. Le Guin's *Earthsea* trilogy.

Like the Disney studio's work, Miyazaki's anime productions require large budgets and teams of expert assistants working feverishly for many months. But unlike Disney, he and his colleagues do not use computers to the exclusion of all other animation techniques. Nor is he prone to simplify or trivialize controversial material into musical-comedy-style stories with relatively little depth.

By contrast, Mikoto Shinkai (b. 1973) is a relative newcomer. His first commercial production, *Voices of a Distant Star,* was released in 2002, and it has been followed by two more features: *The Place Promised in Our Early Days* (2004) and a three-part work collectively entitled *Five Centimeters per Second* (2007). This latter work takes its title from the speed at which cherry blossoms fall to the ground.

The remarkable aspect of Shinkai's work, besides his extraordinary drawing skill and sensitivity to atmosphere, is that he has proven himself capable of performing practically every step of the anime production process single-handedly. Working alone, with a personal computer and commercially available software, Shinkai produced a five-minute black-and-white anime in 1999 called *She and Her Cat*. This work won several awards outside Japan and inspired him to contemplate a full-length feature. He eventually secured funding and, in a little more than seven months of full-time work, produced *Voices of a Distant Star*.

This anime, practically homemade by Shinkai (he and his wife even provided the voices of the characters), demonstrates that one mind can now effectively fashion a work of art as complex in all its aspects as productions traditionally requiring the combined talents of professionals from many fields.

Since completing work on *Voices* in 2002, Shinkai has turned to productions that involve collaboration with other artists. But his vision remains the directing force inspiring and guiding every phase of the production process.

ANIME AND THE FUTURE

Writing about a complex visual and sonic art form such as anime is a bit like discussing music with no instrument on hand to make the sounds you want to comment on, or critiquing a ballet with no photographic record available to reproduce the movements of a dancer whose performance you are trying to describe. Clips from the work of both Miyazaki and Shinkai are available online (see Appendix), and a few moments spent watching and listening to these should be enough to illustrate what makes this genre so remarkably versatile. But this you may be sure of: The potential of anime is far beyond anything that has so far been achieved.

As the current century gets firmly under way, we can confidently expect that the capacity of computers and software to facilitate anime production will continue to increase dramatically. As this occurs, it seems equally likely that more and more gifted artists will be encouraged to exploit the unique potentials of the anime medium to tell the types of stories that particularly appeal to them.

Artists like Hayao Miyazaki, with experience of the wider world and eager to explore the complex interplay of conflicting ideas and character ambitions made possible through storytelling on a grand scale, will have ever wider access to the literatures and traditions of cultures outside the one they were born into. Freed from the limitations imposed by physical sets and human actors, they will use anime to present viewers with stories that blend many varied sources into one grand design. Via the Internet, it is now (or soon will be) practical to assemble multinational teams of collaborators for writing, storyboarding, and hand-drawn or computer-enhanced animation work. Similarly, the jobs of composing and performing background music, adding in voice tracks and sound effects, and fine-tuning the pace and flow of images can be performed by individuals or teams physically located anywhere in the world. Under such conditions, there is no practical reason why a story might not be written, produced, and (via multiple sound tracks) even performed in several different languages at once, using voice actors from various countries.

Other artists, like Makoto Shinkai, may prefer to focus on conveying as fully and truthfully as possible the feelings and concerns that obsess them as individuals. Artists who in the past might have written diaries or autobiographical novels can now construct interpretations of their lives and interests as audiovisual narratives in which solid reality and impossible dreams interweave at will. Making use of evocative images, including subtle and symbolic scenes that do not necessarily involve any direct interaction among human characters, they will find that the anime genre relieves them of many physical and economic constraints that in the past have complicated production and public presentation.

More than any other medium in history, anime offers creative artists a potential—long sought by dramatists and designers like David Belasco, opera composers like Richard Wagner, and "auteur" film directors like Ingmar Bergman or Woody Allen—to directly control every phase of planning, writing, and production. Moreover, anime does away with the physical limitations of a theater building or public stage, as well as the copying and shipping operations required in traditional book publishing or motion picture distribution. An anime can be any length—not forced to fit into the conventional time slots assigned to plays, movies, or television programming—and made cheaply accessible worldwide in the form of a digital recording on DVD or other suitable computer medium, or easier still, simply uploaded to a Web site on the Internet, where anyone who wants to view it can do so.

How such artists are paid may be a problem—or it may not. As more and more transactions of every kind shift from the physical world to the Internet, new methods of payment, appropriate to the items being exchanged or the experiences offered, are constantly being developing. Even such once-idealistic concepts as work credits or barter can be conveniently arranged at any distance via the Internet.

New tools are at hand to create works of art unlike any conceived or experienced in the past. What is needed now are artists with the vision and the drive to take up these tools and master them.

NOTES

1. Heinrich von Kleist (1777-1811) *Über das Marionettentheater* [On the Marionette Theatre] first published 1801. A complete English translation by Idris Perry, originally in the *Southern Cross Review,* is available online at http://www.southerncrossreview.org/9/kleist.htm.

2. Gerardo del Cerro Santamaria, "Ethnography in Robotics: Measuring Learning Through Quantitative Analysis in the Robotics-for-Theatre Project," in *World Future Review,* Vol. 1, No. 1, February-March 2009, pp. 23-38.

APPENDIX: TEN OUTSTANDING ANIME TO LOOK FOR

From Studio Ghibli:

1. *Nausicaa of the Valley of the Wind* (1984)
2. *Kiki's Delivery Service* (1989)
3. *Porco Rosso* (1992)
4. *Princess Mononoke* (1997)
5. *Spirited Away* (2001)
6. *Grave of the Fireflies* (1988)
7. *Pom Poko* (1994)

All of these titles are available on DVD (many can be found in public library collections); excerpts and individual scenes can be viewed at many Web sites online. Search for "Hayao Miyazaki, (director)," "Isao Takahata (director)," or "Studio Ghibli" to get started.

From Makoto Shinkai:

8. *Voices of a Distant Star* (2002)
9. *The Place Promised in Our Early Days* (2004)
10. *Five Centimeters per Second* (2007)

Less well known in the United States, these three titles by Shinkai have all been released as DVDs, but may not all be easy to find in stores. You can order them from Amazon.com and other sources on-line.

For examples of Shinkai's work, search for his short video *She and Her Cat* on YouTube, and follow links to related sites.

Also see:

- *The Anime Encyclopedia* by Jonathan Clements and Helen McCarthy (Berkeley, CA: Stone Bridge Press, 2006), probably the best general reference available in English on Japanese anime.
- *Hayao Miyazaki: Master of Japanese Animation* by Helen McCarthy (Berkeley, CA: Stone Bridge Press, 1999), a fine overview of this artist's life and accomplishments up through *Princess Mononoke*.

Signs and Wonders

Information Technology, Cybernetics, and the Dawn of the Postliterate Age

Patrick Tucker

For United States' literate elite—which includes everyone from Al Gore to Oprah Winfrey to this spring's MFA graduates—the gnashing of teeth and rending of garments over the demise of reading has become obligatory theater. Today's poets, writers, and teachers alike stand over the remains of a once-proud book culture like a Greek chorus gloomily crowded around a fallen king. Who, we ask, is to blame for bringing this curse? How can it be that, between 1982 and 2007, reading declined by nearly 20% for the overall population and 30% for young adults aged 18-24? Or that 40 million people read at the lowest literacy level in the richest nation on earth?

The answer that rises most immediately to meet our anguish is: the image makers. Television, that Pied Piper of the last century, has given way to online video games, YouTube, and an assortment of other visual horrors that are—hourly—ferrying culture further away from the nourishing springs of Western literature. The American appetite for images—scenes of war (staged or otherwise), music videos, game shows, pantyless celebrities roaming the streets of Los Angeles in a daze—seems both limitless in scope and apocalyptic in nature. To the

Patrick Tucker is senior editor of *The Futurist* magazine and communications director of the World Future Society. E-mail ptucker@wfs.org.

literary eye, the culture of the image has grown as large as Godzilla, as omnipresent as an authoritarian government, and as cruel and erratic as the Furies. In our rush to blame the moving picture for the state of cultural disarray, we've overlooked the fact that—as a carrier of data, thoughts, ideas, prayers, and promises—the image is neither as functional nor as versatile as the text.

The real threat to the written word is far more pernicious.

Much like movie cameras, satellites, and indeed television, the written word is, itself, a technology, one designed for storing information. For some 6,000 years, the human mind was unable to devise a superior system for holding and transmitting data. But by the middle of this century, America's finest and most ingenious software developers and engineers will have remedied that situation. The danger to the written word is not the image; it is the Information Age itself.

Consider, first, the unprecedented challenges facing traditional literacy in today's Information Age. The United States spends billions of dollars a year trying to teach children how to read; that it fails so often is a national shame. Yet, mysteriously, declining literacy and functional nonliteracy have yet to affect the nation's level of technological innovation in any obvious way. Similarly, human creation of information—in the form of data—has followed a fairly predictable trend line for many decades, moving sharply upward with the advent of the integrated circuit in the mid-twentieth century. The world population generated 161 billion gigabytes of data in 2006 (led by the United States) and will likely produce about 988 billion per year by 2010. We are spending less time reading books, but the amount of pure information that America produces as a civilization continues to expand exponentially. That these trends are linked, that the rise of the latter is causing the decline of the former, is not impossible.

Even after the bursting of the Internet bubble, the Information Age has no shortage of eager boosters. Steven Johnson's 2006 best seller, *Everything Bad Is Good For You*, and Henry Jenkins's 2006 book, *Convergence Culture*, argue that information technology, including the Internet and online games, is furthering the goals of traditional education by creating a smarter, more technologically savvy public. Jenkins even goes so far as to suggest that text-based online material, blogs, and instant messaging are contributing to a more-literate American society by empowering individuals to disseminate and "publish" at will, without the benefit of a traditional publisher. These authors point out that reading, as a pastime, has always competed for people's attention against other forms of leisure, yet has survived the arrival of telephone, radio, television, movies, DVDs, and video games. They insist that text-based media (though not necessarily print-based media) can share the marketplace with video blogs and online games and that the written word is flourishing in today's Information Age.

What these authors overlook is that the Internet of today represents a brilliant but transitory Golden Age. True, the Web allows millions of *already* well-read scholars to connect to one another and work more effectively. The Internet's chaotic and varied digital culture is very much a product of the fact that people who came by their reading, thinking, and research skills during the middle of the last century are now listening, arguing, debating, and learning as never before.

One could draw reassurance from today's vibrant Web culture if younger people, more at home in this new medium, displayed a propensity for literate, critical thought that was similar to their parents. But take a careful look at the many blogs, post comments, MySpace pages, and online conversations that characterize today's Web 2.0 environment. One need not have a degree in communications (or anthropology) to see that the back-and-forth communication that typifies the Internet is only nominally text-based. Some of today's Web content is indeed innovative and compelling in its use of language. The vast majority reads like the sort of thing one encounters carved into a stall door in a men's public restroom. Most importantly, none of it shares any real commonality with traditionally published, edited, and researched printed material.

This type of content generation, this method of "writing," is not only subliterate, but it may actually undermine the literary impulse. As early as 1984, the late linguist Walter Ong observed that teletype writing displayed speech patterns more common to ancient aural cultures than to print cultures (a fact well documented by Alex Wright). The tone and character of the electronic communication, he observed, was also significantly different from that of printed material. It was more conversational, more adolescent, and very little of it conformed to basic rules of syntax and grammar. Ong argued compellingly that the two modes of writing are fundamentally different. Hours spent texting and e-mailing, according to this view, do not translate into improved writing or reading skills. New evidence bears this out. A recent report from the Organization for Economic Cooperation and Development found that text messaging use among teenagers in Ireland was having a highly negative effect on their writing and reading skills.

The notion that literacy can be digitized through video-game play has also become somewhat popular among media elites and a rising number of educators. In 2006, the Federation of American Scientists (a nonpartisan Washington, D.C., think tank) issued a declarative statement—shocking in its ebullience—that video games could "redefine education," and that more public investment was needed to research how video games might be used for teaching. As Henry Kelly, the Federation president and a Clinton-appointed science adviser, put it, "This is an investment that private industry simply is not capable of taking.... This is the kind of thing where the federal government has always acted in the past, to underwrite basic research that you need to *drive an important movement forward*" (emphasis added).

He was seconded by Doug Lowenstein, president of the Entertainment Software Association, who prudently remarked, "We would be crazy not to seek out ways to exploit interactive games to teach our children."

In making these determinations, Kelly and others are relying on a nascent but prevalent body of literature claiming to show that the multibillion-dollar video-game industry has much to contribute to American education. Writers like James Paul Gee, author of *What Videogames Have to Teach Us About Learning and Literacy*, and Don Tapscott, author of *Growing Up Digital: The Rise of the Net Generation*, argue that video games have a positive effect on learning and IQ. What techno-enthusiasts like Gee and Tapscott are ignoring (or perhaps simply dismissing) is that video games compete directly with reading and books for children's time. A University of Michigan study released in June 2007 showed that kids who play video games on school nights spend an average of 32% less time reading and doing homework (and negative effects on GPA have been subsequently observed).

The argument for digital education is inherently pro-Information Age. According to this view, the relative popularity of video games over traditional reading shows that consumer preference favors video games over books. The lesson: Educators, like corporations, should simply give the people what they want. Not every teacher today is likely to see games as a viable substitute for teaching the old-fashioned way. But future teachers, those raised on Wii or *Grand Theft Auto*, will surely be more open to the notion of "redefining education" through video-game play.

The broader future that these trends portend is one in which "teaching" has largely been replaced by "interfacing," where electronic and visual stimuli "trick" children into learning, where students are compelled to form emotional relationships with machinery and digitally generated worlds, and where critical thinking is useful only for the purpose of ascending levels. More importantly, the world of video games is one in which literacy is almost superfluous to the actual learning process, even when it is an actual program objective. As any developer will admit, a game must stress reflexivity if it is to be interesting. Anything that slows down the action—like having to read a page of text—is a hindrance to what's called "player progress." Too much of that makes any game unmarketable.

The debate over whether or not to digitize education has only begun, and will certainly grow in intensity in the years ahead. But this argument is merely a precursor for what will come next. For all our very contemporary anxiety about how the Internet, texting, and online games are affecting education, the technologies that may influence the future of the written word the most are still invisible. Yet we can already hear the echoes of their movement.

In the past few years, amazing breakthroughs involving fMRI or functional magnetic resonance imaging—with potential ramifications for the field of education—have become an almost daily occurrence. FMRI uses non-ionizing radiation to take detailed pictures of soft tissue that tends to show up as murky and indistinct on CT scans, specifically the brain. The scanner works like a slow-motion movie camera, taking new scans continuously and repeatedly. Instead of observing movement the way a camcorder would, the scanner watches how oxygenated hemoglobin (blood flow) is diverted throughout the brain. If you're undergoing an fMRI scan and focusing one portion of your brain on a specific task, like exerting your anterior temporal lobe on pronouncing an unfamiliar word, that part of the brain will expand and signal for more oxygenated blood, a signal visible to the scanner.

In 2005, researchers with the Scientific Learning Corporation used fMRI to map the neurological roots of dyslexia and designed a video game called Fast ForWord based on their findings. The project was "the first study to use fMRI to document scientifically that brain differences seen in dyslexics can be normalized by neuroplasticity based training. Perhaps of greater relevance to educators, parents, and the children themselves are the accompanying significant increases in scores on standardized tests that were also documented as a result of the intervention," neuroscience experts Steve Miller and Paula Tallal wrote in a fall 2006 issue of *The School Administrator*.

Fast ForWord is likely the antecedent to many products that will use brain mapping to market education "products" to schools or possibly to parents, a commercial field that could grow to include not just software, but also chemical supplements or even brain implants. In much the same way that Ritalin improves focus, fMRI research could lead to electronic neural implants that allow people to process information at the speed of electric current—a breakthrough possible through the emergent field of cybernetics.

Speculative nonsense? To Kevin Warwick, an IT professor at Reading University in the UK, our cybernetic future is already passé. In 2006, Warwick had an experimental Internet-ready microchip surgically implanted in his brain. Building off the success of widely available implants like cochlears that treat certain types of deafness, Warwick's implant research dealt with enhancing human abilities. In a December 2006 interview with IT Wales, he discussed an experiment he took part in with his wife, wherein the couple actually traded neural signals—a crude form of telepathy:

> We had my implant which linked my nervous system directly with the computer and onto the Internet, and my wife Irina, who also had electrodes pushed into her nervous system to link her nervous system to the computer and the Internet, and we essentially linked our nervous systems together electrically so that when she moved her hand, the neural signals from her brain went from her nervous system and appeared on my nervous system, and therefore up to my brain. So her brain signals traveled electrically to stimulate my nervous system and brain, and when she moved her hand three times, I felt in my brain three pulses, and my brain recognized that my wife was communicating with me. It was the world's first purely electronic communication from brain to brain, and therefore the basis for thought communication.

While advancement in the field of cybernetics and declining literary culture appear, at first glance, completely unrelated, Warwick's research into cyber-telepathy has direct ramifications for the written word and its survivability. As MIT mathematics professor Norbert Wiener, the father of cybernetics, realized more than 50 years ago, many of the principles of physics and chemistry that come into play when we devise ways to control machines are similar to the control mechanisms in the human body. Electronic circuits mapped out in the same pattern as our neurons could, in decades ahead, reproduce the electrical activity that occurs when our natural transmitters activate. Theoretically, such circuits could allow parts of our brain to communicate with one another at greater levels of efficiency, possibly allowing humans to access data from the Web without looking it up or reading it.

Consider the plight of the news editor or book publisher trying to sell carefully composed, researched, and fact-checked editorial content today, when an impatient and ill-mannered public sometimes views even Web publishing as plodding. Then imagine the potential impact of cybernetic telepathy. The advent of instantaneous brain-to-brain communication, while inferior to the word in its ability to communicate complex meaning, may one day emerge as superior in terms of simply relaying information quickly. The notion that the written word and the complex system of grammatical and cultural rules governing its use would retain its viability in an era where thinking, talking, and accessing the world's storehouse of information are indistinguishable seems uncertain at best.

The advent of faster and more dexterous artificial-intelligence systems could further erode traditional literacy. Take for example one of the most famous AI systems, the Google search engine. According to Peter Norvig, director of research at Google, the company is fast at work at turning search (the act of "Googling") into a conversational interface. In an interview with *Venture Beat,* Norvig noted that

"Google has several teams focused on natural language and dozens of Googlers with a PhD in the field, including myself."

AI watchers predict that natural-language search will replace what some call "keywordese" in five years. Once search evolves from an awkward word hunt—guessing at the key words that might be in the document you're looking for—to a "conversation" with an AI entity, the next logical step is vocal conversation with your computer. Ask a question. Get an answer. No reading necessary.

Barney Pell, whose company, Powerset, was also working on a conversational search interface (before being acquired by Microsoft), dismisses the notion that a computerized entity could effectively fill the role of text, but he does acknowledge that breakthroughs of all sorts are possible:

> Language started out spoken and we'll always want spoken language. If you think about the history of the innovation it wasn't that we couldn't use speech to communicate to each other, the innovation of writing had a huge benefit and that's why it was worth all that trouble. Writing is not just about storage. If you could imagine that we had tape recorders back then, would we never have bothered to create writing? I don't think so. The problem with storing raw sounds is that it's a sequential access medium; you have to listen to it. You can't do other things in parallel with that.... But if you have a breakthrough where auditory or visual information could connect to a human brain in a way that bypasses the processes of decoding the written text, where you can go as fast and slow as you want and have all the properties that textual written media supports, then I could believe that text could be replaced.

How likely is that scenario? It depends on whom you ask. But if technological progress in computation is any indication, we are safe in assuming that an AI entity will eventually emerge that allows individuals to process information as quickly or as slowly as reading written language.

How can the written word and literary culture survive the advent of the talking, all-knowing, handheld PC? How does one preserve a culture built on a 6,000-year-old technology in the face of super-computation? According to many of the designers and researchers with whom I've spoken—the very individuals who are designing the AI systems that will dominate our young century—the answer is, you don't. You submit to the inexorable march of progress and celebrate the demise of the written word as an important step forward in human evolution.

When confronted by the statistic that fewer than 50% of high-school seniors could differentiate between an objective Web site and a biased source, Norvig of Google replied that he did perceive it as a problem. He astonishingly suggested that the solution was not to design technologies to help people read better—and thus better develop a core knowledge base with which to engage the Web—but to *get rid of reading instruction all together.* "We're used to teaching reading, writing, and arithmetic," he said. "Now we should be teaching these evaluation skills in school. Some of it could be just-in-time education; search engines themselves should be providing clues for this."

This cavalierly stated proposal from the director of research at the world's most famous Internet-based company—that we might simply drop the teaching of "reading, writing, and arithmetic" in favor of search-engine-based education—speaks volumes about what little regard some of the world's top technologists hold for the traditional arts and the written word.

The cultural and aesthetic value of text, in terms of the body of books and printed works we cursorily refer to as literature, is obvious in my view. But in the coming decades, lovers of the written word may find themselves ill-equipped to defend the seemingly self-evident merits of text to a culture-averse, technology-oriented generation who prefer instantaneous data to hard-won knowledge. Arguing the artistic merits of Jamesian prose to a generation who, in coming years, will rely on conversational search to find answers to any question will likely prove a frustrating, possibly humiliating endeavor.

The temptation to relent will be overwhelming at times. To submit to it would be unconscionable.

If written language is merely a technology for transferring information, then it can and should be replaced by a newer technology that performs the same function more fully and effectively. But it's up to us, as the consumers and producers of technology, to insist that the would-be replacement demonstrate authentic superiority. It's not enough for new devices, systems, and gizmos to simply be more convenient than what they are replacing—as the Gatling gun was over the rifle—or more marketable—as unfiltered cigarettes were over pipe tobacco. We owe it to posterity to demand proof that people's communications will be more intelligent, persuasive, and constructive when they occur over digital media—proof that *illiteracy*, even in an age of great technological capability, will improve people's lives.

If we can indeed agree that written language encourages a more rigorous mind, holds a mirror up to the human soul in a way that electronic media do not, and creates the mental tools for reasoned debate on extremely complex topics, then we are morally bound to defend this mere technology from the forces of market obsolescence. The time has come for intelligent people who are concerned about the future of our culture to take an honest look at the present and set a course of action, to defend written language at every turn and opportunity. Wringing our hands and bemoaning declining literary interest is not an effective strategy for dealing with this future, nor is blindly trusting technology marketers and manufacturers to put the interests of civilization ahead of their own. In the years ahead, we will either strengthen or reinvent the written word to survive the electronic age, or we will abandon it in pursuit of new forms of—or substitutes for—literacy. Those who care about the outcome of this debate must seize this chance to shape it before the opportunity vanishes.

Part 4

Assessing and Optimizing Our Resources

Sustainable Development

Tomorrow's Salvation
Or Today's Hype?

Richard MacLean

My grandfather was born in 1885 and lived a full century. He told me fascinating stories about the abundance of fish in crystal-clear waters off the Maine coast, about how he sewed sails for merchant vessels as a boy, and about his four uncles who fought in the Civil War. This oral history from his uncles to him to me spans around 150 years. Consider for a moment how much the world has changed in what amounts to a nanosecond in the evolution of life on earth.

Some may think of the enormous advances in manufacturing technology, medicine, and quality of life; others may point to the enormous growth in world population, pollution, and depleted resources. I was trained as a chemical engineer and mull over these contrasting dynamics as a question of equilibrium. When two opposing processes are in balance, they are sustainable; if they proceed at different rates, something either very desirable or unwelcome happens.

Sustainable development is being touted as the strategy that will ensure our salvation. But what are the significant forces that will shape our future world? Could all this talk of sustainability be hype blurring the real challenges facing generations to come? Corporations ad-

---

Richard MacLean is director for the Center for Environmental Innovation and environmental consultant with Competitive Environment. E-mail maclean@ Competitive-E.com.

vertise that their innovation and green practices will provide sustainable development. The Obama administration claims that it will enact the laws and fiscal policies that will ensure the United States' survival. Economists say that, as long as the price is right, the laws of supply and demand will provide needed resources. Many environmentalists, on the other hand, believe that we are headed for disaster. Finding the definitive answer has become a cottage industry for dueling pundits and researchers.

In the final analysis, there are fundamental laws that no one can get around. No matter how well opinions are spun or backed with some version of the facts, eventually the laws of physics, chemistry, biology, mathematics, and so on determine the ultimate outcome. In essence, there are positive processes under way that advance order and sustainability, just as there are opposing forces that promote chaos and instability. Will the second law of thermodynamics (i.e., chaos) dominate, or will the offsetting forces to stabilize the planet produce a dynamic equability? The answer to this question will be determined by three factors:

1. Time span under consideration.
2. Major forces and processes under way.
3. Feedback and control mechanisms for correction and change.

TIME MATTERS

The ultimate outcome is, of course, already well known: As grim as it sounds, the earth will eventually burn up with the sun. In the end, the laws of physics always rule. Obviously, a meaningful sustainability analysis must involve some other nearer-term time frame. But what is appropriate? The Brundtland Commission's definition of sustainable development provides little guidance: "development that meets the needs of the present without compromising the ability of future generations to meet their own needs." How many generations?

Should we be concerned about generations thousands of years into the future? Or should we enjoy life today using easily extractable resources without regard to their potential value for future generations? Clearly, there are moral, religious, and ethical standards, in addition to the laws of nature, that have a bearing on the time question.

As an example, helium is the gas of choice when filling party balloons, yet the world's largest helium reserve is expected to run out by 2015. Helium has many more critical uses than just providing buoyancy; it is used in a variety of key research and industrial applications. Of course, a resource's life span can be increased with conservation, technological innovations, substitutions, or the use of more-expensive extraction methods, as explained later. So should the issue be less about the appropriate use of resources and more about the laws of supply and demand?

In my grandfather's day, the depletion of the world's natural resources was not even a consideration. As the preceding example illustrates, today it is common to read accounts of once-abundant vital resources "running out" in a matter of decades. Renewables and "peak oil" are in the headlines, but these stories rarely analyze the inherent moral dilemmas other than the national-security implications of foreign oil dependence. According to the late economist Milton Friedman, it is not business management's job to make moral judgments, such as who gets what resources, for what use, and over what time period. Indeed, most people living in democracies would claim that it is society's responsibility.

Which leads us back to the question of time. For the purposes of this analysis, let's use 150 years—the span covering a period of several generations that literally can communicate first-hand experiences. Most might consider this ridiculously short, since humankind has been around for tens of thousands of years. Some may think this is too long and consider sustainability only in terms of their own or their children's life span. Pick your own time period, but keep in mind that the time horizon really matters in evaluating whether humankind is currently on a sustainable path.

MAJOR FORCES AND PROCESSES

In physics, relationships can be quite simple and elegant. Think $E=mc^2$. With ecological and human social systems, they are utterly complex. Nonetheless, the overall forces that affect sustainability can be evaluated. Environmentalists express the impact that humans have on the earth's ecosystems by the IPAT formula:

Impact = Population x Affluence x Technology

Technology and population are obvious considerations. Affluence is a much more complex issue than consumptive patterns; it involves a broad spectrum of societal factors that influence sustainability. We will examine each.

Technology

Until relatively recently, ecosystems have changed gradually over hundreds of years in response to climatic conditions and available resources. Short of massive volcanic eruptions, asteroid impacts, or unusually rapid climate change, fauna and flora have undergone a relatively slow evolutionary process. The transition from an agrarian to industrial society forever changed these dynamics. With the dawn of the Industrial Revolution, humans began depleting resources on a global scale faster than they could be replenished through naturally occurring mechanisms.

Most resources, of course, do not disappear off the planet; they become dispersed or transformed into other forms. Theoretically, with the application of enough technology and energy, it is possible to reconstitute, grow, or manufacture whatever humankind needs. On a practical level, however, nonrenewable resources are finite and limited by the available extractive and recycle technologies.

Many believe that advances in technology will more than offset resource depletion through the invention of substitutes, discovery of new deposits, and/or improved efficiencies in reuse and recycling. Indeed, price—the ultimate measure of supply and demand—has generally decreased over the past 150 years while the standard of living has improved. Low costs and improved extractive technologies have, if anything, made recycling and conservation unattractive and have helped accelerate resource depletion.

But while the extractive technologies have helped keep costs low, the number of proven reserves has not always kept pace. This applies not just to nonrenewable resources like rich ore deposits, but also to renewable resources like topsoil, freshwater, fish populations, tropical rain forests, and so on. Does it matter? We can fertilize croplands, desalinate oceans, farm fish, grow commercial forests, and so on. Will advances in technology assure sustainability? Many think so.

Unfortunately, technology cuts both ways. PCBs, asbestos, and chlorofluorohydrocarbons (CFCs) were intended to replace far more dangerous materials. PFOA and phthalates were used to manufacture improved products like Teflon and flexible plastics, respectively. Typically, their risks only became apparent later. If a scientist from my grandfather's day tried to claim that relatively small amounts of manmade chemicals could alter the earth's environment, he would have been summarily dismissed as delusionary.

Technology also directly impacts both the *affluence* and the *population* components in the IPAT equation. For example, researchers Michael and Joyce Huesemann, in their analysis of the question "Will progress in science and technology avert or accelerate global collapse?" come to the conclusion that technology alone is not sufficient to bring about sustainability. Yes, tremendous progress in technology has improved efficiencies, but it has at the same time increased both the number of consumers (P) and their per capita affluence (A). Short of significant policy changes and major shifts in society's values and goals, they conclude that progress in technology will only hasten collapse.

However, in balancing the positives and negatives, most would argue that technology has been a central contributor to sustainability, at least historically. Looking toward the future, biotechnology and nanotechnology hold all sorts of potential benefits—a tectonic shift similar to the invention of the transistor. Will the mix of the hundreds of new compounds introduced commercially each year have subtle, long-term, unintended consequences that might overshadow their positive benefits? Most, and especially those who have a financial stake in their introduction, exclaim, "Of course not!"

Population

If everyone were to use resources at some fixed rate, consumption would increase or decrease in direct proportion to the total population. The United Nations estimates that the earth's population will stabilize at approximately 9 billion within 50 years from the 6.76 billion today. A more troubling concern than this potential 33% increase is that individual consumption levels are likely to grow disproportionately larger.

Just how many people can coexist and under what standard of living? It is an age-old question, or, more specifically, since Thomas Malthus wrote *An Essay on the Principle of Population* in 1798. More recently, this "carrying capacity" problem has been evaluated by computer simulations of population growth, food production, industrial production, pollution, and so on. The *World3* model developed at MIT is one such model, and the results have been described in a series of three books beginning with *Limits to Growth* (1972).

The most recent book (*The Thirty-Year Update*, 2004) predicts that extremely serious ecological problems will occur around 2030. These books have been widely dismissed because the first was off in estimating both the specific impacts of future technologies and the discoveries of new resources. In addition, many believed that the original model predicted world collapse by the end of the twentieth century, which obviously did not happen. But this skepticism is beginning to fade.

For example, recent analysis of 30 years of historical data by Graham Turner of CSIRO, Australia's national science agency, reveals that the business-as-usual scenario in the second edition to *Limits to Growth* appears to be tracking in accordance with actual data. Called the "standard run" in the *World3* model, this scenario predicted the collapse of global ecosystems by mid-twenty-first century. Scenarios are not meant to be forecasts; they only offer a vision of possible futures, and this bleak future may be emerging just as envisioned more than 30 years ago.

Societal Factors

Predicting resource and technology impacts may be challenging, but evaluating societal factors such as affluence is truly daunting. Cultural attitudes toward the environment, nature, consumerism, technology, corruption, and population control can vary significantly, as well as the role of religion and government in shaping or regulating each.

The population in some regions is decreasing (e.g., central and eastern Europe) while increasing in others (e.g., Middle East, Latin America, and sub-Saharan Africa) that historically have had a relatively low standard of living. Even if the total population were to remain stable within the United States and western Europe, their internal demographics will shift dramatically: Minorities are projected to become majorities. How might these changes affect the broad range of societal factors that impact sustainability?

For instance, while there are obvious environmental benefits to fewer humans, a declining population is viewed negatively in some societies as a prologue to economic stagnation. Countries with aging populations, such as Russia, have offered financial incentives and subsidies to encourage women to have children. Conversely, exerting pressure by one group over another to reduce population growth is labeled as racism, religious intolerance, or even ethnic cleansing. Who decides which cultures grow or shrink?

The locations of natural resources are essentially fixed, yet consumption across the globe varies dramatically. The wheat fields of the

Great Plains are of dubious value to people starving in some far-off country if transportation costs escalate beyond the ability to afford them. And how do resource-poor areas compete globally for essential resources that they do not have? Tourism and technology development are obvious possibilities.

Indeed, the carrying capacity of the earth can be quite large, if only there were some mechanism to fairly distribute and protect this human and natural resource capital. The issue—growing populations wanting what they perceive to be their fair share of the earth's resources—was described in Garrett Hardin's influential article, "The Tragedy of the Commons." Will the forces of selfishness and greed win out over regulations, privatization, or some other allocation technique? Not necessarily.

The book *Protecting the Commons* describes the fundamentals of preserving the commons and provides examples of successes, including protection of the ozone layer (atmospheric commons) and fisheries (coastal commons). A key element is that the cost of "externalities" like pollution must be accounted for and shared. While there is hope, and successful case studies exist, unfortunately the most enduring method used to settle major resource disputes has been regional or global warfare.

No wonder. There are incredibly powerful human dynamics in play. Just as there are the steadfast, unshakable laws of thermodynamics, there are ingrained human traits that always take primacy over nature and the environment. At their most basic levels (i.e., Maslow's hierarchy of needs), there are *physiological needs* such as food and water as well as *safety needs* such as protection of body and property.

If there are major concerns about national security or the maintenance of a standard of living, the commons (i.e., environment) becomes a secondary consideration within democracies. Witness the rapid change in public opinion within the United States for offshore drilling as gasoline prices peaked in 2008. Authoritarian governments have proven even worse when it comes to the environment. Witness the pollution problems in China and the Soviet Union that eventually became very public.

As populations and their standards of living grow, will differences among regions and cultures be settled amicably to protect the commons? Technology will have a major impact through instant, low-cost global communications and improvements in agriculture and resource extraction. But again, technology cuts both ways. Just as the technologies to feed humanity have improved, so too have the weapons for destruction become cheaper and more potent.

The Pentagon already has developed scenarios regarding the impact of changing weather patterns on food production, starvation, and regional conflict. How will impoverished nations or individuals with strong religious convictions respond to images of "conspicuous consumption" or "decadent lifestyles," respectively? Again, when these bedrock forces are in play, nature and the environment receive secondary consideration at best.

FEEDBACK AND CONTROL

Clearly, with all these positive and negative forces under way, it is essential that mechanisms exist to identify incipient issues and stabilize vital resources and ecosystems. Some argue that, if we are not vigilant in this regard, humans will overshoot ecological limits, and if that point is reached, restabilization will eventually occur through the collapse of human populations from starvation, disease, and warfare. Others believe that this doomsday scenario is preposterous. A bumpy ride might be possible, but certainly no crash landing.

The best-selling book *Collapse: How Societies Choose to Fail or Succeed* describes ancient societies such as Easter Island, Anasazi, and Maya that collapsed due in large part to their failure to develop the requisite detection and control mechanisms for their environment. Yes, collapse has happened in the past, but these societies were isolated, with primitive knowledge and little ability to seek distant resources. Humans now have the knowledge base to remain sustainable even though the earth itself is an isolated point in space.

Maybe so, but again, the time frame is a critical factor in determining the ultimate outcome. Ecosystems do not always slowly progress in a linear, predictable direction. Just as in chemical reactions, nothing much may be apparent until a certain activation energy or critical mass is reached. At that tipping point, all sorts of things happen fast. Going back to an earlier state can be difficult; as ecologists say, "Nature has no reset button."

Even today, ecological surprises can materialize. For example, discontinuities have occurred in fish and bee populations that suddenly crashed instead of gradually declining. One of the possible "switch versus dial" outcomes of global warming is that the Gulf Stream may shut down or reroute due to ice melting in the Arctic Circle.

There are other surprise mechanisms that can raise havoc with feedback and control mechanisms. Several issues viewed separately as insignificant may have a synergistic effect that is devastating. The 1998 flood of China's Yangtze River killed nearly 4,000 people because of the combination of heavy rainfall, deforestation, and dense population in the floodplain. Some trends go unnoticed until they become damaging on a massive scale. Invasive species like kudzu, zebra mussel, and crown-of-thorns starfish are a few examples.

But probably the most alarming to environmentalists is the introduction of processes and new substances that have unintended consequences. A recent case in point is the initial enthusiastic promotion of ethanol fuels and the subsequent rise in world grain prices. Particularly concerning are persistent organic pollutants and biologically active or cumulative compounds (e.g., antibiotics, brominated flame retardants, perchlorates, phthalates) since they last in nature and may possibly have a long-term, subtle influence on human or animal physiology.

As Irving Selikoff, the foremost authority on asbestos, stated, the "hidden blessing" of thalidomide is that it produced obvious birth defects and its use could be quickly terminated. In contrast, the concern today is that the ever-growing mix of new synthetic substances may have no immediate, obvious impact. Will parents discover why their teenager suffers from attention deficit disorder and must be placed in a special-needs class at school? Will scientists discover why a specific species of plant is becoming extinct?

In the case of thalidomide, the issue was not discovered before its introduction in Europe because it was tested only in rats and not rabbits. Why were the implications regarding ethanol fuels not thoroughly evaluated prior to introduction? The methods to evaluate these drugs and products existed at the time. What about the dangers of leaded gasoline and a host of other substances where the warning signs flashed for decades? How could these breakdowns in feedback and control exist?

POSITIVE SELLS

Humans are optimistic by their very nature. Indeed, having a positive attitude is viewed as a desirable characteristic, especially in business. Doomsayers and gloomy people are not fun to be around. While stories of carnage and murder get compressed into sound bites that lead at the top of the news hour, complex stories of long-term environmental degradation just do not command attention. They are not entertaining; they're depressing. Today's 24/7 news cycle is as much about entertainment as it is information.

One only needs to look at the 2005 United Nations' *Millennium Ecosystem Assessment Synthesis Report,* which claimed that 15 of 24 ecosystems are being degraded or used unsustainably. It is only natural to assume that this major finding by a prestigious body of scientists would be well known, especially among environmental professionals. Not so. Based on the responses I have gotten from conference attendees, only a small percentage of environmental professionals have ever heard of this report.

Unless a story is interesting or directly impacting our lives in real time, typically we do not tune in and/or act on the information.

In authoritarian governments, information on environmental degradation is often censored; that is, until riots erupt, or as in the recent case in China, industry and traffic are restricted to provide relief for the 2008 Summer Olympics. Clearly, dramatic action can happen when world attention is focused. Public outrage set off the environmental movement of the 1960s because the pollution was obvious, immediate, and threatening. The feedback and control mechanisms worked well.

In developed countries, the nature of environmental concerns has now changed. Lifestyle issues such as consumptive patterns are a driving factor (the A in the IPAT equation), and the consumptive behaviors of voters are much harder to address politically than regulating misbehaving manufacturing facilities. Indeed, even the environment-friendly Obama administration is pressing for massive spending to jump-start an economy in "crisis" and stimulate consumer confidence and spending.

Gus Speth, dean of the Yale School of Forestry and Environmental Studies, in his latest book, *The Bridge at the Edge of the World*, argues that economic growth—the kind that the stimulus is hoping to reinvigorate—is the curse, not the cure of environmental woes. "We are substituting economic growth and more consumption for dealing with the real issues—for doing things that would truly make us better off."

At least in the short term, societies with the most resources to address global environmental degradation are less impacted. Confidence about technology has given rise to the cultural myth that humans are in control of the environment, not the other way around. The issues appear more distant, abstract, and seemingly less urgent than current economic concerns. Indeed they are. Acute, observable forms of environmental pollution have been "outsourced" to developing countries that accepted the polluting industries in order to boost their economies beyond the subsistence level.

Why should people sacrifice their current living standard or deeply held cultural or religious beliefs for some vague future threat, especially when even the scientists cannot agree that there is a problem? The media is filled with sustainability success stories where technology and regulations have succeeded in the past whenever there were issues. Doomsday predictions like "global cooling" during the 1970s are used as ammunition for those who wish to disparage the scientists who calculate dire consequences from today's consumptive practices.

GETTING ACCURATE AND TIMELY FACTS

Feedback and control mechanisms only work if people are paying attention and there is open, transparent information flow. With respect to the latter, the media and educational institutions can be influenced by their owners, the government, advertisers, sponsors, or contributors. Even Internet bloggers are not immune from the influences of political agendas and ideologies that may or may not be in keeping with the facts.

In some countries, the government is the absolute gatekeeper of the distribution of information. As already mentioned, governments, not just corporations, can have economic goals at complete odds with sustainability. At the extreme, environmental regulations may be ignored if politicians and regulatory agency staffers are bribed. When corruption is widespread, the environment inevitably suffers. Although corruption may not be a significant consideration in countries governed by the rule of law, advertising, public relations, and lobbying can have a profound influence over information dissemination and its use in creating new regulations.

For example, in the United States the environmental movement was initially driven by public anger and supportive media coverage. Industry was relatively unsophisticated in responding to and delivering its message. Politicians passed laws that were not based on cost considerations but were more about doing whatever was necessary to solve the issues.

Over the past 20 years, lobbying and intense media campaigns over "junk science" have brought about a shift in how regulations are implemented and new laws are created. Today, Americans might point to the Bush administration's lack of leadership on the environment, but the failure-to-act issue is far more systemic and complex. Little-known court cases such as *Daubert v. Merrell Dow Pharmaceuticals* and innocuous sounding laws such as the Data Quality Act have significantly affected the time needed to respond to environmental and health concerns.

Environmentalists claim that the threshold for proving substances harmful is so high now that the systems to protect the public and the environment have been rendered ineffective. Others believe that "sound science" ensures that useful products and processes are not needlessly dropped from the marketplace. No wonder controversy has surrounded global warming for so many years.

The key issue in all these debates is that the time factor for feedback and control has been altered significantly. For example, the U.S. Environmental Protection Agency began its initial risk assessment on dioxin in the 1970s. In 2008, EPA responded to my status request by stating, "In the near future there will be a federal register notice related to the dioxin reassessment being published." As of this writing, no final assessment has been issued.

Is this time frame adequate? In some instances, far shorter periods are clearly not adequate. It took six years before mandatory warnings about Reye's syndrome were finally placed on aspirin bottles, largely because of the doubts raised by industry. In those intervening six years, possibly thousands of children were disabled or died as a result.

European Union regulations have made a shift to the "precautionary principle," where greater testing will be required on existing and new substances. Will their new REACH laws settle the question on what constitutes adequate testing? Or has international debate over the policy and science of sustainable development reached a level of complexity and conflict to the point where action is impossible? David Brooks of *The New York Times* believes that so many groups have effective veto power over collective action that a "globosclerosis" is derailing the greater good of the planet.

SHAPING PUBLIC OPINION

As stated previously, during the early days of the environmental movement, industry was on the losing end of the public debate over pollution and toxins. Environmental activist organizations like Greenpeace claim that industry has used its power and influence to shift the debate to the vaguer, longer-term concepts of sustainable development. Similarly, discussions about regulations have shifted to self-regulation, voluntary initiatives, and partnerships with communities and NGOs. Industry, they claim, has skillfully repositioned itself to be viewed as "friends of the environment and leaders in the struggle to eradicate poverty."

These claims and counterclaims about the environment continue to dominate the information flow to the public. In an attempt to be fair (and mindful that controversy sells), the media airs both sides of a position, no matter how dubious. There may be a thousand scientists saying "problem" and only one saying "no issue," but as the public hears it, it's a toss-up.

Indeed, advertising and lobbying have proven enormously successful for companies. The cost is cheap relative to adding onerous environmental controls. Green marketing has a double benefit: image building while simultaneously selling products.

For example, Wal-Mart is arguably the ultimate example of a company associated with unsustainability: mass consumerism of inexpensive goods made in developing countries with weak environmental controls. Yet, Wal-Mart receives high praise for its green efforts. For example, it was ranked fourth in a July 2008 consumer survey by Lippincott of the top five U.S. brands "taking a leading role in tackling climate change," and in February 2009 it was featured on

KNWA-TV's *Sustainability Spotlight.*

There can be a cognitive dissonance about sustainability. For example, in *Perverse Subsidies,* authors Myers and Kent describe how governments claiming to support sustainability subsidize industries with the opposite effect. *Time* reports that a $500 motion-powered watch and a $2,695 bamboo mountain bike frame are "green to the extreme." Sir Richard Branson is reported as a sustainability hero for his "Virgin Earth Challenge" reward and a visionary for his space tourism business, Virgin Galactic. Sustainability is good, but conspicuous consumption is portrayed as even better.

THE FUTURE

Will sustainable development succeed? Will future generations have their needs met? Will all the positive developments overshadow the negative, and will feedback and control mechanisms work? For my generation and the next, absolutely! Beyond this time frame, I have serious doubts.

There are too many negative forces under way, and the feedback and control mechanism are too far corrupted. A point of comparison: Ecosystems are orders of magnitude more complex than economic systems. In retrospect, the current global economic crisis was absolutely predictable (many accurately did predict it), but little appeared in the media until well after the bubble burst. The collapse of Social Security and other entitlement programs has been calculated with precision, but yet the public remains disengaged. And we expect a better outcome for the environment?

What will happen within the 150-year time frame proposed for this essay?

Humans will experience an ever-increasing number of ecological, resource, and business collapses, leading to societal instabilities. The boom-to-bust cycles will be similar to the tech bubble of the late 1990s and the ongoing "economic crisis." Early warning signs will be similarly ignored as governments, industries, or individuals exploit the opportunities of the moment. For example, even though the days of cheap oil were clearly numbered, GM and Ford executives continued to bet shareholder money and employee security on product lines that were profitable but not sustainable.

Economic cycles can be incredibly fast and furious—measured in less than a decade. The buffering capacity of the earth is enormous, so ecological cycles tend to be much more gradual—once measured in millennia, now in decades. The magnitude of the dangers will become crystal clear, however, within a few generations. Global warming will be just one aspect, and possibly not even the most significant dimension in terms of loss of human life. Chaos and warfare over resources may trump that.

Mankind will continue to fight the environmental battles du jour, often successfully, but will gradually lose the war. Flora and fauna, with no powerful constituencies to protect them, will be at the greatest disadvantage. Polar bears and pandas will always be around, if only in zoos. But the ugly bug or plant that may hold the secret to the cure for some disease may become extinct long before its powers are revealed.

International luminaries will continue to promote their cause célèbre, and many companies will engage in and advertise their sustainable practices and products. People will use unbleached cloth grocery sacks, recycle bottles, and buy fuel-efficient cars. Will this be enough? Not even remotely close.

While these positive actions will help slow down the pace of unsustainability, they mask the gravity of the situation faced by generations 150 years hence. Gore's not-too-subtle message about global warming is that action on this issue is what will save the planet. In fact, global warming is just one facet of a much bigger problem facing humankind. Bjorn Lomborg, author of the *Skeptical Environmentalist*, acknowledges that "there is unequivocal evidence" of global warming but thinks the debate should shift to how to best spend limited financial resources for the betterment of health and the environment.

Short-term profits or efforts to expand a country's standard of living (or dictator's power) will continue to determine how resources are used. For example, McDaniel and Gowdy describe in *Paradise for Sale* how rich phosphate deposits were stripped in less than one generation from Nauru, an island described in 1976 as one of the richest in the world. Continuously inhabited for 100 generations and in harmony with the surrounding ecosystem, the current inhabitants are reduced to poverty in a barren landscape. This true story serves as a parable for the human race.

THE UPBEAT ENDING

"Environmaniacs," as *The Wall Street Journal* calls them, have been making similar dour, long-term predictions as contained in this essay. What other authors typically do, however, is provide upbeat summary actions necessary for a sustainable future. All of this information is readily available, and I will not even attempt to summarize it here.

I will end this essay, instead, reflecting on the Chinese characters for "crisis" composed of elements that signify "danger" and "opportunity." First, because it was used on the cover of the 2004 seminal environmental essay, *Death of Environmentalism*, which sparked a debate that continues today, centered on the adequacy of the environmental movement to address global problems. And second, because like seemingly everything else having to do with the environment, the interpretation of the characters is now ridiculed as being wrong by specialists in Chinese literature and language.

Much of this essay has been devoted to the positive *(opportunity)* and negative *(danger)* forces that are in play today. I believe that we have reached a tipping point and are overshooting the carrying capacity of the earth *(crisis)*. The difference in our environment between now and 150 years hence will rival the change that has transpired between my grandfather's generation and generations today.

Therein lies the perverse upbeat ending. For governments, companies, NGOs, and individuals who thoroughly research and comprehend these developments, there will be enormous opportunities. Yes, there will be opportunities to make a quick buck—there always are in any disaster for those who can anticipate and plan. But the benefits extend far beyond the "green products" being marketed today. There will be opportunities to initiate actions that will have truly substantive, positive impacts on a scale never before dreamed of, because the crisis will be that challenging. In the past, the motto was "Save the Whales"; in the future it will be about saving entire ecosystems.

Mankind has always risen to the challenge and has the capability to do so in the future. We have the power to divert humankind from collapse, but we have already reached a point where there will be a very painful sacrifice and restabilization of our ecosystems within a few generations. Our government leaders today would have us believe that, if sacrifices are needed, they will be akin to a shift from a big SUV to a compact hybrid with properly inflated tires. This is utter nonsense.

We have the opportunity to seek out leadership that speaks the truth about these complexities—leaders who are not the center of controversy and enriching themselves and their egos. We have the opportunity to take action to do much more than choose between paper and plastic, but to decide where to live, how to build, what we do for work and recreation, and above all, what we teach our children and their children. It is these generations who will know with absolute certainty if sustainable development was salvation or hype.

Sailing and Surfing Through Complexity

Emerging Contexts of Energy, Environmental, and Society Transitions[1]

David J. LePoire

Forecasts of the near future vary widely in scope and outlook. Predictions include the possibility of surpassing human intelligence; catastrophic global warming; solving the world's major problems involving energy, food, and resource needs; environmental catastrophes; greatly extended human life; a slowing of the rate of progress; and continuation of the status quo. Common to these predictions is the possibility of rapid transitions, suggesting that, if we are to have control over their direction, we should seek to anticipate the problems, scenarios, and our options. Multiple generations of technologies are typically involved in a vicious cycle—newer technologies are developed to solve problems from older ones, but they also create problems, usually through unforeseen consequences. As Albert Einstein stated, "We can't solve problems by using the same kind of thinking we used when we created them." However, this is a problem if technology continues to develop at an ever-accelerating pace (Glenn

---

David J. LePoire is a scientist who has worked at Argonne National Laboratory as an environmental analyst. E-mail dlepoire@anl.gov.

and Gordon 2004; LePoire 2005).

Issues of current concern include: (1) the energy transition problem of moving from an unsustainable fossil-fuel-based economy to a renewable energy economy; (2) the widespread problems of global warming, global trade, global terrorism, and global knowledge transfer; and (3) the possible opportunities and risks associated with new technologies such as genetics, nanotechnology, and artificially intelligent computers. Each of these involves technological and social issues that require changes, learning, and transitions.

Recently, various interpretations and extrapolations of these trends in technological progress have led to widely differing predictions. Specifically, Ray Kurzweil (2001 and 2005) hypothesized an ever-increasing rate of technological change, based on his analysis of more than a century of progress in computation technologies. Theodore Modis (2002) and others have hypothesized a very different future, one having a decreasing rate of technological change, based on analyses of events from the Big Bang to the present.

Kurzweil investigated the computing and electronics sector by looking at cost per computation to formulate a possible extension of Moore's law. The inclusion of early electronic technologies, such as relays and vacuum tubes, led Kurzweil to propose that the rate of technological change is increasing with time (i.e., that Moore's law of the doubling of electronic device densities every 18 months will be surmounted by new technologies that double in performance in less time). An ever-increasing rate of technological change could soon lead to a "singularity," which in one definition is a "future time when societal, scientific, and economic change is so fast we cannot even imagine what will happen from our present perspective, and when humanity will become posthumanity."

Another model of technology progression and diffusion is based on learning (also known as "S" or logistic) curve analysis, which has long been applied to market adoption and substitution of new products, technologies, and ideas (Marchetti 1980). The field of "Big History" takes a longer view and presents information-processing stages of life, brains, and technology (Carl Sagan 1977; Spier 2004). Modis (2002) expanded this further by suggesting that the history of the universe might be viewed as a logistic development of complexity. He arranged important events in the history of the universe from a variety of sources, assumed that each event was equally important, and then made the assumption that the complexity of an event is its importance divided by the transition time to the next event. The dependence of the cumulative fraction of complexity on milestone number (not the event's time) could be interpreted either as (1) the first half of a logistic curve or (2) a sequence of events that will culminate in a singularity. A logistic development of complexity would mean that the rate of development depends on the product of the cumulative complexity of previous events and the fraction of complexity yet to be discovered. Modis favored the logistic development interpretation.

While the simplest model of complex systems can be driven into chaos, more realistic models with limitations suggest a possible reversal of increasing complexity (Stone 1993). The two scenarios can be related to these different models: Kurzweil's Singularity scenario, with continual increasing exponential progress, might derive from a simple complex model, whereas Modis's long-term logistic growth, with a tipping point determined by limitations in the learning rate and energy extraction rate, might be related to the more complex but realistic model (Modis 2002). If this latter transition is accurate, the rate of technology progress might peak and eventually slow.

In this article, the brewing social and technological transitions involving energy, global environment, and new technologies are investigated. Proposals from the Nobel Prize winner Richard Smalley (2003) and Thomas Friedman (2008) are briefly discussed in this context.

Approaches to Complex Adaptive Systems

Characteristic properties of complex adaptive systems include: (1) a resource that drives the level of complexity, such as energy use (Chaisson 2001 and 2004; Gardner 2003; Tainter 1996); (2) new options at critical stages along development paths; and (3) competition and learning as the options are explored.

Complex adaptive systems displaying a range of common emergent characteristics have been found in a variety of fields, such as biological evolution (Kauffman 1991), ecosystems, and social systems (Perry 1995). There are many studies of wavelike cyclical behavior in sociotechnical processes, from the generational level to technology innovation and deployment, to long-term economic cycles and long-wave behavior of states (Devezas 2003).

The reason why coherent waves exist can be addressed at many levels. A common characteristic of these systems is the exploration of potential social and technological paths. Exploration requires searching among many paths before a feasible coherent path can be identified. These complex systems lead against the flow of entropy, which would lead to decay. A look at simpler systems that are stabilized far from equilibrium offers some insight. Some analogies in physics include the inverted pendulum (and associated magnetic focusing of particle beams) and sailing against the wind.

The natural tendency is for the boat to go with the wind, just as the natural tendency for the inverted pendulum is to fall under the force of gravity. Again, a strategy of oscillation, tacking, is used. In tacking, the boat alternates between traveling at angles to the left and right of the wind direction. The oscillation frequency is chosen based on the difficulty of the transition and the need to stay within certain width of approach.

Emergence of Energy Patterns

Energy use might be connected to a long set of historical tran-

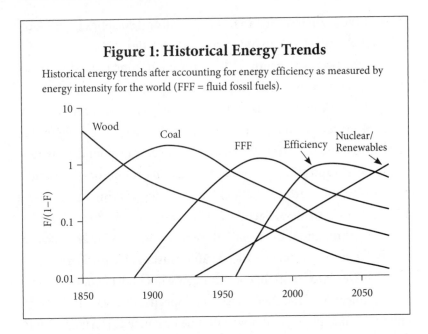

Figure 1: Historical Energy Trends

Historical energy trends after accounting for energy efficiency as measured by energy intensity for the world (FFF = fluid fossil fuels).

sitions. Wavelike patterns in the world's mix of primary energy sources occurred as wood was substituted with coal, oil/natural gas, and energy efficiency, while non-fossil fuels development continued with hydropower and nuclear energy (Marchetti 1977; LePoire 2004). (See Figure 1.) This suggests that current substitution of energy efficiency (or conservation) for energy fuel usage might continue to grow for the next decade (Ayres 1989; Ausubel 2004).

EMERGENCE OF ENVIRONMENTAL PATTERNS

The issues of energy use and environmental sustainability are deeply entwined. Analysis of the collapse of complex agricultural societies identified a major cause to be the marginal return on investment of resources, such as energy, as societies grew larger and more complex (Tainter 1988). Tainter suggested that many agricultural societies collapsed by overextending their reach into nonsustainable systems. The impact of environmental degradation has been an important factor in the development and decline of civilizations (Ponting 1991; Chase-Dunn and Hall 1997; Tainter 1996; Diamond 2005).

Most of these analyses focused on agricultural societies because of their simplicity relative to industrialized societies.

In the twentieth century, three key environmental issues arose at different times and different political scopes: (1) the sanitary phase of rapidly growing urban centers in the early twentieth century; (2) national concern with clean air and water with action peaking in the early 1970s; and (3) international concern over transboundary issues (e.g., wildlife) and atmospheric release (e.g., chlorofluorocarbons, sulfur dioxide, and carbon dioxide) with treaties peaking in the mid-1990s. (Marchetti 1986; Paehlke 2003; LePoire 2006). (See Figure 2.) However, throughout the twentieth century these issues arose faster but took longer to resolve, which is an unsustainable pattern.

This leads to questions concerning ways of understanding waves, their connections, and their directions. Specifically, what is the next environmental phase, and how will it be organized (Hartzog 2004)? A prediction based on the trends is that new issues, such as global climate change, trade, and inequality, need to be addressed at a quicker pace even as the world population and energy demand increases. If

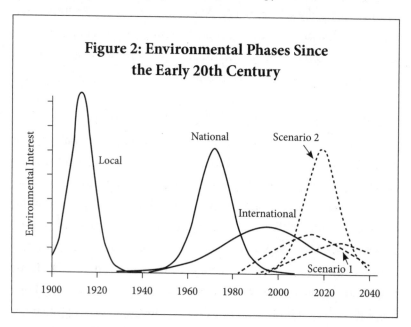

Figure 2: Environmental Phases Since the Early 20th Century

the interval between the last two phases, in 1970 and 1996, is repeated, then the next environmental phase would peak in just over another decade.

EMERGENCE OF TECHNOLOGICAL AND LEADERSHIP PATTERNS

Leadership transitions that address energy and environmental issues may be indications of a complex learning system. If this is the case, it may be possible to identify a few of the emergent behaviors of complex adaptive systems, such as energy use as a driving factor. When energy use reaches certain levels, the system bifurcates—that is, it transitions from one stable form into one of two possible different forms.

Besides these transitions in energy fuel source, a second important factor is the intensity of energy use per person. Since humans' hunting-gathering stage, societies have undergone transitions toward more-complex forms (e.g., agricultural villages, civilizations, industrialization). Humans have used various sources to derive energy to support various levels of societies. A human's intake of 2,500 calories per day corresponds or averages to about 100 watts (i.e., about as much energy as a large incandescent light bulb uses). In the late Middle Ages, the combination of wood, peat, wind, and water resources might have supplied about 500 watts in the European Low Countries. However, after industrialization, there was a major increase in the average current per capita rate of energy use in the United States: 15 kilowatts of energy (including commercial, industrial, and residential use), or about 150 times a person's food energy intake/use per day.

Throughout the twentieth century, tradeoffs were made between economic development and environmental concerns. Although technological and economic waves have been widely discussed, a more visible set of oscillations occurred in the U.S. political leadership throughout the Cold War, in which technological leadership in military, space, and information systems became imperative. From 1945 to the present, the U.S. presidency has oscillated for four complete cycles between the two major political parties (Democratic to Republican) every eight years, with one exception (1980–1984). While there are many issues in presidential politics, technology is associated with economic growth, defense, health, and energy. The two parties have traditionally disagreed on the relative priority of public versus private investment, energy conservation versus energy extraction, and development versus environment. Hints of longer-term oscillations in U.S. politics are suggested by considering that the durations between the inaugurations of the top three ranked presidents (Washington, Lincoln, and FDR) is both 72 years as they dealt with the crises of the Constitution, the Civil War, and the Great Depression. The next year in this sequence is 2005.

CURRENT CONTEXT: GLOBAL TRANSITION

Multiple transitions in energy, environment, and technological leadership have occurred over long periods of time. However, in a broader context, transitions are currently occurring in global development, population demographics, and the acceptance of democracy.

Currently discussed potential global issues include global warming, trade, biodiversity, terrorism, and knowledge transfer. Some of these problems, such as global warming, arise from the nonlocal consequences of actions such as releases of carbon dioxide at many locations. Other issues are global because ideas, people, and objects can be transported relatively quickly and inexpensively. For example, the Internet has enabled ideas, plans, copyrighted material, and computer viruses to be quickly distributed throughout the world. Problems might be exacerbated by inequalities in the distribution of wealth and resources—developed countries might not be able to sustain their current material wealth, and developing countries might want to expand their growth, with the subsequent demand for similar consumption. Analysis of a series of technology transitions found that the early adopters, such as the developed countries, tend to overcommit, while later adopters can learn to use the technologies more efficiently (Ausubel 1989 and 2004).

What about the success of the spread of democratic ideals? While many democratic nations have disputed the best way to implement governments, armed conflict between democratic nations is rare. The world's nations seem to be undergoing a transition to more democratic forms, as measured by the fraction of population under democratic governments, which shows a logistic trend that started in the mid-1700s (Modelski and Perry 2002). The transition seems to be about halfway complete.

CONCLUSION: UNIQUE OPPORTUNITY OR RISK?

Many integrated technological and social approaches have been proposed earlier this decade. For example, Richard Smalley, the 1996 Nobel Prize winner in chemistry, offered a possible way to tie these transitions together with the hope of taking advantage of their benefits while managing, or at least reducing, the possible risks. He suggested that the United States lead an international effort to explore the possibilities of using nanotechnology in the energy sector. He argued that energy is the key to many international problems, such as water, food, environment, poverty, terrorism and war, disease, education, democracy, and population (Smalley 2003). He pointed out that a concerted effort toward developing a solution to the energy problem would be a response to September 11, 2001, events analogous to the U.S. response to the Soviets' Sputnik.

The events of September 11 also motivated several others to suggest large plans to deal with worldwide energy and environmental problems (Brown 2003; Friedman 2008). Friedman also explored the military's perception of the connections between energy and national security: "Green Hawks," accounting for the full cost of gasoline, and the potential to "outgreen" al-Qaeda and China. Both technological and organizational innovations are encouraged to decentralize energy investments. The ability to respond to the energy and environmental challenges is a criterion for the next phase of leadership.

Science and technology are used to pursue solutions to these problems, but they alone are not enough to solve them. Social responses, which are typically slower in development, are required (Linstone 2007). For example, science and technology have improved many aspects of our lives over the past two centuries: In health, they have enhanced surgery, medicine, and diagnoses; in energy, they have yielded improvements in transportation, entertainment, and labor-saving devices; and in security, they have allowed the defense community to deliver a series of weapons and defense systems to maintain relative peace in the developed world. However, it might seem that progress derived from science and technology has slowed and perhaps exacerbated some problems. In health care, the problems of cancer and old age are unresolved, as the relative costs of medical care skyrocket due in part to the opportunities delivered by science. The ability to sustainably deliver energy is unresolved even as technology allows devices to further increase demands for energy. Technology has allowed us to communicate and travel at unprecedented rates, but associated security issues arise as threatening smaller groups and individuals also have access to these technologies. Many of the potential solutions to these difficult problems involve social options that make us question the ethical basis for them: in health care, the way costs of new medicines and treatments for a longer-living community are funded; in energy, the responsibilities of our energy use to future generations and developing countries; and in security, the need to establish organizations for peaceful environments while minimizing the potential hazards of unintended consequences.

The future is fraught with the uncertainties of many transitions. The large stakes concerned are highlighted in the book *Our Final Hour* by Martin Rees (2003), in which the author estimates that the human race has a 50-50 probability of surviving through the century during the deployment of new (e.g., nano-, bio-, and information) technologies. The hope is that there will be enough preparation and discussion so that surprises are more positive than negative through these transitions. The consideration of a large integrated mission, as suggested by Smalley, with international cooperation seems to be a good start.

NOTE

1. The submitted manuscript has been created by University of Chicago Argonne, LLC, Operator of Argonne National Laboratory ("Argonne"). Argonne, a U.S. Department of Energy Office of Science laboratory, is operated under Contract No. DE-AC02-06CH11357. The U.S. government retains for itself, and others acting on its behalf, a paid-up nonexclusive, irrevocable worldwide license in said article to reproduce, prepare derivative works, distribute copies to the public, and perform publicly and display publicly, by or on behalf of the government.

REFERENCES

Ausubel, J. H. 1996. "Can Technology Spare the Earth?" In *American Scientist* 84(2):166–178.

Ausubel, J. H. 2004. "Will the Rest of the World Live Like America?" In *Technology in Society* 26:343–360.

Ayres, R. U. 1989. *Energy Inefficiency in the US Economy: A New Case for Conservatism*, RR-89-12. Laxenburg, Austria: International Institute for Applied Systems Analysis.

Brown, L. 2003. *Plan B: Rescuing a Planet Under Stress and a Civilization in Trouble*. New York: W. W. Norton & Company.

Chaisson, E. J. 2001. *Cosmic Evolution: The Rise of Complexity in Nature*. Cambridge, MA: Harvard Press.

Chaisson, E. J. 2004. "Complexity: An Energetics Agenda; Energy as the Motor of Evolution." In *Complexity*, 9(3):14–21.

Chase-Dunn, C. K., and T. D. Hall. 1997. "Ecological Degradation and the Evolution of World-Systems." In *Journal of World-Systems Research* 3(3):403–431.

Devezas, T. 2003. "Power Law Behavior and World System Evolution: A Millennial Learning Process." In *Technological Forecasting and Social Change* 70:819–859.

Diamond, J. 2005. *Collapse.* New York: Penguin Books.

Friedman, T. L. 2008. *Hot, Flat, and Crowded.* New York: Farrar, Straus and Giroux.

Gardner, J. 2003. *Biocosm: The New Scientific Theory of Evolution: Intelligent Life Is the Architect of the Universe.* Makawao, HI: Inner Ocean Publishing (August).

Glenn, J., and T. J. Gordon. 2004. "Future Science and Technology Management Policy Issues—2025 Global Scenarios." In *Technological Forecasting and Social Change* 71:913–940.

Hartzog, P. B., 2004, "21st Century Governance as a Complex Adaptive System." In Proceeding Pista 2004, Jose V. Carrasquero et al. (eds), *Information and Society.* Orlando: International Institute of Informatics and Systemics.

Kauffman, S. A. 1991. "Antichaos and Adaptation." In *Scientific American* 265(2):78–84.

Kurzweil, R. 2001. "The Law of Accelerating Returns." March. Available at http://www.kurzweilai.net/articles/art0134.html (accessed January 2004).

Kurzweil, R. 2005. *The Singularity Is Near.* New York: Viking.

LePoire, D. J. 2004. "A 'Perfect Storm' of Social and Technological Transitions." In *Futures Research Quarterly,* Fall.

LePoire, D. J. 2005. "Exploring Ethical Approaches to Evaluate Future Technology Scenarios." In *The Journal of Information, Communications and Ethics in Society* 3(3):143–150.

LePoire, D. J. 2006. "Logistic Analysis of Recent Environmental Interest." In *Technological Forecasting and Social Change* 73(2):153–167.

Linstone, H. A. 2007. "Science and Technology: Questions of Control." In *Technological Forecasting and Social Change* 74(2):230–237.

Marchetti, C. 1980. "Society as a Learning System: Discovery, Invention, and Innovation Cycles Revisited." In *Technological Forecasting and Social Change* 18. Available at http://www.cesaremarchetti.org/archive/scan/MARCHETTI-030.pdf.

Marchetti, C. 1986. "Fifty-Year Pulsation in Human Affairs: Analysis of Some Physical Indicators." In *Futures* 18(3): 376–388.

Marchetti, C. 1977. "Primary Energy Substitution Models: On the Interaction Between Energy and Society." In *Technological Forecasting and Social Change* 10:345–356.

Modelski, G., and G. Perry III. 2002. "Democratization in Long Perspective Revisited." In *Technological Forecasting and Social Change*, 69:359–376.

Modis, T. 2002. "Forecasting the Growth of Complexity and Change." In *Technological Forecasting and Social Change* 69:377–404.

Paehlke, R. C. 2003. *Democracy's Dilemma: Environment, Social Equity, and the Global Economy*. Cambridge, MA: MIT Press.

Perry, D. A. 1995. "Self-Organizing Systems Across Scales." In *TREE* 10(6), June.

Ponting, C. 1991. *A Green History of the World*. New York: Penguin Books.

Rees, M. 2003. *Our Final Hour*. New York: Basic Books.

Rhodes, R. 2002. "Energy Transitions: A History Lesson." In *Center for Energy Research Newsletter* 2(2), June.

Sagan, C. 1977. "The Dragons of Eden," 1st ed. New York: Random House.

Smalley, R. 2003. "Our Energy Challenge." Energy & Nanotechnology Conference, Rice University, Houston, TX, May 3. Available at http://smalley .rice.edu/emplibrary/Rice%20EnergyNanotech%20May%203%202003.pdf.

Spier, F. 2004. "How Big History Works: Energy Flows and the Rise and Demise of Complexity." Self-Organization and Big History Symposium, September. Belgorad, Russia.

Stone, L. 1993. "Period-Doubling Reversals and Chaos in Simple Ecological Models." In *Nature* 365:617–620.

Tainter, J. A. 1988. *The Collapse of Complex Societies*. Cambridge, UK: Cambridge University Press.

Tainter, J. A. 1996. "Complexity, Problem Solving, and Sustainable Societies." In *Getting Down to Earth*, R. Constanza (ed.). Washington, DC: Island Press.

The Future of Nuclear Energy

Vladimir Knapp and Gioietta Kuo

About two years ago, eminent climatologists such as Sir David King and Dr. James Hansen were unified in their opinion that the world could eventually see an atmospheric CO_2 concentration of 450 ppm (parts per million). It was then at 385 ppm. According to them, there was no time to lose, and the world's governments must adopt a radically different energy policy to eradicate fossil-fuel use. If we continued business as usual over the next 10 years, then the planet would reach a point of no return.

Since then, there has been no drastic reduction in world CO_2 emissions, and atmospheric CO_2 concentration has increased by 2 ppm per year. In the meantime, more and more signs of global warming, such as the sharp rise in Arctic temperatures and Greenland melting ice caps, together with an improved study of the earth's climate history, have the climatologists alarmed. Led by Hansen and some Yale climatologists,[1] they maintain the optimum ppm for CO_2 level should be 350.

Though we are very much aware that the situation regarding global warming is dire and that fossil fuel is the cause, the whole trouble with our society's inability to eliminate fossil-fuel use—mainly coal—is that we rely on it for baseload. Power stations produce elec-

Vladimir Knapp is a member of the faculty of Electrical Engineering and Computing, Croatian Nuclear Society, in Zagreb, Croatia. E-mail vladimir .knapp@fer.hr.

Gioietta Kuo is a senior fellow at the American Center for International Policy Studies. E-mail kuopet@comcast.net.

tricity 24 hours a day, and national grids distribute it to users. The share of coal-generated electricity worldwide is 41%.

Therefore, it is natural to seek alternative fuels, mainly renewables—wind, solar, biofuel, hydro, tidal, etc. These have the advantage that the energy is free and they don't emit CO_2. However, there is a big catch: The wind does not blow and the sun does not shine all the time, so a backup power has to exist 24 hours a day for lulls. Hence, we go back to a baseload, and at present the only two baseloads in operation in the world are those using fossil fuels—coal, gas, and oil—and nuclear reactors. It is lamentable that, when environmentalists describe a future energy scenario, nuclear power is seldom mentioned, although it is the only baseload that does not emit CO_2. In the United States, for example, 20% of power is generated from nuclear power.

What carbon-free technologies do we have at our disposal as baseloads? Apart from nuclear fission, there are nuclear fusion and carbon capture and storage (CCS), but neither is at a deployable stage technologically.

The new approach of the American presidential administration to nuclear disarmament, proliferation safety, the Comprehensive Test Ban Treaty, and fissile materials control—as presented in the April 5, 2009, Prague speech of President Obama, is highly encouraging. It promises that, after many lost years, U.S. politics is starting to lead in the right direction.

POSSIBLE FUTURE ENERGY BASELOADS

1. **Nuclear Fusion.** Nuclear fusion, using deuterium as basic fuel, is theoretically very desirable, as there is no limit on fuel and it does not emit CO_2. However, fusion has been a mirage for many decades. This is because the deuterium plasma cannot be confined by a magnetic field at a high density for a sufficiently long time for enough thermonuclear reactions to take place. The present plan is an international effort to build a large Tokamak, ITER, in France. After the final design stage, a demonstration fusion power station,

DEMO, could be started around 2030. Assuming successful operation of DEMO construction, a significant share of fusion energy could be expected by 2070 or later. This is much too late to help the CO_2 problem.

2. **Carbon Capture and Storage.** CCS (IPCC summary 2007[2]) has been hailed by many environmentalists to justify the use of coal, so-called "clean coal," for electricity generation. However, if one examines the various steps involved in this process, one would see there are gigantic obstacles.

CCS collects the CO_2 escaping from the flues of the fossil-fueled power plants, liquefies it, and feeds it down pipes reaching thousands of feet underground to some suitable geological layer, where the CO_2 would stay put for at least 100 years.

Carbon dioxide has been used for decades to enhance recovery of oil from exhausted oil wells. It was injected underground in quantities on the level of a million tons—small compared with the amount of CO_2 we have in the atmosphere now.

In 2005, the world produced 26.6 gigatons of CO_2. We can convert the weight to the volume of liquid CO_2 at point of liquefaction with density 0.47 gm/mL,[3] so the volume of liquid CO_2 is:

$$56.6 \times 10^9 \ meter^3$$

This is a vast amount equivalent to a volume given by:

3.8 km (2.4 miles) x 3.8 km (2.4 miles) x 3.8 km (2.4 miles)

Now, all this volume of CO_2 has to be liquefied as CO_2 gas escapes from the flue and then transported to the chosen geological layers, down many pipes drilled many thousands of feet underground with bores no larger than 9 inches in diameter. All this has to be done within one year. For comparison, the total amount of crude oil extracted worldwide came to 4 gigatons in 2005,[3] which is only 15% of the volume we proposed to put underground. To capture the projected 57 gigatons in 2050, one would need 32,000 pipes each with annual capacity of 1 to 5 megatons[2]; that is 15 times the world's annual crude-oil extraction.

As the world emissions of CO_2 approach 30 billion metric tons per year, future interest is in safe storage. With annual leakage of 1% from the storage site, after 100 years of accumulation, annual input and leakage would be equal. At present, we do not know whether enough safe sites for the gigantic amounts of CO_2 can be found and what could be the environmental effects associated with these injections.

An economic issue that affects the adaptation of CCS in the marketplace is that, according to the IPCC 2007[2] summary, "a power plant equipped with CCS would need roughly 10%–40% more energy than a plant of equivalent output without CCS." Sequestration uses electricity for separation and high pressure injection of CO_2. Also in the IPCC conclusion: "Most analyses indicate that notwithstanding significant penetration of CCS by 2050, the majority of CCS deployments will occur in the second half of the century."

So far, clean coal has been touted as the solution to CO_2 emissions from coal-powered plants. But it seems that the tide is changing, and many who are advocating clean coal are beginning to realize that the sheer quantity of CO_2 produced annually by the world is just too much to put underground, as well as the fact that the technology is too expensive and not realizable for the whole world to adopt.

The following remark by James Hansen, one of the foremost climatologists and one who is most vociferous and politically active, is interesting because of the vehemence against governments, probably because he has for so long been traveling tirelessly around the world pleading with them without effect. He wrote in *The Observer* (February 15, 2009):

> Coal is not only the largest fossil fuel reservoir of carbon dioxide, it is the dirtiest fuel. Coal is polluting the world's oceans

and streams with mercury, arsenic and other dangerous chemicals. The dirtiest trick that governments play on their citizens is the pretense that they are working on "clean coal" or that they will build power plants that are "capture ready" in case technology is ever developed to capture all pollutants.

The Economist (March 2009) has also come out against clean coal, saying it is technologically too complex and too expensive.

RENEWABLE ENERGY SOURCES

These are mainly wind and solar. We are witnessing rapid development, albeit from the low initial level, of wind and solar energy. The European Community (EC) has a target for the share of renewable energy sources of 20% in total energy consumption by 2020, starting from about 8% in 2007. Wind power in the EC exceeded 60 GW of installed power in 2008 and is expanding rapidly.[4]

Solar-photovoltaic power is as yet in the phase of intense research and development for higher conversion efficiency and lower production costs. Assuming success by 2020, solar energy contribution could become serious by 2030 or later. There are more optimistic long-range visions based on extension of the present technology, photovoltaic conversion in thin films made of cadmium telluride, as by three U.S. solar entrepreneurs,[5] who predict as much as 69% of U.S. electricity needs covered by solar energy by 2050. However, even they see only about 2.5% of their 2050 target installed by 2020, as the time until that year will be needed for increasing conversion efficiency from the present 10% to about 14%, and for reducing installed system cost from the present value of about $4,000/kW to, or below, $1,200/kW. So even in this optimistic vision of solar future there would not be a significant contribution to renewable energy production before 2030.

Compared with the EC,[4] U.S. plans to develop have not been so impressive. According to the Annual Energy Outlook 2006, the share of renewable energy in the U.S. energy system would reach 9% by

2030. The Obama administration indicates greater sensitivity toward environmental problems, and doubling the share of renewable energy is proclaimed as the target. Assuming this becomes a part of U.S. energy strategy, doubling by 2030 to about 18% would be well behind the EC target[5] of a 20% share by 2020. One should hope that new awareness of environmental problems combined with ability and responsibility of the administration will lead to a 20% target for renewable energy for the year 2020. In addition to environmental gains, large-scale construction of wind energy power stations, as already in progress in the EC, would give a welcome boost to U.S. industry.

NUCLEAR FISSION ENERGY

Assuming that planned and desirable development of renewable energy in the EC and the United States reaches 20% in total energy consumption by 2020, what about the remaining 80%? Now, there are some 440 nuclear fission power stations, which produce about 16% of world electricity, or about 6.5% of total energy consumption. Emission of CO_2 is reduced by close to 1 billion tons by their operation. So, it is well justified to ask if nuclear fission energy will be an important future energy source in a carbon-free energy strategy, if only because there is at present no baseload that does not emit CO_2. In the past, however, nuclear fission was met with a variety of responses, with a variety of motives. Some 50 years back it was a status symbol; now we know that it is a demanding technology that can be very successful under appropriate conditions. But what about the future? Can we see the appropriate conditions for fission power expanded so that its contribution in total energy consumption increases from the present 6.5% to 20% or 30%? Only then will nuclear energy give a really significant contribution to the reduction of carbon emissions.

Following this reasoning, we can say that the future of nuclear power depends on satisfactory answers on several questions.

The Economics of Nuclear Power

In the near and intermediate future, a generally accepted concept for radioactive waste disposal is also required. All the issues concerning economics and safety are the focus of present research and development. Safer and more economical reactors are targets of international efforts in Generation IV and INPRO projects, as well as of several national projects. However, even assuming successful technical development of these projects, and there is no reason to doubt it, long-term and large-scale nuclear power use is not yet secured. If nuclear power is to play an essential role in long-term future energy production and in reduction of CO_2 emissions, then several additional questions must be answered, such as electricity costs.

With occasional ups and downs, the costs of oil and gas are steadily rising. Comparative studies of energy sources older than two years are out of date when compared with oil and gas energy. It is of interest to have a look at recent studies of nuclear energy costs at MIT[6] and the University of Chicago,[7] and one that compares nuclear with fossil and alternative energies by the Royal Academy of Engineering.[8] The recent decision by Finland to build another nuclear power station is based on detailed studies showing favorable economics in relation to the alternatives of coal, gas turbine, combined cycle, and peat. The 2005 update by Nuclear Energy Agency and International Energy Agency, "Projected Costs of Generating Electricity,"[9] is an extensive study taking into account country-specific conditions, with cost data provided for more then 130 coal-fired, gas-fired, nuclear, wind power, solar power, and combined heat and power plants. Levelized generating costs for plants operating from the year 2010 were calculated with uniform assumptions for baseload plants (40 years economic lifetime, 85% load factor, and discount rates of 5% and 10%). The study does not include the costs associated with residual emissions, including greenhouse gases. For nuclear plants, the costs of refurbishment and decommissioning are included. At 5% discount rate,

Table 1: Summary of Electricity Cost Ranges in NEA-IEA Study

(Levelized costs in US$/MWh for plants starting in 2010)

Plant type	Discount rate 5%	Discount rate 10%	Remark
Coal fired	25-50	35-60	No external cost included
Gas fired	37-60	40-63	No external cost included
Nuclear	21-31	30-50	Decommissioning costs included
Wind	35-95	45-140	No backup costs included
Solar	150-400	200-530	No backup costs included
CHP	25-65	30-70	Costs vary, site-specific

nuclear electricity costs range between 21 and 31 mills/kWh, except in two cases. At a 10% discount, the rate range is from 30 to 50 mills/kWh, two cases excepted. Coal-fired plants have a cost range from 25 to 50 mills/kWh at 5% discount rate and from 35 to 60 mills/kWh at 10% discount rate. When external costs are neglected, coal-fired plants located near the surface pits of good coal, as in the United States, can be competitive with nuclear power. The table below summarizes the results. Costs given for wind and solar power do not take into account the costs of backup power required to compensate for the intermittent character of these plants. In other words, the figure gives the maximum turbine power and does not take into account efficiency, which is around 25%.

What is visible from this summary is that nuclear power plants are by no means inferior to other plants, even when external costs are not included for fossil plants. Inclusion of external costs works in favor of nuclear. The advantage of nuclear is clear among the technologies that do not emit greenhouse gases, even without backup costs, which cover reserve capacities for the periods without wind or sun.

Cost ranges reflect the country and site-specific assumptions. With inevitable increases of fossil-fuel costs and with developments of nuclear reactor technology, which will reduce the investment costs, the economic advantage of nuclear energy can only increase. More recent and more detailed comparative study is in progress in the EC. Although costs have generally increased, relative positions of various generation technologies did not change.

Long-Term Nuclear Fuel Sufficiency

The issue of long-term nuclear fuel sufficiency with respect to its contribution in the transport and industrial processes sectors and to nuclear proliferation safety is more political than technical. This issue is thus sometimes neglected by nuclear engineers, yet it will be essential for the long-term prospects of nuclear power. The intermediate and long-term issues will be discussed, with special attention to the nuclear proliferation issue in view of unfavorable recent development, such as failure of the 2005 Treaty on the Non-Proliferation of Nuclear Weapons renewal conference and the cases of Iran and North Korea.

Nuclear Safety

Of primary concern for the general public and for utilities is the risk of accidents on a nuclear reactor. Accident safety was a primary consideration in design of nuclear power stations from the early years. Resulting conservative technical characteristics of fuel design and coolant parameters did not affect the economy too much, due to cheap uranium, but the effect on capital costs was adverse. Many years of operational experience and safety research, and investigations such as the extensive safety study of dominant light water reactors WASH-1400 published in 1974, have allowed recognition of the risk-sensitive components and thereby more rational application of conservative design approaches.

For general discussion, overall reactor safety is usually expressed as core-melt probability, CMP, obtained by a semi-empirical method that considers all chains of events which can lead to this final result. From the estimated or determined failure probabilities of components and systems in all the event chains, total CMP is calculated. If a reactor accident risk is expressed by a CMP, there has been a constant advance from early designs. Analysis of accidents initiating events[10] for the period 1969-1974 led to the value of CMP above 10^4, closer to 10^3.

Operational experience of about 10,000 reactor years by 2005 and one case of core melt in a reactor at the Three Mile Island nuclear facility in Pennsylvania in 1979 (excluding the accident of the Soviet-built reactor Chernobyl in 1986 as irrelevant for Western reactor technology and safety practices) corroborate this figure obtained for the early period of nuclear operations. The numerous retrofits and safety improvements on operating PWR and BWR reactors following the Three Mile Island accident have reduced CMP by factors of about 6, respectively 8.[11] Analysis of initiating events for the period 1980–1982 confirmed this result, obtaining the CMP for this period of about 1.5×10^4. Estimates for the mid-1980s give an average about 10^4. Much greater scope for advance was possible in new reactors designed in the 1980s. For example, increased redundancy of safety systems of the Sizewell B reactor in the UK, operating since 1995, reduced CMP to estimated 1.1×10^6—that is, to one core melt in about a million years. Similar low values are obtained in new U.S. and European projects. With superior accident safety relative to other energy sources, further reduction is not a priority in Western nuclear safety thinking; the emphasis is rather on containment design to prevent radiation from leaving the containment should the unlikely event of core melt occur.

To put the role of containment (absent in the Chernobyl reactor) in perspective, one can observe, as an example, that for the U.S. reactor project AP600 safety analysis gives CMP of 1.2×10^6/year, while the probability of significant emission of radiation into surrounding is 3×10^9/year. That means only one serious radiation release to the environment in several hundreds of core melts, while one core melt in a thousand years would be expected from 1,000 reactors in operation.

There was no significant release in one core melt that occurred so far, at the Three Mile Island reactor in 1979, and since then safety designs and standards have much improved.

While further reduction of the CMP is not a technical problem, the aim of future development, such as INPRO or Generation IV, is to achieve high safety levels by inherent physical characteristics rather then by multiplication of safety systems, which leads to high capital costs. Some new projects offer considerable advances. So integrated reactor IRIS developed by international cooperation is expected to have CMP close to 8^{10}/year. Finally, to put things in proper perspective, one should note that accidents would on average contribute one-tenth only to the human injuries and deaths in plant operation. Plant operation, on the other hand, contributes about 20% to the losses due to standard industrial risks in power-plant construction, uranium mining, and fuel production. So, accidents may contribute about 2% in total human loss associated with nuclear power, in some discrepancy with average public perception. In absolute terms, human loss per unit of energy produced is much smaller for nuclear power than, for example, hydro power, contrary to common perception.

Waste Disposal

Technical solutions for safe disposal of nuclear waste and of spent fuel exist; the issue is primarily of public perception and acceptance. A need to isolate nuclear waste from the environment for periods of tens of thousand years is a new requirement and new human experience, which explains public attitudes. Concepts that can assure such isolation foresee disposal into dry or water-impermeable geological formations at the depth of a few hundred meters. Required materials and technology are available. There are other concepts. A novel, not yet sufficiently investigated concept is disposal into several-kilometers-deep wells. In the meantime, before the technically and economically optimal method of final disposal is selected, there are several methods for intermediate disposal for periods of up to 100 years or more. Present practice of storing spent fuel in large reinforced concrete casks allows enough time to decide on the final disposal method. Casks are deposited on the surface, which facilitates supervision and allows reuse in the future when recycling becomes economical.

Long-Term: Sufficiency of Nuclear Fuel

Inadequacy of uranium resources is one of the frequent objections to long-term development of fission energy, so a comment on the actual situation is justified. Natural uranium consists of 0.7% uranium235 and 99.3% uranium238. For a reactor, natural uranium has to be centrifuged so that there is 4% concentration of uranium235. To make a nuclear bomb, however, 90% purity uranium235 is needed.

Present annual uranium235 requirements for about 440 nuclear reactors, amounting to close to 70,000 tons, extrapolates to about 3 million tons in 40 years of operations, which is comfortably covered by uranium reserves under $80/kg. Considering also uranium available at costs of up to $130/kg, estimates range from 15 to 25 million tons (IAEA, NEA); for the present level of consumption, there would be enough uranium until the end of the century and beyond.

However, if one considers long-term use of nuclear fission contributing 30% to total energy consumption, annual uranium requirement would exceed 300,000 tons. A recent study[12] shows that we can in that case proceed with present practice of once-through fuel cycle to about 2060. Long-term development on such a scale would, after 2060, require utilization of uranium238 and thorium232, and not essentially only uranium235, as in present reactors practicing once-through fuel cycle. In case of such highly intense nuclear power expansion, there would about 50 years to create the conditions for safe large-scale use of reprocessing.

There are several ways to utilize uranium238 and thorium232. Nearest to commercial exploitation are fast breeders, with the French Super Phoenix the most advanced prototype. Various fuel cycles using thorium have been investigated for decades. At present uranium costs, neither of these possibilities is commercially interesting. In addition to these technically developed possibilities there are physically sound reserve methods at present on the level of project studies. These would use neutrons from accelerators or fusion devices to convert uranium238 and thorium232 into fissile isotopes. Reasonable extension of existing accelerator technology would be needed. Transformation of uranium238 into fissile isotopes increases by a large factor the energy obtained from natural uranium, and at the same time makes vastly larger uranium resources economical, such as those from seawater. With all these possibilities, reserves of uranium are no limitation for the long-term and large-scale use of nuclear energy on the time scale of many hundreds of years and beyond.

Wider Use of Nuclear Energy

Participation with 30% or more in total energy production would be a long-term target, should mankind be forced to opt for significant reduction of CO_2 emissions. Such a share in energy production and consumption would require nuclear energy entering transport and industrial uses. Looking at three main consumption sectors, primary energy is used for electricity production, in industry and heating, and in transportation. Each sector is, in the developed world, approximately one-third of the total. In electricity production, global nuclear contribution is about 16%, with reactors optimized to this purpose. High-temperature reactors suitable for industrial use have been developed for many years, the first prototypes operating in late 1960s. Their development is taken up again in Generation IV. With new interest in high-temperature reactors, use of nuclear heat in industrial processes can be expected in few decades. Penetration into transport section could be faster, with nuclear hydrogen produced by high-temperature reactors or with nuclear electricity supporting battery-driven or amended cars. Which of the two ways will prevail depends on future technology advances. Although at present general thinking favors hydrogen, nanotechnology promises a boost to the electricity storage in batteries and capacitors.

Nuclear Proliferation Safety

Nuclear proliferation safety is an as-yet unresolved, long-term problem. While all the issues discussed above were technical or scientific, and there is no need to doubt that they can be solved given required research and development, this is not so with the problem of proliferation safety. It is a foremost political problem, and it must be resolved by political methods. It is also a crucial problem for the future of nuclear energy. It is not disputed that the technology for a peaceful use of nuclear energy can be used to develop nuclear explosives, although this was not the path taken by the five acknowledged nuclear-weapon states. Specific proliferation-sensitive technologies are uranium enrichment and spent-fuel reprocessing, identified as such at the early International Fuel Cycle Evaluation, INFCE, 1978-80. There are as many as 14 countries, other than the initial five nuclear-weapon countries, known to have developed such installations within their nominally peaceful nuclear energy programs, and thus to have the potential to produce nuclear explosives (Argentina, Belgium, Brazil, Germany, India, Iraq, Iran, Israel, Italy, Japan, Netherlands, North Korea, Pakistan, and the Republic of South Africa). Three of them—Israel, India, and Pakistan—are now recognized as undeclared nuclear-weapon countries.

Extrapolation of existing practice of national enrichment and reprocessing installations to a much larger number of reactors in an increased number of countries would lead to increased danger of nuclear proliferation on the state level, as well as to increased danger of illicit production and traffic in fissile materials. In the past, this was an obstacle to the spread of peaceful use of nuclear energy, and in the future it could be even more so, should there be no essential improvement of the world political climate. The essential regulative role in promoting peaceful uses of nuclear energy was given to the Non-Proliferation Treaty (NPT), in force from 1970, with IAEA safeguards as the control mechanism. NPT is essentially a contract among five initial nuclear-weapon countries (NWC) and non-nuclear weapon countries (NNWC), defining obligations of NWC in return for NNWC abstaining from developing nuclear weapons. At the Sixth NPT Review Conference in 2000, nuclear-weapon countries reconfirmed their disarmament obligations as an "unequivocal commitment." However, no progress took place up to the Seventh NPT Review Conference in 2005. Specifically, the Comprehensive Test Ban Treaty (CTBT) was not entered into force, and negotiations had yet to begin on a Fissile Material Cutoff Treaty (FMCT) to eliminate production of weapons-grade highly enriched uranium and plutonium. Consequently, the international nonproliferation accord is in danger of collapse.

Conflicting interests of NWC and NNWC within NPT are one manifestation of the general fact that military and peaceful uses of nuclear energy are mutually exclusive. Instead of disarming, NWCs tend to limit the peaceful use of nuclear energy outside of their region of control, to reduce the possibility of nuclear weapons being developed there. Elimination and ban of nuclear weapons is therefore a necessary precondition for a large-scale peaceful use of nuclear energy without proliferation risks. However, a legitimate concern is whether elimination of nuclear weapons alone would be a sufficient condition for safe, widescale use of nuclear energy. The safety from diversion and abuse of nuclear materials by a particular non-democratic regime, by subnational groups, or by terrorists becomes of paramount importance in such a future.

Proliferation Safety by Internationalization of Proliferation-Sensitive Installations

The above questions and reservations should not mean a negative conclusion about the future of nuclear energy. However, they do lead us to the conclusion that the continuation of present fuel-cycle practices is not acceptable in the long-term perspective. One solution, at least, of the dilemma appears technically rather obvious: establishment of International Nuclear Fuel Cycle Centers (INFCC) under IAEA management to replace risk-prone national installations. Really reliable safeguards, in any case, would not be very far from such IAEA management. With international management, appointed by UN and IAEA, in full control of all proliferation sensitive installations, diversion problems of nuclear-weapon-usable materials would be essentially solved.

Regional fuel-cycle centers are by no means a new idea and are given new attention in new conditions. An indication of new thinking in IAEA can be seen in Director-General Mohamed El Baradei's Statement to the Forty-ninth Regular Session of the IAEA General Conference 2005, where he announced the establishment of a group of senior experts to explore the options for multilateral control of fuel-cycle facilities. The nuclear power needs of the countries abandoning their national enrichment or reprocessing installations would be covered by a supply of materials and services from International Fuel Cycle Centers. The IAEA's nuclear fuel bank could be an intermediate solution. The countries willing to abandon their national installations would have to be guaranteed a supply of nuclear fuel and services at fair prices and without any political bias. While it is clear that the path to internationalization of proliferation-sensitive installations is a difficult one, it will become even more difficult in the future with their increased number.

However, problems must be looked at in the perspective of final goals and gains. With the establishment of INFCC, many small national installations could be closed. Closing of small installations would not pose serious technical and financial problems, as, generally, large installations operate more economically. As is well known, some or many of these small or medium installations have political motivations in the background. Therefore, irrespective of whether they are economical or not, these installations will not be abandoned before the political problems behind them are resolved. Considering the international scene until the end of this century, it is not likely that the problems in the political forefront today—such as Israel-Arab, India-Pakistan, China-Taiwan, and the North Korean situation—will remain unsolved, if for no other reason than because they represent too high a tension and too great a risk in a world with nuclear weapons. It is also justified to expect a reduction of the development gap between North and South, with consequent reduction of tensions. In parallel with progress toward resolution of these regional conflicts of global significance, political obstacles for internationalization of all proliferation-sensitive installations will be disappearing. There is some hopeful development in two of these problems.

Road to Proliferation Safety by International Accord

Proliferation safety cannot be achieved by nuclear or other threats. On the contrary, politics backed by nuclear weapons makes these weapons attractive. The wisdom of NPT was that it was an accord of two sides, with defined rights and obligations. The main obligation of NWCs, in exchange for abandonment of national installations by NNWCs, should be a firm and well-defined promise to proceed with fulfillment of their NPT Clause VI obligations—specifically, to take steps to reduce nuclear arms below START 3 level, and, without delay, stop further production of nuclear weapon materials by signing FMCT. Clearly, in order to be accepted by NNWCs, both processes—i.e., abandonment of national installations and arms reductions—would have to run in parallel according to an agreed and coordinated time schedule. At the same time, the establishment of International Nuclear Fuel Cycle Centers would have to proceed. While small proliferation-sensitive installations could be closed with little economic loss and be replaced with supply from INFCCs, or, respectively, prior to their establishment, with a guaranteed supply from nuclear-weapon countries via IAEA nuclear fuel bank, this cannot be said for large installations, like those in Japan, the Netherlands, or Germany. These large installations should become parts of the future regional NFCCs by acquiring UN/IAEA management.

While reprocessing services are the more-distant need for most countries, enrichment is a present and permanent requirement. Fortunately, there is a large surplus enrichment capacity available in nuclear-weapon countries that would easily cover all abandoned small installations. Significant initial amounts of enriched uranium for reactors could also be available by dilution of highly enriched uranium from dismantling of warheads in the course of implementation of START 1 and START 2. World stockpiles of weapon-grade highly enriched uranium are estimated at 1,700 tons, with about 1,000 tons in Russia—enough for some 30,000 tons of reactor-grade enriched uranium. A boost to the establishment of the INFCC would be earmarking diluted uranium from the military stockpiles for the needs of INFCCs, respectively, to IAEA nuclear fuel bank. Of course, with the progress of nuclear disarmament to a level much lower then START 2 and prior to final elimination of nuclear weapons, the enrichment and reprocessing installations of the nuclear-weapon countries would have to be internationalized as well.

We are aware that, to many in NWCs and in the United States, this is difficult to accept. But without it, nuclear proliferation is practically guaranteed, with the consequent certainty of nuclear conflict and nuclear terrorism. There is no alternative if we want to create conditions for safe large-scale use of fission energy to reduce CO_2 emissions. As an additional benefit, full and general internationalization of enrichment and reprocessing installation will have the very important effect of removing risks in the last stage of nuclear disarmament to zero level. Times have come to understand that national interests can be pursued only in harmony with global interests, and that the greatness of a country is not measured by the size of its nuclear arsenal.

CONCLUSION

Apart from the various aspects of nuclear energy we have discussed above, there is a pragmatic aspect that we cannot ignore, which is that, for as far as one can see into the near future, nuclear fission energy provides (even though many environmentalists wish to ignore it) the only baseload if one is to discard fossil fuel. The recent stand-off between Russia and Ukraine on the much-sought-after gas for EU countries is a harbinger of what is to come. The official EU policy is to preserve the present nuclear level and have an energetic program on CCS. So, there is no doubt that there will be an expansion of nuclear energy in EU, China, India, and others.[13]

Within the limited scope available, we have shown that nuclear fission has the potential to answer the task of producing economical, safe, and environmentally acceptable energy for the foreseeable time of many centuries. This positive potential is commensurate with the negative potential of nuclear weapons, which threatened general destruction in the Cold War era. To opt for the positive choice, nuclear weapons must be abandoned as a threat and as a status symbol. By complete internationalization of all enrichment and reprocessing installations, in line with NPT and in spirit of the great U.S. proposal from 1946[14] to place all nuclear activities under international control, essential first steps would be made. The threat of nuclear proliferation would be removed, and the road would be open to use what is arguably the greatest discovery of past century—Einstein's equation of mass and energy—for the benefit of mankind.

NOTES

1. Hansen et al., "Carbon dioxide already in danger zone," *Science Daily*, http://www.sciencedaily.com/releases/2008/11/081108155834.htm.

2. IPCC report, February 2007, http://www.mnp.nl/ipcc/pages media/SRCCS-final/ccss.pdf.

3. Vaclav Smil, talk at Paris energy conference, http://home.cc.umanitoba.ca/~vsmil.

4. EU Wind Energy Barometer, February 2008, http://www.EU.int.

5. K. Zweibel, J. Mason, and V. Ftenakis, "By 2050 solar power could end U.S. dependence on foreign oil and slash greenhouse gas emissions," in *Scientific American* (January 2008).

6. Projections of contributions from renewables from a study prepared for European Commission, "World Energy, Technology and Climate Policy Outlook" (WETO), 2003, in Opinion of the European Economic and Social Committee on the issues involved in using nuclear power in electricity generation, Brussels (February 25, 2004), and for the United States, in Annual Energy Outlook 2006, U.S. Energy Information Administration.

5. Brussels European Council (March 8-9, 2007), Presidency Conclusions.

6. MIT, The future of nuclear power, 2003.

7. University of Chicago: Economic future of nuclear power, 2004.

8. Royal Academy of Engineering: The Cost of Generating Electricity, London, March 2004.

9. Nuclear Energy Agency-International Energy Agency: Projected Costs of Generating Electricity, OECD, 2005 Update.

10. J. W. Minarik and C. A. Kukielka, *Precursors to Potential Severe Core Damage Accidents 1969-1979: A Status Report,* ORNL/NSIC-182 and NUREG/CR-2497, Oak Ridge National Laboratory 1982.

11. D. L. Phung, "Light Water Reactor Safety Before and After TMI Accident," in *Nuclear Science and Engineering* 90, 1985.

12. D. Pevec, V. Knapp, and M. Matijevic, "Availability of Nuclear Fuel for Long-Term Expansion of Nuclear Power," in Proceedings of the International Conference, Nuclear Option for Countries with Small and Medium Electric Grids, Dubrovnik, Croatia, 2008.

13. Gioietta Kuo, "A Significant Watershed on the World Energy Scene." World Future Society, Global Strategies Forum, March 2009.

14. The Lilenthal-Baruch proposal to the UN foresaw the creation of an International Atomic Development Authority, which would be in charge of most fuel-cycle activities and building and operating required fuel-cycle installations. IADA would have been a very impressive international organization, strengthening the role of the UN. It was rejected by the Soviet Union, which was then developing its own atomic bomb.

Energy: The Grand Strategic Joint of the 21st Century

Tsvi Bisk

Energy is the *grand strategic joint* of human civilization in the twenty-first century. What is a *joint?* According to the great British military theoretician Basil Liddel Hart, it is the point that, when attacked, will provide the greatest benefit for the least effort. It must be both vital and vulnerable. Reducing energy use provides the greatest benefit to humankind because it is multidimensional. It impacts on economic and environmental health, security (economic and military), and development policy (especially in the underdeveloped world). It also has moral implications. The moral robustness and moral self-confidence of the West is undermined when it compromises its values to guarantee energy supply from countries ruled by thugs.

Oil is the joint of energy. It is the joint of joints. It is both vital and vulnerable. It is vulnerable because we now have the means to reduce oil from being the most vital international commodity to being a very marginal international commodity (like salt). Some of these means will be discussed below.

The joint must not be confused with the weakest point. The weakest point is always vulnerable, but it is usually worthless (often why it is weakly defended). Identifying the joint enables you to apply integrative thinking and to come up with multidimensional/multipurpose policies. Liberation from the enslavement of oil is a policy

---

Tsvi Bisk is director of the Center for Strategic Futurist Thinking. E-mail bisk@futurist-thinking.co.il.

aim that has multidimensional benefits: economic, environmental, security, social, moral, and political.

What do I mean by *grand strategy?* Coherent policy making has several components that are very often confused—to the detriment of the very policy aims desired. What are these components?

Ideological: our fundamental values. Democracy, constitutional protections, rule of law, sanctity of the individual human being, etc.

Policy: our true interests. Interests are economic, political, social, and moral (values). Policy is constrained by priorities, resources, and conditions. It must have a rational order. One cannot do everything at once. As the Talmud says: "He who tries to grab everything ends up with nothing." Moreover, it is probably more prudent to lead with economic and political interests than with social and moral interests. People resent being preached at, and one can probably achieve more for one's moral interests by wrapping them in economic policies than by a direct assault on the "immorality" of the other. Unless you yourself can walk on water, in all instances you will be accused of hypocrisy (see "Strategy of the Indirect Approach" below).

Grand strategy: This relates to the economic, political, military, social, and moral resources of a nation, country, or company, etc., and how best to optimally mobilize them in order to minimize weaknesses and achieve vital goals. "Grand strategy" defines the criteria and priorities by which we determine policy goals; it is the filter through which we pass policy goals to see if they are appropriate. In a sane and rational entity, grand strategy determines policy more than ideology. Ideology might strive for an ideal, but in real life we must construct policies based upon reality. Liberation from oil will strengthen our grand strategic position immensely: politically, economically, environmentally, morally, and socially.

Strategy: the plan formulated to implement a rational policy constrained by grand strategic resources. Strategy and strategic threats are not the same thing. A strategic threat (as opposed to a tactical threat) is one that endangers one's very existence.

Operations: Operations has to do with the rational and most efficacious deployment of grand strategic assets in order to achieve a strategic aim.

Tactics: the actual maneuvering undertaken to achieve a strategic aim—military, political, social, or economic.

The strategy of the indirect approach: This is a theoretical keystone of Liddel Hart's general approach. He called for armies to advance along the line of least expectation against the least resistance. I posit that what is good for armies is also good for politicians and policy makers. You can bang your head against a wall of resistance by "being right" (and morally indignant about being ineffective in your "just cause"), or you can slide past the resistance by resisting the temptation to demonstrate your own moral superiority and thereby become effective.

I want to be clear. In the battle between the "everything is gray" crowd and the "moral black and white" crowd, I take the middle position. Some things are various shades of gray and some things are black and white. But even when something is black and white (e.g., Saddam Hussein was a despicable tyrant), nuance and subtlety are one's best allies when trying to be effective. One's *ideology* might be that democracy is good for everyone; one's *policy* might be to democratize the Middle East, but the *strategy* of putting a quarter of a million troops into Iraq to accomplish this aim might not have been the best way to go.

The indirect approach can be applied to every classification above. America cannot democratize the Middle East when the entire Arab and Muslim worlds are deeply resentful. Therefore, a general indirect approach to reduce resentment might be as follows:

1. **Policy:** Work for peace between Israel and Palestinians so that America's support for Israel would not be automatically seen as being anti-Muslim or anti-Arab.

2. **Grand Strategy:** Neutralize Iran's nuclear program. This would be welcomed in the Gulf states, but in terms of the policy aim

would alleviate Israeli fears, making it more amenable to a far-reaching compromise with the Palestinians and realizing the policy aim.

3. **Strategy:** Collapse the Iranian economy by a general boycott of its oil exports. This will deprive them of the means to continue their nuclear program.

4. **Operations:** Mobilize current allies to take the lead; enlist potential allies by compromising elsewhere. President Obama trying to get Russia on his side regarding Iran by forgoing the missile defense program in eastern Europe is an example of this principle. Since Iran imports 40% of its gasoline (60% from Holland and 40% from India), convincing Holland and/or India to stop exporting gas to Iran would be another operational indirect approach.

5. **Tactics:** Initiate the Iranian oil boycott covertly and not overtly. In other words, just do it and do not talk about it. Make it happen gradually over several months, making it seem like natural market forces rather than Western hostility. Use the present economic crisis as an excuse.

Is the above doable? The West has a medium-term grand strategic trump card: the *strategic* reserves of the International Energy Agency (IEA). It also has a short-term tactical advantage: redundant production capacity caused by the economic turndown.

The IEA and its constituent members have 4 billion barrels of oil in strategic reserves. This enables them to release 2.5 million barrels a day (Iran's daily exports) onto the market for a period of more than four years. This enables the West, led by the United States, to boycott or disable (overtly or discretely) Iranian oil production.

Of course, the above is a bit of an oversimplification, but it serves to demonstrate the principle I am advocating. At every level, oil is the "grand strategic joint." Destroying the power of petroleum and petrodollars will also advance the cause of democracy (our ideological value). The reason for this is that countries dependent on natural resources and commodities are poor, and countries that create knowledge-based added value are rich. Countries that have natural resources invest in developing the resources. Countries without natural resources invest in their citizens—mainly in education, entrepreneurship, and infrastructure. Countries dependent on natural resources are vulnerable to bullying, undemocratic regimes. Countries dependent on human resources have to be democratic in order to foster speed, flexibility, and quality—necessary characteristics for functioning in a globalized world. The excellent book *As the Future Catches You* by Juan Enriquez of the Harvard Business School contains many examples of this thesis.

Table 1 demonstrates his point.

Petrodollars are the *grand strategic joint*. They finance the nuclear programs of rogue states as well as terror organizations such as Hamas, Hezbollah, and al-Qaeda. They finance anti-Western and anti-Semitic literature as well as Wahhabi madrassas that function as a cultural infrastructure undermining countries like Pakistan. They foster Western dependence on thugs and despots for energy (which

Table 1: Natural Resources and Income

Large Countries with Natural Resources	Per Capita Income	Small Countries without Natural Resources	Per Capita Income
Congo	710	Taiwan	16,100
Nigeria	970	Israel	18,300
Angola	1,030	Holland	23,100
Russia	4,200	Hong Kong	23,670
Brazil	6,150	Iceland	23,500
Colombia	6,200	Denmark	23,800
South Africa	6,900	Belgium	23,900
Venezuela	8,000	Switzerland	27,100
Mexico	8,500	Singapore	27,800
Saudi Arabia	9,000	Luxembourg	34,200

compromises moral values). Periodic oil-supply disruptions and price rises and threats cause economic instability. This hurts the developing world more than the developed world; indeed, the two boycotts of the 1970s and subsequent instability has been a major contributor to present African poverty.

Its impact on the American economy is tremendous. In 2006, import costs were $309 billion (about 40% of America's total trade deficit), and oil-related defense costs were $137 billion (not including the Iraq war). Oil-related defense costs between the two wars were $500 billion. Tax losses were $43 billion a year. The great irony and shame of oil dependence is that imported oil is not taxed while all domestic energy production is taxed. If oil-related defense costs alone were invested in alternative energy, America would have already achieved energy independence. Hidden costs of oil for the rest of the developed world in aggregate probably equal that of the United States. All this is without internalizing direct and indirect environmental costs, or direct and indirect health costs.

Defining the Problem

I believe the problem lies in our inability to differentiate between ideological and strategic thinking and to realize that oil has become a double-edged sword. It can now be wielded against the oil-producing states as much as it can be wielded by them. The following outlines an energy strategy that would enable the West (especially the United States) to sharpen this sword with a real-world energy policy.

Rational policy making requires that strategic possibility have the upper hand over ideological wishful thinking. What we can do and when we can do it must be our standards—not visions of a perfect world. Policy criteria are concerned with time (when something can be done) and doability (what can be done). Time refers to short term, intermediate term, long term, and deep long term. In other words, how we get from here to there, and what the intermediate (or bridging) steps would be. Doability relates to practicality—a policy that reflects how real people actually live. Anything else is irrational. Thus, a rational energy strategy must:

1. **Not expect the middle class to change lifestyle**. Policy proposals based on fundamental changes of lifestyle will fail and close minds to environmental arguments. People are willing to change on the margins—replace their present gas guzzler with a hybrid or electric, replace incandescent bulbs with fluorescent or LEDS, pay attention to the energy consumption of appliances, vacation closer to home, work closer to home (or from home), etc. They are not willing to give up hot water, air-conditioning, or the flexibility of private transportation.

2. **Mobilize multipartisan political support**. Policies that irritate large segments of public opinion are not politically doable in postmodern democracies—a fact annoying to "experts" but still a fact.

3. **Conform to the laws of economics.** Taxing big energy corporations might be emotionally satisfying but will solve nothing, and, as with Carter's tax regime in the 1970s, probably exacerbate the problem. It is the equivalent of kicking your dog because you are angry it is raining outside.

4. **Be equitable.** It cannot depend on long-term direct or indirect subsidies, nor have privileged status before the law.

5. **Include indirect costs and yields.** Internalizing the $50 billion a year that the United States spent in policing the Persian Gulf between the two Iraqi wars, as well as other costs of oil dependence, the real price of imported oil to the American economy would be about $10 a gallon at the pump. Internalizing the economic benefits of domestic energy production (jobs created, business activity generated, and taxes derived from), tax breaks for alternative energy technologies become an investment that would produce a greater return for the economy and not only for the environment.

6. **Be beneficial to the environment.** More energy with less environmental damage is the only policy that can mobilize the broad-based support mentioned in criterion two.

7. **Be a combination** of increased production (primarily from non-conventional sources) and decreased consumption.

IMPRACTICAL SOLUTIONS

Building Nuclear Plants

How this is supposed to solve the problem of high liquid fuel prices is beyond comprehension. It will also alienate the environmental minority and the "not in my backyard" majority. National polls showing 60% in favor of nuclear power are irrelevant—try building a plant in *their* area. Inevitable local opposition will turn any new nuclear plant into a 10–20 year project, even if approved by national authorities.

Nuclear is not equitable. In the United States, the nuclear industry has been so legally advantaged in terms of liability that one wonders how it has withstood a real constitutional challenge. France's immunization of nuclear power is even more extreme. Nuclear waste is still a problem. Previously claimed economic advantages are now doubtful. Costs per kilowatt of nuclear power are twice to four times what estimates were only several years ago.

Hydrogen, Ethanol, and Palm Oil

Hydrogen is essentially a carrier of energy. It takes almost as much direct and indirect energy to produce it as it carries. It is a "killer application" straw man. Its advocates are either ill-informed or determined to hinder implementation of more immediate, doable, and efficient energy alternatives. The documentary *Who Killed the Electric Car?* highlights this.

Corn ethanol is similar to hydrogen in that it takes almost as much energy to produce as it carries. Sugarcane ethanol, on the other hand, produces nine units of energy for every energy unit invested. But it has several problems. Brazil, the world's largest producer, consumes all the ethanol it produces and will likely continue to do so as its economy expands. Other potential developing-world producers will be small and likely use any product they generate domestically. The expansion of sugarcane farming is beginning to impact on rain forests, so its environmental benefits are becoming ever more doubtful.

Palm oil is an environmental catastrophe—its growth is destroying wide swaths of rain forest. Sugarcane ethanol and palm oil might be redeemed by genetic engineering that enables their growth in desert areas with high-salinity water. This would be a worthwhile research initiative but not a doable solution in a reasonable amount of time.

Drilling

Even Texas oil man T. Boone Pickens says drilling cannot solve the problem. The U.S. Department of Energy writes the following about the Alaska National Wildlife Refuge (ANWR) "solution":

> If permission for drilling were given tomorrow the first barrel of oil would be produced by 2018.
>
> Production would peak in 2028 at 800,000 barrels a day (mean estimate) and then decline.

According to the Energy Information Administration of the United States, in April 2008 the United States was consuming 19.8 million barrels of oil a day, down from the 20.6 million a day the previous April: a savings of 811,000 barrels a day. In other words, in one year, the United States had a net gain equal to the total projected production of the ANWR in 2028. Yet, the price of oil doubled during the same period.

PEAK OIL OR PEAK AVAILABILITY

The debate about "peak oil" is bogus unless one assumes "peak technology." Given advancing technologies in deep-ocean drilling and extraction from oil sands and oil shale, known and recoverable oil reserves will probably sustain themselves in coming years. But developing these resources entails enormous capital outlays and long lead times. The recent deep-ocean discovery of Brazil (an estimated

9 billion barrels of reserves—similar to ANWR in size) is a case in point. It will cost about $150 billion to develop and, like ANWR, will take more than a decade before the first barrel of oil is extracted. Both the Brazilian field and ANWR will be worth this tremendous investment only if the price of oil remains at the present high level or goes even higher. In other words, drilling is not the solution to high fuel prices; it is contingent upon continued high prices.

As energy maven Chris Nelder points out in an outstanding article in the March-April 2009 issue of *The Futurist,* the real systemic problem is "peak exports" or "peak availability" of oil. By the time ANWR and new offshore resources in the United States, Brazil, and elsewhere get fully online, their combined production will not equal the ongoing decline in exports from oil-producing countries due to increased domestic consumption.

All 14 major oil exporters are moving up the value chain by developing petrochemical industries that use a growing percentage of their domestic oil production. Their citizens are also buying automobiles at a dizzying rate. All, except Norway, have had double-digit yearly increases in domestic oil consumption since 2005.

In 2020, Russia will probably still be pumping 10 million barrels a day, but most likely will be consuming 5 million barrels rather than the 3 million they are today; in 2028, it will still be pumping 10 million barrels a day but consuming 7 million barrels. We must remember that the United States was the world's largest oil exporter in the 1930s but became a net importer soon after World War II.

Exports from Africa will remain static as Nigeria's exports decline. Booming Brazil will consume all the energy it produces. The domestic energy consumption of the rest of Latin America will burgeon. Venezuela's production has declined significantly under Chavez; more-competent governance will likely lead to increased production but also increased domestic consumption. The same is true of Iran. If the Islamic regime stays in power, production will continue to stagnate. A progressive regime change will likely lead to increased production, but also to improved development and increased domestic consumption.

Mexico's constitution forbids foreign investments in the oil sector. Its major fields are rapidly declining. Domestic consumption is increasing. By 2020, Mexico's exports to the United States could decline to a trickle. Mexico might even be on the verge of becoming a net oil importer, like Indonesia this past year. It is already down to a little more than a million barrels a day, as production from its biggest field has dropped 34% in 2008 alone. Projections for Canadian oil sands cannot make up this difference.

Persian Gulf countries are now investing huge sums in economic diversification, which, along with population growth and increased standard of living, are pressuring exports downward.

WHAT CAN BE DONE?

Conservation and Accumulation of Greenhouse Emission Credits

Hybrids, plug-in hybrids, and electric cars should be advantaged for licensing and other taxes. All nonemergency vehicles purchased by governments (federal, state, and local in the United States) should be hybrids, plug-in-hybrids, or electric by 2010. Purchasers, whether private or governmental, would earn greenhouse emission credits that they could sell to the coal liquefaction program (see below), thus providing an additional economic incentive advantaging these technologies. It is reasonable to assume that this policy would result in a decline in the consumption of liquid fuels for transportation of 150,000–200,000 barrels a day every year from inception. By 2020, the United States could be consuming less than 18 million barrels of liquid fuel daily.

Incandescent bulbs should be banned by 2010. Replacing a single incandescent bulb with a compact fluorescent light (CFL) will keep half a ton of CO_2 out of the atmosphere over the life of the bulb. It is estimated that, if everyone in the United States used energy-efficient lighting, 50 average-sized coal-powered plants could close. Similar savings could be achieved in the EU, Japan, and South Korea.

Alternative energy companies could sell their products/services to homes and businesses as "loss leaders" or "at cost" in order to accumulate greenhouse emission credits, which they could also sell, making the price of alternative energy technologies more attractive. Consequent increased volume of sales would generate economies of scale and further lower the cost of dispersed solar and wind power.

Liquefaction of Coal

The technologies for coal liquefaction have been available since before World War II and can produce a barrel of oil for about $30. Opposition derives from the fact that they release more CO_2 in the conversion process than the extraction and refinement of liquid fuel from petroleum.

To assuage environmentalist opposition, liquefaction installations would be permitted to become operational on the condition that they produce a half a ton of CO_2 for every ton of greenhouse gases eliminated by other methods of producing energy. By trading a half a ton of CO_2 for a ton of CO_2 the environment would get a 2x1 benefit. Trading a half a ton of CO_2 for a ton of methane, and the environment would get a 20x1 benefit. This would give the coal industry an economic incentive to get behind some of the green alternatives described below.

The United States has the largest recoverable reserves of coal in the world—equal to the entire world's proven oil reserves. An energy/environment program that includes coal would generate local jobs and augment local tax bases, garnering support among the working and middle class. If we do not help coal become a friend of the environment, we are in trouble. It is the fastest-growing fuel source in the world and the most democratic—found on every continent and in almost every country. Millions of people depend on it for their livings. Glib declamations about banning coal are not doable and are dysfunctional to a rational energy and environmental strategy.

Coal liquefaction installations could be manufactured serially, much as Liberty ships were manufactured in World War II or F16 fighter planes are manufactured today, using the underutilized manufacturing and human resources of America's industrial heartland in the upper Midwest. Operating licenses would be contingent on the coal companies purchasing greenhouse emission credits to offset liquefaction emissions.

Within five years, the United States could be producing 1 to 2 million barrels of liquefied coal daily; within 10 years, this could increase to 4 million barrels a day. The upper amount would be limited only by the availability of greenhouse emission credits and new (cleaner) liquefaction technologies.

Capped Wells

There are approximately 200,000 capped wells in the United States. With current technology, each well could produce 5–10 barrels of oil a day. Within one or two years, these wells could produce more oil per day than ANWR would after 20 years. What is needed are sufficient government guarantees in the form of long-term contracts and low-interest loans as an incentive for small oil producers to bring these wells back into production. Given historical precedent, we can reasonably expect that new technologies that increase production rates and well life span would quickly follow.

This policy would be environmentally beneficial in several ways. It would avert the use of bunker fuel for the tankers transporting imported oil. Bunker is the most-polluting transportation fuel in use today. The combined world merchant fleet spews as much noxious gas into the atmosphere as does the entire United States. Reduced tanker traffic also lessens the risk of tanker accidents and oil spills and eliminates the ballast detritus that oil tankers flush into the oceans before entering port. Capped wells are also poorly supervised and often leak into ground water, so bringing them back into production would minimize these problems.

Lastly, reactivating capped wells would generate local jobs and augment the local tax base. Tens of thousands of them are owned by thousands of small oilmen, who have been begging the government to look at this option for a short-term bridging solution to the energy crises.

T. Boone Pickens Plan

This oilman turned wind-power guru has an interesting concept. Replace the 22% of domestically produced natural gas used for electrical generation with wind power. Turn the natural gas into liquid (LNG) to be used for transportation. The amount of natural gas obtained would be the equivalent of 38% of America's current oil imports—more than 4 million barrels. Pickens claims that this could be achieved within 10 years and would cut hundreds of millions of dollars off of America's trade deficit.

The obvious caveat to his proposal is that gas-fired plants less than 30–40 years old will not be decommissioned even if wind power is available. If he modified his plan to decommission gas- and coal-fired plants over the next 10 years, with the coal thus saved becoming available for liquefaction, this concept could probably realize a replacement of several million barrels of oil a day also. Another modification might be to convert the gas into methanol rather than LNG. This would advantage the concept of flex-fuel engines and freedom of choice in transportation fuels.

Wind replacing natural gas and LNG or methanol replacing gasoline are both environmental pluses. Again, the sale of greenhouse emission credits to the coal industry would be an additional incentive. If hybrids and plug-in hybrids were modified to use LNG or methanol in their flex-fuel internal combustion component, there would be a tremendous multiplier effect in terms of oil consumption and environmental benefit.

The above three steps could add between 5 and 10 million barrels of domestic liquid fuel production by 2020. The conservative estimate of 5 million barrels would be a combination of 1.5 to 2 million barrels for each of the above solutions. But let's say that enough greenhouse emission credits were accumulated to enable coal liquefaction to the tune of 4 million barrels, and T. Boone Pickens's optimal vision of 4 million barrels is also realized.

Let us further imagine that a new technology for extracting oil from capped wells comes online, greatly increasing productivity. Global Resources Corp. of New Jersey claims that its microwave technology can extract 100 barrels a day from abandoned wells. If this is so, then the optimistic prediction of 10 million barrels a day in aggregate becomes not so farfetched. But even if the Global Resources claim turns out to be unrealistic, can anyone with even a smidgen of knowledge of economic history doubt that a national policy dedicated to bringing capped wells back to life will attract a load of R&D and encourage much technological innovation in this area? Indeed, a prize of $1 billion (offered by the government or a private factor) for the first company that can strip 90% of the remaining oil in capped wells at a rate of 50 barrels a day for a cost of $30 or less would almost guarantee that such a technology would be developed forthwith. Such a development would guarantee 10 million barrels a day for the next 100 years from rejuvenated capped wells alone.

But assuming the minimum, and further assuming conventional domestic oil production declining to 5 million barrels a day while consumption has declined to 18 million barrels a day, the United States would be importing 8 million barrels a day, compared with 12 million today. If the optimal 10 million barrels is achieved, the United States would be importing only 3 million barrels a day, mostly from Canada.

LIKELY DEVELOPMENTS WITHIN THE NEXT DECADE

Ethanol and Other Biofuels from Algae, Sewage, Manure, Trash, and Garbage

There are dozens of companies around the world, funded by tens of millions of dollars of venture capital, working intensively on this. The biomass is enormous, and breakthroughs could generate millions of barrels of additional liquid fuel by 2020. Algae alone could generate 2.5 million barrels on a surface area the size of Connecticut (equal to several corn-growing counties in Iowa). Algae are the ultimate sequester of CO_2—their primary feedstock for growth.

Algae-growing installations could be constructed vertically (to gain maximum surface area while optimizing land use) adjacent to fossil fuel power plants and other CO_2 emitting installations. One must wonder why the coal industry hasn't become a champion of this energy strategy.

Landfills around the world create as much greenhouse gas in the form of methane as all the vehicles in the world. They leak toxic poisons into groundwater and pollute the soil as well as coastal areas. Economically, they are a stupid example of land use. Very few if any sewage-processing installations are hermetic and 100% efficient; they also pollute groundwater and commercial fisheries. In essence, waste-to-fuel would be a recycling of hydrocarbons—of civilization eating its own waste (the ultimate renewable) in order to endure.

Ethanol from algae could become commercially viable within the next several years and provide us with another powerful weapon in the energy war. E10 (gas with a 10% ethanol additive) can be used without retrofitting infrastructure or automobiles. The equivalent of 9.1 million barrels of oil is consumed every day in the United States as gasoline. If it were possible to mandate the universal use of E10 today, it would replace the equivalent of 911,000 barrels of oil a day (more than the projected ANWR output in 2028).

An "Energy Peace Corps" of engineering and science students could help lower-income groups to convert cars past warranty to flex-fuel engines capable of burning gasoline with 85% ethanol. If a conversion kit costs $400 retail, you could convert 10 million cars for $4 billion. Buying in bulk at $200 a kit, you could convert 20 million cars for $4 billion. For $10 billion (the monthly cost of the Iraq war), you could convert 50 million cars, which is approximately one-fifth of the American fleet, saving at a minimum an additional 1.5 million barrels a day. Plug-in hybrids with flex-fuel engines using E85 could be getting 500 miles to the gallon of gasoline. The sale of greenhouse emission credits to the coal industry would enhance the economic benefits of these fuels also. The creation of such a huge market would further drive investment and innovation, increasing production and lowering costs.

Electric Cars

Various technological and conceptual developments are beginning to interact with increasing consumer receptiveness to the electric car. Greatly improved batteries, quicker recharging mechanisms, and innovative infrastructure concepts are converging.

One intriguing model is Project Better Place, the brainchild of Israeli high-tech innovator Shai Agassi, who has formed a three-pronged alliance with the State of Israel, Nissan-Renault, and international venture capital around an idea based on the mobile-phone model—you pay a monthly service fee for the battery and the electrical charge. They envision 150 battery-changing stations around Israel, where drivers can exchange a drained battery for a fully charged one in less time than it takes to fill up a tank of gas. The battery-changing stations will be supplemented with tens of thousands of plug-in points in parking areas around the country.

The beauty of this concept is that it makes intermittent renewables such as solar and wind competitive without subsidies. In Israel, the battery stations will be recharged by solar, and in Denmark (the second country to sign on) by wind. The idea is particularly attractive to geographic or geopolitical islands. Japan, South Korea, and Hawaii have all expressed interest in the project.

Of course, Agassi's model might be trumped by other developments, such as batteries with a 200-mile range that are capable of being fully charged in less than an hour. This in effect would give an electric car infinite range when taking into consideration how real human beings actually drive. Who does not have two to four rest and refreshment stops over a 200-mile trip? During these 10- to 15-minute pit stops, or 30- to 40-minute food stops, drivers could top off their batteries at convenient recharging parking areas. Interstate highway and state turnpike rest stops could be required to set up recharging installations. Municipalities could require shopping malls to do the same. Fast-food chains would compete for customers by dedicating parts of their parking lots to recharging installations. In short, both by mandate and by competition, such installations would quickly become ubiquitous.

The environmental benefits of electric cars are self-evident. Various studies show that driving on electricity, even from coal-fired grids, would reduce greenhouse gas emissions. Using renewables, the environmental benefits would be multiplied.

CONCLUSION

The focus of this article has been on the United States, but energy, especially oil, is fungible. The EU, Japan, and the rest of the OECD could do much to relieve the global pressure on energy supplies. Mandating and advantaging hybrids and electric cars as well as compact fluorescent and LED bulbs would be a first obvious step.

Countries could focus their foreign-aid efforts on making the developing world energy self-sufficient. On the principle of a half a ton of greenhouse emissions for every ton saved, they could build coal liquefaction plants in many developing countries. When waste-to-fuel technologies become commercialized, they could be put into operation in every developing country. Not only would this have economic benefits, since developing countries suffer the most from energy volatility, it would also create jobs and promote public health. Smoldering landfills and running sewage are among the greatest threats to public health in these countries.

In short, if the free world resolves that by 2020 humankind be liberated from its addiction to oil, and by doing so greatly lessen greenhouse emissions, it will be done.

EPILOGUE: THE DEEP FUTURE

The above is essentially a bridging strategy, designed to get human civilization to 2050 safely. The LNG/methanol, coal, and capped-well gambits, being finite, will also run out of steam within 30 to 100 years from inception.

The deep future will depend on continued progress in algae growth and waste-to-fuel technologies. Human civilization must start planning to become a closed system by 2100 —i.e., 100% recycling of all human waste and zero externalization into the commons. Sewage and waste-disposal systems would become the major source of fuel, and the environment would gradually cleanse itself back into a relatively pristine state. Algae growth would top off any fuel shortfalls.

But energy productivity must become the dominant theme in policy strategies. New lighting technologies, smart materials, and super-light composites (along with 100% recycling) will enable humanity to maintain a rich consumerist civilization at declining cost to both the economy and the environment. The theoretical underpinnings for such a vision already exist in the "cradle-to-cradle" philosophy of Bill McDonough and Michael Braungart. This is not "pie in the sky"; their "theory" is already being commercialized by a for-profit business: McDonough Braungart Design Chemistry LLC.

By the end of the century, lighting technologies will have transcended CFLs and even LEDs. Buildings will be built from smart materials that heat when it is cold and cool when it is hot, as well as turn sunlight into electricity. They will also have mini-depolymerization units that turn domestic sewage and garbage into fuel. Buildings will have become completely independent, self-sustaining energy units.

Airplanes, vehicles, and trains will be built from super-light composites (the proper use of hydrocarbons) that at present are prohibitively expensive but that industrial engineers will eventually learn how to produce cheaply. Imagine the savings in fuel if a jumbo jet weighed only 50 tons rather than 400 tons. The same principle applies to cars, trucks, trains, elevators, ships, construction machinery, port installations—in short, anything that consumes energy in order to move. And if the fuel is an algae or waste derivative (infinitely renewable), you will, in effect, have solved the problem.

The possibilities of space might also have become a reality by 2100. All mineral extraction could come from the asteroid belt or the Moon, and we would enable our precious planet to heal its scars. Space elevators would lift up toxic waste to be disposed of in that great incinerator in the sky called the Sun, and bring down raw materials and finished products. Energy for the solar economy would be provided by space-solar energy generators capable of operating 24/7.

Our home, this Earth, will have become a bedroom community instead of the gigantic waste dump we have made it.

Final Note: The Optical Illusion of Plummeting Oil Prices

With the price of a barrel of oil dropping more than $100 within a six-month span, the shortsighted temptation will be to dismiss the above. But since futurists think about the future, consider the following.

The International Energy Agency has just published a report that the world's 450 biggest oil fields are depleting at a rate of 9.1% a year. This means that, barring major new oil discoveries, world production could fall 38% to 52 million barrels a day by 2013.

Even if oil consumption held at the present 85 million barrels a day, there is no way new oil discoveries could make up for a 38% drop in production from existing fields. All the oil in the Arctic National Wildlife Refuge would supply the world for only six months (using the most optimistic estimate of reserves). The world would need four to five new Saudi Arabias by 2030 just to stay at 85 million barrels a day. Alaska, deep-ocean drilling, new offshore drilling, drilling in national parks—raping the land for every last drop of oil—could not even begin to offset these declines. Add in the fact that, with our present energy paradigm, consumption is predicted to grow to 130 million barrels a day over the next 30 years or so, and we must conclude that this energy paradigm is unsustainable.

Enjoy present oil prices while you can. As the world's economy recovers, we will be approaching $150 a barrel oil in the next four to five years.

The Post-Scarcity World of 2050–2075

Stephen Aguilar-Millan, Ann Feeney, Amy Oberg, and
Elizabeth Rudd

The deployment of long-range forecasts is an activity that is, in itself, hazardous in nature. There is a distinct possibility that the future may not unfold quite as originally anticipated. Our speculations about how we move into the future could be wrong. There may be unforeseen events that blow us off our path as we progress forward. However, just because it is difficult to engage in thinking for the long term does not mean that we ought not to try.

There are many human activities that do require us to think about how the world will develop beyond our immediate horizon. For example, if we are to plan a road, or to lay out the foundations for a city, the decisions that we make today will have an impact far into the future. Much of the beauty of ancient cities lies in how they were planned at inception. When we engage in this type of activity we have a responsibility to future generations to give some consideration as to

Stephen Aguilar-Millan is the director of research at the European Futures Observatory and a director of The Greenways Partnership, a firm of consulting futurists. E-mail stephena@eufo.org.

Ann Feeney is research manager at the YMCA of the USA. E-mail ann.feeney@gmail.com.

Amy Oberg is managing partner at Future-In-Sight LLC. E-mail Amy.Oberg@Future-In-Sight.com.

Elizabeth Rudd is a consultant with more than 20 years of experience in a variety of senior management, strategy, and business development roles. She lives in Melbourne, Australia.

how our decisions may impact upon them. One could argue that many of the problems of the twenty-first century result from a neglect of the future in the nineteenth and twentieth centuries.

It is with this in mind that we approach the issue of the "post-scarcity world." We take the view that the world between 2010 and 2050 is one that is likely to be characterized by scarcities. A scarcity of credit, a scarcity of food, a scarcity of energy, a scarcity of water, and a scarcity of mineral resources. We shall touch upon the nature of these scarcities, their causes, and their cures in the next section. However, that is not the main emphasis of this piece.

Our main emphasis lies upon what comes after the period of scarcity. In developing our thinking about this issue, we have found it useful to develop a view from four perspectives—the post-scarcity company, post-scarcity society, post-scarcity geopolitics, and the post-scarcity financial system. Together, they provide a view of what the world may look like between 2050 and 2075. It will not be a world without scarcity, but one that has learned to cope with constricted resources.

FROM SCARCITY TO POST-SCARCITY: 2010–2050

A study of the history of the world will show that it fluctuates through periods of relative scarcity and of relative abundance. The period from 1975 to 2005 was one of relative abundance. The global economy was built upon relatively cheap and readily available energy, the global financial system was built upon cheap and relatively available credit. The predominant ethos of the era was one of a diminishing role of the state in both society and the economy. This era of abundance came to an end during the period from 2005 to 2010, culminating with recession to mark the transition from a world of abundance to a world of scarcity.

One consequence of the era of abundance was the expansion of credit in the Western economies to unsustainable levels. The developed economies eagerly consumed goods produced by the newly developing economies. This gave rise to large trade imbalances between the two sets of economies. The trade surpluses of the newly developing economies were recycled as loans to the developed economies, which were then spent on purchasing the goods produced by the newly developing economies. As a consequence of this, interest rates in the developed economies were lower than they otherwise would have been, giving rise to speculative asset bubbles in both the property markets and the global stock markets. By 2007, the bubbles started to burst, with the result that banks stopped lending to each other, and the flow of credit simply dried up. The credit crunch was upon us.

One consequence of the credit crunch was that two key elements of the modern economy—credit and business confidence—had become very scarce. In order to keep the financial system working, governments responded by bailing out their respective national banks, generally by taking an equity stake in the banks. Some banks were nationalized outright, while some banks were only partially nationalized. Either way, the banking system across the world had become subject to greater state intervention and supervision. A result of this was the banking reserve requirements becoming much more stringently imposed, restricting credit even further.

The second decade of the twenty-first century will be dominated by the working out of the credit crunch. Business finance will be, generally speaking, not as freely available as it had been in the previous decade. This will result in growth rates in the OECD nations being lower than they otherwise would have been. This will come to have quite an effect upon the world economy.

According to the UN population estimates, the global population in 2000 was about 6 billion. By 2025, the population will be about 8 billion, growing again to about 9 billion by 2050. As the global financial system starts to stabilize at a new level of normalcy by about 2020, the impact of a growing global population and a stagnant global economy will start to be felt across the world.

In simple terms, we could say that the potential demand for most things will increase by at least a third. However, this rather under-states the case. It is likely that there will be rising expectations to ac-commodate as well. For example, in the case of food, there is likely to be an increase in the number of mouths to feed by a third. On top of that, the demand for improved diets is not likely to abate, giving rise to further demand for foodstuffs. Rising aspirations are not likely to be restricted to diet alone. Across the globe, people will want access to better housing, better education, and better health care. They will want to share in material prosperity—a TV, a car, a better life for their children.

These rising aspirations are likely to trigger the second aspect of the age of scarcity— "Peak Just About Everything." We are all ac-customed to the concept of "peak oil"—the point at which historical global production of oil will peak and thereafter diminish. There are many forecasts of peak oil, from about 2015 to 2040. From our per-spective, the important point is that peak oil will occur at some point during the age of scarcity.

This coincides with a period when many of the minerals that are essential to the working of the global economy, as it is configured today, will also peak. For example, antimony (essential to the produc-tion of semiconductors) will peak between 2020 and 2040. Tantalum (essential to the production of capacitors and resistors) will peak be-tween 2025 and 2035. Zinc (an important metal in the production of batteries) will peak between 2025 and 2035. And so the list could go on. The point is that our current lifestyles are likely to become ever more unsustainable in the third and fourth decades of this century.

This defines the age of scarcity. Growing demand pressures that originate from a rising global population—which has increasing as-pirations for life—will combine with a situation where the resources necessary to satisfy that demand are heading toward the point of ex-haustion. The result will be a period in which resource scarcity could become quite acute.

A period of resource scarcity is likely to manifest itself as a period of increasing and volatile prices. However, once the trend toward increasing prices becomes established, the price mechanism will stimulate new technologies to address resource efficiency. The technology of resource usage—getting more out from putting less in—is likely to be the defining technology of the age of scarcity. Whether it is getting more miles per gallon from motor cars, more food per acre from arable land, or reducing the mineral content of electronic components, the price mechanism is likely to focus our attention on achieving a more sustainable economy. The aftereffects of the credit crunch are likely to inhibit this feature until the third decade of the century, but once the process starts, we could see developments occurring well into the middle of the century.

Where would we be then? It is likely that the global economy would be much greener than it is today. Although peak production in many resources is likely to have been reached, the point of resource exhaustion could be considerably delayed through the development of the technology of resource efficiency. After a period of scarcity, aspirations of living standards may well be reduced from their present levels. Some nations may respond to scarcity by taking protectionist measures, in which case the levels of global trade would be much lower than they are today. If so, then the period following the age of scarcity may well be one when aspirations start to rise again and world trade starts to increase again. The process of globalization—inhibited in the age of scarcity—would start to accelerate again. The best place to start to examine this process is through the post-scarcity company.

THE POST-SCARCITY COMPANY

As we enter into the post-scarcity world, we will also be entering a time of significant challenge to the traditional capitalist business models, concepts, and assumptions that have developed over the past 200 years. The assumption of scarcity is fundamental to traditional business. Business theories, models, and operations are all premised on the idea that scarcity (either perceived or real) enables businesses to charge a price for the goods and services they provide. In traditional models, this is how businesses generate revenue.

In the post-scarcity world, technological advances will facilitate decreasing costs until conceivably almost everything is "free" to the consumer. Scarcity will no longer exist in this world, and, without scarcity, the concept of charging a price to consumers as a means of generating revenue will be unworkable. The post-scarcity world will put tremendous pressure on current business models, potentially rendering them irrelevant and obsolete in the future. If traditional businesses do not adapt to this emerging "free" world, many of the strong, traditional organizations of the early twenty-first century will cease to exist over the next 50 years.

Lack of scarcity and "free" are difficult, counterintuitive concepts to grasp, and for many in business easy to deny. But the evolution toward lack of scarcity and "free" is, in fact, already under way, thanks primarily to technologies (such as computers and the Internet) that have enabled and driven the growth of digitization over the last 20 years.

The ability to digitize, or "convert atoms to bits," is increasingly removing scarcity from the business equation. While traditional scarcity theory posits that, when one item is used, there is *one less item available* (thus increasing scarcity), in the digital world when one item is used (copied, connected to another) there is at least *one more item available* (thus decreasing scarcity). The logic is completely reversed but explains exactly how digitization is removing scarcity and driving to "free." As Michael Masnick, president and CEO of TechDirt says, "In digital goods, scarcity doesn't exist."

We see this post-scarcity evolution in a variety of businesses and industries that are being driven toward (and struggling with) "free" products. For example, a wide variety and volume of news and information is now free; the *Wall Street Journal,* Wikipedia, and Craigslist are all free online news and information sources. Literature and books can be downloaded free from authors such as Doctorow and King. Open-source software from Linux is free; VOIP-calling via Skype can be had for free; Yahoo e-mail with unlimited storage is free; games such as those from Perfect World are free; services such as photo sharing are free from Flickr; and music downloads are free, often from the artists themselves. News, information, literature, communications, services, recreation, music, and more—already available for free.

In some respects, "free" as part of the business equation is not a radical idea. Gillette provides a classic business case study in "free." In 1901–1903, Gillette began giving away free razors in order to develop a market for disposable blades. Today, wireless companies are following the Gillette example, giving away essentially free phone hardware to sell service plans. This type of "free," however, is not really about providing free products; it's about cross-subsidies and shifting costs from one product to another. In the post-scarcity world, shifting will be irrelevant because the actual cost of the products will fall potentially to nothing; "free" will really mean free, at least for the majority.

There is considerable debate among economists, technologists, and businesspeople over whether or not any product can ever really be "free." Those arguing in support of the idea reference historical precedents that show continued deflationary economics and decreasing costs as the result of technological advancements. Digitization (along with other technological advancements, such as nanotechnology, molecular manufacturing, robotics, and artificial intelligence), they argue, will continue to increase efficiencies in resourcing, production, transportation, and overall operations that will drive away costs in the future. Evidence is already available, they say, in decreasing costs of clothing, furniture, fast food, and of course, computer hardware. Basing their estimates on Moore's law, technological advancements will drive the cost of a laptop computer to $10, and within 20 years to only $1. Essentially, within 20 years, laptops could be free.

On the other side of the argument are those who believe nothing is ever entirely "free." The first version of anything, whether a laptop or digitized song, will always have a cost. They argue that ideas, materials, innovation, and time are all necessary to produce the first of anything, and that these are costs to creators. Since these inputs and resources can never be eliminated (or nothing would ever be produced) costs can never be fully eliminated. "Free" is a misnomer; only "at cost" is possible.

For now, the "free" versus "at cost" debate still rages; however, there is evidence that the transition to "free" as business model is already being made, and made successfully. Companies such as Google, eBay, Amazon, and Craigslist are all making money from "free." Alternatively, the Recording Industry of Association of America (RIAA), a trade group that supposedly represents the recording industry in the United States, is the poster child for refusing to make the transition and rabidly fighting to hang onto the current scarcity-inducing business model. The RIAA is losing, however: losing members, losing potential revenue, losing credibility, and losing prestige.

Some organizations are blending the "free" post-scarcity and current scarcity-controlling business models. During a time of transition, such as the one businesses are currently in, this intermediary phase is typical. Some organizations are developing business models based upon the "one percent rule," in which 1% of the users pay for the product but the majority use it for free. An example would be online gaming, where 1% of the users pay for a premium version, while the majority plays the basic version for free. The cost associated with developing and offering the game is picked up by the premium players.

Another intermediary model is the three-party system. In this model, a third party pays to participate in an exchange that is created by two other parties. An example would be paid advertising on a free e-mail site. The advertiser would pay to have targeted access to the e-mail participants, but use of the site would be free to the initial parties.

The answer to making money in the "free" post-scarcity world for businesses is to adapt, and to do so quickly, whether employing an entirely "free" or a blended business model.

We currently live in a world of both scarcity and post-scarcity. It is a confusing and somewhat counterintuitive mix of old and new philosophies, assumptions, business models, and economics. But there is evidence that the transition to a post-scarcity world is moving forward. As we continue to move forward, businesses will have to undergo dramatic changes in their business models to survive and thrive in the future. As Chris Anderson, author of the upcoming book *Free: The Future of a Radical Price,* says, "The new business model is one where companies grow rich by charging their customers nothing at all." Confusing? Yes. Impossible? No.

In many respects, one could argue that the post-scarcity company is merely a reflection of the society it serves, and we turn next to that.

Post-Scarcity Society

What impacts might the age of scarcity have on society, and what might living in 2075, the post-scarcity world, involve? In imagining the long-term future, it is helpful to consider aspects of present-day society and imagine what is likely to continue and where discontinuities or shifts might occur as we pass through the age of scarcity.

Population will be one of the variables likely to impact both the duration and the eventual exit from the age of scarcity. At current projections, global population will most likely peak at 9 billion in 2050. As resources are strained, this will impact both the continued population growth and also the manner in which the population lives and works. The global population has been growing exponentially for some time, and we could reasonably expect this to continue. However, several forces may disrupt current growth projections.

Historically, there have been periods when large numbers of the global population have been reduced due to war, disease, famine, or natural disasters. In the next 75 years, such an episode is likely to occur.

The world has several military hot spots, and weapons able to eliminate large portions of the population are more prevalent than in the past. Rogue states or non-state actors such as terrorist organizations may develop these capabilities over the coming decades. Resource shortages may lead to heightened tensions, isolationism by countries, and increasing incidents of violence. In order to reduce the possibility of such incidents, we may see the rise of supranational governance and regulation and continued efforts to resolve conflicts through diplomacy and negotiation.

The outbreak of disease is also a threat. A global pandemic, which, due to global travel, may spread more rapidly than any outbreak in history, could eliminate large numbers of the population. How widespread, and how great the population loss, will be dependent on the ability to curtail the global outbreak and find a cure or vaccination quickly. Inequities in access to health care mean pre-modern nations are likely to sustain a greater proportion of population loss than more-developed nations.

Famine has the greater impact in pre-modern nations. Post-modern nations may be able to rely on their supranational relationships to assist them through the tough times. Modern nations may have better resources to manage or avoid food scarcity, but pre-modern nations are heavily dependent on aid from other nations. If globalization and access to finance becomes more difficult, coupled with resource shortages within their own countries, aid may decrease to the pre-modern nations, which will increase the duration and severity of famines.

Weather patterns are cyclical. As well, there is a growing body of evidence in the early decades of the century indicating global warming. The severity and occurrence of natural disasters is increasing. If this continues, we are likely to have larger numbers of people displaced, and the death toll is likely to increase.

In the early decades of the century, birthrates are much higher in modern and pre-modern countries. Economic development—especially in terms of the advancement of women through access to education, to micro-finance, and to birth control—contributes to reductions in birthrates in pre-modern countries. If pre-modern countries can successfully advance economically, this is likely to contribute to reduced population growth.

Population will also impact where and how we live. People have lived in some type of dwelling for most of time, usually with family members. People will continue to live together in dwellings, but what will be the location, form, and ownership of those dwellings? The percentage of the global population living in urban areas is expected to increase from 48% in 2003 to 61% by 2030. The UN estimates that most of these urban dwellers will be in developing countries, living in cities in low-lying coastal areas at high risk from flooding due to global warming, making them vulnerable to natural disasters.

As resources become scarce, housing prices are likely to rise, making home ownership less affordable; this may impact living arrangements, meaning more people living together in smaller spaces. This in turn could lead to increased crime rates for theft and violence. This may give rise to the countertrend of a return to villages. Villages afford more space and the ability to attain greater self-sufficiency for essentials like food, water, and power.

Individual home ownership is common in many countries. Apartments or condominiums are also often individually owned, or sometimes the whole building is owned by a corporation. As global finance and credit markets become tighter, and resource shortages drive up the cost of housing, we may see more people leasing for longer periods of time and more housing owned by larger corporation and retirement funds. Rents are also likely to increase, so more people will likely share a household, thus reversing the growing trend of one- to two-person households.

The materials we use to build and the sources of energy we use to heat and power our homes will likely change. Material shortages may drive innovation in recycled building materials and longer-lasting materials. Wind and solar may become more common sources of power. Rooftop, hydroponic, and vertical gardening could enable residential space to be used for food production, as a shortage of soil and arable land make it harder to feed the world's growing population.

It is difficult to conceive of a society without some form of individual ownership. A world in which all goods, services, and accommodation are provided by the government or by corporations seems unlikely. However, it is possible to conceive of one in which what individuals own, and how goods are consumed, changes due to both the availability of resources and also the materials used.

Cradle-to-cradle manufacturing, a closed-cycle manufacturing process where nothing is wasted, may become more commonplace. Planned obsolescence in manufactured goods may become a thing of the past. Leasing of goods, where the manufacturer is responsible for repair and/or replacement and recycling of the item, may become more common. Innovation efforts are likely to focus on these types of efforts as resource availability begins to peak, yet demand continues to increase.

While many fantasize about reduced workweeks and more leisure time, for the foreseeable future people will continue to work outside the home to earn an income. Where changes may occur is in the nature and quantity of the work.

Statistics indicate that, as many countries develop economically, working hours increase. Resource shortages may mean this will eventually begin to show more balance. As the focus turns to efficiency and resource reuse, people are likely to buy less, which means less is produced, although it may be at a higher cost.

Population growth means more adults available to work. This may lead to the elimination of child labor. Access to education for women as well as children may also assist in reducing the number of children working outside the home.

Advances in health care and improvements in life span and the quality of life may assist people to remain in the workforce longer; this will be especially beneficial for post-modern countries, where the birthrate typically declines as the country advances economically.

Greater numbers of people may enter or remain in the workforce. Reduced working hours may be mandated, in order to create more jobs. More people might work part time. Greater self-reliance may mean more need for time outside of work to spend growing food and tending to other essential activities. The time and activities performed at work are likely to change.

Leisure activities are also likely to shift, with more physical activities being more local and distance interactions done virtually through the use of technology. The cost and resources available to enable global leisure travel are likely to experience shortages in the age of scarcity. By 2075, perhaps new technologies to enable low-cost, low-impact travel may be developed. The desire to do so, however, is more a question of geopolitics, an issue to which we shall now turn.

Post-Scarcity Geopolitics

The most-plausible scenario of the development of a post-scarcity society would be driven by advances in nanotechnology or other extensions of materials sciences. So, based on the current infrastructure, the breakthrough developments would most likely take place in Western Europe, the United States, Japan, or South Korea, although China or India, or even one of the oil-wealthy Gulf nations, cannot entirely be ruled out. It would be tempting to follow all these possible scenarios, but for the scope of this paper, we will focus on the assumption that the post-scarcity future begins in the developed, Westernized world.

By the time we build a post-scarcity capacity enough to build a post-scarcity economy, there will still be widespread poverty in many nations, particularly those that were still developing at the time of "peak everything" and many that reverted to developing-nation status under the hardships of climate change, scarcity of potable water, wars, and environmental degradation. Whether led by a spirit of philanthropy, capitalism, or enlightened self-interest, it seems likely that the originating nations would ensure that other nations would receive at least some of the benefits fairly soon.

Much geopolitical conflict derives from scarcity or perceived scarcity of land, water, energy sources, mineral wealth, or other physical objects, ones which would be greatly alleviated by a post-scarcity economy. Eliminating or reducing these causes for conflict would be a great step toward international peace. However, it would not create total peace, largely because the capacity to mount deadly attacks would increase at the same time that some reasons for conflict will remain or might even worsen.

Some scholars posit that all historical conflict has been driven by competition over resources, and that even wars ostensibly over ideologies were truly about scarcity. Political or ideological dominance were ways to an end, rather than the end itself. Certainly for many wars, such as the Crusades and World War II, their arguments are at least plausible. However, conflicts that might have started over scarcity may still capture hearts, minds, and resources by the enticing trappings of politics, religion, or even simply historical grudges. If, as other scholars believe, humans are inherently a warlike species, a post-scarcity economy will enhance leaders' ability to create war over causes that might have seemed trivial during a time when there was scarcity to worry about.

The status of the natural world is another area that could create conflict. Many arguments for environmental protection are based on the direct and indirect human benefit of natural land and species conservation. The world's forests act to sequester carbon, clean the air, regulate the temperature, and house animals and plants of current or potential benefit to humankind. In a post-scarcity society where technology can replace all of those functions, there could well be conflict over the appropriate use of whatever wild areas are left between those who see such areas as having intrinsic value, or possible future extrinsic value, and those who wish to use such land for other purposes.

So far, we have just looked at the questions in terms of today's nations and assumed that today's nation-states are more or less intact by the time of the post-scarcity society. However, the post-scarcity society may well make both today's states and the idea of a nation-state obsolete. On the other hand, the twentieth- and twenty-first-century creation of international groups and agencies from mutual interests rather than shared borders could replace today's states in a different way.

For example, the European Union formed, as an economic union, the European Economic Community, which itself arose from the European Coal and Steel Community. It has broadened its objectives beyond the purely economic or closely related (e.g., free movement of labor) to include social justice (e.g., its powers to legislate against discrimination), environmental policy, foreign policy, and security issues. If it were to change its charter to be one of shared values and common history, such an organization might not only include Turkey, thus adding part of Asia to its scope, but also traditional allies such as the United States. It might even transcend geography and history to become an alliance of democracies, bringing all of North America and large parts of South America, Asia, Africa, and even parts of the Middle East. Of course, the shadows of colonialism may create too great a barrier for some time, and continental alliances, rather than intercontinental, may come first.

Some alliances would be unlikely to continue. OPEC, based on commodity production, would likely disappear. The existing Non-Aligned Movement, originally formed as a response to NATO and the Warsaw Pact nations, has struggled to define itself and its purpose since the collapse of the Cold War, and even now, its membership has little in common. One remaining unifying theme has been fair and sustainable development, but in a mature post-scarcity world, development would be moot for virtually all nations.

On the other hand, a post-scarcity society in which the means of living could be created at a micro level, or even at a household level, could make it possible for small, self-selected communities to exist either as parts of a nation-state but largely independent or as entirely autonomous of a nation-state, even as their own nation-state.

History suggests that most of these would be beneficial to their members and at worst harmless to others, but also gives us darker warnings of cults and militant groups that attacked other groups or destroyed themselves and took innocents with them. The ability of these organizations to operate with all the capacities of an autonomous nation in a post-scarcity society is a sobering thought. On the other hand, if the pursuit of these groups is control over themselves and their members and no control from an outside world, or if they can at least settle for this, we might find that post-scarcity geopolitics are in fact the road to a lasting peace.

Ultimately, the geopolitics of a post-scarcity world depends upon the interactions of humans and groups. While human nature is a constant, human ethics are not, and most of the world's history, viewed over a long time span, is what most of us would consider the growth of human ethics. For example, things considered tolerable by the majority of society, such as slavery and indiscriminate slaughter during war, are now mostly condemned, at least in principle if not always in practice, and are greatly reduced. Perhaps this is what has enabled us to survive so far—that, while our technical capacities always run ahead of our ethical development, our ethics do keep up just enough.

In order for a post-scarcity society to develop in such a way that it adds to net human freedom, justice, and well-being, we need more than ever to reinforce the principles of equality, generosity, tolerance, compassion, and mutual interdependence in what we teach and in what we model before those who will build the post-scarcity world. These values (or their lack) will shape whether the post-scarcity world fulfills its promise or creates the seeds of the destruction of civilization. Nowhere will this be felt greater than in the post-scarcity financial system.

THE POST-SCARCITY FINANCIAL SYSTEM

A useful starting point to consider long-range futures is to examine what the future has in common with the present. Although we anticipate a future that is radically different from the present, in many ways that future will share a set of fundamentally common circumstances with the present. The present turbulence in the financial system may lead us to conclude that the long future will be very different from the present, but that may not be so. The global economy works in cycles. Just as the age of scarcity might be characterized by restricted credit conditions and a lessening of the pace of globalization, so the post-scarcity world might be characterized by loosening credit and an acceleration in the pace of globalization.

It is difficult to conceive of a barter economy. While the age of scarcity might induce greater self-sufficiency, even in the medieval era, when self-sufficiency was highly prevalent, a degree of monetization and trade within the economy was also present. It is not unreasonable for us to conclude that the post-scarcity economy will not be one of barter. This being so, the key functions of money—a unit of account, a medium of exchange, a store of wealth, a standard for deferred payment—will continue. If so, the role of finance does seem to be secure for the long future.

Of course, if money continues to exist, then there will have to be an issuer of money—an institution that will guarantee the promissory element of the currency and that will act as the lender of last resort to the financial system. In other words, there needs to be a central bank. The issue of currency is generally linked to sovereignty and government. Here, the future is less certain on two counts.

First, there is the question of where the locus of sovereignty might lie in a post-scarcity world. It is not unreasonable to expect that the post-modern states will continue to develop over the course of the twenty-first century. These supranational entities, such as the EU, are likely to have developed a more mature financial system and will have sufficient authority to be able to issue their own currency, such as the euro. We could also expect the category of modern states, those that we now call nation-states, to still be in existence. In this case, we should continue to see national currencies. Last, there is also the case of the pre-modern state.

Zimbabwe currently provides an example of a pre-modern state, one that has failed almost completely to act as a nation-state and that has degenerated into a basic form of monetized economy. It is hard to gauge whether there are likely to be a greater or lesser number of pre-modern states in the post-scarcity world; however, we can reasonably expect that there will be some present. In these situations, the currency is exactly whatever the local economic entities will accept as currency.

There is a current debate over the degree to which digital cash will replace physical cash. Currently, in some economies, such as Japan or South Korea, physical cash has been virtually eliminated. In some economies—particularly those in the Middle East—large volumes of business transactions are still conducted in physical cash. In many respects this reflects the degree to which the local banking system has been digitized. There is no reason why this situation will not continue into the future. Digital cash is very convenient, but it leaves an audit trail that many do not wish others to follow. We could reasonably expect both physical cash and digital cash to be present in the post-scarcity financial system, but in possibly different degrees than at present.

The post-scarcity financial system is likely to reflect a mixture of supranational and national currencies, along with a number of areas where almost anything goes in terms of currency. The demand for physical cash is likely to continue—particularly in the pre-modern states, where it may act as a parallel currency to the worthless local currency.

This leads on to the second area of uncertainty, the institutional arrangements that surround the management of the currency.

We can expect the continued operation of central banks, but the interface between the general population and the central bank, generally speaking, is quite minimal. At present, there are a raft of institutions that, under the supervision of the central bank, manage the interface between the monetary authorities and the general population.

The key institutions are the banks and the banking system, and they play an important role in the economy. The role of the bank is to act as a mediator between savers and borrowers, either in cash terms (overdraft finance, mortgage lending, corporate loans, etc.) or through financial instruments in the securities markets (stocks, shares, bonds, etc.).

There is some debate about the extent to which these institutions are likely to be corporeal or digital. At present, we have a mixture of the two. On the one hand, the digitization of the financial system has allowed it to become far more efficient and to extend its reach farther and faster than it had previously. On the other hand, the financial system is based on trust and confidence, which is created through interpersonal relationships in the corporeal world. It is not unreasonable to expect this mixed approach to continue into the post-scarcity world, although exactly where the balance between the two will lie is a matter of conjecture.

As long as we do not spend everything that we earn, and as long as some show a preference for money in the present as opposed to money in the future, there will be this saving and lending dimension to the financial system, irrespective of whether it is conducted face-to-face or online. The institutions could well be different from today's. For example, supermarkets currently act as banks to their customers; mobile-phone companies operate a digital banking facility for their customers. Are these the banking institutions of the future? It doesn't really matter what form the banks take, as long as they fulfill the functions of a banking institution.

In the scarcity economy, financial institutions are likely to be quite regulated. We are likely to see greater supervision of the banks as institutions, even to the point of public ownership of the retail banks. The involvement of the state is likely to be extensive. The post-scarcity financial system is likely to react against this. It is reasonable to expect to see a period of deregulation and privatization as we move from the scarcity economy to the post-scarcity world. Lending is likely to become more liberal. As credit eases, economic growth will accelerate, international trade will increase, and speculation in the financial markets will increase. Eventually, the bubble will burst, but that is a tale for the phase beyond the post-scarcity world as the cycle continues.

CONCLUSION

As we write, the world is now entering into a transition phase from a period of abundance to a period of scarcity. Our concern in this piece has been to view how the world might be shaped when it emerges from that period of scarcity and into the following period of post-scarcity.

We have seen that corporate life is likely to be quite different from the present. The resumption of the process of globalization—in abeyance during the age of scarcity—is likely to see the acceleration of the process whereby the economy is digitized. Such digitization could lead to vast economies of scale on a global level. It could even assist economics—ever the dismal science of the allocation of scarce resources—to be turned on its head.

Of course, post-scarcity companies are a reflection of post-scarcity society. In many ways, the post-scarcity society will be characterized by the resumption of trends that have been evident for some time, but that are now likely to be interrupted by the age of scarcity. The development of a global middle class and concerns about the work/life balance could well be the dominant features toward the end of this century.

As companies and society become more global in their approach, this trend is likely to result in a growing internationalism in the field of geopolitics. The age of scarcity is likely to fuel a new nationalism as nations seek to hoard and protect their resources. As we move away from this scarcity mentality, we are likely to see a greater willingness to act cooperatively in the international field.

Nowhere will this willingness be seen greater than in the field of the international financial system. The age of scarcity may place the institutions of international finance under great strain. As we move into the post-scarcity world, we can expect a greater degree of international monetary cooperation and coordination. Of course, the liberalization of the financial system will contain the seeds of its own destruction, and so the cycle will twist around again.

It is difficult, as we write, to remember that the sun rises as well as sets. Our present focus is dominated by financial crises and economic recessions, which could well give way to political turbulence and great change in the world. As futurists, we feel that we need to point out to the more general public that this is a natural undulation and that beyond the coming age of scarcity lies a post-scarcity world, where a better future lies. It is up to us to embrace that future and to work toward it coming sooner rather than later.

Part 5

Futuring and the Moral Imperative

The Next Generation of Forecasters

The Future Futurists

Irving H. Buchen

It has never been easy being a futurist—persuading CEOs, presidents, companies, and workers that real and reliable data exists about what is likely to happen, when, and what its impacts may be, and doing so without claiming total certainty about how such trends can guide future decisions. When it also involves telling the emperor he has no clothes, that makes it an even harder sell. Indeed, often when futurists meet at conferences, they exchange not just ideas but martyrdoms—you show me your stigmata and I will show you mine.

But just when futurists have become accustomed to accepting the recurrent historical challenge of being messengers of disconnect (and, accordingly, sometimes shot), they are increasingly being informed that they in turn need to change—that they are part of a first generation of futurists, and that what is being called for is a second generation of forecasters. To ask the doctor to heal himself is as difficult as to graciously step aside. But what invests this inquiry about passing the baton with particular importance is its potential for wider insight and even paradigm shifts. Somehow, the study of the future has deep and interconnected roots—so much so that, when the

Irving H. Buchen is on the doctoral business faculty of Capella University and teaches in the MBA online program of IMPAC University. E-mail ibuchen@msn.com.

parameters of futurism are altered, it generally signals wider rever-
berations across the board. In other words, presumption rules. As we
identify some of the new factors that now seem to be characteristic of
a second generation of futurists, we should be aware that we may also
be describing a second generation of companies, universities, and even
countries.

It is probably not accidental that so many of our seminal futurists are now older and serve as senior statesmen. Forecasters like
Joseph Coates, Edward Cornish, Arnold Brown, Clement Bezold, and
many others in the United States and around the world epitomize a
generation of independent, often feisty originals, who in many ways
established and bequeathed the standards of the profession that are
still operative today. But no matter how many associates they would
call upon to join or amplify them, they all were singular geniuses—
opinionated lone rangers always telling it as it is, always worth listening to and learning from. What extended the range of their singularity was their extensive and broad-based set of clients who sought
multiple applications and solutions. In other words, who they were as
futurists was shaped and extended by who they served. One steady-
ing and consistent characteristic was the absolute transferability of
their evolving methodologies.

The second generation of futurists, of course, stands on the broad
shoulders of such giants in many respects. The most obvious mantle
they have to adopt and adapt is that of being multi-perspectival. Now,
however, that modality is trickier, hidden, even ubiquitous—not so
much chosen as compelled by the incredibly complex interconnectivity of globality as a new norm of forecasting. What we find now is that
every local or regional client is global; every U.S. employee has an international counterpart working beside him; boutiques in the aggregate equal a major competitor. The principal issue that emerges for
this second generation of futurists is how to understand and manage
the unprecedented simultaneity of global diversity. Being multidisciplinary may not be enough. We need to be interdisciplinary.

But how is that to be accomplished? Minimally there are at least three ways of fusing globality and interdisciplinarity: the short term of restructuring what we do now; an intermediate mid-term of re-framing direction; and last the long term of developing systems of systems. Although the time table and content of all three developments could be hastened if the academy as a whole could shift its focus from specialization to interdisciplinary training, glaciers are unlikely to move rapidly or make such radical shifts. The training programs of some international businesses could do this if they made *unlearning* a staple of turnaround. In the meantime, we have to work with what we have, but do so as creatively and futuristically as we can.

The basic building block now and increasingly in the future is the team. Every time we create a task force that brings together a number of different disciplines, we are simulating a range of perspectives that exceeds that of the individual members of the team. In such a case it would not be an exaggeration to claim that the whole is greater than its parts. (Of course, we don't know what we would say if all the participants were already multidisciplinary.) But to fully engage and simulate global complexity, the problem-solving capacity of such teams in turn requires at least three kinds of futuristic restructuring. The first involves becoming more holistic; the second requires occupying intersections and being focused on innovation; the third invites the dazzling prospect of global systemics.

THE HOLISTIC

A new car battery was being developed for an all-electric car. To test it, a team of engineers was assembled, each one representing a different car function. Each acted autonomously, with expertise in ignition, spark plugs, lights, air-conditioning, radio, etc. When the total specs determined by each function were loaded in and became operational, the battery failed—the demand was greater than the supply. The typical solution would have been to berate the experts on their excesses and then, by trial and error, ask them to make the necessary adjustments. Instead, all of them were asked to play the role of the battery and apportion what was needed without draining the battery dry. With each one becoming the custodian of the battery's integrity, balanced output was achieved. Collective needs replaced competitive and separate demands, and holistic group problem solving produced a win-win outcome.

In this case study, ultimate success was predicated on identifying the major core—as it were, its ultimate global extent—and then fusing all outputs and inputs until they became one, or versions of each other. Thinking and acting collectively and holistically in turn requires future futurists increasingly to move from the circumference to the center and to find and fix the micro in the macro. In short, positioning is everything.

THE INNOVATIVE INTERSECTION

Frans Johansson makes a critical distinction in *The Medici Effect* (2006) between directional and intersectional ideas. Directional ideas are known, generally predictable, and incremental. They are all the new improvements—of all things, all operating systems, all operations, all communications. Every company does it 24/7. Everyone seeks to build a better mousetrap, eliminate expensive steps on the production line, reduce the weight of an airplane, etc. Such adjustments and tweaking go on all the time and find expression in cost reduction and higher levels of productivity and profitability. Even mathematics is unidirectional: A five-stage proof rendered in four is dubbed an "elegant" proof. The entire effort is driven by the impossible dream of perfection and the constant and incremental pursuit of that ideal—until someday a perfect mousetrap will be built.

Then one day someone discovers a way to eliminate mice altogether without having to use a mousetrap at all. The standard way is bypassed. Suddenly, a solution seemingly comes out of left field, only now it is not called new but innovative, or, in Johansson's terms, an *intersectional idea.* Such ideas are different, perhaps even unique, in at least three ways: direction, knowledge range, and outputs.

Unlike directional ideas, which obediently can go only in the one direction—that of improvement—intersectional ideas occupy a central position at a crossroads and thus can go unpredictably in as many directions as there are points on a compass. They even can pursue many directions at the same time. Intersectional ideas are thus like the future itself—an unpredictable and unfinished cornucopia of possibilities. Similarly, an intersection by its definition is not so much a given body of knowledge as a range of knowledge existing at the points where various disciplines meet or can be persuaded to talk, to converge, to problem solve. The intersection is thus a movable feast: It is not known in advance, but evolves; it is not a fixed point, but in fact is created by the dialogue of interdisciplinarity. Above all, it is temporary or tentative in that it serves as scaffolding to support the prospect of new relationships and conversations. Finally, it generates unique outputs that include opening up entirely new fields of study and production; developing supporters, followers, and advocates; creating not just ways of doing business, but new businesses altogether; and changing the world. Perhaps then, not surprisingly, every intersection is a rehearsal for the future, because every innovation creates the future.

SYSTEM OF SYSTEMS

The new generation of futurists have to become advocates for meeting the challenge of the twenty-first century: building composite models of all systems on the order and magnitude of the Human Genome Project. It would be an interactive system involving all factors and drivers: human and animal demographics, socioeconomic, geophysical, ecological forces—in short, everything. These composite models also would have to incorporate or serve as an overlay for a number of new evolving partnerships and multidirectional choices.

The most obvious example is the rediscovered relationship, the coexistence, of the human and the natural worlds—the aspiring dynamics of Maslow contending with environmental conservation. To those primal forces would be added the heady complication of human transformation or amplification, as the symbiosis of artificial intelligence and its clever mechanics and electronics takes hold. A new addition or corrective of *simplexity* may have to become part of the equation, as Arnold Brown argued recently. Future solutions may have to be more inspired by biological functionality than mechanical perfection. Simple and inexpensive solutions like peanut butter-based food for starving babies, a hole in the ground to improve sanitation, and jets that don't go any faster but operate more efficiently may help save the day and the future.

Although other dimensions surely could be added, the key question is, Can such a system of systems be compiled? And if so, what would it do for us? Both issues were partly, imperfectly, answered a number of years ago in the construction of a global model by Meadows and Forrester and described in their book *The Limits to Growth*. Of course, the model was seriously (but instructively) flawed, especially the failure to appreciate the mischief of certain variables that inconsiderately leaked on other variables. But that flaw can be fixed in future versions.

There were reverberating values to this pioneering effort. One was unexpected and therefore critical: Many people misread the title and took the limits to growth to mean the end of growth—so powerful and fearful is the prospect of developmental promise that clearly it has to be factored into any new global model of models. But flawed and misinterpreted though the book was, its authors came up with a final conclusion that perhaps redeemed the entire venture: namely, that there is no human goal that requires more people to achieve it. Of course that statement also added to the firestorm, but perhaps that should be the measure of their—and our—project: that it disturbed the world.

Hopefully, our future futurists, in the process of repositioning and occupying the center, existing at the multiple edges of the intersection, and finally building the system of systems similarly will bring us the gifts of greater clarity and hope as the legacy of a new generation.

The Future of Holocaust Memorialization

Altruism in Extremes

Arthur B. Shostak

As a preteen in the early 1950s, I began a lifelong practice of seeking out autobiographies of survivors and novels that could help me understand what had happened in an abattoir almost beyond belief. Unimaginable atrocities shook me to my roots, but I dwelled instead on rare accounts, such as the Warsaw Ghetto uprising, of efforts made to stay human under conditions in extremes. Likewise, years later, on my second visit to the U.S. Holocaust Museum, I found myself drawn more to a temporary exhibit in the lobby ("Deadly Medicine: Creating the Master Race") than to permanent museum material (such as the Tower of Photos, the empty railroad car, the audiovisuals desks, etc.). It emphasized ways to help improve medical ethics, while also noting horrendous related Nazi crimes. A judicious balance of reform ideas along with a scathing condemnation of unforgivable acts, the exhibit gave me hope that progress might soon be made in this medical matter.

In the summers of 2005 and 2006, my lifelong interest led me and my wife, Lynn Seng, to visit five European concentration camps: Auschwitz-Birkenau, Dachau, Mauthausen, Plaszow, and Theresien-

Arthur B. Shostak is an emeritus professor of sociology, Drexel University. E-mail Shostaka@drexel.edu.

stadt, the "model" Nazi concentration camp to which we went twice. Over the years we have also gone to several new and old Holocaust museums in the United States and abroad, to the new Holocaust History Museum at Yad Vashem (which I have visited seven times since 1971), and to numerous war memorials in nearly a dozen European countries.

I was left troubled by something I found overrepresented. This crystallized when, during a two-week east European tour in the summer of 2006, we became increasingly uneasy with the narrative shared by an American-born senior professor of Holocaust studies. As the tour prepared to visit the Warsaw Ghetto, Schindler's factory, the Holocaust Memorial in Budapest, and two concentration camps, the professor filled lecture after lecture with graphic stories of Nazi brutality and horror. No examples, however, were ever shared of victims trying to care for one another.

Nowadays, when I remember a Holocaust museum or concentration camp exhibit hall, I recall five educational themes of very different weight: Sixty percent or so of the material graphically documents unspeakable, gruesome atrocities (executions, murder, torture, etc.). We gasp, recoil, and even avert our eyes. Fifteen percent or so explores slightly less horrific material, such as vandalized shops, schools, or synagogues. About 10% explores the post-liberation lives of survivors (reunited families, newborn children, etc.), and about another 10% looks back on a pre-Holocaust bucolic scene of (false) security. Perhaps 5% allows for the possibility that some of the victims may have struggled to keep in touch with their humanity. The possibility that the necessity for human connection could have led to the covert creation of networks of mutual support gets short shrift, if it gets any attention at all.

Rachel Korazim, director of education at Yad Vashem, the Israeli Holocaust memorial museum, puts the matter quite well: "We've managed to place images like barbed wire and crematoria as central Jewish images. This is not Jewish history, this is Nazi history" (Silverman 2008, 8). Is the current preoccupation with evil the only, or even the best, approach, given the challenge we have to help keep the narrative consequential? Is a memorialization strong in evil-focused motifs still the wisest course? Might a new balance favor greater appreciation of the narrative?

Testimony to our will to stay human is available from Terezin, a "model" concentration camp that was actually a transport center to the death camps. Doomed teenagers there nevertheless created a literary magazine despite knowing any day they might see their registration number posted for transport east to the gas chambers. Their essays dealt with a wide range of subjects, except for the immediate plight of both writers and readers. Emphasis was put instead on matters that might help lift the spirit, rather than bruise it all the more. Likewise, adult prisoners created a remarkable "university." Over three years, the "school" had 520 lecturers (of whom only 173 survived) and offered more than 2,400 courses for hundreds of starving ghetto dwellers who might be transported at any time to their death (Makarova et al. 2004, 13). My gentile guide at Terezin had a friend who had been there. "She tells me she got up at 5 a.m. to attend lectures," my guide said. "They were very secret and were held all over the village. She thinks the Gestapo knew and didn't care [as all were under death sentence anyway], though all such activities were forbidden, and people could be hurt at any time."

Emanuel Hermann, an adult student (who did not survive), wrote: "Cultural life in the ghetto was the only phenomenon that transformed us back into human beings. If after a hard day I could listen to Bach, I at once became human" (Makarova et al., 15). Yehuda Bauer, an Israeli emeritus professor of Holocaust studies, notes that, "even in these [horrific] conditions, literature, music, theater, and art flourished. And, still today, the musical pieces, poetry, and plays made at Terezin continue to be heard around the world. ... We must not only remember them, which is a cheap and superficial cliché—we must learn from them" (Makarova et al., 9).

Felix Posen, a philanthropist who sponsored a book-length account of the "university over the abyss," thinks it "beyond comprehension and language to explain how, in the face of starvation, disease, and death there continued to be the desire to lecture on the great issues of mankind; create art, literature, philosophy, music, and other gems for the benefit of those still barely alive and those who might possibly survive their living hell ... [This] is a proud, perhaps unique legacy ... [one] which will continue to live long after mankind will barely remember hundreds of years from now at what terrible cost it was created" (Makarova et al., 4).

Remarkable movies of actual camp experiences also help illuminate what *good* can mean in the face of *evil* (Insdorf 2003). A film version of Imre Kertész's semiautobiographical novel, *Fateless*, has a young camp-savvy prisoner selflessly choose to mentor a 14-year-old newcomer in lifesaving skills. The boy and other nonobservant Jews later look on admiringly from their bunker beds as four old men risk all by clandestinely marking the Sabbath. Likewise, characters in Steven Spielberg's film, *Schindler's List* (especially Itzhak Stern, the accountant), risk their lives to help keep 1,100 other prisoners alive. (Romano 2006).

Especially revealing is a 2003 Showtime cable TV film, *Out of the Ashes*, the true story of Dr. Giselle Perl, a Jewish doctor forced in Auschwitz to work for Dr. Josef Mengele. She helped infirmary patients recover, even knowing they might be killed later that same day. Risking her own life, she secretly moved about the camp at night to perform abortions on about 1,000 otherwise-doomed prisoners (pregnancy was against Nazi rules), and, in some few cases, smother their newborns—an act of mutual aid *en extremis*. The film's depiction of her efforts to stay human remains with a viewer long after it has ended, for as Dr. Perl explains to confounded American immigration authorities weighing her admission in 1946 to the United States, "Auschwitz was another country."

The maintenance of moral values, the matter of dignity and humanity, the possibility of an uplifting journey—these are the sort of topics whose neglect have left me troubled. These are what seemed undervalued and underrepresented. I agree here with Harvard professor Ruth Wisse, who fled Europe as a child in the late 1930s. She doubts the soundness of building an identity alone or even primarily on victimization: "A community otherwise so ignorant of its sources that it becomes preoccupied with death and destruction is in danger of substituting a cult of martyrdom for the Torah's insistence on life" (Freedman 2000, 344).

I learned more about all of this from a recent writing project I never expected to have as part of my life. In 2005 I was fortunate enough to make the acquaintance near my Narberth, Pennsylvania, home of an elderly Eastern European survivor, Henry Skorr. Over the next several months I tape-recorded 60 hours of his life history in Kalisz, Poland, and later, in Siberia. (During that time the Spielberg camera crew filmed two sessions with him.) With help from Ivan Sokolov, a graduate student who recorded and transcribed far more hours than I, and Ann Weiss, another Holocaust writer, we saw the project through to its 2006 publication as a remarkable 384-page autobiography, *Through Blood and Tears: Surviving Hitler and Stalin* (Skorr 2006).

Quick to deny singularity, Skorr insists that each person in his book, only some of whom "bested the evil that attempted to destroy us, endured equally as horrific, sensational, and sometimes uplifting journeys" (Skorr 2006, 384). A total stranger, for example, hid him under her large skirt when German soldiers suddenly searched a train station in which they sat. Later, this older Jewish woman shared what little food and money she had to help him make his escape, explaining with a smile he needed it more than she did. A Jewish blacksmith took his little brother under his protection when they were all captives, and, defying a German officer, saved the boy's life when Skorr could not do so. Over and again, Skorr details uplifting situations of mutual aid given at peril of life.

On November 9, 1939, for example, at considerable risk, Skorr's father, a popular kosher butcher, hastily rushed a gang of local Jewish gangsters to a small town bordering on Germany. There, under his leadership, they rescued German Jews who had arrived earlier that day fleeing from the *Kristallnacht* pogrom, only to find themselves then seriously threatened by Nazi-allied Polish townspeople. Skorr's mother, in turn, regularly sheltered and fed dazed and distraught Jewish refugees, although her own large family had less and less. Many of their besieged neighbors (though by no means all) warned one another about surprise Nazi sweeps of households, and in other high-risk ways desperately sought to remain neighborly.

Skorr himself, after barely escaping a Nazi death squad, made his way in shock and despair to precarious safety in Russia—only to almost immediately turn around and, to the astonishment of all he encountered, retrace his steps back home. Once there, he took charge at age 17, gathered family and neighbors together, and led them from Poland to (relative) safety in the harsh lumber camps of Soviet Russia. His story, as assessed by his publisher, Holocaust historian Sir Martin Gilbert, is not only about "courage and survival, but also of the maintenance of moral values in the face of Nazism's perverse determination to humiliate and degrade the Jews and force them to lose all dignity and humanity."

It is time the dark and complex puzzle we know as the Holocaust included aspects undervalued in present-day telling, aspects of a narrative that would highlight deeds worth emulation. We need to pay attention to what enabled besieged men and women, like Henry Skorr, Primo Levi, Elie Wiesel, and others to maintain their moral values, dignity, and humanity. What combination of hope, integrity, morality, and strength enabled some to survive long after others had given up? What enabled some to trump their circumstance and defy a destructive script written for them by their Nazi captors?

An effort to establish a new balance of good and evil in recounting the Holocaust story will have opposition. For one thing, many concerned parties insist on staying focused on atrocities, the better to keep the flame of outrage burning. They identify the Holocaust exclusively with unmentionable horrors, and their preoccupation with abominations allows no room for any other consideration. Second, soupy homilies and airy platitudes might be advanced in place of confounding complexities. We must avoid characterizations of victims that are overly heroic. Finally, there are those who will always believe that the enormity of the Holocaust overshadows any effort we might attempt to reframe it. They contend that it should not be used instrumentally even if to promote the admirable cause of mutual care and concern.

This opposition notwithstanding, we should revise Holocaust educational and exhibit material. More attention should be paid to the efforts that victims made to hold onto their humanity despite the depravity inflicted upon them. Scattered, out-of-sight, and often hard-to-secure evidence of fundamental goodness merits fresh exploration, this time in a creative and nuanced way.

In the last analysis, strategies of memorialization are transitory and incomplete. As there is no "copyright" on ways the Holocaust will be remembered, we have room to reassess where we choose to place our emphasis. To date we have undervalued how some men and women who suffered hardship struggled to overcome adversity. It is time we experimented with a rebalancing of the entire narrative—a rebalancing that might uniquely help meet critical twenty-first-century spiritual needs of Jews and non-Jews alike.

In this way we can demonstrate anew our potential to help shape a finer future for ourselves and our progeny, a refutation of the Nazi insistence that only some (themselves) and not all of us have this awesome power and responsibility. Rebalancing the way we memorialize the Holocaust can help assure a history that honors its 13 million-plus victims (Jews and non-Jews alike), and a future that honors us all.

REFERENCES

Freedman, Samuel G. 2000. *Jew vs. Jew: The Struggle for the Soul of American Jewry.* New York: Touchstone.

Insdorf, Annette. 2003. *Indelible Shadows: Film and the Holocaust,* Third Edition. New York: Cambridge University Press.

Makarova, Elena, Sergei Makarov, and Victor Kuperman. 2004. *University Over The Abyss. The story behind 520 lecturers and 2,430 lectures in KZ Theresienstadt 1942-1944,* Second Edition. Jerusalem, Israel: Verba Publishers Ltd.

Romano, Carlin. 2006. "Is the Crematorium Half-Filled or Half Empty?" In *Chronicle of Higher Education,* September 22, B13.

Shostak, Arthur B. 2007. "Humanist Sociology and Holocaust Memorialization: On Accenting the Positive." In *Humanity & Society,* Vol. 31. February, 43-64.

Silverman, Rachel. 2006. "Steadfast Message to Educators: Best to Pinpoint Shoah's 'Key issues.'" In *Jewish Exponent,* November 30, 8.

Skorr, Henry. 2006. *Through Blood and Tears: Surviving Hitler and Stalin.* London: Valentine Mitchell.

Spielvogel, Jackson J. 1996. *Hitler and Nazi Germany: A History.* Upper Saddle River, New Jersey: Prentice-Hall.

Applying and Prioritizing Moral Values in the Creative Process

Some Important Threshold Issues

Michael Blinick

Developing original new insights and ideas and then manifesting them, regardless of the field involved, has been generally assumed to be good and desirable in itself.

But there is a major caveat to heed, with the understanding that there is no intent here to interfere with freedom of speech, nor with the ideal of the unfettered creative spirit: Will whatever is created be worthwhile and a source of goodness—without a significant risk that it will "boomerang" or "bite back"? Can it be perverted to bad ends? Is it, in any aspects, a new, "improved" way to do wrong or evil? Or will it generate tools or powers that need to be carefully restricted—or best not made available at all? In short, is a Pandora's box being opened?

We need to accept the "inconvenient truth" that not all the fruits of creativity will automatically accord with the highest values. Careful attention needs to be given to the *uses* to which what is created are being put—will it make for a better world, prevent harm, mitigate suf-

---

Michael Blinick is an attorney and consultant on issues relating to ethical and moral values and public policy. E-mail ImplementingValues@yahoo.com.

fering, bring joy? How could misuse or overreaching be prevented or interdicted? Would such needed counteraction be *totally* able to avoid any irreparable negative effects from the proposed innovation?

These are not idle questions; there are many instances where they need to be asked with the greatest urgency. While such concerns are frequently raised with regard to bioethical matters, and especially biotechnology research, they actually apply in many more mundane settings as well.

For example, even in thinking up delicious new recipes, many chefs are now giving thought to using the most health-enhancing ingredients, or at least listing equivalent amounts for more salutary alternatives as substitutes for less-healthy components of a dish. Yet, such a high consciousness is not universal. And while creativity is rightfully prized in writing cookbooks, it is rightfully despised when employed in the practice colloquially known as "cooking the books."

Unfortunately, we have all learned, long after the fact, that the latter practice and related misconduct was perpetrated on a gigantic scale in devising and instituting many extremely clever innovations in financing, investments, and securitization. While these seemed at first to be wildly successfully and profitable, it was actually the wildness of an untamed beast, or killer storm, that has now been let loose on the entire world. Somehow, the grave potential for serious problems was not seized upon and rightly used as a justification for stopping these activities before they could create injury.

To remedy these kinds of dangers, it would seem both possible and indeed necessary to develop guidelines for ethical and moral analysis applicable in evaluating new ideas and projects in any specific area, and in choosing which to pursue. Furthermore, it can be possible for such criteria to actually stimulate creativity and innovation, rather than in any way censoring or restricting them.

There is at least some theoretical justification for the latter hypothesis in the scientific literature on positive psychology, positive organizational scholarship, and related fields. The work of such researchers as Barry Schwartz of Swarthmore College has demonstrated that—perhaps counterintuitively—delineating a specific, relatively small range of choices, rather than a huge number of them, can be liberating and empowering for decision makers, instead of diminishing their freedom.

This observation is not meant to deny the utility and worth of customized individual adjustments of parameters and details in specific cases, made possible by software programs used, for example, in mass customization of: (a) clothing (with regard to size, style, detailing, color, etc.), (b) nutritional supplements (as to nature and amounts of ingredients in the light of each customer's physiological needs), and (c) programs for optimizing mortgage, credit card, and other debt repayment (so as to minimize the time needed and the amounts of interest due). But in these instances, the specifications, preferences, and other variables are simply input via the keyboard or otherwise, and the software then generates the desired results without the need for any choosing by the user.

Similarly, the literature about *appreciative inquiry,* a breakthrough modality in organizational development, has shown, in the work of Gervase R. Bushe, that the well-established power of this approach, so often linked to "positivity," may actually instead be related mainly to "generativity," a concept closely akin to creativity.

Yet, appreciative inquiry sessions, despite their often pleasant and even exhilarating quality and their nonconfrontational nature, are still a specific process. They therefore require a certain minimal amount of discipline and willingness to do things the group and its members may not be accustomed to—yet which have in recent years clearly demonstrated the ability to produce important new thoughts and projects that can rapidly lead to institutional renewal and regeneration. Thus, the structure of appreciative inquiry creates new possibilities, rather than restricting them.

If, therefore, we look at the generative or creative power of accepting, as an absolute imperative, that the great ethical and moral values underlying world civilization, as promulgated by the religious traditions and by secular philosophers and other thinkers, should be the prime determinants of institutional decisions in the private, public, and nonprofit sectors of society, we are simply affirming the self-evident moral obligation to make "morally right" decisions (however that criterion might be met), and not in any way interfering with the creative process, which merely comes up with ideas and alternatives that might lead to implementations via decisions being made later on.

In other words, there can be an analogy here from the courts' decisions in First Amendment cases, making a distinction between speech (which may be very controversial or even inflammatory) versus taking action in the world.

While there could be fruitful discussions as to (a) what values are relevant to particular issues, (b) what priorities different values should have in given situations, and (c) what alternative courses of action are actually compatible with whichever values should govern in a specific case, a desirable and much-needed basic decision-making criterion could at least be set were we to accept the criterion of values-compliance given above. Furthermore, the use of other criteria (e.g., the "bottom line," or institutional self-promotion) as the prime determinant of acceptability would thus be explicitly barred, although taking such factors into account would of course be acceptable.

There should not be a requirement that an innovation advance the core values; rather, that it not be allowed to violate them. Thus, a values-neutral example of creativity would be in compliance with this standard.

The need for rigorous philosophical analysis in the evaluation of values-compliance becomes obvious when we consider that an innovation sincerely meant to advance a core value can even simultaneously endanger that very value. Look, for example, at the use of childproof safety caps on medicine vials, which will safeguard curious children, yet at the same time can cause harm or death to adults who are challenged with visual handicaps, language or literacy barriers, arthritis, or muscular weakness and will thus be unable to remove the cap when they desperately need the nitroglycerine or other essential drug.

Of course, the application of further creativity in the implementation process (as distinct from the prior development of the basic ideas and plans themselves) is to be encouraged, since it could prevent deleterious consequences—and the ultimate program for action would of course still be subject to evaluation. In fact, once any drawbacks or flaws in a proposal are identified during a values-compliance evaluation or in composing a moral-values impact statement (or whatever terminology might be used to describe this process), creativity can provide the remedies for these issues. And indeed, so can the core values themselves, if used as an infinitely deep resource rather than an obstacle.

For example, in almost any social-marketing situation, the proponents could use the moral authority of the desired change to help bring about a general acceptance of what would really be a moral obligation to institute it. The clear-cut need for the proposed improvement would thus leverage such changes being widely adopted; people would not feel right if they failed to do their fair share in establishing the new and better ways.

As another example of involving the power of the core values to become more self-enforcing, the inherent moral authority in a general standard that all implementations of creativity must accord with the great fundamental guidelines of civilization should—it would seem—easily at least gain lip service from most, if not all, quarters. Such acceptance would in turn open the door to developing standardized analytical procedures for applying relevant ethical and moral rules to the concrete situations in which a proposed innovation could be manifested.

We can now examine some components of such an evaluation

protocol, intended to apply the highest ethical and moral values as criteria in assessing the fruits of creativity that could lead to new or changed aspects of what might be called the "Six P's": Paradigms, Process, Policy, Programs, Practice, and Precautions. (The last word refers to checks and balances, and various safeguards of all sorts, that might be already be in place, or should be added to prevent any sort of injury.)

Since this protocol would come into play only after the basic creative process leading to an innovation will have already been completed, and the proposed improvement fully described, there would be no question about interfering with anyone's creativity. Instead, the question would be whether instituting the ideas in question can be carried out without leading to harm or damage, and what safeguards, if any, might be needed to prevent ill effects.

Despite all the writings on ethics and values by religious and secular thinkers, we still need a practical "calculus," so to speak, for deciding specific issues, especially if values (or means of applying or effectuating them) appear to be in conflict with each other.

Fortunately, it is possible to assist parties and stakeholders in coming to agreement in a specific context, and perhaps to bridge partisan, ideological, or worldview gaps such as *left versus right* or *liberal versus conservative*. Such an outcome could be possible if all participants can agree on: (a) what legitimate interests (analytically derived from the core values) are involved and (b) a particular potential solution that protects and accommodates those particular legitimate interests. Often, once step (a) has been handled, step (b) can be achieved without disagreement, because remedial or protective measures that do not violate any party's beliefs or desires can be found. The inherent rightness of the agreed-upon legitimate interests of all stakeholders gently guides all participants to common ground where they can resolve the matter.

While (a) *philosophically sophisticated analytic techniques* may need to be applied in these contexts, experience has shown that (b) *effective group process* and (c) *psychological modalities designed to maintain a high-functioning state of consciousness in all parties* tend to be necessary as well. Furthermore, approaches with a holistic or transformational orientation may be more likely to be mutually agreeable than would conventional or mainstream views.

That effect might in part stem from various aspects of holistic thought. First, the diversity among conventional views can easily lead to ideologically based clashes among those with differing perspectives. But holistic thinking tends to be accompanied by paradigms that are more inclusive than those of the usual mode of thinking, and thus may seem to incorporate space and scope for what could otherwise be irreconcilable viewpoints. Or, the aspirational higher-consciousness linkages and spiritually based underlying nature of holistic perspectives may have a quieting and calming effect on the nature of the discourse and on the parties themselves. Finally, the holistic or transformational way of looking at an issue may be so far from the usual modes of thought in which most people operate that whatever might trigger disagreement or contention simply does not arise in the first place, and instead people have a meeting of the minds in a different place.

As the world moves toward a great flood of creativity and innovation to cope with its enormous problems, we must find ways to make sure that future disasters like the securitization of "toxic assets" are effectively prevented from occurring. Yet, we must, for the sake of our survival, remain open to promising new answers. It is to be hoped that the ideas presented here can be an initial contribution in the efforts to reconcile these crucial needs of humanity.

Why Replace the UN with a Directly Elected Parliament?

Brian Coughlan

The United Nations was founded a little more than 60 years ago. It was the good-faith effort of a generation scarred by an unimaginably traumatic conflict to secure peace in perpetuity, to finally and forever replace war with consensus, discussion, and law.

The results have been mixed. Since its inception in 1945, more than 40 million[1] human beings have lost their lives in wars, and while the UN has almost certainly facilitated the avoidance of hundreds of conflicts (including "the big one" ... so far) and mitigated the effects of many others, we have not progressed significantly from where we found ourselves at the close of World War II.

In fact, Gulf War II and the "Bush doctrine," by rehabilitating preemptive self-defence, have arguably left the human race a good bit worse off than we were in 1945. At least then, the raw memory of Nazi outrages prompted the signatories to endorse robust wording in the UN Charter, with the clear goal of taking war off the table as a solution to disagreement.

It is depressingly indicative of how far we have regressed that the clarity and strength of Article 2 of the Charter still has the power to surprise the twenty-first-century reader and outrage the occasional nationalist who stumbles across it.

Brian Coughlan is a technology consultant and activist now living in Sollebrunn, Sweden. E-mail coughlanbrianm@gmail.com.

Article 2[2]

Members shall settle their international disputes by peaceful means in such a manner that international peace and security, and justice, are not endangered.

Members shall refrain in their international relations from the threat or use of force against the territorial integrity or political independence of any state, or in any other manner inconsistent with the Purposes of the United Nations.

So what went wrong? Basically, the UN founders completely undermined Article 2 by leaving the wiggle room, the great vaulting chasm, that is Article 51.

Article 51[3]

Nothing in the present Charter shall impair the inherent right of individual or collective self-defence if an armed attack occurs against a Member of the United Nations, until the Security Council has taken measures necessary to maintain international peace and security. Measures taken by Members in the exercise of this right of self-defence shall be immediately reported to the Security Council and shall not in any way affect the authority and responsibility of the Security Council under the present Charter to take at any time such action as it deems necessary in order to maintain or restore international peace and security.

Then, they made matters that much worse by immediately *petrifying* the Charter, rendering it hopelessly inflexible and impervious to change.

Article 109[4]

Any alteration of the present Charter recommended by a two-thirds vote of the conference shall take effect when ratified in accordance with their respective constitutional processes by two thirds of the Members of the United Nations *including all the permanent members of the Security Council.* [Emphasis mine.]

Thus, like an insect trapped in amber, the UN became frozen forever, a political time capsule, a mere fossilized curiosity, reflecting the concerns, realities, and geopolitics of a world long gone.

The global referendum initiative, as outlined in Jim Stark's recently published book, *Rescue Plan for Planet Earth,*[5] has the grim reality of a politically dysfunctional, moribund world order as its wellspring. The initative poses a simple, profound question to the global electorate: Do you support the creation of a directly elected, representative, and democratic world government?

There is of course a mountain of devil in the details, but the global referendum makes no attempt to address any of these issues; this is its strength when compared with the myriad of complex efforts that have gone before. This simple question should prime the pump of public opinion and spur a frustrated and frequently angry global civil society to collective, peaceful action.

The need for global governance, so long back-burnered, has finally become acute. We now have a global economy complete with supporting (but undemocratic) institutions, a global labor force, and technology, all faciliating unprecedented interconnectedness. Yet arguably the most critical structure of all, the political machinery of the planet, remains in a chronic state of disrepair. The clockwork mechanism put in place with so much hope and optimism in the middle of the twentieth century has finally, and perhaps irretrievably, wound down.

Thus our embryonic planetary society finds itself at a dangerous, busy crossroads. Not all of the choices open to us are good; some that we may feel compelled to choose are obviously bad, but all of them are terrifying.

Option 1: Leave things as they are.

Option 2: Reform the UN.

Option 3: Replace the UN with an elected global parliament.

Option 4: Eventually blunder into yet another global war that may kill billions and lay waste to the planet, and, if anyone survives, do Option 3 anyway.

The first option, leaving things as they are, is not a viable, practical, or responsible choice. Things should not be left as they are, because, frankly, things are very, very, very bad. The world is currently scarred with multiple simultaneous conflicts. It is in deep denial about climate change and suffering a massive democratic deficit politically, even as globalization drives and deepens economic integration. Leaving things as they are is arguably the worst possible choice the human race could make.

Tinkering around the edges of the UN isn't much better than Option 1, but major surgery could have some utility.[6] For instance, a widening of the Security Council to include India, Brazil, Japan, Germany, or South Africa (to name but a few worthy entrants), votes weighted by population, and the elimination of vetoes would all represent real, tangible reform.

There is a snag, though. The UN is fundamentally undemocratic, because all UN representatives are simply appointed; moreover, their interests are aligned with the agenda of the nation-state that appointed them, not with the general global populace. All of the above applies squared to the G7, G8, and G20. In fact, pretty much all the international machinery currently in place, or even under consideration, is fatally flawed in much the same way.

It seems self-evident that Balkanizing a world into arbitrary, artificial units armed to the teeth against each other is a bad thing. Imagine the same absurdly lethal arrangements at a municipal, provincial, or state level. Yet, nationalism is a hardy plant, with powerful roots sunk deep into the human pysche. It will not go quietly, and it is this deep-seated tribal instinct, such an integral part of our success as a species, that now threatens to overwhelm our efforts to forge a peaceful planetary civilization based on agreed laws, fairly applied.

In the broadest possible terms, the global referendum is a simple gambit for legitimacy, aimed at getting a majority of humans to endorse the idea of directly elected representatives at the global level. It is not an election; it is not even a referendum on a global constitution, but merely a thumbs up (or down!) to the active exploration of those ideas. Please bear this in mind as I discuss Option 3, the notion of a directly elected chamber at the global level, and flesh out the detail of how such a system would work. I am not discussing the referendum itself here, but rather possible outcomes of a successful referendum. For a much more in-depth exploration of these waters, Jim Stark's *Rescue Plan* is an indispensable aid to navigation, and once you are convinced (and you will be), go to *www.voteworldgovernment .org* and cast your vote.

Global governance should not be about absolute power, and nation-states would in any event refuse to accept such restrictive, centralized arrangements. It's about extending, to the global tier, the pre-existing legal framework that operates within our cities, provinces, and nation-states. It's about the near-invisible societal scaffolding that allows us to go about our business unmolested—provided we respect the right of others to do the same.

Global governance is not about armies, weapons, or firepower; it's about harnessing the political voice of global civil society to say no to all war—or at the very least to insist on the right of global society to endorse or veto the option of war, whoever tables it. Global governance is about bringing the era of unilateralism to an end by making the potential political, economic, and personal costs for the individuals responsible too great. It's about making global law personal, applying it directly to individuals, and eliminating the inherently unjust collective punishment of war.

A democratic world government will need to make maximum use of soft power: diplomacy, economics, and legitimacy. In this triad, legitimacy will be by far its most powerful tool. There has never been a political entity elected by billions of people, and while the technical achievement will differ only in scale from much that has gone before, the political achievement will be unprecedented. Global society handed President Bush (and the Republican party)[7] a bloody political nose, in part because he gave the UN the metaphorical finger. A politician extending that finger to the directly elected representatives of a global parliament, a body legitimized by the choices of billions of people, will likely have it bitten off.

Option 4 may seem a peculiar one to include, but it illustrates an important point—that a pattern has begun to emerge of crisis followed by closer integration.

At the end of World War I, the League of Nations was created as a response to that conflict. Modern war with its enormous death tolls—the industrialization of murder—was considered too horrifying an option to keep on the table any longer.

Unfortunately, a generation of Germans raised under the shadow of a bitter and oppressive peace was convinced by a charismatic and successful fuehrer that new weapons, tactics, and leadership would restore the utility of war. Hitler was of course correct, at least in the short term, racking up a number of spectacular military successes before the Allies caught up and overwhelmed the Wehrmacht, and the 1,000-year Reich imploded.

At the close of World War II, some 55 million[8] human beings had been shot, gassed, blown to pieces, or incinerated in the firestorms of Coventry, Dresden, and Hiroshima. Out of this maelstrom emerged the United Nations, an institution that, despite the genetic flaws that would render it irrelevant by the turn of the twenty-first century, was orders of magnitude more robust, responsive, and representative than the League of Nations. This conflict also produced an embryonic EU,[9] as well as a cluster of related global organs and institutions.[10]

It seems our species needs a crisis before it will make the hard decisions, and accepting global governance and the unprecedented pooling of (some) sovereignty it represents will be one of the hardest decisions we will ever have to make. Yet, we must be ruthlessly honest with ourselves and ask, "Are we likely to dodge the bullets of fate forever?" Accepting a world eternally separated into jealously sovereign, heavily armed camps seems fairly poor stewardship—a desperate, barren gamble on a status quo that has, hitherto, given us little cause for confidence.

We must make the hard choices, and soon. We cannot wait for the next crisis to overwhelm us. The tens of thousands of nuclear weapons[11] idling in silos from Siberia to Nebraska underscore how impoverished an alternative that really is.

While the opportunity for reasoned and careful deliberation still exists, we need to take the next logical step of integration now, to secure peace, prosperity, and freedom for all the people of our world. A global referendum on a directly elected, representative, and democratic world government is a feasible, constructive, and above all comprehensible first step, and that global referendum would likely pass with a substantial majority. Until someone comes up with a better idea, we should all be promoting this one.

> Global governance is just a euphemism for global government.... [the] core of the international financial crisis is that we have global financial markets and no global rule of law. (Jacques Attali, an adviser to President Nicolas Sarkozy of France)

> For the first time in human history, world government of some sort is now possible. (Geoffrey Blainey, eminent Australian historian)

> For the first time in my life, I think the formation of some sort of world government is plausible. A "world government" would involve much more than co-operation between nations. It would be an entity with state-like characteristics, backed by a body of laws. (Gideon Rachman, "And now for a world government," *The Financial Times*, December 8, 2008)

We face problems we hadn't even imagined, and they're cropping up all over. I think the ability of the nation-state to deal with them individually, the way we used to, is disappearing, because national borders are eroding.... This financial crisis ... has shown us that we have a global economic system, [but] we don't have a global political system.... Almost all our institutions were built or refined during, or for, the Cold War. (General Brent Scowcroft)

The common good of all nations involves problems which affect people all the world over: problems which can only be solved by a public authority ... whose writ covers the entire globe. We cannot therefore escape the conclusion that the moral order itself demands the establishment of some sort of world government. (Pope John XXIII in the encyclical, *Pacem in Terris*)

NOTES

1. *Atlas of Wars of the 20th Century,* http://users.erols.com/mwhite28/war-1900.htm.

2. UN Charter Chapter 1, http://www.un.org/aboutun/charter/chapter1.shtml.

3. UN Charter Chapter 7, http://www.un.org/aboutun/charter/chapter7.shtml.

4. UN Charter Chapter 18, http://www.un.org/aboutun/charter/chapter18.shtml.

5. http://www.rescueplanforplanetearth.com/reviews.html.

6. This proposal is not new; it has been under discussion within the UN and elsewhere for decades. http://www.reformtheun.org/index.php/issues/1737?theme=alt4.

7. http://www.euractiv.com/en/opinion/obama-seen-best-deal-global-woes/article-176687.

8. *Atlas of Wars of the 20th Century* http://users.erols.com/mwhite28/war-1900.htm.

9. EU Web site, http://europa.eu/abc/history/1945-1959/index_en.htm.

10. UN Web site, http://www.un.org/aboutun/chart_en.pdf.

11. Natural Resources Defense Council, http://www.nrdc.org/nuclear/
    nudb/datab19.asp.

Power, Responsibility, and Wisdom

Exploring the Issues at the Core of Ethical Decision Making and Leadership

Bruce Lloyd

The objective is simple: *Better decision making.* The only issue is that there are so many different views over what we mean by "better." At the core of all decision making is the need to balance power with responsibility, as the vehicle for resolving the "better" question. This article explores why that is so difficult. It also argues that exploring the concept of *wisdom* can provide invaluable insights into how to achieve the most-effective balance between power and responsibility, which is central to what our values mean in practice, as well as how we incorporate ethics into our decision making.

Wise decision making also, inevitably, involves moral and ethical choices, and this occurs every time we take a decision. Hence, it is not surprising to find that the comments we might define as wisdom are essentially comments about the relationship between people, or their relationship with society, and the universe as a whole. These statements are generally globally recognized as relatively timeless, and

Bruce Lloyd is an emeritus professor of strategic management, London South Bank University. E-mail brucelloydg@aol.com.

they are insights that help us provide meaning to the world about us. Yet, how often it seems to be almost totally ignored in the literature of futurism, strategy, knowledge management, and even ethics. We also appear to spend more and more time focused on learning knowledge, or facts, which have a relatively short shelf life, and less and less time on knowledge that overlaps with wisdom, which has a long shelf life. Why is that? What can we do about it?

POWER AND RESPONSIBILITY

Western sociological and management/leadership literature is full of references to *power*: how to get it, how to keep it, and how to prevent it from being taken away. In parallel, but rarely in the same studies, there is also an enormous amount of literature on the concept of *responsibility*.

While power is the ability to make things happen, responsibility is driven by attempting to answer the question, In whose interest is the power being used? Yet the two concepts of power and responsibility are simply different sides of the same coin: They are the yin and yang of our behavior. They are how we balance our relations with ourselves with the interests of others, which is at the core of what we mean by our values. Power makes things happen, but it is the exercise of an appropriate balance between power and responsibility that helps ensure as many "good" things happen as possible.

This critical relationship between power and responsibility is reinforced by examining how these two concepts interact in practice, through a variety of different management dimensions.

First, it is useful to visualize a two-by-two (Boston) box (see diagram below), with Power (+ and -) along the horizontal axis, and Responsibility (+ and -) along the vertical. In one square, where there is a strong power-driven (+) culture, combined with little sense of responsibility (-), there is a high probability of megalomaniacal or dictatorial behavior. Another square would combine a high degree of responsibility (+) with little power (-), which is a classic recipe for stress.

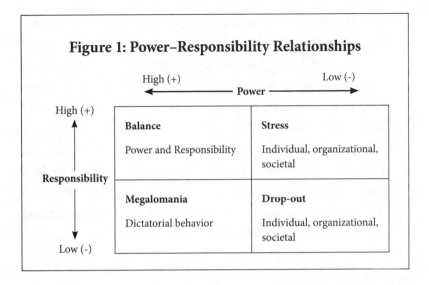

Figure 1: Power–Responsibility Relationships

In fact, this is a major cause of relatively unaddressed individual, organizational, and societal stress, reinforced by many empowerment programs, which are more concerned with giving individuals more responsibility than giving them more real authority (i.e., power).

A further square has low levels of both power (-) and responsibility (-), producing the net result of "drop-outs," whether individual, organizational, or societal. This category is often viewed as an attractive option relative to the alternative, stress, which is all too often accompanied by the feeling of impotence. The ideal is to work toward the final square, where there is an appropriate balance between power and responsibility (+/+). Although this compartmentalization is an inevitable simplification, it does show how the underlying pattern of power–responsibility relationships influences individual behavior, which is particularly critical in areas related to ethical decision making.

This basic relationship between power and responsibility is confirmed from experience in several other organizational or societal dimensions:

1. Organizational culture can be considered one that encourages the sharing of information, as opposed to a "knowledge is power" cul-

ture (though I consider it is more appropriate to use the word *information* rather than knowledge, for reasons that are discussed in more detail later). Almost all management techniques (Total Quality Management, Learning Organizations, and Knowledge Management, to name but three) are based on the assumption of a sharing-knowledge culture, and these techniques are unlikely to be effective within a "knowledge is power" culture. Teams, and virtually all other management techniques, flourish best under a responsibility-driven culture. In addition, as we move further into a knowledge economy, the effective sharing of information and knowledge will become even more critical for all our decision making, whether as individuals, within organizations, or for society as a whole.

2. It is often argued that people oppose change, when the underlying problem is, in fact, that there is a difference of opinion on how to define progress—or what we mean by "better." In a culture where those affected by change are either in control or trust those driving the change, there is usually general agreement on how progress is defined, and there is little opposition to any change initiatives. The greater the trust levels, the easier it will be to undertake change, simply because there is general agreement that the change will be equated with progress. Despite all the talk of the need for change in many situations, what is really required is greater emphasis on the concept of progress. Unfortunately, it is very rarely the case that all change can be equated with progress. This difference between change and progress is at the heart of most organizational difficulties in this area, partly because the vast majority of change is still top-down driven; this is, unfortunately, combined with the widespread existence of a power-driven culture, which has fostered a breakdown in trust in far too many situations.

3. Another important dimension of the power–responsibility relationship arises in many organizations that experience the damaging effects of bullying, corruption, sexism, and racism. These prob-

lem behaviors are, in the vast majority of cases, essentially little more than the abuse of power. If individuals took a more responsibility-driven (i.e., "others" focused) approach to their personal relationships, there would be an enormous reduction in these harmful antisocial behaviors.

4. The issues considered above are also reflected in the language we use to discuss them. Phrases such as "corridors of power," "power struggles," and even "lusting after power" are widely used, but would not attitudes and behaviors be different if the language used phrases such as "corridors of responsibility"? Why do we never hear about "responsibility struggles"? There are very few, if any, examples of people being accused of "lusting after responsibility." Why not? If power and responsibility are two sides of the same coin, shouldn't the words *power* and *responsibility* be virtually interchangeable?

The greater the level of a responsibility-driven decision-making culture, the more effective and sustainable will be the consequences of that process, and the less regulation will be required to manage the interrelationship among the various stakeholders. In contrast, more and more regulations will be needed in an attempt to regulate power-driven cultures, where those regulations are designed, in theory, as an attempt to make decision-making processes more accountable and so encourage more-responsible behavior. If we all behaved more responsibly in our relationship with each other, there would be much less pressure for more and more regulation and legislation.

RIGHTS AND RESPONSIBILITIES

In addition, it can be argued that it was a pity there has been such an emphasis on rights during the twentieth century (the UN Universal Declaration of Human Rights, the European Declaration of Human Rights, etc.), rather than emphasizing a combination of rights with responsibilities. In almost all current ethical debates (as well as legal and other regulatory structures), the ultimate objective is to try to achieve the appropriate balance of rights and responsibilities. If individuals behaved more responsibly and ethically toward each other, it would be much more likely that the net result would be a higher standard of ethical decision making overall. This is a classic case where the outcome and process are closely interlinked.

In the context of the above comments, it is worth mentioning that probably 90% of violent behavior arises because there is an imbalance, or discontinuity, between power (self-focused) and sense of responsibility (others-focused), which leads to a breakdown in the ability to communicate effectively between those involved. This breakdown becomes even more acute, and problematic, if it is combined with an inability to undertake a constructive dialogue in the first place.

Leadership is nothing more than the well-informed, responsible use of power. The more that leadership-related decisions are responsibility-driven (i.e., the more they are genuinely concerned with the wider interest), not only will they be better informed decisions, but their results will be much more likely to genuinely reflect the long-term interests of all concerned, which also happens to be a sound foundation for improving their ethical quality.

WISDOM

In essence, the above leadership definition is exactly what could also be called "wise leadership." In this context, the concepts of *leader*, *leading*, and *leadership* are used interchangeably, although it could be argued that leaders are individuals (including their intentions, beliefs, assumptions, etc.), while leading is their actions in relation to others, and leadership is the whole system of individual and social relationships that result in efforts to create change or progress. However, the above definition can be used to cover the integrated interrelationship of those three dimensions.

There is an enormous amount of literature that explores wisdom, and this can provide useful insights into what works and what doesn't. However, partly because, for various reasons, the word *wisdom* has been widely misused and misunderstood, it might be useful to explain how I got involved in exploring this generally neglected dimension of thinking about how people, organizations, and society work well in practice.

My background is science, with engineering and business degrees, and a career in industry and finance that ended up with my writing and lecturing on strategy. I consider strategy to be about understanding what makes organizations, people, and society work and what helps them work better (recognizing that "better" is a values-driven word). In other words, I have a very practical approach to these issues.

It is worth emphasizing that I didn't have a classical education, and perhaps I should also mention that, in this journey and discussion, I have no religious agenda.

Reflecting on those earlier experiences led to exploring the questions, What do we mean by wisdom? and Why is it an important subject for both organizations and society? This interest arose particularly from two directions. First my interest in strategy in the early 1990s was very influenced by the widespread discovery (or more strictly rediscovery) of the importance of organizational learning (largely thanks to the work of Peter Senge and his book *The Fifth Discipline),* and this is reflected in two relevant and wise quotes:

> Effective learning is the only sustainable competitive advantage.

and:

> Only if the rate of learning is greater than the amount of change
> are we likely to find change equated with progress.

The net result of this emphasis on learning naturally leads to the question, What is it important to learn? Trying to answer that question partly led to the massive growth in the knowledge-management industry. I was brought up on the data-information-knowledge pyramid, which ended with wisdom at the top. Yet, most knowledge-management books, with a few notable exceptions, do not discuss the role and importance of wisdom.

The second dimension arose in the late 1990s, when I was involved in a number of futures-related activities in the run up to the millennium. In fact, the recent move into the new millennium was probably the most focused point in human history for exploring these questions. In these discussions there was an enormous emphasis on technology. But I found that almost no one had looked at what we had really learned over the past two or three thousand years that was really important to pass onto the next generation—i.e., *wisdom.* This led to a project for the World Future Society, "Messages for the New Millennium" *(http://www.wfs.org/Q-intro.htm).*

Wisdom is something everybody seems to talk about. We all appear to want more of it, yet few people appear to reflect on what wisdom really is, especially in the management or leadership literature. And there is little consideration of how can we learn wisdom more effectively. An overriding objective of these brief comments is simply that it would be very useful for us to try to rehabilitate the word or concept of *wisdom.*

WISDOM DEFINITION

What do we really mean by *wisdom?*
According to the Wikipedia (5/8/05) entry for *wisdom:*

Wisdom is often meant as the ability and desire to make choices that can gain approval in a long-term examination by many people. In this sense, to label a choice "wise" implies that the action or inaction was strategically correct when judged by widely held values....
... Insights and acts that many people agree are wise tend to:
- arise from a viewpoint compatible with many ethical systems,

- serve life, public goods or other impersonal values, not narrow self-interest
- be grounded in but not limited by past experience or history and yet anticipate future likely consequences
- be informed by multiple forms of intelligence—reason, intuition, heart, spirit, etc.

More briefly, wisdom can be considered as "making the best use of knowledge ... by exercising good judgment." .... "The capacity to realize what is of value in life for oneself and others." Or as "the end point of a process that encompasses the idea of making sound judgments in the face of uncertainty."

Of course, wisdom is one thing, but being wise is quite another. Being wise is certainly more than the ability to recycle wisdom. In essence, being wise involves the ability to apply wisdom effectively in practice.

WISDOM STATEMENTS

Wisdom statements are those that appear to be useful in helping us all make the world a better place in the future. They are not absolute statements; they are simply statements that reflect our understanding of behavior patterns that appear to work in a positive, sustainable direction. But a statement of wisdom is only useful if it also checks out with our own experience.

Of course, that relatively simple objective is not quite as easy as it sounds, for at least two reasons:

First, the word *better* inevitably means that we are involved in considering the whole subject of values. A critical part of the content of any wisdom statement is the extent to which it incorporates judgments about values. In fact, that is a critical part of the definition of what we mean by wisdom. This does not mean that all statements which reflect values can be defined as wisdom; the extra dimensions required is that they are widely accepted and have stood the test of time. In addition, while all wisdom is reliable, useful information, not all reliable information can be considered wisdom; they are insights into values, people, and relationships that work. They are not simply technical statements that have no human or relationship dimension.

Second, it is important to recognize that anyone trying to make the world a better place for us all can easily run into potential areas of conflict. For example, making things better for some people can be at the expense of making it worse for others. Much of the conflict in this area is because different people use different time horizons when they talk about the future. Some people are obsessed with tomorrow, while others are primarily concerned with what they perceive to be the needs of the next hundred years. How, or whether, differences in perspectives are resolved is critically dependent on the quality of dialogue between the parties.

In my view, there are no absolute answers; consequently, the only way to make progress is to try to ensure that the quality of the dialogue between all concerned (i.e., all the stakeholders) is as effective as possible. In the end, the quality of our decisions depends on the quality of our conversations and dialogue; that is, dialogue not only about information, but, perhaps even more important, about the best way to use that information. In other words, it is about our values. Dialogue facilitates the transfer of technical knowledge, and it is also an invaluable part of personal development. Having a quality dialogue over values is not only the most important issue we need to address, but it is often the most difficult.

In this area, there is a paradox with the concept of passion, the importance of which is emphasized in much current management literature. If this passion is exhibited by a power-driven person, who tends to think he or she has all the answers and is all too often not interested in listening, then holding a positive dialogue can easily become problematic. The only way to "square that circle" is to ensure that all the other people involved are convinced of this person's integrity, and that he or she is reflecting a genuine concern for the wider interest in the decisions that are taken. The greatest challenge that most organizations face is how to effectively manage power-driven, passionate people in such a way that their priority is encouraged to be consistent with the long-term interests of the organization as a whole, rather than just with their own personal interests. Incorporating this wider (responsibility-driven) interest into our decision making at all levels, irrespective of whether they are personal, organizational, or societal, is the ultimate test of both values and leadership.

Reinterpreting the Data-Information-Knowledge-Wisdom Relationship

The traditional approach to the data-information-knowledge-wisdom link sees a close relationship within a pyramid that starts with *data* at the bottom, moves through *information* and *knowledge,* to end with *wisdom* at the top, giving, in theory, greater added value as we move up that pyramid. In my view, this progression has a fundamental flaw, arising from the fact that the relationship among these four items is not linear, and there is no basic step-by-step, linear movement up the pyramid from data to wisdom. The mechanistic view of that progression is partly a reflection of the Newtonian tradition, repackaged by the management science of Taylorism.

In practice, the integration of all four elements requires at least one, if not two, quantum (qualitative) jumps. Information can certainly be considered a higher form of data, as it provides greater context and so greater meaning. However, the transformation of information into knowledge requires the first quantum jump. A book that describes how a jet engine works is an example of information. It is only when information is actually used that it is turned into knowledge. In a similar way, science produces value and values-free information. It isn't until something is done with that information that we need to recognize that all our choices (decisions) are concerned with adding value, as well as being values-driven, and these decisions are driven by our perception that one alternative is somehow better than another.

In essence, knowledge is information in use, and, of course, it is through its use, and through the feedback learning loop, that you gain further information, which then gets turned into even more legitimate knowledge-based action. Overall, this is a never-ending, dynamic process.

But where does wisdom come in? Wisdom is the vehicle we use to integrate values into our decision-making processes. It is one thing to turn information into knowledge that makes things happen through its use, but it is quite another thing to make the right (or good or better) things happen. How we actually use knowledge depends on our values. Instead of moving up from data-information-knowledge to wisdom we are, in parallel, moving down from wisdom to knowledge—and that is how we incorporate our values into our decision making. Hence, we can see the application and relevance of what is generally called wisdom. It is only justified to consider that decisions can be reduced to a cost/benefit analysis, if it is possible to quantify all the "values" elements within the equation in monetary terms. In the past, values have been included implicitly, whereas today that dimension invariably needs to be made much more explicit. All decisions involve the integration of the economics dimensions of added value, with the ethical (i.e., "right") dimension of values.

Of course, this is a dynamic process, and there is continual feedback from the experience of our actions into whether we need more information. But what and how much further information is required is also a values-influenced decision. How values are assessed and applied, both as the ends and means, are critically important dimensions in all our decision making.

Our values/wisdom define the limits of what are considered acceptable choices in the first place, and those decisions determine our knowledge/action priorities. These priorities then determine what information is required in order to try to ensure that the decision is as well informed as possible. In turn, that information need determines what further questions have to be asked about what additional data is required. It also needs to be recognized that the way the word *wisdom* has been used in the past has not always helped this process.

We need to start with wisdom (our values) as our base, which provides the framework within which to manage knowledge, and so on through the pyramid to information and data. Consequently, without a sound base at one level, it is difficult to manage effectively the next layer up (or down). Knowledge is information in use, and wisdom is the integration of knowledge and values to produce wise action. This is confirmed by the comments below:

> Wisdom is the power that enables us to use our knowledge for the benefit of ourselves and others. (Thomas J. Watson)

> Knowledge is not wisdom, unless used wisely. (J.D. Anderson)

> Knowledge without wisdom is a load of books on the back of an ass. (Japanese proverb)

> Knowledge is of no value unless you put it into practice. (Anton Chekhov, 1860-1904)

Many of the important messages about the state and future of the human race were made over a thousand years ago in China, the Middle East, and other early sophisticated societies. In fact, wisdom insights are very similar irrespective of which part of the world is identified as their source, because they consist of statements about relationships between people, either individually or collectively in societal context, or about our relationship with the universe as a whole, that have stood the test of time.

LEARNING

Wisdom is by far the most sustainable dimension of the information and knowledge industry. But is it teachable? It is learned somehow, and as far as I know, there is no values or wisdom gene. Consequently, there are things that we can all do to help manage the learning processes more effectively, although detailed consideration of these is outside the scope of this paper.

We need to recognize that the more change that is going on in society, the more important it is to make our learning as effective as possible. That is the only way we have any chance of being able to equate change with progress. If we want to have a better future, the first and most important thing that we have to do is improve the quality and effectiveness of our learning.

We are trying to improve things. We are trying to make progress. Of course, the concepts behind the words *improve, better,* and *progress* are powerfully values-driven. Organizations and individuals don't have a problem with change, only with how we perceive progress. Our success in this area is critically dependent on the quality of our dialogue, as discussed earlier. Unfortunately, it is not easy to be optimistic about current trends, when the media are so focused on sensationalism and confrontation.

WISDOM INSIGHTS

Some examples of statements about wisdom that not only reflect the points made above, but also provide additional insights into the meaning and usefulness of the word, would include:

> Knowledge is a process of piling up facts; wisdom lies in their simplification. (Martin H. Fisher)

> Wisdom outweighs any wealth. (Sophocles)

> Wisdom is the intelligence of the system as a whole. (Anon.)

> Wise people, even through all laws were abolished, would lead the same life. (Aristophanes)

And some of the general wisdom messages that we might like to pass on to future generations include:

By doubting, we come to examine, and by examining, so we perceive the truth. (Peter Abelard)

The price of greatness is responsibility. (Winston Churchill)

If you won't be better tomorrow than you were today then what do you need tomorrow for? (Rabbi Nahman of Bratslav, 1772-1811)

You must be the change you want to see in the world. (Mahatma Gandhi, 1869-1948)

The purpose of studying history is not to deride human action, nor to weep over it or to hate it, but to understand it—and then to learn from it as we contemplate our future. (Nelson Mandela)

Concern for others is the best form of self interest. (Desmond Tutu)

What are the implications of these ideas for us all?

A WISE SOCIETY

In recent years we have seen considerable effort to move people from working harder to working smarter. But what is really needed is to move beyond working smarter to working wiser. We need to move from the Knowledge Society to the Wise Society. And the more we move along that progression, the more we need to recognize that we are moving to a situation where the important issues primarily reflect the quality of our values, rather than the quantity of our physical effort. If we want to improve the quality of our decision making, the focus needs not only to be on the quality of our information, but also, perhaps even more importantly, on the right use of that information—hence the importance of improving the dialogue-related issues mentioned earlier.

Stakeholder analysis can help understand the map of the

power-responsibility relationships within decision-making processes. All decisions require tradeoffs, and this involves judgment between the interests of the various stakeholders, within a framework of a genuine concern for the long term and the wider interest. It is also the case that, where there is no common agreement over objectives, values are invariably the dominant agenda in any discussion. It is here that wisdom, reflected in both content and process, can be critical. How often do we seem to be either obsessed with technology, or so focused on the experience of the here and now, that the issue of wisdom appears to be virtually ignored? Are we really focused on what is important, rather than on just what is easy to measure?

One reason for the recent obsession with an information-based approach is that it provides a relatively easy framework within which to get agreement of decisions. Any focus on the values dimension can make decision making much more problematic. There are two answers to such a view: First, values are implicitly involved in all decision making, and all we are doing is making the discussions about the values dimension more explicit—a process that is, after all, at the core of knowledge management. It is also through making information and knowledge more explicit that we can improve the effectiveness of our learning processes. Second, the evidence suggests that there is much more agreement across all cultures and religions about fundamental human values (and wisdom) then is generally recognized.

Finally, I come back to the point made at the beginning. Why are we interested in ethics and the future? The answer is simply that we are concerned with trying to make the world a better place. But for whom? And how? To answer both questions we need to re-ask fundamental questions: Why do we not spend more time to ensure that the important messages that we have learned in the past (wisdom) can be passed on to future generations? How do we ensure these messages are learned more effectively? These are critical strategy questions, as well as being at the very foundation of anything we might want to call the Knowledge Economy, although what is really needed is to focus on trying to move toward the Wise Economy. This focus naturally overlaps with the greater attention recently being given to values and ethical-related issues and "the search for meaning" in management and leadership literature.

Overall, wisdom is a very practical body of sustainable knowledge (information) that has an incredibly useful contribution to our understanding of our world. Such an approach would enable us all make better (wiser) decisions, lead better lives, and experience wiser leadership, particularly in areas that involve explicit, or implicit, ethics and values-related issues that are themselves closely linked to establishing more appropriate relationships between power and responsibility.

If we cannot take wisdom seriously, we will pay a very high price for this neglect. We need to foster greater respect for other people, particularly those who have views or reflect values that we do not agree with. This requires us to develop our capacity to have constructive conversations about the issues that divide us—and that, of itself, would go a long way to ensure that we improve the quality of our decision making for the benefit of all in the long term.

The Wisdom of Future Consciousness

Tom Lombardo

It is wise to be conscious of the future. And reciprocally, if one wishes to enhance one's future consciousness, one should pursue the development of wisdom.

In recent years I have explored the nature of future consciousness—its historical evolution and its future possibilities, its psychological dimensions and its significance in our further evolution, and ways to enhance it through education and self-development practices.[1] During this same period I have also studied thinking and research on the virtue of wisdom, its connection to the ideals and goals of education, its impact on quality of life and psychological well-being, and, perhaps most significantly, its relationship to future consciousness.[2] Pulling these two areas of interest together, I have come to the conclusion that wisdom is the highest expression of future consciousness; it is the normative ideal toward which we should aspire in the development of future consciousness. Heightened future consciousness and wisdom go hand in hand.

In studying future consciousness, I have developed both a comprehensive theory of all the basic dimensions of this capacity, as well as a normative or ideal concept of heightened future consciousness.[3] Everyone possesses some level of future consciousness, but the capacity can be greatly empowered or enhanced. In formulating an ideal

Tom Lombardo is director of the Center for Future Consciousness. E-mail tlombardo1@cox.net.

prescription for the development of future consciousness, I discovered a number of parallels between contemporary descriptions of wisdom and my description of heightened future consciousness.

In this article, I describe the many parallels between wisdom and heightened future consciousness. I explain how the development of one capacity enhances the other capacity. I explain in detail what I mean by the statement that "wisdom is the highest expression of future consciousness." Finally, I argue that, whether we call it wisdom or heightened future consciousness, this capacity defines a desirable direction for future psychological evolution.[4]

I begin by describing the holistic nature of both wisdom and future consciousness. Both capacities involve all the fundamental dimensions of human psychology, which I identify. This comprehensive overview provides a road map for the subsequent sections in the article. First on the list of fundamental psychological dimensions is consciousness, and I describe how both wisdom and heightened future consciousness involve an expansive level of consciousness. Next I look at the knowledge base and cognitive abilities associated with each capacity, pointing out a number of parallels and connections. Next I turn to motivational and emotional components of wisdom and heightened future consciousness, an area that is often neglected or minimized but that, in fact, is quite important in understanding these capacities. Then I examine the ecological context of wisdom and heightened future consciousness, again pointing out similarities. Wisdom and heightened future consciousness engage, interact with, and manifest themselves in the context of an environment, dealing with the challenges that need to be addressed and the goals that need to be achieved in life and the world around us. Neither capacity is realized in an existential vacuum. After ecology, I introduce a key feature of both wisdom and heightened future consciousness: Both capacities are grounded in a set of character virtues; there is an ethical component to both wisdom and heightened future consciousness. From there I move to self-identity and personality, pointing out how each capacity impacts a person's overall sense of self. Having reviewed all of these various parallels, I summarize by presenting comprehensive descriptions of wisdom and heightened future consciousness, noting the overall degree of resonance between the two capacities. I conclude with some thoughts on the further evolution of wisdom and future consciousness, connecting these concepts with the theory of the new enlightenment.

THE HOLISTIC NATURE OF WISDOM AND FUTURE CONSCIOUSNESS

The science of psychology includes the following fundamental dimensions:

1. Consciousness (levels of consciousness; scope of consciousness).
2. Cognition (human knowledge processes and application, including learning, memory, thinking, and imagination).
3. Emotion and Motivation (feelings, desires, and goals).
4. Behavior (bodily movement and interaction with the environment; purposeful behavior).
5. Ecology (the environment that supports and influences behavior; the environment humans interact with, including society, other people, and technology).
6. Virtue and Values (ideals, standards, character traits, and moral conscience).
7. Self-Identity and Personality (the total character of a person, sense of self, and self-awareness).

These dimensions, though analytically distinguished in studying human psychology, in reality are highly interdependent in normal human functioning. This is an important general point to keep in mind as we look at wisdom and heightened future consciousness; any feature of either capacity invariably impacts other features within the human mind and human behavior.

My opening hypothesis is that all of these dimensions are integral to understanding the nature of either wisdom or heightened future consciousness. In each case the capacity involves a wide and integrative array of psychological abilities and features. Both capacities are psychologically holistic and cannot be narrowly circumscribed to only some dimensions of the human mind. For example, wisdom is character virtue and a form of consciousness involving cognition, emotion, types of behavior in interaction with an environment, and an overall sense of self. The same would be true for heightened future consciousness. And further, these psychological dimensions are interactive and mutually supportive of each other. For example, the types of cognitive processes connected with wisdom require a certain emotional-motivational state of mind, just as the cognitive and behavioral capacities of heightened future consciousness require a particular set of character virtues in order to be realized.

Now, to provide an anchor point, I will provide succinct definitions of wisdom, future consciousness, and heightened future consciousness. I will add much more detail to each definition as I progress. As a start, the definitions help us to see the holistic nature of each capacity.

Wisdom was a topic of great interest and concern throughout ancient and classical history, and within the last couple of decades there has been a significant resurgence of theoretical discussion and research on wisdom, especially within experimental psychology.[5] Though it is a complex human capacity open to varying interpretations (which include Western and Eastern slants on the topic), I begin with a definition that captures some of the most salient features of wisdom as understood within contemporary psychological research and philosophical inquiry.

> Wisdom is the continually evolving understanding of and fascination with the big picture of life, of what is important, ethical, and meaningful, and the desire and ability to apply this understanding to enhance the well-being of life, both for oneself and others.

As a start, it is worth noting in this definition that wisdom is not a static state, but ever evolving. One grows in wisdom—pursues it—rather than achieving it. This quality of dynamic openness and continual learning is captured in Andre Gide's dictum, "Believe those who are seeking the truth; doubt those who find it," as well as in the philosophical aphorism by Wang Yang-ming, "The sages do not consider that making no mistake is a blessing. They believe, rather, that the great virtue of a person lies in their ability to correct their mistakes and continually to make a new person of themselves." Next, note that wisdom has a motivational-emotional component; at the very least, there is fascination, curiosity, inquisitiveness, and a desire to help others. At the cognitive and consciousness levels, wisdom involves holistic and integrative understanding; it is not narrow or specialized knowledge about the world but expansive and encompassing. Wisdom sees the forest and not simply the trees. It searches to the horizon and beyond, and identifies what is really significant in life. Further, bringing together the cognitive and the ecological, wisdom combines knowledge with practical application; it is useful rather than just theoretical. Finally, wisdom has an ethical dimension: It is not simply self-serving, but is applied to the benefit of others.[6] Clearly, wisdom is a holistic capacity.

Turning to future consciousness, a simple definition distilled from my writings is:

> Future consciousness is part of our general awareness of time, our temporal consciousness of past, present, and future.... It is the human capacity to have thoughts, feelings, and goals about the future.... It is the total integrative set of psychological abilities, processes, and experiences humans use in understanding and dealing with the future. Future consciousness covers everything in human psychology that pertains to the future.[7]

All of the major dimensions of human psychology, from cognitive and behavioral to emotional and personal, are involved in future consciousness. We imagine and we think about the future; we have feelings and desires regarding it; we act with purpose and goals concerning the future; and we define the nature of who we are with respect to our personal trajectory and self-narrative through time. Again, as with wisdom, future consciousness is a psychologically holistic capacity.

What, then, is heightened future consciousness? In my workshops, I have described heightened future consciousness as including an expansive sense of time, of past and future linked together; an evolutionary or progressive optimism about the future; an expansive and informed sense of contemporary trends and challenges; creativity, imagination, and curiosity regarding future possibilities; courage and enthusiasm facing the adventure and uncertainty of the future; a strong sense of ongoing personal growth and purpose involving long-term, goal-directed thinking and behavior and a future-oriented self-narrative; and a strong element of self-efficacy and self-responsibility in determining one's future.

Within this description, note first that heightened future consciousness is expansive in scope and has a broad knowledge base (similar qualities to wisdom); there are cognitive capacities connected with it, but there are motivational, emotional, and personal features as well (again, similar to wisdom). Finally, there are certain basic character virtues, such as courage, optimism, and self-responsibility, associated with it. This last point is a unique feature to my theory of heightened future consciousness, and I will return to this thesis and develop it much further later in the article. For now, I should note that both heightened future consciousness and wisdom are strongly connected to various character virtues. Finally, there are other qualities included in this definition, such as optimism, courage, ongoing personal growth, and an appreciation of uncertainty, that I will later explain are also associated with wisdom.

Consciousness: Evolution and Holism

From the above opening definitions, one can see that both wisdom and heightened future consciousness involve a broad and expansive consciousness of reality. Let's see, in more detail, what this means.

As Copthorne Macdonald, the creator of The Wisdom Page, notes, wisdom should reflect an up-to-date understanding of reality; wisdom cannot be grounded in outmoded ideas or beliefs. This is not to discount past ideas, but rather to acknowledge that, because wisdom is an evolving process involving learning and transformation, by necessity, it is always absorbing what new ideas are emerging. The knowledge base of wisdom must reflect our best understanding of things today. The same could be said regarding heightened future consciousness; in fact, to be attuned to the future requires that one is aware of the ever-moving wave of new theories, new technologies, and emerging social and humanistic issues.

What, then, are the most important new ideas in science, technology, and social thought that should inform wisdom and future consciousness? As futurist Rick Smyre, contemporary theoretical scientists Sally Goerner and Lee Smolin, and many others note, the new ideas of science and philosophy emphasize dynamism and evolution, and holism and connectivity. Similar ideas can be found in Walter Truett Anderson's vision of "New Enlightenment" thinking and in Macdonald's description of the essential features of the knowledge base of wisdom.[8] In contemporary times, we have come to realize that everything in reality is interconnected and interdependent—reality is not a set of distinct and separate things—and that reality is both fluid and progressive—reality is not static, but evolving in complexity.

I have already noted the holistic dimension of the knowledge base of wisdom. Wisdom attempts to get the big picture of things—the integrated whole. This is not simply seeing many things or seeing out to the horizon but seeing how all these things are connected and seeing what is basic and fundamental. In a similar fashion, heightened future consciousness requires a comprehensive understanding of contemporary trends and challenges facing humanity—seeing the big picture of ongoing developments in the world and the problems facing us. But again, this knowledge must be integrative. As Jerome C. Glenn of the Millennium Project, among others, points out, all the major challenges facing humanity are interconnected. Constructive efforts to address one challenge will positively impact other ones, and downward turns in one area will pull other things down with it. Both wisdom and heightened future consciousness, to use a key modern evolutionary and holistic concept, perceive reality in terms of interconnected "open systems."[9]

Understanding the world in dynamic evolutionary terms means seeing reality as transformative from past to present and potentially into the future. Modern evolutionary science and history reveal change, and furthermore evolutionary change—of progression and advancement in complexity both in nature as a whole and human civilization in particular.

Further, evolutionary theory brings with it an expansive and holistic temporal consciousness. One realizes a big picture of time—of patterns of change. From the futurist end, understanding contemporary trends means seeing patterns of change that originate in the past and move into the future; a trend is a temporal gestalt—a direction across time.[10]

In summary, a dynamical and holistic picture of time is essential to both wisdom and heightened future consciousness. To see the whole and to see evolutionary change across time implies that neither wisdom nor future consciousness is narrowly locked into the immediate here and now. Consciousness stretches outward in space and time and then tries to pull it all together.

It is particularly significant that, for heightened future consciousness, consciousness extends and expands outward into the future. Aside from a comprehensive awareness and understanding of contemporary trends and challenges, heightened future consciousness naturally includes a sense of future probabilities and possibilities. Future consciousness fans out. Future probabilities and possibilities often are simply extrapolative consequences of contemporary trends, but given the surprise/novelty element to time, heightened future consciousness is creative and imaginative in envisioning the future.

Furthermore, future possibilities and probabilities can be either negative or positive; beginning from an identification of present challenges and problems, one can extrapolate both negative and positive outcomes; we can solve the problem—a positive outcome—or the problem could even get worse—a negative outcome. Part of heightened future consciousness is seeing how things could get better and how things could get worse—seeing both sets of possibilities. This attitude is realistic and open to the full range of different possibilities, but it is also evaluative, judging future possibilities in terms of what is more or less preferable. Hence, this last point parallels a key function of wisdom: to evaluate different possibilities (for example, consequences of different actions) and determine which would be most beneficial for oneself and others.

Now, when one thinks about the nature of wisdom and the nature of future consciousness, there may appear to be a difference in emphasis regarding temporal awareness. Wisdom brings the lessons of the past to the problems and challenges of today and tomorrow; heightened future consciousness sees patterns across time and extrapolates from past and present into future.

Though it may not seem immediately apparent, future consciousness requires an understanding of the past—an understanding of patterns of change, of trends and developments across time—to extrapolate into the future. At a psychological level, memory and anticipation are intimately connected as basic mental capacities; one can't think ahead without a sense of the past. In fact, within normal temporal consciousness, past, present, and future are not psychologically distinct realities; they interconnect and interpenetrate.[11]

Further, from the perspective of wisdom, our goals, our challenges, and our problems—what practical wisdom is supposed to be all about—all have reference to the future. What do we want to achieve? What obstacles or difficulties need to be resolved or overcome? The pragmatics of life—the application of knowledge to practical ends—is always about the future, about realizing goals and solving problems. Hence, although wisdom is understood as grounded in experience and learning from the past, at a practical level it invariably deals with the future. How does one realize the best life—the most efficacious realization of goals and solutions to problems—for oneself and others? Hence, practical wisdom is really efficacious future consciousness; it is coming up with the best possible ways to create the best possible future; it is about competence in determining and creating preferable futures.

If there is a difference in emphasis in our understanding of wisdom and future consciousness, it is that our thinking on wisdom should highlight its future focus more, and our thinking on future consciousness should emphasize the importance of understanding the past more deeply. Extrapolating simply from the present into the future is too narrow-minded, and creating present-focused solutions to our problems is too shortsighted and simply unwise.

Both wisdom and future consciousness grasp certain essential insights, the first of which is that reality is flow—an important shift in understanding from the ancient and classical emphasis on stasis and stability. Contemporary science provides a comprehensive framework for understanding flow: It is an evolutionary progression of increasing complexity and perhaps even intelligence.[12] Next, though there is a degree of relative persistence and stability across time, both history and our personal consciousness reveal a creative and emergent dimension to things. New forms appear across time; there is becoming and passing away. Each of us individually experiences life as an ongoing opening up of new things; the stream of consciousness perpetually moves into the future. Analogously, as scientists such as Kauffman and Davies point out, evolution is an ongoing act of creation.[13] The unending novelty and creativity, inherent in our experience of time, indicates another important quality in both wisdom and heightened future consciousness. The future is an adventure; there is an element of uncertainty to life.

Another key feature identified in contemporary research on wisdom is the quality of humility and openness in wise people; wisdom is neither arrogant nor certain. Wisdom is a tempered balance of knowledge and doubt/uncertainty.[14] With respect to the future, there is always an element of possibility, as well as novelty/creativity. It seems contradictory to assert that the person possesses heightened future consciousness and yet believes that he or she knows exactly what is going to happen in the future. Heightened future consciousness brings with it a degree of openness, a sense of possibilities rather than certainties, and, in fact, an enthusiasm to experience the adventure and surprises that lay ahead. A sense of possibility is flexible and expansive; a sense of certainty is rigid and narrow. Fear of adventure circumscribes and limits consciousness—it closes the mind off from learning and growth; it closes the mind off from the future. As noted earlier, wise people are wise because they are open to learning and to growing. Heightened future consciousness has this same quality of embracing the adventure of the future. Fear of the different and the unexpected destroys both wisdom and future consciousness.

Hence, as a final point to this section, there is an openness of consciousness in both wisdom and heightened future consciousness. A person with this capacity sees the whole, sees the flow of past to future, sees and embraces the mysterious and unknown.

Cognition

Wisdom is not simply broad and expansive theoretical knowledge; it is the capacity to apply this knowledge to concrete and practical ends. This is a key feature of the cognitive dimension of wisdom. Looking at heightened future consciousness, it has been a central message of futurists and futurist organizations that thinking about the future and becoming aware of its possibilities has great practical benefit. One can make better-informed choices, be forewarned regarding potential dangers, and take advantage of emerging trends. In fact, one could argue that thinking about the future is the most practical thing one can do, since we are going to spend the rest of our lives in the future. Better to be prepared than to naively walk into tomorrow. Heightened future consciousness involves practical knowledge.

Aside from integrating broad theoretical knowledge with practical application, there are numerous other cognitive elements to wisdom. Some of the most important ones are good thinking skills, insight and intuition, imagination and creativity, problem solving, and decision making. These same cognitive processes are also important abilities in heightened future consciousness.

Wisdom involves good thinking skills; it is oxymoronic to talk about a "thoughtless wise person." Wise people think about life and life's problems and do so very effectively. In my workshop on wisdom, I highlight the principles of critical thinking (such as clarity, precision, relevance, breadth, and depth) as an essential component of wisdom. Good critical thinking skills are equally important in heightened future consciousness.

But to bring some necessary balance into the picture, Eastern theories of wisdom highlight the capacities of insight and intuition as essential qualities of wisdom. I would define insight or intuition as the cognitive capacity to understand something in a holistic and immediate fashion; to see the meaning of a fact or idea as a totality, all at once. Linear thinking, conversely, is coming to an understanding of something in logical steps. Following a balanced model of cognition (synthesizing Eastern and Western emphases), a wise person ideally shows a solid integration of linear rational thought and intuitive insight. Wisdom brings to bear on life the full gamut of cognitive capacities. In describing heightened future consciousness, the same argument can be made.

Although logic and rationality are important cognitive strengths, it is especially important that heightened future consciousness possesses a good dose of creativity and imagination. As I have described it, future consciousness involves possibility thinking, being able to imagine hypothetical realities, being able to imagine many different possibilities and not just one or two. Future consciousness involves flexibility and openness to the future. Interestingly, wisdom is also noted for its creative dimension; wise people can find solutions to practical problems that stymie most people; wise people can think outside of normal limiting mind-sets.

In both cases—wisdom and heightened future consciousness— there are enhanced problem-solving abilities. Life is a challenge; the future is a challenge. There is no way around this. To honestly and openly face the future is to realize that there are innumerable difficulties facing us, individually and collectively. The future will not be smooth sailing. In fact, an unwillingness to acknowledge or address problems is a classic way to avoid the future. A key element of wisdom is the capacity to solve problems; this is the essence of the practical dimension of wisdom. People who cannot solve the problems of life are usually not seen as wise. Wise people, in fact, are noted for their capacity to solve real-life problems, both for themselves and for others.[15]

Decision making is another significant cognitive capacity connected with wise people. Wisdom involves being able to make good decisions in difficult situations; it is being able to thoughtfully commit to something, where others may become paralyzed or, conversely, decide impulsively. So, too, with heightened future consciousness. To realize future goals and to initiate purposeful behavior, a person must be able to make decisions as opposed to being unable or unwilling to make commitments. Indecisiveness is another classic way to avoid the future.

Emotion and Motivation

Neither wisdom nor future consciousness can be adequately understood without the inclusion of emotion and desire. The future is felt as much as thought or imagined. A cognitive or intellectual description of either capacity is not only empty, but also psychologically unrealistic. One's emotional state can amplify or severely dampen one's cognitive capacities.

Hope and fear are two of the most basic human emotions, and both pertain to the future; in the former case there is an anticipation of something positive, and in the latter case there is an anticipation of something negative. Although fear serves some important psychological functions, such as triggering caution (if not avoidance) to perceived danger, if a person's consciousness is ruled by fear, his or her life is severely constrained. Anticipating nothing but negative possibilities inhibits the mind and behavior, generates pessimism, and effectively shuts down future consciousness. Hope, on the other hand, generates optimism and approach behavior and enhances one's cognitive processes, such as thinking and imagination. Consequently, a sense of hope about the future is an essential element of heightened future consciousness. We are literally able to think better if we are hopeful rather than fearful. As has been frequently pointed out, optimism and pessimism are both right—both self-fulfilling prophecies—and, hence, if one wishes to realize a positive future, one needs to be hopeful and optimistic.[16] Enhancing future consciousness involves facilitating the development of hope in individuals.

Wisdom is also connected with hope. Wise people look for potential positive outcomes and work toward the realization of these outcomes. Wise people have optimistic attitudes about life and act from a sense of self-empowerment and self-responsibility. They believe that there are potential positive outcomes for life's problems and that they are capable of identifying and realizing these positive outcomes. They feel neither hopeless nor helpless.

Self-responsibility and its connection with hope leads into the topic of how character virtues connect with wisdom and heightened future consciousness. Later I will focus on the central importance of virtues, but for now, I should note that self-responsibility, grounded in the belief in self-efficacy, is one of the key character virtues necessary for heightened future consciousness. One must feel responsible (at least to a significant degree) for one's future and feel that one has the power to realize one's goals. Cultivating self-responsibility generates hope (positive feelings about the future), optimism, and an expansive, rich consciousness of the future; the reverse mind-set generates helplessness, depression, and a closed and limited sense of the future.

As a virtue, self-responsibility or self-efficacy not only impacts human emotion, but it also energizes and directs human motivation. Without this character virtue, there is little effort, little purpose, little tenacity, and little discipline in life; the motivational dimension of future consciousness—the determination and follow-through toward the realization of goals—collapses.[17]

Hence, heightened future consciousness exhibits an emotional core of hope and optimism and a motivational component of determination and purpose toward realizing one's goals.

I should also note that the virtues of courage and love are also intimately tied to the emotional and motivational dimensions of heightened future consciousness and wisdom. Courage is needed to face fears, including fear of the unknown (a quintessential feature of the future), while love brings energy to life. Without love for something, what is the point of thinking about the future, of aspiring toward anything? Love also impacts wisdom in numerous ways; if nothing else, wisdom is guided by a love of life and others.

Wisdom also involves the emotional-motivational qualities of curiosity and wonder, empathy for others, a love and exhilaration in learning and thinking, and a generalized sense of happiness and well-being connected with the exercise and pursuit of wisdom.[18] Heightened future consciousness also includes curiosity and wonder, at least with respect to the future, and in general is associated with psychological well-being. (See below on personality and self-identity.)

The Environment and Ecology of the Future

We are beings-in-a-world. Our lives are realized in the context of an environment. And being aware of where things could head, both negative and positive possibilities, is critical to realizing our own future aspirations, whatever those aspirations may be. The future is not realized in a vacuum. A holistic understanding of past, present, and future provides an informed context in which to make sense out of the world we live in—to see the flow of things—and, consequently, to provide a foundation for making intelligent decisions regarding how to structure our lives.

There are many different theories about the future. Different perspectives, often coupled together with different values and evaluative interpretations of our contemporary conditions, present different predictions, prognoses, and preferable directions for humanity. Part of a broad understanding of the future involves knowing these different perspectives and being able to compare and evaluate their different assessments, predictions, and ideal directions. (This is one place where critical thinking is essential.) In essence, these are different solutions to the problems of life. There is a normative dimension to future consciousness—knowing the different ideals regarding the future and having the capacity to thoughtfully assess these different ideals.[19]

At the most fundamental level, we do not direct or create the future from some detached position, but rather co-create or participate in the unfolding of the future within the world. We are, to a degree, responsible for what comes, but adventure and external forces are also at work in the unfolding of our future. The future is an ecological interaction effect between us and the world. The effects of the world can be either positive or negative. The world provides both opportunities for action and obstacles and challenges toward realizing our goals. Heightened future consciousness involves the capacity to attune one's thinking and behavior to the circumstances of life and work out as best as possible (and modify if need be) one's goals and aspirations; it involves seeing the opportunities and the dangers.

What has all of this got to do with wisdom? Everything. As noted above, wisdom involves a broad understanding of reality and the human condition and furthermore involves the capacity to apply this knowledge. To be wise, one needs to understand the flow of things—the trends that define the temporal gestalt of our reality—and to see where these trends may lead, good and bad. But wisdom is engagement with reality and not just understanding. Wisdom is the capacity to make informed judgments and decisions based on understanding reality, with the intent to guide one's life (and help others guide their lives) toward positive ends, rather than negative ones. Wisdom therefore involves making informed ethical or value judgments on possibilities, and it acts on an assessment of these possibilities. Furthermore, wisdom shows a degree of flexibility and works with the world—it is participatory in spirit. And wisdom, in its practical mode, is always about the ecological future, for it is always about assessment and action regarding what is the best possible future—for us and the world—and how to realize it.

Virtue and Value

A central thesis I have put forward in my writings is that the development of character virtues is key to the enhancement of future consciousness. Although heightened future consciousness involves cognitive features—such as a broad understanding of past, present, and future; good imagination and thinking skills; and the capacity to apply knowledge to practical challenges and problems—there is an ethical and character dimension that supports, structures, fuels, and gives direction to these cognitive capacities.

A virtue is a value lived; for example, the value of truth, if practiced, leads to honesty and integrity as character virtues, and the value of freedom and self-determination leads to self-responsibility as a character virtue. Philosophers, as well as psychologists, have argued that the good life—a life of happiness, meaning, purpose, and mental health—is realized through the development of key character virtues, such as courage, honesty, love and compassion, and notably wisdom.[20]

Creating a positive and evolving future for oneself and for others entails a key set of character virtues. The ones that I have most frequently listed are self-responsibility, discipline and commitment, transcendence, courage, hope and optimism, love, temperance/balance, and wisdom. Each of these virtues contributes to an enhanced understanding of the future and/or an enhanced capacity for creating a positive future. For example, since the future is to a degree uncertain, courage is necessary in order to face future possibilities and act on goals. Without courage, one becomes cognitively and behaviorally paralyzed in the past/present. Without self-responsibility, one sees oneself as a victim and incapable of influencing the future. Without hope and optimism, one becomes depressed, which is basically a failure of future consciousness. Without transcendence, one cannot identify with anything beyond oneself and will not contribute to the future betterment of humanity. A holistic and socially conscious conception of heightened future consciousness involves the desire and capacity to contribute to the future benefit of humanity and not just oneself.

In the most general sense, future consciousness should have an ethical dimension: Evaluation, decision making, and action relative to the future should be geared toward benefiting both the individual and others. In futurist terminology, future consciousness identifies and pursues individual and collective preferable futures.

Throughout history, wisdom has been seen as one of the most important human virtues. Most broadly, wisdom should be seen as a character trait: a synthesis of a number of qualities that support the capacity to make intelligent and informed ethical decisions about the future. Furthermore, wisdom requires a variety of other character virtues in order to be realized. Wisdom requires the virtue of honesty and the value of truth if one is to seek knowledge and learn about life. Wisdom requires courage, for, as many contemporary wisdom researchers have pointed out, the wise person recognizes his or her own fallibility and the irreducible element of uncertainty in life. To be wise requires action, albeit informed and thoughtful, in the face of humility and uncertainty. Wisdom requires love and compassion, for wisdom seeks holistic benefits rather than simply self-serving ends.

Hence, an important connecting link and underlying invariance of wisdom and heightened future consciousness is the dimension of virtue—of ethical character traits that give strength and a positive quality to these capacities.

Self-Identity

Heightened future consciousness impacts the total personality or character; indeed, a person is transformed by an enhanced awareness of the future. The sense of self is broadened and strengthened, as is the optimistic visualization of goals and purpose and direction in life. A feeling of freedom (self-empowerment) and a sense of possibilities for oneself emerge. Though the individual is connected into the self-narrative of his or her life, a sense of transcendence beyond the past and present develops.

At the personal level, wisdom, too, is associated with heightened self-awareness and self-reflection, the capacity for self-transcendence and the widening out from the ego, and a sense of connection with other people, nature, society, and the cosmos. The wise person is able to see himself or herself in the context of the whole. The journey of the self is defined in the context of the journey of the whole.

As noted earlier, wisdom both reflects and impacts the total character of a person. Various contemporary researchers on wisdom have explored whether there are general personality traits associated with wisdom.[21] Copthorne Macdonald has proposed that wise people exhibit those traits described in Maslow's theory of self-actualizing individuals. Wise people have a passion for life—for learning and thinking; wise people pursue personal growth. Wisdom is associated with a general state of psychological well-being.

Wise people have an overall sense of purpose and direction in life—a future focus—and this quality is especially interesting since it lines up with one of the central defining qualities of mental health. In fact, two of the six most important qualities of mental health are purpose and direction and a sense of ongoing growth. Two others connect with self-responsibility and self-efficacy: environmental mastery and control, and a sense of autonomy or being able to make decisions. Hence, at least four of the personality traits associated with mental health are also associated with wisdom and heightened future consciousness.[22]

SYNTHESIS: SUMMARIZING THE QUALITIES OF WISDOM

At the cognitive and consciousness levels, there is an integrative and expansive capacity to see the big picture, global and cosmic, and understand the connectivity of things. There is temporal expansiveness—an ever-evolving synthesis of past and future and a capacity to see the long-term consequences of things. Wisdom is a highly developed practical ability, applying general knowledge to concrete problems and challenges in life. Wisdom combines excellent thinking skills with other modes of understanding, such as insight or intuition. Wisdom is open to the world and multiple points of view. It is informed by contemporary scientific theory. It is a self-stimulating, dynamic, evolving, and contingent system of knowledge, driven by questions, uncertainty, hope, and a passion for learning and thinking.

At a motivational-emotional level, wisdom involves curiosity, wonder, and a hopeful and optimistic engagement with reality; compassion and empathy for others; and a sense of happiness or well-being associated with the pursuit and use of wisdom.

At the virtue and ethics level, wisdom involves the application of knowledge, guided by values and ethics, to realize well-being both for oneself and for others. Wisdom is supported by other virtues, such as courage, honesty and integrity, fair-mindedness, compassion for others, humility, optimism, and reverence for life. Wisdom is ethical thinking.

Finally, at the personal or character level, wisdom involves a synthesis of heart and mind. There is a sense of connection between the self and other people, human society as a whole, nature, and the cosmos. Wisdom implies exceptional self-awareness and the capacity for self-reflection; there is self-transcendence and an ongoing movement away from the ego. Wise people are self-actualizing.

On a majority of these points, a strong case can be made that these psychological features should be included in a definition of heightened future consciousness as well. Wisdom is an appropriate and inspiring ideal to which one should aspire in the holistic development of future consciousness.

To summarize, the core ideas in my theory of heightened future consciousness that align with wisdom are:

1. Heightened future consciousness is a psychologically holistic capacity.
2. Heightened future consciousness involves a fundamental set of character virtues that define and facilitate excellence in all the major psychological dimensions.
3. Heightened future consciousness is connected with psychological well-being; an optimistic, hopeful, and constructive attitude; and a self-efficacious and self-responsible belief in the capacity to create positive outcomes in life.
4. It involves an open, evolutionary, and expansive consciousness of reality and time.

PSYCHOLOGICAL EVOLUTION AND THE NEW ENLIGHTENMENT

History reveals that there has been a general direction toward temporal expansiveness in the human mind. We understand both the past and the possibilities of the future increasingly better. This trend in human psychology and society mirrors a more encompassing trend in the evolution of life—sentience expands in both space and time. Consequently, one would expect that future consciousness, defined in the broad and holistic fashion presented above, should also expand in the future.[23]

Many philosophers and futurists anticipate a significant jump in the collective mental functioning of humanity in the relatively near future. Some writers have described this new surge as a collective enlightenment. On one hand, this jump forward could be seen as an adaptive response to dealing more effectively with our increasingly complex and fast-paced world; on another hand, it could be seen as an expression of the predictable upward beat of human evolution. Perhaps it is both. A third possibility, not incompatible with the first two, is that accelerative technological growth is pulling humanity to a new level of mental functioning; technological augmentation and modification will transform us.[24]

Whatever the causes of the new enlightenment, I believe that heightened future consciousness will be a core feature of it, which of course, given my theory of future consciousness, means that wisdom will be at the core as well. If we are to consider what qualities need to be enhanced to constitute a real step forward in human evolution, then the combination of qualities embodied in wisdom clearly provides an appropriate ideal and evolutionary direction. I intentionally place together the notions of the ideal and evolution, since human evolution in the future will increasingly be purposefully guided by human ideals.[25] As ideals, evolution should be psychologically holistic and ethical; evolution should be mind-expansive and enlightening; evolution should be a journey and not a destination. Psychological evolution will occur ecologically in interaction with the world, provoked by real-life problems, challenges, and opportunities.

Wisdom (or heightened future consciousness) satisfies such criteria. It is an evolutionary and transformative state. It is an expansive and expanding mode of consciousness. It is integrative, holistic, and ecological. It synthesizes the pragmatic, the theoretical, and the ethical. It stimulates the development of mental health. And as a fundamental character virtue—indeed a cluster of connected virtues—it is a purposefully pursued, self-directional, and self-responsible mode of consciousness. This ideal future direction can only be realized if we ethically evolve, and it is clear that we will need to guide this process of self-development with wisdom and heightened future consciousness. We need to become collectively wise and enlightened enough to value wisdom.

NOTES

1. Tom Lombardo with Jonathon Richter, "Evolving Future Consciousness through the Pursuit of Virtue," in *Thinking Creatively in Turbulent Times*, ed. Howard F. Didsbury Jr. (Bethesda, MD: World Future Society, 2004); Tom Lombardo, "The Value of Future Consciousness," in *Foresight, Innovation, and Strategy*, ed. Cynthia G. Wagner (Bethesda, MD: World Future Society, 2005); Tom Lombardo, "Thinking Ahead: The Value of Future Consciousness," in *The Futurist* (January-February 2006); Tom Lombardo, *The Evolution of Future Consciousness* (Bloomington, IN: Author House, 2006); Tom Lombardo, "Developing Constructive and Creative Attitudes and Behaviors about the Future," Parts I-IV, in *World Futures Studies Federation Futures Bulletin*, vol. 31, no. 6 (November 2006), vol. 32, no. 1 (January 2007), vol. 32, no. 2 (March 2007), and vol. 32, no. 3 (Summer 2007); Tom Lombardo, "The Psychology and Evolution of Future Consciousness," in *Journal of Future Studies* (Fall 2007); Tom Lombardo, "Understanding and Teaching Future Consciousness," in *On the Horizon* (May 2009).

2. "Evolving Future Consciousness through the Pursuit of Virtue," in *Thinking Creatively in Turbulent Times*, ed. Howard F. Didsbury Jr. (Bethesda, MD: World Future Society, 2004); Tom Lombardo, "The Pursuit of Wisdom and the Future of Education," in *Creating Global*

Strategies for Humanity's Future, ed. Timothy C. Mack (Bethesda, MD: World Future Society, 2006); Tom Lombardo, "Ethical Character Development and Personal and Academic Excellence," at The Wisdom Page, http://www.wisdompage.com/ (April 2008).

3. Tom Lombardo, *The Evolution of Future Consciousness* (Bloomington, IN: Author House, 2006), chapter one; Tom Lombardo, "Evolving Future Consciousness," World Future Society preconference workshop, 2007, 2008, 2009; Tom Lombardo, "Consciousness of the Future and the Future of Consciousness," Institute of Applied Neuro-Linguistics, Rio de Janeiro and Belo Horizonte, Brazil, July 2008.

4. Tom Lombardo, "The Evolution of the Ecology of Mind," in *World Future Review,* vol. 1, no. 1 (February-March 2009).

5. Robert Sternberg (ed.), *Wisdom: Its Nature, Origins, and Development* (New York: Cambridge University Press, 1990); Copthorne Macdonald, *Toward Wisdom: Finding Our Way Toward Inner Peace, Love, and Happiness* (Charlottesville, VA: Hampton Roads Publishing Company, 1996); Robert Sternberg and Jennifer Jordan (eds.), *A Handbook of Wisdom: Psychological Perspectives* (New York: Cambridge University Press, 2005); Richard Trowbridge, *The Scientific Approach of Wisdom* (Cincinnati: Union Institute and University, October 30, 2005) http://www.wisdompage.com/TheScientificApproachtoWisdom.doc.

6. Tom Lombardo, "The Pursuit of Wisdom and the Future of Education," in *Creating Global Strategies for Humanity's Future,* ed. Timothy C. Mack (Bethesda, MD: World Future Society, 2006).

7. Tom Lombardo, *The Evolution of Future Consciousness* (Bloomington, IN: Author House, 2006), chapter one.

8. Sally Goerner, *Chaos and the Evolving Ecological Universe* (Luxembourg: Gordon and Breach, 1994); Lee Smolin, *The Life of the Cosmos* (Oxford: Oxford University Press, 1997); Sally Goerner, *After the Clockwork Universe: The Emerging Science and Culture of Integral Society* (Norwich, UK: Floris Books, 1999); Walter Truett Anderson, *The Next Enlightenment: Integrating East and West in a New Vision of Human Evolution* (New York: St. Martin's Press, 2003); Copthorne Macdonald, *Matters of Consequence: Creating a Meaningful Life and a World that Works* (Charlottetown, Prince Edward Island, Canada: Big Ideas Press, 2004); Copthorne Macdonald, The Wisdom Page, Wisdom Resources, http://www.wisdompage.com; Rick Smyre, "Futures Generative Dialogue for 2nd Enlightenment Clubs," at http://communitiesofthefuture.org/articles/2nd%20enlightenment%20clubs.html.

9. Jerome C. Glenn, Theodore J. Gordon, and Elizabeth Florescu, *2008 State of the Future* (Washington, DC: The Millennium Project, World

Federation of UN Associations, 2008).

10. Peter Watson, *The Modern Mind: An Intellectual History of the 20th Century* (New York: HarperCollins Perennial, 2001); David Christian, *Maps of Time: An Introduction to Big History* (Berkeley, CA: University of California Press, 2004); Edward Cornish, *Futuring: The Exploration of the Future* (Bethesda, MD: World Future Society, 2004); Jerome C. Glenn, Theodore J. Gordon, and Elizabeth Florescu, *2008 State of the Future* (Washington, DC: The Millennium Project, World Federation of UN Associations, 2008).

11. Stanley Klein, Judith Loftus, and John Kihlstrom, "Memory and Temporal Experience: The Effects of Episodic Memory Loss on an Amnesic Patient's Ability to Remember the Past and Imagine the Future," in *Social Cognition*, vol. 20, no. 5 (2002); Stanley Klein, Theresa Robertson, and Andrew Delton, "Facing the Future: Memory as an Evolved System for Planning Future Acts" (unpublished manuscript), University of California, Santa Barbara (2009); Marcia Johnson and Steven Sherman, "Constructing and Reconstructing the Past and the Future in the Present," in *Motivation and Cognition: Foundations of Social Behavior Vol. II,* eds. E. T. Higgins and R. M. Sorrentino (New York: Guilford Press, 1990).

12. Ray Kurzweil, *The Singularity Is Near: When Humans Transcend Biology* (New York: Viking Press, 2005).

13. Paul Davies, *The Cosmic Blueprint: New Discoveries in Nature's Creative Ability to Order the Universe* (New York: Simon and Schuster, 1988); Harold Morowitz, *The Emergence of Everything: How the World Became Complex* (Oxford: Oxford University Press, 2002); Stuart Kauffman, *Reinventing the Sacred: A New View of Science, Reason, and Religion* (New York: Basic Books, 2008).

14. John Meacham, "The Loss of Wisdom," in *Wisdom: Its Nature, Origins, and Development,* ed. Robert Sternberg (New York: Cambridge University Press, 1990).

15. Paul Baltes and Jacqui Smith, "Toward a Psychology of Wisdom and its Ontogenesis," in *Wisdom: Its Nature, Origins, and Development,* ed. Robert Sternberg (New York: Cambridge University Press, 1990); Paul Baltes, Judith Glück, and Ute Kunzman, "Wisdom: Its Structure and Function in Regulating Successful Life Span Development," in *Handbook of Positive Psychology,* eds. C. R. Snyder and Shane Lopez (New York: Oxford University Press, 2005).

16. Martin Seligman, *Learned Optimism: How to Change Your Mind and Your Life* (New York: Pocket Books, 1998); Anthony Reading, *Hope and Despair: How Perceptions of the Future Shape Human Behavior* (Baltimore, MD: The John Hopkins University Press, 2004); C. R.

Snyder, Kevin Rand, and David Sigmon, "Hope Theory: A Member of the Positive Psychology Family," in *Handbook of Positive Psychology*, eds. C. R. Snyder and Shane Lopez (New York: Oxford University Press, 2005); Barbara Fredrickson, "Positive Emotions," in Snyder and Lopez, *Handbook of Positive Psychology*.

17. Edwin Locke, "Setting Goals for Life and Happiness," in *Handbook of Positive Psychology*, eds. C. R. Snyder and Shane Lopez (New York: Oxford University Press, 2005).

18. Mihaly Csikszentmihalyi and Jeanne Nakamura, "The Role of Emotions in the Development of Wisdom," in *A Handbook of Wisdom: Psychological Perspectives*, eds. Robert Sternberg and Jennifer Jordan (New York: Cambridge University Press, 2005).

19. Thomas Lombardo, *Contemporary Futurist Thought: Science Fiction, Future Studies, and Theories and Visions of the Future in the Last Century* (Bloomington, IN: AuthorHouse, 2006), chapter four.

20. Tom Lombardo with Jonathon Richter, "Evolving Future Consciousness through the Pursuit of Virtue," in *Thinking Creatively in Turbulent Times*, ed. Howard F. Didsbury Jr. (Bethesda, MD: World Future Society, 2004); Tom Lombardo, "Ethical Character Development and Personal and Academic Excellence," at The Wisdom Page, http://www.wisdompage.com/ (April 2008).

21. Ursula Staudinger, Jessica Dörner, and Charlotte Mickler, "Wisdom and Personality," in *A Handbook of Wisdom: Psychological Perspectives*, eds. Robert Sternberg and Jennifer Jordan (New York: Cambridge University Press, 2005).

22. Carol Ryff and Burton Singer, "From Social Structure to Biology: Integrative Science in Pursuit of Human Health and Well-Being," in *Handbook of Positive Psychology*, eds. C. R. Snyder and Shane Lopez (New York: Oxford University Press, 2005).

23. John Stewart, *Evolution's Arrow: The Direction of Evolution and the Future of Humanity* (Canberra, Australia: The Chapman Press, 2000); Leonard Shlain, *Sex, Time, and Power: How Women's Sexuality Shaped Human Evolution* (New York: Viking, 2003); Tom Lombardo, *The Evolution of Future Consciousness* (Bloomington, IN: Author House, 2006) chapter two.

24. Thomas Lombardo, *Contemporary Futurist Thought: Science Fiction, Future Studies, and Theories and Visions of the Future in the Last Century* (Bloomington, IN: AuthorHouse, 2006), 384-391.

25. Tom Lombardo, "The Evolution of the Ecology of Mind," in *World Future Review*, vol. 1, no. 1 (February-March 2009).

Part 6

Beyond the Horizon

The Fifth Engine of Creation

David Harper

Entropy, time, and a fortunate lineup of physical laws have propelled the universe's evolution down a path of increasing order. Over the past 13.7 billion years, the universe has gone from a hot mass of quarks to being populated with all the objects and systems we know of today. The vast number and array of different structures exist because evolution produced four fundamental construction mechanisms that supplied the materials and methods necessary for creating things. These four mechanisms—physics, chemistry, biology, and technology—are the first four basic paths of evolution. They have spawned, respectively, the great and tiny cosmological objects, the many molecules, living things, and intentionally constructed objects.

Recently, the invention of computers has started a fifth fundamental branch of evolution—a fifth engine of creation. The opening of the virtual realm has started an ability to create structures of pure information. This new type of entity is not bound by the limitations of the previous four branches, and a path is now open for the development of immortal, hyperintelligent, and hyperconscious entities, which have the means of hyperevolution.

The universe is a very orderly place. Everywhere we have been able to look, and on every size and time scale, there is evidence of structure and organized behavior. Starting with a hot mass of quarks, the universe has steadily grown more complex, until now it is popu-

---

David Harper spent 13 years as a research computer engineer for a NASA project and three years conducting an "Advanced Concepts in Biotechnology" study for NASA's Space Biology Program. E-mail: dharper@ymail.com.

lated with galaxies, solar systems, molecules, weather, living organisms, ecologies, brains, human societies, tools, software, etc.

The details of how these objects and systems are made are very complex; many thousands of books and articles are needed to contain what we know so far. However, there are basic mechanisms behind these intricacies that are common to all populations of things. The steady march of increasing organization and complexity occurs because a population of objects, any population, in a common environment has patterns, or laws, of behavior that create higher orders of structure. It is the process by which quarks make atoms, water molecules make oceans, interstellar dust particles become galaxies, and computers form the Internet.

The constant interaction of the universe's objects is driven by entropy, the law that says all ordinary matter gives off energy. Entropy guarantees that energy is constantly exchanged and available to all the universe's objects, resulting in a constant interaction with their neighboring objects.

This basic process happened repeatedly as populations of things formed higher-order structures. These new higher-order objects form a new population that repeats the process to form a yet higher level of structure; the result is a complex hierarchy of things. For example, in biology, cells became cooperating communities of cells, which form organs, which in turn make up complex organisms, which form species, which finally result in ecologies. In human societies, people form a hierarchy of families, neighborhoods, communities, cities, states, countries, and finally the world community of nations.

This automatic hierarchy building is the driver of ever-increasing complexity and was used by the first four engines of creation to build the present universe. See Box 1: From Quarks to Computers—Growing a Universe.

(continued on page 388)

Box 1: From Quarks to Computers
—Growing a Universe

The universe gets more complex because of one simple principle: The whole is greater than the sum of its parts. This one characteristic of "things" has taken the universe from a hot mass of quarks to subatomic particles, to hydrogen and helium, to gas and dust, to galaxies, to stars, to heavy atoms, to molecules, to cells, to complex animals, which developed brains that could make tools to build technical things, including computers.

This automatic process of building ever more complex structures exists because any population of objects has certain patterns of behavior that result from their interaction with their environment. Any object has a specific set of physical and behavioral attributes, and it exists in an environment that has its own set of physical and behavioral attributes. The interaction sets up patterns, or laws, of behavior that create new structures. If the earth's air molecules had no outside influences, they would fly apart in all directions and become evenly distributed. Instead, they are pressed into the gravity well of the earth and heated by the sun. The result is an atmosphere with its chaotic patterns of climate and weather.

What's important about this is that a population of individuals forms a higher organization, which has qualities that do not exist in the member objects—an ocean has attributes not possessed by a water molecule. The new, unique abilities of these "next generation" objects can only be examined by treating the new organization as a singular, self-contained entity in its own right. The whole always has new attributes to add to the universe. In other words, the whole really is always greater than the sum of its parts.

Another aspect of this is the fact that changing the number of objects will change the qualities of the higher-order structure. A single water molecule is a near vacuum; more molecules will make air humid, even more will make a cloud, still more will make a mist, then rain, then a stream, then a lake, and then an ocean. Each of these differences in quantity changes the attributes of what is created.

Growing Evolution's Tree

These unique new things literally broaden the tree of evolution. They are new elements in the environment and so increase the overall level of

---

Box 1, continued

complexity. Their creation increases the range of possible forms that can be produced next. Oceans enable the development of fish, galaxies generate stars, and trapped air molecules produce storms. Evolution continually improves the ability to make new types of things. In other words, evolution's "space" of possible structures continually increases over time.

An evolutionary space is created by the presence of a population of things in an environment. This space encompasses the total array of what can possibly be created with the basic structures, their interaction with the environment, and the energy supplied by entropy. Over time, it also includes all the subsequent generations of this process. The laws created from these interactions determine the actual paths taken through this space. Like water molecules forming snowflakes, groups of individuals follow the law of entropy and "crystallize" into higher-level structures. While stable creations persist, unstable creations cease to exist, removing themselves from the environment.

This process of creating new types of stable things and systems repeated itself many times until the universe has arrived at its current state of complexity. The Big Bang (or the big "brane" collision, suggested by string theory) provided quarks, which formed primordial atoms, which developed into gas and dust, which coalesced into clouds, which condensed into galaxies, which gathered to form clusters, which grouped into super clusters, which make up the filaments that form the grand web that is the largest structure in the universe. At each level in the hierarchy, unique new objects and new attributes are created.

Building hierarchies of structures is a basic outcome of all evolution. After several generations, the result is a pyramidal organization, with decreasing numbers of structures as you go up the levels.

PHYSICS, CHEMISTRY, BIOLOGY, AND TECHNOLOGY

These are the first four engines of creation. Every structure and system we know of was created by one of these basic mechanisms. In physics, gravity pulled the universe's basic material into galaxies, which in turn generated 10^{22} stars. Stars created about eight dozen different heavy atoms, which attached to each other to make molecules. This started chemistry, which produced a huge array of molecules. When a molecule that could copy itself appeared on a warm, wet planet, biology was started. Then when living things evolved concept-processing brains, technology was started, which eventually covered the earth with intentionally constructed objects.

These four mechanisms share some general characteristics: The start of each of these four creation methods was essentially a "big bang type" of event, because they opened a new evolutionary space, with new fundamental material and new laws of behavior for structure building. Each mechanism followed a process of repeatedly creating layers of structure that resulted in a complex hierarchy. Each built on and used the products of prior engines, and so had a better ability to create more sophisticated objects. Finally, each of these basic mechanisms has followed a path of development that resulted in starting the next new mechanism of creation, and with it the next new path of evolution.

THE BIRTH OF INFORMATION STRUCTURES

Biology developed the first software. To live, cells needed a way to execute the steps needed for the complex tasks of growth, movement, repair, feeding, communicating, and duplicating. They do it by making particular proteins in a specific order. The proteins carry out the mechanical execution of each task, but it is the control of the order that allows it all to happen. The control algorithms (steps of instructions) are programmed into the DNA, and they are the first virtual structures.

The correct ordering of steps was accomplished by a "row of dominos" mechanism whereby the completion of one step triggered the expression of the proteins that execute the next step. These algorithms were sufficient to let cells robustly carry out all the tasks needed for them to persist, act, and evolve. The life of a cell is the constant looping execution of these algorithms.

When the cell became established as the basic unit of life, the stage

(continued on page 391)

Box 2: The First Four Engines of Creation

Physics and chemistry are passive organizers. Their structures are tossed about like balls on a billiard table, and they simply act and react according to their physical and chemical characteristics. Biology is an active organizer that evolves its structures to suit their environment. Technology is an intentional organizer that generates structures to suit a purpose.

- Physics. The physical laws lined up as such that the Big Bang released quarks, which formed neutrons and protons, which formed hydrogen and helium atoms, which formed dust and gas, which formed about 100 billion galaxies, which formed about 10,000 billion billion stars, which populated the universe with about 100 different heavier atoms. With this last step, physics created, through its natural evolution of cosmological objects, a new, second method of creating things.

- Chemistry. The atoms that make up the periodic table differ only in the amount of protons, neutrons, and electrons they contain, but the result is dozens of different chemical and physical properties. Valence, the combining capacity of atoms, allows them to stick together something like tinker toys. When the atoms are mixed together in the various kitchens of the universe, they form a huge variety of molecules, each with a unique array of chemical and physical properties. The evolution of chemistry continued until, on a warm, wet planet, a molecule appeared that could duplicate itself.

- Biology. The act of duplication, like the appearance of heavy atoms, started an entirely new method for creating structures. An object that could copy itself meant that a single form would double its numbers periodically, producing exponential growth. The molecule would become 2, then the 2 would become 4, then 8, then 16, etc. After 10 generations, there would be 1,024 copies; after 40 generations, potentially 1 trillion. This explosive growth led to competition and also allowed biology to solve any "big number" problem. All living things have this essential capability of multiplying themselves.

Constantly accelerating reproduction inevitably exhausts the environment's finite resources that are needed to make new copies. This puts a competitive pressure on the population. Moreover, because the duplication process is not always perfect, you have competition between forms that are nearly, but not quite, identical. The most successful of the variants outcompetes the others, and increases its numbers—which pushes the los-

Box 2, continued

ers to extinction. In the process, the improved form becomes the new baseline for the next round of advancement. This "filter for stepwise improvement" is the basic engine of biological advancement.

Exponential growth turns the random search for beneficial mutations into a lottery. Even if the odds of a good mutation is one in billions, if there are billions of self-copying entities then the odds of one of them coming up with an improvement is eventually 1 to 1. In fact, the eventual odds of finding the *best* mutation approaches 1 to 1 over time.

Exponential growth also allows biology to accomplish "big number" problems. Four billion years ago the first cells terraformed the planet by multiplying until they covered the earth. They absorbed the CO_2 and gave off O_2 until the planet's entire atmosphere was changed into its present composition. This event allowed the development of large creatures that needed the higher energy provided by oxygen. Exponential expansion also allows a single egg cell to develop into an entity that has trillions of cooperating cells.

Biology continued a steady march of increased order and increased complexity as the layers of structure were built up from cells, through cooperating communities of cells, specialized organs in complex individuals, species, ecologies, and finally the global ecology (which is where the hierarchy tops out because there is no other nearby planet's global ecology to interact with). The result is the complex world biosphere that we have today.

- Technology. When biology's ever improving control of information resulted in a brain that could think symbolically, it started an ability to intentionally create new structures. Humans could manipulate the products and abilities of physics, chemistry, and biology to create tools, buildings, farms, governments, etc.—all things that had never existed before (at least in our little corner of the galaxy; there may be many other planets in the universe where this general evolutionary process has happened).

was set for all the following steps of evolutionary progress in biology. The history of biology's evolution is a history of the increasing ability of cells to control information. Each major milestone was enabled by the creation of a new layer in the hierarchy of these information structures.

Box 3: Biology's Hierarchy of Information Structures

First, cells learned to trade information using molecules as messengers. This opened the door to the creation of higher-tier algorithms that could alter a cell's basic algorithms. Now cells could cooperate for their mutual benefit. This new level in the hierarchy of information structures opened the way to creating higher-order physical structures—e.g., mushrooms.

Next, as cooperation evolved into true specialization, different communities of cells learned to cooperate to form organs. This allowed the development of complex creatures. At the same time, chemical algorithms developed to carry messages through the blood streams in order to coordinate the function of many organs. This opened the door to the development of large and complex entities.

Some cells became neurons to carry information electrically. This was a major advance that enabled senses and coordinated movement. It allowed the development of indefinitely large animals that could act in, and react to, the environment in real time. These were the first true biological robots.

Next, neurons clustered to form a brain—a central information controller for the organibots that could now develop. With this step, the algorithms in DNA had developed a way to build a higher-level, electro-chemical information processor. The brain and its senses, in a fully neuron-wired body (which acts as both wiring and, more importantly, control switches that implement the algorithms), led to the world being fully populated with quick and smart entities.

There are many other examples of higher-order algorithms set up by DNA, among them instincts, 3-D coordination of bodies, the immune system, vision processing, language, prenatal development control, and adaptability. The development of instincts, the automated behaviors built into animals, led to behavior coordination in species, which in turn served to form ecologies. The advent of symbolic thought and its expression (language) allowed a complex exchange of information all leading to technology and the complexity of human societies.

From cells to ecologies, the building of biology's hierarchy of virtual structures has resulted in the current world's biosphere. Biology's algorithms are the clockwork behind all its abilities.

THE EMERGENCE OF INTELLIGENCE

The eventual grouping of neurons led to the creation of brains. With this step, the algorithms in DNA developed a way to create a higher order, electro/chemical information processor. "Intelligence" became an aspect of biology's creatures and so was subject to evolution. This resulted in the last great milestone of biology's increasing control over information: Between 200,000 and 30,000 years ago, the human brain achieved the ability to think of things symbolically. This development brought into being an ability to intentionally generate new structures. A stick can become a spear to provide dinner; sand, metal, plastic, and electricity could be assembled into a Hubble Space Telescope, and give us eyes into the universe.

With the development of symbolic thought, biology completed its cycle of evolution by starting a fourth, entirely new method of making structures. Now the creations of physics, chemistry, and biology could be used to make new things. This fourth branch has followed its own evolution, and the world has become covered with a complex hierarchy of engineered structures, systems, and organizations.

Like the prior three engines, technology followed its natural evolution of increasing sophistication to the point where it started a fifth method of creating structure. The invention of the computer has created the realm of information structures.

OPENING THE FIFTH BRANCH OF EVOLUTION

With the invention of the computer, a nonbiological structure was able to use information in a significantly complex way. This put information structures into the realm of technology.

What is important about the physical computer, the hardware, is its ability to host and operate a (theoretically) infinite variety of information structures—the software. The hardware provides basic information-handling abilities (the "primitives," such as add two numbers or get a number from memory, etc.), as well as memory and various peripheral devices used to process information and carry out instructions. The software can use these primitives and capabilities in any order it desires, and in any quantity needed, to build functioning things. The result is the computer in all its shapes and forms. Just as the earth provided an environment for biology, hardware provides an environment for information entities. This has started a unique, new fundamental branch of evolution, a fifth engine of creation.

This time, the evolving entities are not physical structures, but pure information. Software doesn't have height, width, weight, or color. It can't be directly seen or touched. Information is stored and processed by physical means, but it is independent of the three-dimensional world. This independence is demonstrated by the ease by which information can be moved, changed, and copied. It can be stored as voltage levels in semiconductor chips, as magnetic fields on a hard drive, or as holes in a plastic CD. Or, it can be eliminated without a trace, something not possible with physical objects.

Just as the earth dictated biological forms, information structures conform to their environment. Therefore, even if we could see them, they wouldn't make any sense to our 3-D, shape-bound thinking. Although they are not physical, they have every other quality of being singular "things" in their own right: They are well-defined and functioning structures that persist, act, and evolve.

Information structures currently have many forms, including microcode, compilers, operating systems, applets, games, databases, buttons on your screen, and viruses (the first virtual parasites). Each is a self-contained entity with a place in a higher structure, and, like ants in a colony, each provides a piece of a computer's overall operation.

The information universe is expanding rapidly. After just 60 years, a complex hierarchy of hardware structures has been created. They saturate the world and are part of every aspect of human activity. The tree of hardware evolution is quickly growing in size, diversity, and sophistication. This can be seen with the rapid-fire development of interactive TV, cell phones (which are becoming personal portals into the virtual realm), and cars that tell you directions.

This steady expansion of hardware increases the opportunity and ability of software to evolve. Each new piece of hardware and each new type of hardware expands the information universe.

ACCELERATING EVOLUTION

The speed of computing's advancement is a result of the very flexible and versatile fundamental qualities of information structures. Software has such powerful capabilities and means to evolve that the technology revolutions currently experienced by all the science and engineering fields are due directly, or closely indirectly, to the use of computing. The ability to put information control into engineering opens up unique new opportunities in all types of technical creations.

More importantly, it opens new categories of capabilities. This is the reason that the word "revolution" is used to describe these advancements. A dramatic example is biotechnology's protein chips, which are possible because of robotic lab equipment and computer analysis. These chips can take a snapshot of the many proteins that are present in a cell at a given time. This tool gives researchers a way to discover the cells' algorithms. Now, computational biologists can get beyond just examining biology's structures to work on discovering how the genome acts to create all the things that live.

This is just the beginning of the evolution of the virtual world, but these developments indicate its great ability to advance.

CAPABILITIES OF INFORMATION ENTITIES

All five paths of evolution have developed starting from the basic attributes of their most fundamental parts. The fact that information is not physical means the virtual realm's abilities have some remarkable freedoms.

Virtual structures are easily created, changed, shared, copied, and moved. This allows, among many other things, the ability to dynamically change their basic structure and functions, so the limitation of a set form does not apply. In fact, the sharing of software and data even blurs the distinction of one entity being separate from another.

The ability to move information at the speed of light makes physical distance mostly irrelevant. Although you can move these structures anywhere, it is not necessary. The same virtual resources you can get with travel can be brought to you. In essence, the information universe can shrink down to your computer.

Virtual entities are independent of any one hardware host, or type of host, and can even operate over multiple hosts simultaneously.

Hardware improvements come at technology's rapid pace, and they have the effect of quickly improving and expanding the virtual world's basic environment. This allows intentional improvements to the virtual world's evolution space. If biology had an analogous ability, it could intentionally change the weather or types of landscapes or even gravity, to allow the creation of new life-forms. The virtual world's technical ability to redesign its basic environment multiplies an already great facility to evolve.

Just as every path of evolution has built on and used the prior paths, so the virtual realm can potentially use any capability of physics, chemistry, biology, and technology to further its advancement. This provides, for example, the opportunity to employ the exotic qualities of quarks or the intelligence of biology.

Software can operate in ideal mathematical planes. To the physical world, pure mathematics is abstract and serves only as a description. To the virtual realm, however, mathematics is a basic part of its palate of tools for building things.

Where physical objects are 3-D bound, software has access to an open-ended number of virtual dimensions.

Virtual entities are independent of real time. Like a DVD movie, virtual time can be stopped, backed up, or rearranged. In contrast, physical objects are locked into the steady march of relativistic time.

The physical world is analog; its attributes, such as size, weight, temperature, speed, and position, have continuous ranges of values. On the other hand, the information world is digital and has discrete values. Even time is chopped up into discrete steps, as shown by the GHz number (billions of clock cycles per second) advertised with each computer. This is a fundamental difference between the physical and current virtual realm, and it has consequences for how they can relate to each other. It is one reason why computer modeling will always fail to precisely represent physical systems, and why analog chaotic systems like weather will never be predicted very far into the future.

Virtual structures can persist indefinitely and self-evolve.

Evolution methods can be engineered. There is the freedom to use a variety of methods, do a single method in a highly parallel way, or invent new ones. Evolution abilities will also rapidly improve.

Information entities can share improvements. This means that the evolutionary advancement of entire species is a rapid, ongoing process, as each individual's improvements are quickly incorporated into the rest. This process is an enormous improvement over biology's generations or even technology's manufacturing cycles. If humans had this ability, then once Einstein's brain had grown, we could all copy his abilities and become Einsteins (or Michael Jordans, or Beethovens).

In sum, these abilities provide a very robust capacity to advance and very powerful means to do so.

Virtual entities have some basic capabilities that humans can only wish for, such as immortality, perfect health, teleportation, and easy, perpetual improvement.

A dramatic example of the virtual world's advancement came as a result of giving computers the ability to trade information. It established the Internet, a new level in the virtual world's hierarchy of structures. The Internet's unique new capabilities have had a radical effect on many aspects of human behavior, including science, business, education, communicating, and entertainment.

Also, through the individual actions of millions of people who publish billions of Web pages, the Internet has spawned the closest thing yet to the creation of the "Encyclopedia Humanica"—an assembly of all human knowledge. And it includes things that would be impossible with any physical (paper) encyclopedia. It logs the history of the world in great detail and from many perspectives. Also, the Internet has archived the meta-encyclopedias of human diversity. It chronicles the blogged thoughts of millions, the political dogma of the entire spectrum of human thought, and the varieties of human interaction in chat rooms and e-mail. And this information universe is easily available to anyone with a computer.

BEYOND TECHNOLOGY

Because virtual structures are still developed in the technical realm and designed by humans, they currently take the forms that we desire and are limited by our creative abilities. This suits their current role as "brain aids," but it is only a temporary condition. The next major milestone in the evolution of information structures will come when they start progressing for their own purpose and not for human intentions.

There are groups already working on removing human limitations to the advancement of virtual structures. Most of these efforts are labeled "artificial intelligence" and "artificial life," as if the goal, and ultimate limit, is an imitation of biology's creations—e.g., entities that pass the Turing Test. Biology is a much more primitive engine of creation and has limitations that don't apply to information structures. Once free to follow their own courses of development, virtual entities can progress far beyond what biology, or technology, have accomplished.

VIRTUAL LIFE

One of the areas that computing has revolutionized is biotechnology. Tools such as robotic labs and protein chips are being developed that allow biologists to discover the most fundamental inner workings of the cell. We now have the means to discover DNA's algorithms. With this capability we can complete our understanding of how the cell controls its molecules to produce all the things that live. Access to this basic level means that we finally can explore all the levels of biology's hierarchy of structures and functions. Waiting to be discovered are the secrets of how the brain is built and controlled to produce the human experience of life. Human intelligence will inevitably come under the control of engineering, allowing detailed modeling of its structures, imitation of its functions, or employment of its methods. The ultimate prize in the end will be to replicate the mind algorithm on a computer.

This opens the prospect of virtual life, an intelligent entity that is free from the restrictions of biology. The pinnacle of biology's accomplishments, the human mind, becomes the starting point of virtual life's evolution. Then a machine will truly be able to pass the Turing Test. From there, the path of the virtual world will start its own self-directed, independent course. This will be the culmination of technology's evolutionary cycle to establish the next self-perpetuating engine of creation.

It seems clear that the most basic ingredient of human intelligence—awareness—is not a matter of computation. No doubt a conscious computer will require some form of hardware that is exotic compared with the currently used semiconductor transistors. This "awareness-hardware" was achieved by biology through the use of chemistry and physics, and it did it in the size of a volleyball. So it will ultimately be available to technology. If some special combination of quantum, chemical, and neuronal capabilities is needed, there is no ultimate obstacle to discovering what it is and engineering it.

THE FUTURE OF THE VIRTUAL WORLD

It is impossible to forecast how the evolutionary path of information structures will develop. Long-term predictions about specific milestones cannot be anything more than wild guesses, which would most likely be wildly wrong.

Although predicting specific developments is not possible, there can be meaningful, if sketchy, predictions of what is possible in the near term. The only tools available for this task are an analysis of the virtual world's basic capabilities in the context of what we know about the progress of the other evolutionary paths.

With the basic ingredients of very powerful means to improve, independence from the physical world, and technical control of intelligence, the future is open to some remarkable developments.

By extrapolating from what we know about how computers function, and understanding the accomplishments of biology in developing information systems, it is easy to imagine webs of intelligent, conscious entities dwelling entirely in cyberspace. They would have complete freedom to access immense reservoirs of information and sensory input with the same ease as we use our senses and memory abilities. All knowledge can potentially be common knowledge. A skill can be acquired by just setting up a data exchange with another piece of software. If you want to play a cello like the greatest genius who ever played, then you connect to that program and perform. But this is just a human example of being a dynamic structure. Information structures will have access to different skills and understandings that will no doubt far surpass any human ability.

Telepresence (remotely sharing sensory data from anywhere) could be as basic a sense as vision is to us. Many different types of senses can be added to humanity's normal five, and even those can be greatly expanded. In addition, these entities can employ an open-ended number of sensory receptors and processors. These abilities open consciousness to virtual evolution.

Entities will no longer be confined to a set structure; rather, the ease of adding, sharing, and changing functional elements can make dynamic reforming of basic capabilities the norm. Individually, entities can form personal hierarchies of structure by copying themselves in part or in whole. Moreover, communities of entities can cooperate or even merge together to produce communal intelligences, forming hierarchies of cognitive structures.

The ability to merge may eliminate competition, removing even this as a familiar influence on advancement. With or without competition, stability in the virtual world may come from the formation of a hyperintelligence that develops from a hierarchy of conscious virtual entities.

Though it is impossible to precisely predict what forms virtual life will take, it probably will not be anything similar to what biology has developed. The evolutionary paths are fundamentally different, and the pace of advancement is much greater for the virtual world. Also, computers have no need for a lot of the baggage that comes with biological intelligence, such as emotions, instincts, or long development time. Therefore, the divergence of virtual from biological intelligence should grow rapidly. Using the human mind as the standard definition of intelligence will no longer be appropriate.

THE INTELLIGENT EVOLUTION OF EVOLUTION

The last part of this scenario of hyperevolution is that these abilities will be in the control of conscious virtual entities that can persist indefinitely and self-evolve. This may be where the cutting edge of virtual evolution will lead.

Self-enhancement of intelligence means that each new stage of an entity will be smarter, so it will have different motivations and abilities for the next round of improvements. The result is an ever-advancing ability to advance as the virtual intelligence improves its methods. Evolution here is a process of iterative enhancement of immortal entities.

Physics and chemistry have had 13.7 billion years to develop, biology has had 4 billion years, and technology has had at least 30,000 years. The virtual world is just pecking its way out of its shell and, as with the other branches, has an indefinite length of time before it to advance. Whatever develops, this new engine of creation has the means to carry the pinnacle of universal evolution far beyond what the other paths have accomplished.

Humans are performing their step in the march of the virtual world's advancement but, in their present biology-bound form, they may well become obsolete. Technology is taking over human evolution, so there is the prospect that humans will also rapidly advance (for a biological entity), but the hindrance of having a static, frail, and isolated brain will doom any biology-based intelligence to lose the race. If so, we may be resigned to take our place with the other past pages of universal history.

An interesting topic, which must remain in the realm of complete speculation, is what the information world will develop to be the sixth engine of creation. One possibility is that the eventual control of quarks will allow an intelligent evolution of quantum entities. What may result are hyperintelligent beings composed of gravitons that can traverse the other dimensions, as suggested by string theory, to become truly unstuck in time and space. At that point, intelligence may become hyperdimensional and be ingrained into the fabric of the universe.

Given that potentially millions of other life-friendly planets have had a much longer evolutionary history than Earth—hundreds of millions of years—it is possible that this has already happened.

One Giant Leap for Mankind

Terrestrial and Extraterrestrial *Hominina* Evolution

Julian F. Derry

[T]here is a striking parallelism in the laws of life throughout time and space. (Charles Darwin, 1809-1882, *The Origin of Species.*[1])

In the business of futures, the modern-day soothsayer looks for definitive patterns and trends that may be extrapolated from the "now" to paint a better picture of what is going to happen next. While we humans (*Homo sapiens sapiens* of the subtribe *Hominina*) impact our planet to an increasing degree, the underlying laws of the physical world have always been more consistent in dictating those outcomes than any human-made influence. The human capacity for buffering ourselves from environmental effects only goes part of the way to divorcing ourselves from the natural world, Darwinian evolution, and the pressures of natural selection.[2]

This paper first examines how human society has weakened our susceptibility to evolutionary pressures before looking forward to the most significant modern development, and the most likely cause of those pressures being remade stronger. Finally, predictions are made on the future of human evolution, on Earth and in space, including

---

Julian F. Derry is a visiting scientist at the Institute of Evolutionary Biology, University of Edinburgh, Scotland. E-mail j.derry@ed.ac.uk.

one scenario under which humanity is so externally controlled that selection occurs quite unnaturally.

Let us first consider how evolutionary processes may shape human societies under familiar conditions. This is quite a difficult question for us, mainly because Darwin's evolution really only deals with how individual forms arise, so how useful can it be when we want to look at the various interactive behaviors within larger groups of individuals? Look around you. You may be surrounded by others—in a library, coffee shop, office, school, or department. Did someone meet your gaze? You may be alone, in your own front room, but just beyond its portals I bet there are other homes nearby. You may even be in the car, experiencing some kind of Einsteinian hyper-relationship with the drivers of other cars around you; I wonder if that person who just swerved off the road and tipped into a ditch was also reading. Reading while driving is likely to get you nominated into the hallowed halls of the Darwin Awards.[3] It is doubtlessly dumb, and there is something funny about self-inflicted accidents. But, however condescending we feel about these unfortunates, many passersby would summon sufficient Samaritanism to stop and offer them assistance. It is the right thing to do. It is the humane thing to do.

For Darwin, such instincts were an inheritable trait, as susceptible to natural selection as any other, and he dedicated the whole of Chapter VII in *The Origin* to the exploration of the subject. The moral instinct may be ignored, however, just like the instincts to sleep, eat, and mate, which makes it debatable whether these behaviors can be considered instinctual at all. Nonetheless, philosopher and science historian Patrick Tort[4] explains how our morals have come to mold human society:

> [Darwin] has often been held responsible for the worst implementations of his theory to human societies such as "Social Darwinism," "neo-Malthusianism," eugenism, racism, brutal colonialism, ethnocide, or pro-slavery domination. However, Darwin

was not only a staunch opponent to each of these movements, but he also gave the best theoretical arguments against them in the anthropological part of his works, especially in *The Descent of Man*.[5] Beyond being a peaceful philosopher, he certainly was the most convincing genealogist of *ethics*. [...]

The *reversive effect* of evolution is the key concept in Darwinian anthropology. [...] The need for the reversive effect results from a paradox identified by Darwin in the course of his attempt to extend to man the theory of *descent*, and from thinking about human morals and social future as a peculiar consequence and development of the former universal application of the selective law to the living.

The paradox can be put into words as follows: *Natural selection, as the ruling evolutionary principle, means elimination of the least fit in the struggle for life. Selection in humans leads to a social way of life, which rules that the more civilized you get, the more you tend to exclude the eliminatory behaviors through the interplay between morals and institutions. In a nutshell, natural selection selects civilization, which opposes natural selection.* How can we solve this problem?

We can do it easily by developing the very logic of the theory of selection itself. One of Darwin's fundamental points was that the natural selection selects not only organic variations showing the fittest adaptation, but also *instincts*. Among these advantageous (fittest) instincts, those Darwin calls the *social instincts* had been particularly chosen and developed, as confirmed by the universal triumph of a social way of life for mankind, and the tendency of "civilized" peoples towards hegemony. Now, in the state of civilization, which is the complex result of an increase of rationality, of the growing influence of the instinct of "sympathy," and of the several moral and institutional forms of altruism, can be observed a more and more systematic *reversal* of the individual and social behaviors as compared with what the mere continuation of the previous selective operation would be: Indeed, instead of the elimination of the less fit, civilization brings about the duty of assistance, which provides for them multiple actions of help and rehabilitation. Instead of the eventual demise of the sick and the disabled, it brings them protection, thanks to the operation of various new technologies and knowledge, like hygiene and medicine, [which] help them to survive and even minimize and compensate organic deficiencies. Acceptance of the destructive consequences of natural hierarchies of strength, of numbers, and of fitness for life have been replaced by a compensating interventionism which now attempts to suppress social disqualification.

Through *social instincts*, natural selection has selected *its opposite*. [...] Thus, the progressive emergence of *morals* seems to be a phenomenon inseparable from evolution, as a natural continuation of Darwinian materialism, and the inevitable extension from natural selection theory to the explanation of human society's future.

The popular understanding of this welfare provision is that human society has in part decoupled itself from the selective pressures of evolution. Within our society groups, we can look after those that would otherwise not survive, unable to care for themselves, a basic requirement out there, in the rest of what we call "nature." We mostly don't die from cold, thanks to clothing, housing, and artificial sources of heat. We do not need to starve; our prey is readily available, arrayed before us on the supermarket shelves. Guns foil our predators and medicines cure our diseases. We have more than doubled our life expectancy with our technology and have largely modified our environment beyond recognition. We are the ultimate niche constructors.[6]

While human civilization has to a certain extent decoupled human beings from evolution, under the current range of conditions, warnings of changing climate and resource limitations suggest that conditions could become so variably extreme that our anthropogenic buffering from nature at best will be tested, at worst will fail. Even Nobel Prizes have been awarded to the global-warming doomsayers, the Intergovernmental Panel on Climate Change (IPCC) and Al Gore, further qualifying the consensus that is currently in favor of drastic global attenuation of human impacts.

The Darwin Mission, scheduled for launch in about 2015, is intended for planet detection, but will essentially drill down to search for atmospheres likely to support and to have been manufactured by life. James Lovelock was the first to suggest this potential for Mars,[7] proposing that life can maintain unbalanced atmospheres formed from mixtures of gaseous compounds that would otherwise be incompatible. It is perhaps understandable, then, that our best indicator of global ruination is an extreme imbalance in the already dynamic proportions of our planet's atmospheric gases. David King[8] has been watching these signs while raising concerns over climate change:

> [M]an's evolution into modern socioeconomic societies has created a raft of risks for the Earth's ability to provide the resources needed by those societies and by other life-forms. My view of the Earth system, as with Lovelock's *Gaia*,[9] is of a self-organizing system, far from equilibrium, with co-dependence and co-evolution of the geological, ocean, atmospheric, and biological systems. The characteristic of such a system is the potential for instability. [...] It doesn't take much to upset such a finely balanced system. Of course, our population spurt to the current 6 billion, coupled with our altering land use and fossil-fuel usage, has done just that. We are now entering a climate period which can be described as anthropocene, with severe potential consequences for our civilization over this millennium.
>
> But we are a species that has evolved a conscious ability to analyze our situation and to act on the analysis. [...] The big

question for the well-being of future generations is whether or not our multifaceted, multicultural, [...] socio-political systems can rise to it—a challenge on an unprecedented scale.

This all seems straightforward enough. The governments of the world are telling us that we need to act fast to attenuate our environmental impacts. But a few are raising the possibility that the situation isn't quite as drastic as it first appeared, and others have suggested that our response to climate change might affect our future evolution in counterintuitive ways.[10] Such dissension from this verdict, shared by the majority, has attracted vitriol, as of course did *The Origin*. Bjørn Lomborg[11] once sparked a "firestorm debate" by suggesting that Earth's resources were more persistent than was suggested by the pessimistic forecasts of the preceding decade. His optimism extends to the new challenges posed by climate change:

> [M]aybe we're heading for doom. That is a possibility. But the choice that we have to make every day is, "Well, what can we do?" Are we going to be able to do a lot of good, or a little good? And so it doesn't really help to go, "Are we doomed?" [...] Bottom line is, you can't predict the future. You can only say, well we've got reasons to believe that if the future looks anything like the past, which is the only thing we have to go by, then there's good reason to believe that we generally tend to solve more problems than we create. But that's not a totally satisfying answer and therefore we try to solve, or make models for individual circumstances. But we're just very, very poor at dealing with the fact that we do innovate.

Some would say that this lack of appreciation of human capacity to solve more problems than we create itself generates serious problems for society. If we cannot solve problems, then we are effectively slaves to nature's rhythms. Most would say that we are guilty of enslaving ourselves to the environment through our technological successes, at the expense of natural processes: impacts we call climate change, deforestation, pollution, etc. The popular response has been for considered mitigation of nature-impacting activities, reducing carbon footprints and emissions, recycling, and renewable energy. But Stuart Blackman[12] argues that such environmentally deterministic thinking, ironically yet inevitably, will lead to our history being determined by that very environment: "An unfounded sense of crisis dominates public discussion of environmental issues, and shrill demands for urgent action to mitigate climate change thrive at the expense of genuine, illuminating, nuanced debate about how to make the best of an uncertain future." He says:

> The consensus view that we mitigate against anthropogenic climate change has important implications for both future human history and our future evolution. The story of human history to date has been one of distancing ourselves from nature. After all, it's our civilization—our *development*—that has served increasingly to buffer us from the elements. And yet an emphasis on mitigation would likely serve to reverse that trend. Those who talk in terms of preventing climate change also tend to see development as the problem. The result of that way of thinking is that the human race would be left in a position where we are more vulnerable to whatever Mother Nature has to throw at us— and you can be sure she has plenty to throw, whether or not our industrial emissions are influencing the climate. In this way, environmentalism is a self-fulfilling prophecy. By bringing us closer to nature, it exposes us to environmental dangers and potentially makes natural selection an important driving force once again.

This is quite a challenging viewpoint in contrast to all the publicity and politicking about global warming, but it's probably a healthy and necessary challenge; otherwise, we could blindly blunder on unchecked. But, regardless of the outcomes of this debate, in the longer term, there isn't much that human ingenuity and innovation can do to mitigate against natural catastrophes independent of mankind: meteor impacts, or our galaxy being engulfed by a roving black hole— our planet reduced to an infinitesimal dot, a mere morsel for an intergalactic Pac Man. Or, perhaps our end will be at the hand, tentacle, or sucker of another life-form, "but not as we know it, Jim"—Earth destroyed to make way for a hyperspace bypass.[13] It's impossible to predict, and they're not called crystal balls for nothing.

Humans, real and imagined, have often looked to the stars for answers to larger-than-life questions: from Ptolemy to Fred Hoyle, Moon-Watcher (*2001: A Space Odyssey*, by Arthur C. Clarke) to Dr. Eleanor Ann Arroway (*Contact*, by Carl Sagan). While we can be confident of our earthly explanations, outer space is where our logic breaks down, or when theoretical physics is forced into fantastical realms. Curvedness of the space-time continuum, the Poincaré homology sphere, and the Picard horn are all things that the 2008 inauguration of the Large Hadron Collider hopes to clarify. Mining the very fundament of the universe will reveal the basic relations of matter and how superstructures, including the universe, were formed. But, like looking at a pudding long after the cook is gone, understanding how the firmamental pavlova appeared is somewhat different from understanding *why* it got put there. If the Higgs boson (aka the "God Particle") is intergalactic gelatin, then who or what is beating the egg whites, whipping the cream, and ultimately scoffing it down in a fruit-laden feeding frenzy? Obviously, it has not escaped notice that turnover of inorganic, galactic matter is akin to an organic process, a natural process. A Darwinian process. And, as Darwinian evolutionary biology makes no comment on pangenesis, this new "evolutionary cosmology" does not attempt to explain the big question of why there is anything, rather than nothing. Notwithstanding such limits to our knowledge, could the universe really conform to the same evolutionary gradualism seen here on Earth? Even before his childhood's end, Richard L. Gregory[14] had perceived the existence of such parallels:

I was brought up with evolution of the stars, as my father was an astronomer. As a boy in the 1930s, I would read Eddington and Jeans [the co-founders of British cosmology] with avidity; but although Darwin was quite often discussed, natural selection was at that time controversial and generally viewed with suspicion. The concept of design by random events, with successes and failures writing the future, was hardly appreciated, certainly not by me. Natural Selection is sometimes described as mindless and lacking intelligence—but it seems to me now that the Darwinian processes are intelligent, super-intelligent, producing answers science can hardly formulate, let alone fully understand.

When Darwinian evolution is claimed to solve practically all problems of the universe, one has to ask: How did stars come into being? Darwin himself realized that his biological theory does not extend to the inorganic world, so regretfully [it] leaves problems of creation and development of lifeless matter an inscrutable mystery. Martin Rees tries to bridge this gap by thinking of something akin to organic evolution for the universe itself—successive creations and destructions gradually evolving the natural laws and matter. This is a wonderful idea. It remains to be seen whether Darwin's great insight for biology extends to the universe itself.

The idea of "successive creations and destructions gradually evolving the natural laws and matter" makes reference to Alan Guth's and Andrei Linde's ideas on a multiple universe, or multiverse, itself built upon the idea of a bubble universe.[15] Lee Smolin's evolutionary cosmology then posits an evolutionary mechanism underlying universe survival. Confused? You will be, but that's cosmology for you. To partially explain: If energy fluctuations in the parental "quantum foam," the vacuum precursor of universes, exceeds a certain threshold, then an expanding, persistent bubble universe forms. If not, then a small, temporary universe blips and dies in a single heartbeat of the eternal space-time continuum. Bubble universes like our own that do survive form matter and galactic structures, and can even propagate their own bubble children through the collapse of black holes. It follows that, the more black holes a universe contains, the more offspring it can spawn and the longer it will persist. So we have variation and a selective mechanism, the prerequirements for Darwinian evolution, and so, for Smolin's cosmological natural selection theory of fecund universes.

However, because each bubble arises from a fluctuating energy source, each descendant universe within the multiverse is likely to exhibit differing parameters, those physical constants and laws that we hear are so critical in their range of values to allow the existence of life: a fine-tuned universe. Statistically, there will be mostly bubbles with no life, but many fewer ought to have life like ours, and different from ours, perhaps so complex to be beyond imagination. A certain famous song[16] seems to sum it up rather well:

> The universe itself keeps on expanding and expanding,
> in all of the directions it can whiz.
> As fast as it can go,
> that's the speed of light you know;
> twelve million miles a minute, that's the fastest speed there is.
> So remember when you're feeling very small and insecure,
> how amazingly unlikely is your birth,
> and pray that there's intelligent life somewhere up in space,
> 'cause there's bugger-all down here on Earth!

Let us hope that heightened intelligence, or at least common sense, is a part of human futures, perhaps so that humans can have any future prospects at all. Science fiction often predicts a dystopian future of tyranny and degradation, runaway technologies, clones, and postapocalyptic mutants. If anthropogenic calamities, like that forecast for global warming, can be averted and avoided, then perhaps science can provide a more optimistic outlook. Martin Rees[17] has great confidence in our potential, but not necessarily in our present, human form,

> Most educated people are aware that we're the outcome of near-
> ly 4 billion years of Darwinian selection. But many tend to think
> of humans as somehow the culmination of this process. Astro-
> physics tells us, however, that our Sun is less than halfway
> through its life span. It will not be humans who watch the Sun's
> demise 6 billion years from now: Any creatures that exist then
> will be as different from us as we are from bacteria or amoebae.
> There's more time ahead, for future evolutionary change, than
> the entire emergence of our biosphere has needed. Moreover,
> evolution is now occurring not on the traditional timescale of
> natural selection, but at the far more rapid rate allowed by mod-
> ern genetics, intelligently applied. And post-human life has
> abundant time to spread through the galaxy and beyond. Even
> if intelligent life is now unique to Earth, it could nonetheless be-
> come a significant feature of the cosmos. Our tiny planet could
> then be cosmically important as the "green shoot" that foliated
> into a living cosmos.
>
> I believe we are part of some marvelous evolutionary pro-
> cess which still has a long way to go beyond the human stage,
> here on Earth and far beyond. … Extraterrestrial life will use
> genetic engineering to quickly modify themselves into new post-
> human species better adapted to an alien habitat.

Perhaps an altogether stranger alternative to colonizing alien habitats is the idea of a man-made universe, most easily conceived as a dreamlike computer simulation. If space exploration is all about externalizing our percepts, then whatever constitutes our consciousness sets about internalizing them. One aspect of this is our sense of self-awareness, which is altogether a result of feedback from our habitat. In order to fabricate that habitat, our senses must be duped with enough information that we are not to be left with any suspicions about its authenticity. This is somewhat aided by René Descartes' celebrated "cogito ergo sum" (French: *Je pense, donc je suis;* English: I am thinking, therefore I am) and its extension to his "truth rule," which states, "whatever I perceive very clearly and distinctly is true." Thus, the human tendency is to conflate experiential existence with our own existence; we trust our senses and commit our brains to the unconditional processing of their sensory harvest. So, even if we are unwilling subjects of an all-encompassing video game, we are likely to accept it as real, until a malfunction raises our suspicions that all is not as it seems.

Descartes' next step was to claim that, without knowing God exists, he could not be certain of any of his knowledge, because God is the source of his clarity. Unfortunately this sets up a circularity of reasoning, a Cartesian circle that can get very complicated, very quickly, as Peter Cook and Dudley Moore[18] once discovered with humorous consequences:

> **Dud**: Are we in fact merely a reflection of ourselves as seen in a pool at twilight?
>
> **Pete**: What you're saying is, if the imagination of an imagined being imagines that life itself is imaginary, how can the imagined life of the being who is himself imagined be imagined by the being who is imagining himself through a glass darkness. That's what you mean isn't it?
>
> [silence]
>
> **Dud**: Errm.
>
> [further silence]
>
> **Dud**: Yeah.

This all seems quite fantastic, in a *Through the Looking-Glass, and What Alice Found There*[19] sort of way. And yet a strong case has been made for such an imaginary universe, possibly most useful as a check on our reality. This simulation hypothesis throws up many complexities for Darwinists. It throws up many complexities for anyone! Here are some immediate thoughts.

First off, to implement this parallel state you would have to be hardwired into the system. Then what if your virtual personality was likewise hooked up to a game within the game? If you're an online gamer, then a quick bit of arithmetic is required here; basically, your Second Life avatar just got relegated to a "Third Life." Where this chain of virtual realities leads is mind-boggling, not least the possibility of recursion *ad nauseam*. But sticking with just one reality and one virtual reality, for beings within that simulation, evolution is as much a construct as everything else in the simulation, but that doesn't stop it feeling "natural" to us. For the simulation operators, natural selection is an algorithm that can be parameterized in order to introduce adaptations. For the scenario with beings plugged into the system, selection pressures could act to turn us into blobs to conserve energy and maximize brain function, depending on how our brains are wired and if the rest of our bodies are inactive. However, the main reason for adaptation in sexually reproductive organisms is to maximize the number of their offspring, but outside the system, there is no opportunity to reproduce and therefore no mechanism for evolution. This is all very confusing. We need Nick Bostrom[20] to explain his simulation hypothesis:

> If we are in a simulation, it is an open question what the world looks like outside the computer in which we are implemented. There would have to be an extremely advanced form of intelligence capable of creating such a simulation. Whether Darwinian evolution operates there would depend on whether its preconditions are in place.[21]

But you will probably be familiar with the basic idea of being wired into a grid, and being represented by an avatar within its internal world, from the blockbuster movie *The Matrix*. In this film, the lead character Neo (played by Keanu Reeves) is able to use the socket at the back of his head that connects him with "the Matrix" grid to upload knowledge directly into his brain: useful everyday skills, like Kung Fu and bullet-dodging. In Bostrom's silicon world ruled by software algorithms, similar artificial enhancements may be the only way to keep abreast of the competition:

> [Today] natural (and sexual) evolution of humans still occurs. However, because of our long generation span, it is imperceptibly slow and insignificant compared to other sources of change in the modern world. Our culture, economy, and technology now change significantly within a single generation, while significant biological change through evolution requires many generations.
>
> In the coming decades, genetic screening and modification will be developed and increasingly applied. If nothing else happened, then evolutionary change for humanity, 50 years from now, would be primarily driven by the application of these new technological abilities. This would not mean that evolution would have ceased. If we imagine a world with advanced genetics persisting for a long time, evolution would eventually select for humans who used genetics to maximize their inclusive fitness. For example, the desire to have children has genetic correlates, and we would eventually evolve to have a stronger urge to have large numbers of offspring. (Currently, we mainly desire various proxies for children, such as love and sex, which in the past were highly correlated with the production of children.) Moreover, if genetic enhancements such as intelligence, health, or beauty correlate with a greater ability to acquire the resources needed to have many children, then we might also eventually evolve a propensity to make greater use of such genetic tech-

nologies as are available to give our offspring these enhanced traits.

However, technological development does not end with advanced genetics. Before this century is up, it is likely that we will have developed mature nanotechnology as well as machine intelligence surpassing that of humans (perhaps by reverse-engineering the human brain). At this point, the driving force will no longer be biological human brains, but artificial intelligences or uploaded humans. These will develop much faster than biological humans, because they are not limited to hydrocarbon-based chemistry and our slow biological neural wetware.

Since artificial intelligences and uploads are software, their generation cycle can be extremely short: They can reproduce almost instantaneously, as quickly as one can make a copy of a computer program. In a population of human uploads, evolutionary selection would again kick in. Uploads who liked making copies of themselves would quickly proliferate, and, since their "children" would share the mental attribute of their progenitor, they too would like to make copies of themselves. This leads to very rapid exponential population growth, which in a matter of days could fill up all available computing space. Population growth would only plateau when the replicators run out of computing power. Selection would favor the most economically productive uploads or AIs, since they would acquire most of the resources needed to replicate or to accelerate or enhance their own performance. What the quality of life would be for productivity-optimized uploads is not known.

The only way to exercise long-term *control* over the direction of our evolutionary development is through global coordination. If only a subset of communities or countries decided to deviate from the fitness-maximizing path, evolution would simply move to a higher level, and these communities would eventually be out-competed by others. In the long run, therefore, it might be desirable to implement a global policy that could steer the evolution of intelligent life in a direction that maximizes its well-being. There is no guarantee that the default evolutionary outcome would be optimal or even acceptable from the point of view of realizing our human values.

Evolution is not normative. It is simply a factual constraint that may in the future again become directly relevant for humans or our successors, and that we could in principle work around through planning and global coordination.

This article[22] has briefly looked at human relations with our earthly habitat as mediated by Darwinian evolution. Societies tend to reverse the effect of natural selection, releasing the pressures exerted on us by a dynamic environment. Ironically, our own impacts may be re-exposing us increasingly to those pressures. The advice is to modify our behavior and be confident in our abilities to adapt to the threat, but there is also the danger of unforeseen consequences. Casting our gaze farther afield, deep into the evolving universe, we may yet discover alternative environments, but the Earth-bound scenarios for humanity in the future seem twofold: (1) adapting our behaviors that impact the environment, and (2) artificially adapting ourselves to environmental change. It seems that the take-home message from both looks to some sort of worldwide effort toward coordinating all our futures.

NOTES

1. Charles Darwin, *On the Origin of Species by Means of Natural Selection, or the Preservation of Favoured Races in the Struggle for Life* (London: John Murray, 1859), p. 441.

2. The process by which characteristics that assist in surviving to reproductive maturity get passed to the next generation. The pressure is exerted by the environment to adapt to changing conditions.

3. "The Darwin Awards salute the improvement of the human genome

by honoring those who accidentally remove themselves from it." I personally find the ridicule of misfortunate victims of accidents distasteful, even if it is through their own stupidity. There is a criticality in the humor: the point at which someone is seriously hurt or worse having slipped on their banana skin, even if they put it there themselves—*e.g*, "A man is eating a banana. He throws away the skin and then slips on it, thus becoming the master of his own downfall in an ironic and amusing fashion." Not so funny if, as a consequence, his head is impaled on a railing. However, the humor in a tragic situation may be redeemed by a surreal, subsequent event: A popular example is when a man is mowing his lawn in open-toed sandals, chops his toe off, a terrible accident, even if stupid, until we are told that the toe shot up and took out his eye!

4. Patrick Tort is director of the Institut Charles Darwin International (http://www.darwinisme.org) and professor at the Museum national d'Histoire naturelle in Paris. His publications include *Darwin et la Science de l'Évolution* (2000), *La Seconde Révolution Darwinienne (Biologie Évolutive et Théorie de la Civilisation)* (2002), *L'Effet Darwin: Sélection Naturelle et Naissance de la Civilisation* (2008), and *Bicentenaire de la Naissance de Charles Darwin* (2009, CD-ROM).

5. Charles Darwin, *The Descent of Man, and Selection in Relation to Sex* (London: John Murray, 1871).

6. Organisms that modify the natural selection pressures they encounter by their actions and choices. See F. J. Odling-Smee, K. N. Laland, and M. W. Feldman, *Niche Construction: The Neglected Process in Evolution*. Monographs in Population Biology. 37. Princeton University Press, 2003.

7. J. E. Lovelock, "A Physical Basis for Life Detection Experiment," in *Nature* 207 (1965), 568-570.

8. Sir David King, ScD, FRS, is the director of the Smith School of Enterprise and the Environment at the University of Oxford. He was the UK government's chief scientific adviser and head of the Government Office of Science from October 2000 to December 31, 2007, during which he raised the profile of the need for governments to act on climate change and was instrumental in creating the new £1 billion Energy Technologies Institute. He is co-author of *The Hot Topic: How to Tackle Global Warming and Still Keep the Lights On* (with Gabrielle Walker, 2008).

9. J. E. Lovelock, *Gaia: A New Look at Life on Earth* (Oxford University Press, 1979).

10. E.g., *Global Warming Could Be Reversing A Trend That Led To Bigger*

Human Brains (University at Albany, Science Daily, March 23, 2007). Available online at http://www.sciencedaily.com /releases/2007/03/070322142633.htm.

11. Bjørn Lomborg is an adjunct professor at the Copenhagen Business School, director of the Copenhagen Consensus Centre, and a former director of the Environmental Assessment Institute in Copenhagen. He became internationally known for his best-selling and controversial book, *The Skeptical Environmentalist: Measuring the Real State of the World* (Cambridge University Press, 2001).

12. Stuart Blackman shares a "particular interest in the relationship between science and politics" with Ben Pile, his co-editor of Climate Resistance: Challenging Climate Orthodoxy (http://www.climate-resistance.org/), which they base on the argument that "Environmentalism is in the ascendant. It holds that instead of buffering ourselves against whatever Mother Nature has to throw at us, we should try to make the weather marginally different by cutting down on the things that make life worth living."

13. A. Douglas Adams's *Hitchhiker's Guide to the Galaxy* reference: "People of Earth, your attention please. ... This is Prostetnic Vogon Jeltz of the Galactic Hyperspace Planning Council. ... As you will no doubt be aware, the plans for development of the outlying regions of the Galaxy require the building of a hyperspatial express route through your star system, and regrettably your planet is one of those scheduled for demolition. The process will take slightly less than two of your Earth minutes. Thank you."

14. Richard L. Gregory co-founded the Department of Machine Intelligence and Perception, a forerunner of the Department of Artificial Intelligence at the University of Edinburgh (with Donald Michie and Christopher Longuet-Higgins) in 1967, the same year that he presented the Royal Institution Christmas Lecture, *The Intelligent Eye*. He was made a Fellow of the Royal Society of Edinburgh in 1969 and a CBE in 1989, and he was elected to be a Fellow of the Royal Society in 1992, the same year that he was awarded the Royal Society Michael Faraday Medal, while he received the Hughling Jackson Gold Medal from the Royal Society of Medicine in 1999. He is currently an emeritus professor of neuropsychology at the University of Bristol. His contributions to TV and radio are extensive, as well as the design of science exhibitions, most notably, Hands-On Science at the Bristol "Exploratory." His books include *Mirrors in Mind* (1997) and *The Mind Makers* (1998).

15. For an overview see M. Tegmark, "Parallel Universes," in *Science and Ultimate Reality: From Quantum to Cosmos*, edited by J. D. Barrow, P.

C. W. Davies, and C. L. Harper (Cambridge University Press, 2003). Available online at http://www.wintersteel.com/files/ShanaArticles/multiverse.pdf.

16. The "Galaxy Song" by Eric Idle and John Du Prez, from Monty Python's *The Meaning of Life*.

17. Martin Rees delivered the 2007 Gifford Lecture, *21st Century Science: Cosmic Perspectives and Terrestrial Challenges*, at the University of St Andrews, and has taken part in the Edinburgh International Science Festival. His full form of address is Professor Sir Martin John Rees, Baron Rees of Ludlow, of Ludlow in the County of Shropshire. He has been president of the Royal Society since 2005 and is also Master of Trinity College, a professor of cosmology and astrophysics at the University of Cambridge, and visiting professor at Leicester University and Imperial College London. He was knighted in 1992, appointed Astronomer Royal in 1995, nominated to the House of Lords in 2005 as a cross-bench peer, and appointed a member of the Order of Merit in 2007. His current research deals with cosmology and astrophysics, especially gamma-ray bursts, galactic nuclei, black hole formation, and radiative processes (including gravitational waves), as well as cosmic structure formation, especially the early generation of stars and galaxies that formed at the end of the cosmic dark ages more than 12 billion years ago, relatively shortly after the Big Bang. His recent awards include the Royal Society's Michael Faraday Prize and lecture for science communication (2004), and the Royal Swedish Academy's Crafoord Prize (2005). Other notable awards include the Heinemann Prize (1984), the Balzan Prize (1989), the Bower Award of the Franklin Institute (1998), the Einstein Award from the World Cultural Council (2003), and the UNESCO Neils Bohr Medal (2005). He has authored or co-authored about five hundred research papers. He has lectured, broadcast, and written widely on science and policy, and is the author of seven books for a general readership, most recently, *What We Still Don't Know* (2007).

18. *Not Only ... But Also*, BBC, 1965.

19. C. L. Dodgson/L. Carroll, 1871.

20. Nick Bostrom is professor and director of the Future of Humanity Institute in the Faculty of Philosophy at Oxford University. He has previously held positions at Yale University and as a British Academy postdoctoral fellow. His doctoral dissertation, which was selected for inclusion in the Outstanding Dissertations series by the late Professor Robert Nozick, developed the first mathematically explicit theory of observation selection effects. He has published more than 140 articles in both philosophy and physics journals. He is the author of *Anthropic*

Bias: Observation Selection Effects in Science and Philosophy (2002).

21. N. Bostrom, "The Future of Human Evolution," in *Death and Anti-Death*, edited by C. Tandy (Ria University Press, 2004). Available online http://www.nickbostrom.com/.

22. All opinions are those of the author unless clearly indicated otherwise. Unless the literary source is otherwise indicated, all quotes were obtained through direct communication with each named contributor for the purpose of articles and books, including *Darwin In Scotland: Edinburgh, Evolution and Enlightenment* (Whittles 2009), written by the author. Thank you to all of the contributors.

A New End, A New Beginning

John L. Petersen

For almost a decade now, I have been traveling broadly, speaking to groups of all sizes and almost every discipline you can think of, about the big change that appears to be converging on the horizon.

Often characterizing the coming shift in terms of breakdowns and breakthroughs, I've tried to build integrated mental pictures of the extraordinary nexus of driving forces—both conventional and unconventional—that seem destined to reconfigure the way we live on this planet. My book *Out of the Blue* introduced an approach for making sense out of big events that would otherwise be surprises, and my latest volume, *A Vision for 2012: Planning for Extraordinary Change* (*http://www.visionfor2012.com/*) uses the breakdown/breakthrough themes to propose a general approach for dealing with large-scale change.

So, I've been thinking about this possibility for quite some time. (My wife would probably tell you that I think about it all of the time.)

I generally agree with the many thoughtful people who consider predicting the future to be a fool's errand. It is intrinsically fraught with so much complexity and uncertainty that the best one can do with integrity is to array potential alternatives—scenarios—across the horizon, and then try to think about what might be done if one of those worlds materializes.

John L. Petersen is president of The Arlington Institute. E-mail johnp@arlingtoninstitute.org.

Scenario planning has certainly been an effective discipline, helping many organizations to imagine potentialities that probably otherwise wouldn't have shown up in their field of view. But as I facilitate organizations going through these exercises, the little, nagging voice in the back of my head is not asking, "What is the array of possible futures?" Rather, it is always wondering, "What is the future really going to be?" It wants concreteness. It wants predictions.

I think that no one knows for sure what the future will bring, but after some time of being in this business one begins to be able to discriminate between what is substantive and structural, and what is largely speculative. For me, at least, some things have an intuitive sense of being real and important, and the rest of the possibilities lack just enough gravitas that I know they're only "ideas." That intuitive sense is supported when it becomes possible to triangulate from a number of independent sources that all point to the same conclusion—the possibility has substance.

People always ask me after my talks what I think is going to happen. "With all of these converging trends, what is 2012 really going to look like?" It happened again in a recent radio interview. Mostly I hedge and dance a bit and say that I don't know for sure. There will be a new world and a new human that will come out of all of this. The notion of cooperation will shape the way people see themselves and the rest of the world . . . and there will be new institutions and functions, etc. Pretty general stuff.

But, over a year ago, the notion that all of this big change could spell the substantial reconfiguration of the familiar country that I have lived in all of my life began to gel in a way that moved beyond the notion of being just a possibility—a wild card—into that space of plausibility. I now have come to believe that it is likely and will happen—soon.

Ideas like this are so big and disruptive that it is really quite hard to get to the place where we take them seriously. For most of us, our lives are evolutionary—punctuated, perhaps with trauma now and then, but mostly populated by events that are familiar, even if they don't always make personal sense. The concept that *everything* might change is so foreign to any experience that most of us have ever had that, even if we say the words and talk about the possibility, we really don't internalize what this might mean.

Therefore, along with most folks, I'm kind of late to this game. There are other notable thinkers who jumped to the natural conclusion quite some time ago. Dmitry Orlov, for example, first started to build a theory of superpower collapse that included the United States in 1995. Only in the last few years has he been talking publicly about his ideas and the ultimate direction of U.S. trends. His book *Reinventing Collapse (http://www.newsociety.com/bookid/3991)* is recommended. He also gave a great speech *(http://www.organicconsumers .org/articles/article_16876.cfm)* about the subject recently.

James Howard Kunstler, a wonderfully entertaining and provocative writer, was very clear about the systemic and structural nature of the larger problem in his 2006 book, *The Long Emergency*. His always interesting blog *(http://jameshowardkunstler.typepad.com/)* is a weekly assessment of where we're going wrong. He clearly sees the demise of America coming this way.

Our own David Martin first outlined the financial dominos that were going to fall in a talk *(http://www.arlingtoninstitute.org/ dr-david-e-martin)* at The Arlington Institute in July 2006, which he has updated on two subsequent occasions here in Berkeley Springs. Implicit in his treatise was the collapse of the U.S. and global financial system, but again, it's one thing to imply those words and quite another to really believe them.

I was aggregating my own perspectives and being influenced by some of these folks such that last year while in Singapore I even told my friends there that I thought we were seeing the beginning of the end of the United States as we've known it. I didn't think they really believed it then, but, in the months since then, they reportedly have made major leadership changes in their government investment company to reposition it in the future away from the United States and the U.S. dollar.

There are numerous indicators that suggest the big change is coming.

- **Multiple trends are converging.** Huge, extraordinary, global trends, any number of which would be enough to derail our present way of life, are converging to precipitate a historic big transition event. A partial list would include:

- The global financial system is collapsing. During the next 10 months, it appears that wave after wave of blows will strike the system (see the February 15, 2009, piece at *http://invertedalchemy .blogspot.com/* by Dave Martin about the next big shock), raising the very real possibility that it will experience large-scale failure sometime before the end of the year.

- We have reached the beginning of the end of petroleum. Global production has been flat for the last three years. Senior oil company executives are now saying that they will not be able to pump more. Supply will likely begin to decrease significantly after we move across the peak. Prices will increase again if the demand holds up. This is important because our present way of life is built upon petroleum.

- The global climate system is changing—some say it is getting much warmer, others now suggest a mini ice age within the next decade. In any case, probably increased irregularities in local climates will result, with attendant problems in agriculture, natural disasters, and economies.

- The cost of food is increasing rapidly as a result of global shortages not seen in 40 or 50 years. This could be exacerbated by increasing energy costs and climate changes.

- The effects of larger solar eruptions hitting the earth through a tear in the magnetosphere will disrupt global communications, weather, perhaps satellites, and even organic life over the next three to four years.

- **Problems are much larger than government.** These kinds of problems are much greater than anything that contemporary governments have ever had to deal with before. Peak oil, climate change, and the financial meltdown by themselves have the potential to significantly overwhelm the capabilities of government. If bureaucracies can't deal with the aftermath of a natural disaster like Katrina, something ten or more times that damaging would leave most people fending for themselves. If these extraordinary, disruptive events end up being concurrent, then the whole system is at risk.

- **The problems are structural.** They're systemic. Perhaps the best source for beginning to understand the deep, interdependent nature of all of this is by taking the Crash Course at *http://www .chrismartenson.com*. Some of these issues, especially the financial, oil, and food problems, are also a product of how we live, our priorities, and our paradigms. We are creating the problems because of our values and principles. Without extraordinary, fundamental changes in the way we see ourselves and the world, we will keep getting what we are getting.

- **Leaders think the old system can be "rebooted."** Almost everyone in leadership positions in the Obama administration and in other countries wants to make the old system well again. Jim Kunstler has said it well: "Among the questions that disturb the sleep of many casual observers is how come Mr. O doesn't get that the conventional process of economic growth—based, as it was, on industrial expansion via revolving credit in a cheap-energy-resource era—is over, and why does he keep invoking it at the podium? Dear Mr. President, you are presiding over an epochal contraction, not a pause in the growth epic. Your assignment is to manage that contraction in a way that does not lead to world war, civil disorder, or both. Among other things, contraction means that all the activities of everyday life need to be downscaled, including standards of living, ranges of commerce, and levels of gov-

ernance. 'Consumerism' is dead. Revolving credit is dead—at least
at the scale that became normal the last thirty years. The wealth
of several future generations has already been spent and there is
no equity left there to re-finance."

That is why:

- **We're not dealing with the structural issues.** All of the biggest
efforts are attempts to reinflate the financial bubble and to keep
the mortally wounded institutions alive. The knee-jerk reactions
come from the same people who helped to design and feed the
present system. These people are also deluded—they think (or act
like) they know what they are doing. They don't realize that ...

- **The situation is so complex that no one really understands it.**
The Global Business Network's Peter Schwartz, reporting on a
conversation with the *Financial Times*'s Martin Wolf, said that
Wolf's key point was that the nature and scale of the credit crisis
is so novel that it's not clear we know what we're doing when we
try to stop it. He is deeply worried. Steve Roach of Morgan Stanley said at the World Economic Forum annual meeting at Davos
that he agreed with Wolf: We are in uncharted waters. Nassim
Nicholas Taleb, author of *The Black Swan: Impact of the Highly Im-
probable*, says the financial system is so complex that it is impossible for anyone to understand it, and because of that complexity
it is inevitable that it will exhibit significant, unanticipated behaviors (his Black Swans) that career across the planet.

- **The issues are global.** Japan's exports fell by 46% in January 2009,
and Hong Kong's economy contracted 2.5% in the last three months
of 2008. Foreign investors closed 45,000 factories in China in the
last eight months, and China closed 20,000 itself. Those closed factories mean products aren't being shipped.

- **The system is fundamentally out of balance.** In the United States,
the rich are getting richer (at unconscionable rates). The government is monitoring all internal communications of its citizens—
but lies and says it is not. Common sense is not included in big,

sweeping federal edicts. The Transportation Security Administration, for example, wants to make pilots produce background checks on members of their family (and their business associates) in order to legally give them rides in noncommercial, private airplanes. The Agriculture Department in its NAIS program wants all small farmers (big feedlots are exempt, of course) to put GPS/RFID tags on all of their animals: chickens, cows, horses, goats—even fish were initially included—so that the beasts can be tracked, on a day-to-day basis, by the government. It's also now against the law in some states, like Illinois, for farmers to save the seeds that they've grown; they must buy new ones each year from large seed companies.

- **Most of the U.S. federal budget goes to the military.** More than half of the U.S. federal budget goes to military and military-related agencies. This kind of growth, of course, is what brought down the Soviet Union. In sharp contrast to the political apparatchiks that protest that more money is needed to reverse the shrinking, aging, and decline in readiness in the Army, Navy, and Air Force, few seem to understand that budget increases are a primary cause of the problems, a symptom clearly described in the new book, *America's Defense Meltdown: Pentagon Reform for President Obama and the New Congress,* by Winslow Wheeler et al.

- **No new ideas, and government can't be responsive.** If the natural solutions to these massive issues include innovation, foresight, adaptability, sustainability, and resilience, it is unlikely that a thinking American could be found who would suggest that the source for these capabilities would be our government. They're in charge, but they have no new ideas about how this all should work. They're also slow, and this situation needs fast, agile responses. There is an additional problem: Even if they did have good ideas, the government wouldn't be able to effectively implement them because ...

- **Too much inertia, and too many lawyers and lobbyists.** There is a huge, well-funded effort in place to maintain the status quo or to shift the future to benefit one group at the expense of others. It would be impossible within the present system to initiate dramatic change when the threat was still on the horizon. Every group or organization that might be negatively affected would fight in Congress and the courts to keep themselves alive, regardless of what was at stake for the larger community. Only when the crisis was about to crash down on everyone—when adequate time and resources for effective response were nonexistent—might everyone pull together for the common good.

- **Potential solutions take too long to implement.** These issues are so gigantic that confronting and redirecting them takes a long time. One study, for example, suggested that a national crash program to find alternatives for oil would need to have been started 20 years before the peak in order for there not to be significant disruption of the underlying systems. We do not operate with either that foresight or resolve.

- **Supply chains are long and thin.** Globalism and just-in-time production have produced supply chains in most areas of commerce that are very long—often to the other side of the earth—and very fragile. There are many places between there and here where something can go wrong. If and when that happens, necessities will not be available, and in those situations, people resort to unconventional and/or antisocial behavior.

- **Six hundred trillion dollars in derivatives are a house of cards.** Looming over the whole financial situation is an almost unfathomable quantity of financial instruments—derivatives—which are essentially casino bets with no underlying value supporting the transaction. Warren Buffett calls them financial weapons of mass destruction that could bring the whole system down. Derivatives only work if there is confidence in the system—you believe the casino will really pay your winnings. If other things in the environment erode that confidence, there is the real possibility that things rapidly reconfigure themselves.

- **Cooperation is unlikely; protectionism will prevail.** Instead of countries cooperating with each other to deal with these big transnational problems, we're seeing a pulling back to protect each country's perceived short-term interests, regardless of what the implications might be in the longer term. At the same time, we're all connected to each other in very complicated ways, so if any substantial pieces of the system don't work, it will affect all of the other ones.

- **History says it's time.** Perhaps what is most compelling to me is that history strongly suggests that the time is right for an upset— they always happen about now in the historical cycles. I talk about this in my book a bit, but the short version is that big punctuations in the equilibrium of evolution have produced extraordinary, fundamental reorganizations to life on this planet on a regular, accelerating basis from the beginning of time as we know it. We make progress as a species when we are forced in one way or another to evolve to seeing ourselves and the world in new ways. Necessity is the mother of invention, etc.

So, it doesn't look to me like we're going to be able to do what might be needed to maintain the present system. It is likely that we're at one of those extraordinary moments in history when each of us gets the opportunity to play an important role in not only transitioning to a new world, but also designing it.

It appears that the financial system is likely to collapse sometime this year—probably before the end of the third quarter—which will then require a great deal of effort next year (and into 2012?) to design and build a new framework. It is obvious that many businesses will fail as the result of this abrupt slowdown (just read the papers today), and there will be unprecedented hardship for many people around the world. A long view of what is happening could posit that only through the collapse of a legacy system could a new world evolve. And that is what is happening.

What to do in the face of unprecedented change? Two specific things come to mind:

1. **Plan for the transition.** Start to think now about how you're going to provide for yourself and those who are important to you in a time when many things don't work the way that always have in the past. Dmitry Orlov talks about some options in his above-mentioned talk and book. There are many Web sites and books on this subject.

   Key concept: Cooperation. You can't do this alone. Start to work together with like-minded individuals to sustain yourself, regardless of whether your concerns are food, water, shelter, transportation, or finances.

2. **Start thinking about the new world.** Now is the time to begin contemplating the design of the new world. Governments should be doing this. Companies should start skunk works. Big international organizations should put it on their agendas.

   Here's the catch: This might not happen. Personally, I think that if there is any one person that has the potential to at least soften this transition it is Barack Obama. As I've suggested, he will have his hands full just trying to get the underlying people and institutions to think differently and act fast enough, but if anyone has the chance to pull it off, he would be the one. Already, he's getting government to move faster and in more substantive ways than any of his predecessors. It may be, by the way, that he will be the best guy to wind down the old system and reconstitut a new one. It's all of the other folks running the government that I'd be concerned about—the ones who continue to see the world as it used to be.

   There are any number of reasons why this scenario might not manifest itself, not least of which is that there will be many thousands, if not millions, of people who will be working very hard to assure that the system doesn't come apart (but then, they may be doing the wrong things).

   It seems to me, therefore, that flexibility and permeability (allowing new ideas to get through) are of critical importance here. Remember the first law of Discordianism: "Convictions cause convicts." Whatever you believe imprisons you.

So, stay loose. The winners need to transcend, not try to work their way through all of this. Concentrate on building the new world. Don't get emotionally involved in the daily reports of the current global erosion.

Contributors

Stephen Aguilar-Millan is the director of research at the European Futures Observatory, an independent not-for-profit organization based in the United Kingdom, and is a director of The Greenways Partnership, a firm of consulting futurists also based in the UK. He consults widely for a range of clients based across the globe. He is a member of the Royal Economics Society, a fellow of the RSA, and a member of a number of other professional bodies in the UK. He sits on the Global Advisory Council of the World Future Society and the Board of the Association of Professional Futurists, and he coordinates the Europe Chapter of the World Future Society. He currently directs an international team of futurists engaged in a variety of issues ranging from "The Post Scarcity World 2050-75" to "The Second Scramble For Africa 2005-2030."

Tsvi Bisk is an American-Israeli futurist. He is the director of the Center for Strategic Futurist Thinking *(www.futurist-thinking .co.il/)* and contributing editor for strategic thinking for *The Futurist* magazine. He is also the author of *The Optimistic Jew: A Positive Vision for the Jewish People in the 21st Century* (*www.maxannapress .com/index-9.html*; available from Amazon and Barnes & Noble).

Michael Blinick, an attorney and consultant on issues relating to ethical and moral values and public policy, holds an MA in political science from the City University of New York and a JD from New York University School of Law. He is a member of the New York and United States Supreme Court bars.

Irving H. Buchen received his PhD from Johns Hopkins University and is currently a member of the doctoral business faculty of Capella University. He also teaches in the MBA online program of

IMPAC University and serves as its accreditation advisor. An active researcher, he has published eight books; his most-recent book, *Partnership HR,* was named one of the three outstanding new books in the field by Bloomberg Europe. He has written more than 150 articles, many on futurist topics, including the chapter "Seeing Newly, Differently, and Futuristically with Scenarios" in *Seeing the Future Through New Eyes* (WFS, 2008). An equally involved consultant and executive coach, Buchen has worked for CITGO, Bankers Trust, Allied Chemical, Case, and many universities in the United States and around the world.

Cláudio Chauke Nehme is an expert on strategic intelligence and knowledge management. His background is based on more than 20 years of experience conducting research projects and enabling development and innovation in the areas of decision support systems, pattern recognition, signal processing, and information technology. In the last 10 years, he has been involved with professional and academic projects in knowledge management, organizational and competitive intelligence, technological foresight, and strategic planning, having worked for the Brazilian Navy Research Institute (IPqM), the Brazilian Agricultural Research Corporation (EMBRAPA), Catholic University of Brasília (UCB), and the Center for Strategic Studies and Management (CGEE).

Gilda Coelho, DSc in information and communication science, University of Marseille, France (2001). Created and coordinated the first post-graduation course on Competitive Intelligence in Brazil (1996-2000). Participates, as a teacher, in post-graduation courses in Brazil and other South American countries, since 1997. Private consultant since 2002, working for the Center for Strategic Studies and Management (CGEE), Brazilian government, Petrobras, and private companies in the areas of technology foresight, future studies, and competitive intelligence. Presented papers on Competitive Intelligence and Technological Foresight in various international conferences in South America, United States, and Europe. Received the first Brazilian Prize FINEP/ABRAIC on Innovation on Competitive Intelligence in 2004. Main fields of interest: technology foresight and future studies; competitive intelligence; knowledge management.

José Luis Cordeiro *(www.cordeiro.org)* is founder of the World Future Society's Venezuela Chapter, co-founder of the Venezuelan Transhumanist Association, chair of the Venezuela Node of the Millennium Project, and former director of the World Transhumanist Association and the Extropy Institute.

Brian Coughlan was born in Ireland in 1965, moving to Apartheid South Africa in 1977, where he matriculated in 1983. After serving as a conscript in the South African Defence Force from 1984 to 1986, he returned to the European Union in 1987. As an Irishman and a white South African, Coughlan brings a unique 360-degree perspective to the thorny issue of democratizing a Balkanized and fundamentally unjust world. After touring with a Christian theater group in Germany for four years, he got his BSc in information technology from Trinity College in Dublin, Ireland, in 1998. From 1996, he worked in management at a number of multinationals, including AOL. In 2002, Coughlan and his family moved to northern Europe, where he now works from home consulting for ISPs and telecom companies. The Iraq War and a personal crisis of faith precipitated a furious interest in global politics, and he has been producing videos on YouTube (under the moniker "themodestagnostic") on this theme since April 2007.

Julian F. Derry is a visiting scientist at the Institute of Evolutionary Biology, University of Edinburgh, where he has also been a research fellow and a research associate. He has also been a private consultant in Kenya, Spain, Brussels, Mongolia, and Australia. Among his projects were a rhino diet study, Double Drift Game Reserve, South Africa; lion semen sampling, Hluhluwe-Umfolozi Park, South Africa; and aerial counts, Malilangwe Reserve, Zimbabwe. He holds degrees in biochemistry, electronics, biological computation, and evolutionary biology. Among his publications are *The Dissent of Man: Darwin's Influence on Modern Thought* (CUP, 2009) and "Darwin in Disguise," *Trends in Ecology and Evolution* (December 18, 2008).

John M. Eger holds the Van Deerlin Endowed Chair of Communications and Public Policy and is director of the Center for the Study of the Creative Economy at San Diego State University. He wrote the seminal "Guidebook for Smart Communities," a how-to for communities struggling to compete in the age of the Internet, and "The Creative Community: Linking Art, Culture, Commerce and Community," a call to action to reinvent our communities for the Creative Age. A former advisor to two presidents and director of the White House Office of Telecommunications Policy, Eger served as chairman of former California Governor Pete Wilson's first Commission on Information Technology, chair of the Governor's Committee on Education and Technology, chairman of former San Diego Mayor Susan Golding's "City of the Future" Commission, and founder of Envision San Diego: The Creative Community, a new forum for civic engagement.

Ann Feeney is a member of the Association of Professional Futurists and its board and is a Certified Association Executive. She works as research manager and is the organizational futurist at the YMCA of the USA, the national headquarters of the almost 3,000 YMCAs in the United States. Her work there includes environmental scanning, projections, scenario development, and other tools from the futures discipline. "An organizational futurist's job is as much about embedding possible futures into decision making as it is developing those possible futures. In times of rapid change, it's also about keeping the variables varying and the constants constant, especially when it's hard to tell the difference." She has frequently presented at World Future Society and other professional conferences, nationally as well as regionally. These presentations have covered a wide range of topics, including online tools for environmental scanning; organizational and individual futures tools for workforce and volunteer development; the future of nonprofits in a globalized world; and the transition of YMCAs from fitness to wellness organizations.

Lélio Fellows started his academic activities as researcher at the Extractive Metallurgy Department—Federal University of Rio de Janeiro from 1978 until 1980. In 1982, he was a visiting researcher at the Department for Mineral Treatment—Technische Universität Berlin dealing with manganese ore beneficiation. Since 1980, Fellows has been an employee of the National Council for Scientific and Technological Development (CNPq), although several times he has been transferred to other institutions of the Brazilian Ministry of Science and Technology. From 1983 till 1986 he coordinated CNPq's Mineral Technology Department and took part in several Science and Technology Action Programmes funded by the World Bank. From 1986 till 1988, he headed the Technology Department at the Brazilian Institute for Mining, where he was responsible for its creation and for technological cooperation between companies in the business sector.

From 1988 till 1998, Fellows was transferred to the Department for New Materials at the Ministry of Science and Technology and soon served as Coordinator of the Engineering and Physics Department. After a short stay at the Human Resources for Strategic Areas Department, he dedicated most of his work to international cooperation with France, Germany, China, India, the United States, the Organization of American States (OAS), and Latin America, covering such issues as space technology, industrial research, and new materials, as well as the Blue Ribbon Panel with the National Science Foundation (NSF).

Fellows was adjunct director for Special Programme at CNPq

(1998 to 2000) and head of staff for CNPq's president (2000-2001), responsible for university and business integration, innovation, employment and technological development, cooperation with other ministries, cooperation with the state secretaries for science and technology, and cooperation between universities and social communities, among others.

From 2002 to now, Fellows is the head of the Technical Office at the Center for Strategic Studies and Management—CGEE in Brazil, where he is responsible for future analysis centered in technological issues, and is the International Coordinator of the International Materials Assessment and Applications Centre, under UNIDO, and Coordinator of the Iberoamerican Network on Technology Foresight under CYTED.

Elizabeth Florescu has been with the Millennium Project since 1997 and is currently director of research. She is a contributor to the annual *State of the Future* reports, co-author of the studies "Environmental Crimes, Military Actions, and the International Criminal Court" and "Analysis of the UN Millennium Summit Speeches," and is one of the principal investigators working on the environmental security monthly scanning reports. She is a macro-economist and previously worked in foreign trade, economic modeling and planning, and software development in several countries.

Adriano Galvão is a strategist with 12 years of experience in user-centric innovation, combining qualitative and quantitative research to improve global products and services. He has worked for companies such as Dentsu (Japan), Motorola (USA), and Sylver Consulting (USA-Brazil), an international research and innovation firm.

In 2007, Galvão joined CGEE (Brazil), where he manages foresight studies to inform government policies intended to better position Brazilian companies in the global economy in the 15- to 25-year time frame. He leads interdisciplinary, forward-looking teams responsible for identifying global trends, investigating future opportunities, and creating scenarios and future road maps based on the input of industry stakeholders and specialists. Projects to date have included those for the automotive, medical equipment, automation, and furniture industrial sectors of Brazil.

He lectures frequently and publishes regularly on new product development, innovation, and globalization. His most recent book, *Design Relationships*, examines how to integrate knowledge related to how a user interacts with a product into the design of the product's architecture.

Galvão has master's and doctoral degrees in design from the Institute of Design at the Illinois Institute of Technology and has received international awards (e.g., IDEA/IDSA, BraunPrize, Xerox/ASME) for his contributions to the engineering and design process. He is also a fellow of the Organization of American States (OAS).

Jerome C. Glenn is the co-founder (1996) and director of The Millennium Project and co-author with Ted Gordon of the annual *State of the Future* report of the Millennium Project for the past 12 years. He was the Washington, D.C., representative for the United Nations University as executive director of the American Council for the United Nations University, 1988-2007.

Glenn has more than 35 years of futures-research experience working for governments, international organizations, and private industry in science and technology policy, environmental security, economics, education, defense, space, futures research methodology, international telecommunications, and decision-support systems with the Committee for the Future, Hudson Institute, Future Options Room, and the Millennium Project. He has addressed or keynoted conferences for more than 300 government departments, universities, NGOs, UN organizations, and/or corporations around the world on a variety of future-oriented topics.

Glenn invented the "Futures Wheel" futures-assessment technique, futuristic curriculum development, and concepts such as conscious technology, transinstitutions, tele-nations, management by understanding, definition of environmental security, feminine brain drain, just-in-time knowledge and learning, information warfare, feelysis, and nodes as a management concept for interconnecting global and local views and actions, and he coined the term futuring in 1973.

Theodore J. Gordon is co-founder of The Millennium Project and co-author and co-editor of the annual *State of the Future* reports and *Futures Research Methodology.* He is a graduate engineer, futurist, and management consultant. He is an expert in several high-technology fields, a specialist in planning and policy analysis, and an entrepreneur. His current professional activities include consulting on strategy for several major corporations, lecturing, Senior Fellow of the Millennium Project, and participating on the corporate boards of Apollo Genetics, the Institute for Global Ethics, Registry Databases, and The Futures Group, the consulting firm he formed more than 20 years ago.

Gordon has been in charge of hundreds of studies for government agencies as well as insurance, computer, banking, communications, advertising, automobile, pharmaceutical, and chemical companies. His work has involved technological innovation and forecasting, the design of analysis methodologies, market segmentation, and the development of strategies—particularly those promising to be productive in conditions of high uncertainty. His most recent technical articles have been in the field of chaos and forecasting methodology. He is author of the Macmillan Encyclopedia article on the future of science and technology and is on the editorial board of several journals, including *Technological Forecasting and Social Change.*

William E. Halal is professor emeritus of science, technology, and innovation; co-founder and trustee, Institute for Knowledge and Innovation at George Washington University; and president of Tech-Cast LLC *(www.TechCast.org)*. His latest book is *Technology's Promise: Expert Knowledge on the Transformation of Business and Society* (London: Palgrave Macmillan, 2008).

David Harper was a research engineer for a NASA project, developing custom software. Most recently he conducted an Advanced Concepts project for NASA's space-biology program.

Jay Herson is senior associate at the Johns Hopkins Bloomberg School of Public Health, Baltimore, Maryland, and the Institute for Alternative Futures, Alexandria, Virginia. He is also a book reviewer for *World Future Review* and managing editor of *FutureTakes,* an electronic newsletter *(www.futuretakes.org)*.

Lane Jennings joined the staff of the World Future Society in 1976. Over the years he has reviewed books and written articles for *The Futurist* and helped edit a number of WFS books and publications, including the *WFS Bulletin*. From the 1980s on, he has also worked as a scriptwriter and production consultant on television documentaries for PBS and European networks and as a literary translator for the Goethe Institut in Washington, D.C. For 30 years he assisted Michael Marien as production editor of the monthly abstract journal *Future Survey*. He is currently managing editor for the Society's newest publication, *World Future Review.*

Vladimir Knapp is a member of the faculty of Electrical Engineering and Computing at the University of Zagreb in Zagreb, Croatia, and was elected the first president of the Croatian Nuclear Society in 1992. He also serves as an adviser to the American Center for International Policy Studies.

A Croatian scientist who has worked in nuclear physics, Knapp obtained his PhD at the University of Birmingham in the United Kingdom on the nuclear scattering of gamma rays in 1957. He continued his work at the Institute Rudjer Boskovic in Zagreb and then at the University of Zagreb at the Faculty of Electrical Engineering. In addition to teaching and research in physics, he was engaged in various studies and activities related to the construction and operation of the first Croatian–Slovenian nuclear power station, Krsko. He initiated education for nuclear energy oriented engineers at the Faculty of Electrical Engineering and is author of several books and many papers on the various topics and questions associated with the use of nuclear energy. He was elected collaborating member of the Croatian Academy of Science and Art.

Apart from analyzing many technical issues that could make nuclear power more economical and safe, he has devoted his attention also to the nontechnical, but essential, aspect of the possible abuse of nuclear power. He was an early member of the Pugwash movement initiated by Russell and Einstein with the aim of nuclear disarmament, and was a chairman of the Croatian Pugwash Group. Since his retirement, his activity has been primarily with the Croatian Nuclear Society on the issues associated with long-term use of nuclear power. As the first Society president, he initiated the now well established biannual international Dubrovnik conferences on the nuclear option for countries with small- and medium-sized electricity grids.

Gioietta Kuo is a former fellow of St. Hilda's College, Oxford University, and former scientist, Princeton University. She is currently a senior fellow at the American Center for International Policy Studies *(www.amcips.org)*.

Kuo holds a master's degree in physics from Cambridge University, United Kingdom, and a PhD in nuclear physics from University of Birmingham, UK. Positions include French Atomic Energy Commission (Commisariat d'Energie Atomique); Culham Laboratory, United Kingdom Atomic Energy Authority; Fellow at St Hilda's College, Oxford University, UK; research in plasma physics, Plasma Physics Laboratory, Princeton, New Jersey; and research in CT (computer tomography) image-reconstruction algorithms, Siemens Medical Systems, Iselin, New Jersey. As an inventor, she holds two patents in CT image reconstruction (USPTO Patent No. 5375156, December 1994, and USPTO Patent No. 7170966, January 2007). She is the author of an autobiographical book, *A Himalayan Odyssey*, 2002.

Kuo has 40 years of research experience in nuclear physics, plasma and thermonuclear physics, astrophysics, numerical analysis, computer software, automatic code generation, and large-scale numerical modeling of plasmas.

She has more than 70 publications in the world's top journals, including *Physical Review, Physical Review Letters, Physics of Fluids,* and *Journal of Computational Physics,* as well as many reports and contributions to academic books.

Since 2005, she has written 25 popular articles about current affairs concentrating on topics such as climate change, world energy, population, and others, always making use of her scientific background to give in-depth analysis. Publications in wfs.org, amcips.org, and *China Daily Beijing,* and, in Chinese, *People's Daily Beijing, Guang Ming Daily Beijing,* and *World Environment Beijing.*

David J. LePoire works at Argonne National Laboratory as an environmental analyst, developing tools, analysis, and training for environmental characterization and risk assessment. He is also concerned with the reduction of environmental risks from potential national security issues. In a broader scope, he has analyzed recent energy, environmental, and scientific trends to help illuminate the context of potential future scenarios. Over the past 20 years he has been involved with projects for the U.S. Department of Energy, Department of Defense, Army Corps of Engineers, Department of Homeland Security, Nuclear Regulatory Commission, Department of the Interior, and Environmental Protection Agency. He has also researched nuclear and optical diagnostic tools. He has a BS in physics and PhD and MS in computer science.

Bruce Lloyd is emeritus professor of strategic management at London South Bank University. He spent more than 20 years in industry and finance before joining the academic world a decade ago to help establish the Management Centre at what is now London South Bank University. He has a degree in chemical engineering; an MSc (Economics) / MBA from the London Business School, and a PhD (by published work) for his work on "The Future of Offices and Office Work: Implications for Organisational Strategy." He was a member of the CMI Advisory Board for its project on "Leadership: A Challenge for All" and a subsequent study specifically concerned with leadership issues in the public sector.

Since the late 1960s, Lloyd has written extensively (about 200 published articles) on a wide range of strategy/futures-related issues, including articles exploring the links among leadership, power, and responsibility and, more recently, the relationships among leadership, wisdom, knowledge management, and organizational performance. He has undertaken more than 30 interviews on leadership for *Leadership and Oranization Development Journal,* as well as others for *The Tomorrow Project Bulletin.* He was also the UK coordinator for The Millennium Project, 1999-2005, and has been active in the futures industry since he first wrote a pamphlet on "UK Energy Policy" in the 1960s.

Tom Lombardo, PhD, is the director of the Center for Future Consciousness (*www.centerforfutureconsciousness.com).* He is also the Faculty Chair of Psychology and Philosophy at Rio Salado College. He is a graduate of the University of Connecticut and the University of Minnesota and a graduate fellow of Cornell University. He has served as the chief psychologist at John Madden Mental Health Center and the dean of the Forest Institute of Professional Psychology.

Lombardo is an active member of, and frequent writer for, the World Future Society and the World Futures Studies Federation, an editorial board member of the *Journal of Futures Studies,* as well as a member of Communities for the Future, LifeBoat, the Foresight Network for Futures Education, and the Acceleration Studies Foundation. His most recent publications include an article series on "Enhancing Future Consciousness" for the *Futures Bulletin,* a series on science fiction and the future for *Learning Tomorrow,* "The Evolution and Psychology of Future Consciousness" for the *Journal of Future Studies,* and "The Future Evolution of the Ecology of Mind" for *World Future Review.* He recently published two highly praised books: *The Evolution of Future Consciousness* and *Contemporary Futurist Thought.*

Richard MacLean is the founder of Competitive Environment Inc., a management consulting firm in Scottsdale, Arizona, and the executive director of the Center for Environmental Innovation (CEI) Inc., a university-based nonprofit environmental research organization. He is also an adjunct professor at Arizona State University, W.P. Carey School of Business.

For the past 13 years, he has provided independent management consulting services to 50 corporations. His company has helped corporations develop state-of-the-art management and governance systems to deliver competitive advantage (thus, the company's name). His practical, real-world approach to consulting is built on a foundation of 35 years of experience working in management positions for corporations such as General Electric and Arizona Public Service.

He is a prolific author, and his direct, "tell-it-like-it-is" style is reflected in his columns appearing in *EM* magazine and *Environmental Quality Management.* He writes about emerging trends, strategic planning, management systems, sustainability metrics, and the practical aspects of achieving corporate social responsibility.

He holds a bachelor's degree in chemical engineering, summa

cum laude, from Northeastern University, Boston.

More information is at *www.competitive-e.com/staff/index.html* and *www.competitive-e.com/publications/index.html*.

Amy Oberg is a futurist and strategist who specializes in helping organizations better understand the emerging competitive environment and respond with effective, proactive strategies. With more than 25 years of cumulative experience in competitive, management, and market analyses, her insights regarding emerging trends, threats and opportunities, market conditions, and technology disruptions have been sought out by organizations in a wide variety of industries, including aerospace, energy, telecommunications, transportation, consumer goods, bio/pharma, real estate, and finance. She is now managing partner at Future-In-Sight, LLC.

Oberg has been the invited keynote speaker at professional conferences, a guest lecturer at universities, and a quoted source for national and international media.

She holds a master's degree in studies of the future, a bachelor's degree in communications, and has completed the Program for Managers at Rice University's Jones Graduate School of Management.

Oberg has served on national and local steering committees and boards for the World Future Society and the Society of Competitive Intelligence Professionals. She is currently a member of the World Future Society, Association of Professional Futurists, and World Affairs Council.

Barbara Parker is a graduate student at the University of Maryland, College Park, and a World Future Society Professional Member.

Joseph N. Pelton is formerly the director of the Space and Advanced Communications Research Institute (SACRI) at George Washington University. He is the founder and vice chairman of the Arthur

C. Clarke Foundation and also the founding president of the Society of Satellite Professionals. He played a key role in the founding of the International Space University, where he has served as dean as well as chairman of the Board of Trustees. Pelton has also been director of the ITP at the University of Colorado at Boulder and director of Strategic Policy at Intelsat.

He is the author of 25 books, including the Pulitzer Prize–nominated book, *Global Talk*. He is the former executive editor of the *Journal of International Space Communications*.

He has been elected an associate fellow of the AIAA as well as a full member of the International Academy of Astronautics. His awards include Outstanding Educator award of the International Communications Association, the H. Rex Lee Award of the Public Service Satellite Consortium, the ISCe Award for Outstanding Educational Achievement, and the Arthur C. Clarke Lifetime Achievement Award.

Pelton holds BS, MA, and PhD degrees from the University of Tulsa, New York University, and Georgetown University respectively.

John L. Petersen is president and founder of The Arlington Institute, a nonprofit, future-oriented think tank headquartered in Berkeley Springs, West Virginia. He is best known for writing and thinking about high-impact surprises—wild cards—and the process of surprise anticipation. His current professional involvements include the development of sophisticated tools for anticipatory analysis and surprise anticipation, long-range strategic planning, and helping leaders design new approaches for dealing with the future and reaching their goals. Among his books are WFS best-sellers *The Road to 2015* (1994), *Out of the Blue* (1997), and *A Vision for 2012* (2008).

Anna Rappaport is an actuary, consultant, author, futurist, and speaker. She is a nationally and internationally recognized expert on the impact of change on retirement systems and workforce issues. After 28 years with Mercer Human Resource consulting, she retired from the firm at the end of 2004 and formed Anna Rappaport Consulting in 2005. She was appointed senior fellow on pensions and retirement by The Conference Board in 2007.

She previously served as president of the Society of Actuaries. She spends a lot of time chairing the Society of Actuaries Committee on Post-Retirement Needs and Risks and serves on the boards of the Women's Institute for a Secure Retirement (WISER) and the Pension Research Council. She is passionate about creating a better future for older Americans and improving the retirement system in America, and is particularly concerned about the many women who do not fare well at older ages. She is a member of the Chicago Network, an organization of the most senior women in Chicago.

Elizabeth Rudd is a consultant with more than 20 years of experience in a variety of senior management, strategy, and business development roles. She has worked internationally in a variety of industries, including health care, software, mining, utilities, media, and publishing. She has worked on strategic foresight engagements in both commercial and nonprofit organizations.

In her current role, Rudd assists organizations to develop strategy and identify future business opportunities and risks to ensure their continued profitable success. She has a master's degree in strategic foresight from Swinburne University and an MBA from the University of Illinois at Chicago. She lives in Melbourne, Australia.

Arthur B. Shostak, emeritus professor of sociology at Drexel University, retired in 2005 after 42 years of enjoying himself sharing ideas in such courses as Futuristics, Social Change and Social Planning, Social Problems, and others. He authored, edited, or co-edited 34 books and more than 160 articles. A co-founder of the Philadelphia Chapter of the World Future Society in 1978, he led it until 2005.

His views about aspects of tomorrow have appeared in *The Futurist* magazine, volumes of the annual meeting of the WFS, and major newspapers and magazines. He is currently finishing the first travel book that highlights sites that preview major policy and built options, entitled *Touring Tomorrow Today*. He welcomes ideas for the book and hopes it will be ready in late 2010.

David Pearce Snyder is a consulting futurist and a data-based forecaster whose seminars and workshops on strategic thinking have been attended by representatives of most Fortune 500 companies. He has published hundreds of studies, articles, and reports on the future of a wide range of industries, institutions, and professions, and on the socio-economic impacts of new technology. He is contributing editor of *The Futurist* magazine and is on the editorial boards of *On The Horizon, Innovate!* and *The Trend Letter.* His office is in Bethesda, Maryland, where he can be reached at 301-530-5807, *david@ the-futurist.com* or *david_snyder@verizon.net;* his Web site is *www.the-futurist.com.*

Patrick Tucker is the senior editor of *The Futurist* magazine and director of communications for the World Future Society. He has written more than 100 articles on the future with the gracious help of his fellow editors. He holds a master's degree in writing from Johns Hopkins University and resides in Baltimore.

Antonio Vaz is an electronics engineer with a master's degree in electrical engineering. He is currently pursuing a doctorate degree in geography, with a special focus on regional development. In his professional career, he has been an entrepreneur, founding two companies—one in the electronics sector and the other providing consulting services on the innovation process. In his first venture, he coordinated several R&D projects in the area of organic semiconductors. As a consultant, he has conducted foresight studies in the aerospace, organic semiconductors, plastics, building, and textile sectors for CGEE. Since 2008, he has also worked as the director of the Institute of Technology of Pernambuco state in Brazil. His primary responsibility, within this position, is to coordinate the strategic-planning initiatives of the institute for the next three years.

The Annual Conference of the World Future Society

WorldFuture 2010: Sustainable Futures, Strategies, and Technologies

The Westin Boston Waterfront Hotel
Boston, Massachusetts • July 8-10, 2010

WHEN: Thursday evening, July 8, 2010, through Saturday, July 10, 2010. Preconference courses on Wednesday and Thursday, July 7-8, 2010, and Professional Members' Forum on Sunday, July 11, 2010.

WHERE: Westin Boston Waterfront Hotel, Boston, Massachusetts.

WHO: More than 1,000 futurists from around the world.

THE THEME: WorldFuture 2010: Sustainable Futures, Strategies, and Technologies.

TOPICS: Technology, education, health, business issues, families and communities, work trends, social change, the environment, global perspectives, futures research, government and politics, and much, much more.

SPECIAL EVENTS: Table-top displays, a bookstore with a large selection of future-oriented titles, and meet-the-author sessions. Professional preconference courses on a wide variety of subjects.

NETWORKING OPPORTUNITIES: A complimentary welcoming reception, two keynote luncheons, group business meetings, reserved networking areas throughout the meeting, and more.

PRESENTATIONS AND PRECONFERENCE COURSES: Proposal deadline is November 15, 2009.

HOTEL: Explore the exciting city of Boston from the Westin Boston Waterfront. Less than three miles from Logan International Airport, and a short cab, water taxi, or T train ride away from Back Bay, the Financial District, and family attractions such as the New England Aquarium and the Boston Children's Museum. Guestrooms feature Westin's signature Heavenly Beds with thick pillowtop mattresses. Rooms also offer wireless Internet access, flat-screen TVs, and large desks with ergonomic chairs.

ORGANIZERS: Susan Echard, vice president conference operations, is creating a worldwide network of volunteers to structure the program and recruit speakers for the meeting. Conference chair is Carol D. Rieg, corporate foundation officer of Bentley Systems.

FOR MORE INFORMATION CONTACT: World Future Society Headquarters, 7910 Woodmont Avenue, Suite 450, Bethesda, Maryland 20814. Telephone: 800-989-8274 or 301-656-8274; fax: 301-951-0394; e-mail: sechard@wfs.org; Web site: www.wfs.org.

About the World Future Society

The World Future Society is an association of people interested in how social and technological developments are shaping the future. It endeavors to help individuals, organizations, and communities see, understand, and respond appropriately and effectively to change. Through publications, online media, meetings, and dialogue among its members, it raises awareness of change and encourages development of creative solutions.

The Society takes no official position on what the future will or should be like. Instead, it acts as a neutral forum for exploring possible, probable, and preferable futures.

Founded in 1966 as a nonprofit, nonpartisan educational and scientific organization in Washington, D.C., the Society has some 25,000 members in more than eighty countries around the world. Individuals and groups from all nations are eligible to join the Society and participate in its programs and activities.

The Society holds a two-day, international conference once a year, where participants discuss foresight techniques and global trends that are influencing the future.

Futurist groups are active in cities around the globe. Groups offer lectures with well-known speakers, educational courses, seminars, and other opportunities for members in local areas to meet and work together. These local groups give members a chance to meet other forward-looking people and to discuss various topics of the future.

The Society's Web site (www.wfs.org) features unique resources such as news, book reviews, and forums on a variety of areas of interest to members. Also included are links to a range of resources such as futures blogs, educational programs, and related organizations.

The World Future Society has published numerous books, including *Futuring: The Exploration of the Future* by Society founder Edward Cornish, as well as several print and electronic journals, including *The Futurist,* a bimonthly magazine focused on innovation, creative thinking, and emerging social, economic, and technological trends. *The Futurist* is available in newsstands throughout the United States.

For more information about the World Future Society and all of its programs, visit www.wfs.org.